SCOTT FORESMAN

Everyday Spelling

Authors

James Beers

Ronald L. Cramer

W. Dorsey Hammond

PEARSON

Scott Foresman

Editorial Offices: Glenview, Illinois • Parsippany, New Jersey
New York, New York
Sales Offices: Boston, Massachusetts • Duluth, Georgia
Glenview, Illinois • Coppell, Texas • Sacramento, California
Mesa, Arizona

■ ACKNOWLEDGMENTS

ILLUSTRATIONS

Cover: Pablo Bernasconi; **pp. 12, 13, 15, 19, 23, 27, 31:** Roger Chandler; **pp. 12Center, 20, 38C, 39, 76, 90, 146:** Randy Verougstraete; **pp. 14, 26, 40, 66, 92, 118, 142, 143, 144, 145, 149, 153, 157, 161:** Thomas Kovacs; **pp. 16, 36Bottom, 113, 166B:** Paul G. Somers; **pp. 17, 47, 137, 151:** Margaret Sanfilippo; **pp. 18, 44, 64, 65, 67, 70, 71, 75, 79, 83, 96, 122, 148:** David Wink; **pp. 21, 35C, 36C, 60, 121, 159:** Marianne D. Wallace; **pp. 22, 24, 48, 50, 74, 100, 126, 152:** C. K. Poedtke; **pp. 28, 158Top, 158C:** Richard Syska; **pp. 29, 51, 73, 77, 85, 86BR, 88, 102, 120, 124, 133, 141, 160, 163:** Yoshi Miyake; **pp. 30, 56, 82, 95, 108, 134, 160:** Donna Ingemanson; **pp. 30, 56, 82, 129, 133:** Randy Chewning; **p. 32:** Gil Ashby; **pp. 33, 43, 55:** John Manders; **pp. 34, 60TL, 86TL, 112, 138, 164:** Maria Stroster; **pp. 35B, 87, 103, 107, 150:** Joe Rogers; **pp. 38T, 41, 45, 49, 53, 57:** Kelly Hume; **p. 42:** Melinda Levine; **p. 46:** Craig Rex Perry; **pp. 52, 59B, 78, 104, 130, 156, 166T:** Teresa R. Jonik-Heine; **pp. 54, 58, 72, 90, 91, 93, 97, 101, 105, 109, 110, 139, 154, 162:** Corasue Nicholas; **p. 68:** Jack Wallen; **p. 80:** Terry J. Sirrell; **pp. 94TL, 94CL:** Susan J. Shipley; **p. 95:** Richard Syska; **p. 98:** Laura Derichs; **pp. 99, 116, 117, 119, 123, 127, 131, 135:** Rebecca Brown; **pp. 107, 111, 167:** Mary Jones; **pp. 114, 136:** Kees de Kiefte; **pp. 115, 132:** Paul Sharp; **p. 125:** Patti Green; **p. 140:** Ann Rebidas; **pp. 147, 155:** Shelley Dietrichs; **pp. 196, 197:** Mark Sobey; **pp. 198, 199, 218, 219, 225:** Kelly Booth; **pp. 200, 201, 216, 217:** Larry Frederick; **pp. 202, 203:** Charles Thomas; **p. 204:** Susanne Beringer; **pp. 205, 208, 209:** Damien Reynolds; **pp. 206, 207:** Connie M. Eichberger; **pp. 221, 222:** Randy Minor; **p. 318:** David Tamura; **p. 320:** Liz Wheaton; **p. 324:** Christine Mortensen; **p. 326:** Bob Radigan

PHOTOGRAPHS

Every effort has been made to secure permission and provide appropriate credit for photographic material. The publisher deeply regrets any omission and pledges to correct errors called to its attention in subsequent editions.

Unless otherwise acknowledged, all photographs are the property of Scott Foresman, a division of Pearson Education.

Photo locators denoted as follows: Top (T), Center (C), Bottom (B), Left (L), Right (R), Background (Bkgd).

170 (L, R) Library of Congress; **171 (BL)** ©Anne S. K. Brown Military Collection/Brown University Library, **(T)** ©Currier & Ives, 1876/Library of Congress, **(BR)** *Surrender of Lord Cornwallis at Yorktown*, 19 October 1781, John Trumbull (American 1756-1843), oil on canvas, 20 7/8 x 30 5/8 inches/Yale University Art Gallery; **172** Corbis; **173 (C)** American Philosophical Society, **(T)** "Lewis and Clarke at Three Forks" by E.S. Paxson, 452-803 image #4, Montana Historical Society Archives/Montana Historical Society, Helena, MT; **(TR, C)** Missouri Historical Society; **177** Schomburg Center for Research in Black Culture/Astor, Lenox, and Tilden Foundations/New York Public Library Picture Collection; **178 (R)** Library of Congress, **(L)** Coffrin's Old West Gallery; **179 (C, TL, B)** Corbis, **(TR)** ©Jim Strawser/Grant Heilman Photography; **182 (BR)** Collection of The New-York Historical Society, **(CL)** ©The National Police Gazette/New York Public Library Picture Collection/Art Resource, NY; **183 (R)** ©Norman Owen Tomalin/Bruce Coleman Inc., **(C)** The Hogan Jazz Archive, Tulane University; **184 (R)** ©George Roger/Getty Images, **(L)** From the collection of The American Legion National Headquarters; **185 (TR)** Corbis, **(L)** ©Poinsett/Getty Images; **186** ©Robert Kelly/Getty Images; **188 (CL, BL)** Getty Images, **(BC)** ©Rubberball Productions; **189 (TR)** ©Martha Swope, **(TL)** ©Rubberball Productions; **190 (L)** ©Runk/Schoenberger/Grant Heilman Photography, **(R)** ©Biophoto Associates/Photo Researchers, Inc.; **191** Lowell Hess/©1964 *Marvels and Mysteries of our Animal World*/Used by permission of The Readers Digest Association, Inc., Pleasantville, NY; **193** ©George Disario/Corbis; **194** Custom Medical Stock Photo; **195** Custom Medical Stock Photo; **200** ©Runk/Schoenberger/Grant Heilman Photography; **204** ©The Science Museum/Science & Society Picture Library; **205** Lee Milne, Palomar Observatory; **208** ©Ken Ross/Viesti Associates, Inc.; **209 (BR)** ©Don & Pat Valenti Photography, **(BL)** ©Michael Shay/Polara Studios; **214** ©Universal/The Kobal Collection; **215** ©Don Ornitz/Globe Photos, Inc.; **260** ©Don Dixon; **262** Official U.S. Naval Photograph; **267** National Museum of American History/Smithsonian Institution; **275** ©Leo Ainsworth/National Oceanic and Atmospheric Administration; **280** National Park Service; **295** The White House; **301** Official U.S. Naval Photograph; **312** ©Baldwin H. & Kathryn C. Ward/Corbis; **315 (T)** ©Robert Frerck/Odyssey/Chicago, **(B)** ©Steve McCutcheon/Anchorage Museum of History and Art.; **316** Michael K. Nichols/©Magnum Photos

ISBN 0-328-22305-0

Copyright © 2008 Pearson Education, Inc.

5 6 7 8 9 10 V042 16 15 14 13 12 11

CONTENTS

UNIT 3

■ CONTENTS

UNIT 5

■ CONTENTS

Cross-Curricular Lessons

🖐 SOCIAL STUDIES

🍎 HEALTH

💡 SCIENCE

CONTENTS

✳ FREQUENTLY MISSPELLED WORDS!

Lots of words on your spelling lists are marked with green asterisks ✳ . These are the words that are misspelled the most by students your age.*

Pay special attention to these frequently misspelled words as you read, write, and practice your spelling words.

a lot	we're	TV	Christmas	friends
too	finally	until	clothes	know
it's	there's	something	I'm	outside
you're	where	going to	no one	always
their	can't	through	our	beginning
that's	usually	they	than	college
there	doesn't	to	especially	maybe
they're	really	which	let's	now
because	allowed	different	then	wear
probably	didn't	everything	weird	
don't	off	believe	favorite	

* **Research in Action** is a research project conducted in 1990–1993. This list of frequently misspelled words is one result of an analysis of 18,599 unedited compositions. Words are listed in the order of their frequency of misspelling.

strategy Workshop

Developing Spelling Consciousness

DISCOVER THE STRATEGY Everyone misspells words like these—words we know how to spell, or ought to.

know	now	I'm	outside
our	which	their	Christmas
we're	don't	let's	friends
where	they	to	there
you're	than	they're	off
always	too	then	TV
can't	until	there's	it's
didn't	wear	that's	

They're called **frequently misspelled words** in this book. Students your age misspell them again and again when they write.

> Which three of these words did the writer misspell in the LOST notice above? Find them and write them correctly.

These mistakes are mostly with easy words we know how to spell, such as leaving the apostrophe out of a contraction, so misspelling these words makes us look bad. If we could learn too notice these mistakes, we'd catch them. (Did you catch the misspelling in that last sentence?)

We need to make ourselves aware of these words. We need to develop our **spelling consciousness.**

TRY IT OUT Find the nine misspelled words in these notices and write them correctly. *Hint:* A word that looks right may actually be the wrong word, so proofread carefully for meaning.

FREE KITTENS!
You may choose from six cute kittens. Thay all need a good home. Dont wait untill all six are gone. Hurry! Call me right away at . . .

FOR SALE
See the stars through a telescope in almost perfect condition. It would make a great Chrismas gift or buy it for yourself. It will provide hours of entertainment and has educational value to. Call no for the best deal.

FOR RENT
If you cant afford to buy a boat, rent one. I'm the proud owner of a 20-foot luxury cruiser. Fish of the bow or sunbathe on the deck. Sleep in a cabin or out side under the stars. Call me at . . .

LOOK AHEAD More frequently misspelled words appear in the spelling lessons that follow. Each one is marked by the asterisk symbol you see in this lesson. You'll also find them in proofreading exercises. Look through the lists for the next five lessons and write down any frequently misspelled words that are spelling problems for you.

Getting Letters in Correct Order

SPELLING FOCUS

Watch for letter combinations that are hard to keep in order. Pay special attention to those parts: **believe, doesn't.**

■ **STUDY**   Say each word. Then read the sentence.

1.	**tremendous**	The loss was a **tremendous** letdown.
2.	**doesn't** ✳	The broken clock **doesn't** chime.
3.	**collapse**	Floods caused the bridge's **collapse.**
4.	**because** ✳	We can't play **because** of the rain.
5.	**believe** ✳	Do not **believe** every rumor you hear.
6.	**thoroughly**	We **thoroughly** cleaned up the mess.
7.	**through** ✳	She walked **through** the doorway.
8.	**retrieve**	A computer can **retrieve** a file.
9.	**glimpse**	We caught a **glimpse** of the sun.
10.	**weird** ✳	I play **weird** music on Halloween.

✳

WATCH OUT FOR FREQUENTLY MISSPELLED WORDS!

11.	**mediocre**	The play received **mediocre** reviews.
12.	**perception**	My **perception** of the problem is clear.
13.	**irrelevant**	I found the story's details **irrelevant.**
14.	**perspective**	Put problems in the proper **perspective.**
15.	**neutral**	Since I'm **neutral,** I can't take sides.
16.	**preliminary**	They revised the **preliminary** report.
17.	**naive**	Like a **naive** child, he feared nothing.
18.	**perceive**	I did not **perceive** how upset they were.
19.	**deceitful**	A liar is a **deceitful** person.
20.	**preferable**	Blue is the **preferable** color choice.

CHALLENGE!

kaleidoscope
surveillance
inconceivable
preposterous
interpretation

■ **PRACTICE**   Look over the list words carefully. First, write the words that you think are most difficult for you to spell. Then write the rest of the words. Underline letters you sometimes confuse.

■ **WRITE**   Choose two sentences to write an advertisement, slogan, or saying.

SYNONYMS Write the list word that means the same as each pair below.

1. completely, totally
2. unimportant, trivial
3. fall, plummet
4. recover, regain
5. sense, detect
6. trust, be certain

7. neither side, objective
8. beforehand, prior
9. since, whereas
10. simple-minded, trusting
11. misleading, false
12. better, favored

RHYMES Write a list word that rhymes with each underlined word or phrase and makes sense in the sentence. Underline each list word in which the rhyming part is spelled differently from the word it rhymes with.

13. Just as I had <u>feared</u>, my new hairdo is ____.
14. We caught a ____ of the performing <u>chimps</u>.
15. Is it your ___ that the game was won through <u>deception</u>?
16. The wait in line was <u>horrendous</u>, but the roller coaster ride was ____.
17. Please don't sit and <u>stew</u>. I'll take you there when I'm ____.
18. It took a new <u>detective</u> to give the case a fresh ____.
19. If you want to <u>provoke her</u>, say the show was ____.
20. It should make sense, but it____. He was here when he said he <u>wasn't</u>.

Developing Spelling Consciousness

We sometimes misspell familiar words that we shouldn't miss. Proofread this passage. Write the four misspelled words correctly.

21–24. You can't beleive everything you hear. Just becuase a word is short dosen't mean it's easy to spell! In fact, really easy words are the ones we're most likely to spell wrong. When you're threw writing something, make sure you proofread for easy words too!

FREQUENTLY MISSPELLED WORDS * *FREQUENTLY MISSPELLED WORDS*

Believe is a frequently misspelled word because students often misspell it. Maybe this will help: Don't bel<u>ie</u>ve a l<u>ie</u>.

■ PROOFREADING AND WRITING

☰	Make a capital.
/	Make a small letter.
∧	Add something.
℮	Take out something.
⊙	Add a period.
¶	New paragraph

PROOFREAD FOR PUNCTUATION

When you write a contraction, remember to include an apostrophe. For example:

I dont like baby-sitting anymore because the kids just wont listen to me.

Check Contractions Read each sentence. Add apostrophes to contractions that need them. If they are correct, write "Correct."

1. Its a tremendous responsibility to be a baby-sitter.
2. You cant be too naive around little kids.
3. I have found that theyll try to get away with a lot.
4. I believe, however, that kids aren't ever really too bad.
5. Ive found it to be the best way to earn extra money.

PROOFREAD A JOURNAL ENTRY

Find the eight misspelled words in Mariko's journal entry. Write them correctly. Some may be words you learned before. Three are contraction errors.

> I cant believe the kid I baby-sat for. She was decietful, dishonest, and disrespectful. It was wierd. She didnt want to watch teevee (TV), so I had to play with her all night. When I got home, I was throughly (truely) exhausted and ready to collaspe. I don't think Ill ever stay with her again.

WRITE A JOURNAL ENTRY

Write a journal entry about your most recent baby-sitting experience or about a time you've spent with young children. Use three spelling words and a personal word.

Word List

preliminary	perception	perceive	naive
preferable	believe	glimpse	because
tremendous	retrieve	collapse	neutral
mediocre	deceitful	through	doesn't
perspective	weird	thoroughly	irrelevant

Personal Words 1.___ 2.___

16

tremendous
believe
doesn't
collapse
because
thoroughly
through
retrieve
glimpse
weird

Review

RIDDLES Write the list word from the box suggested by the clues in each riddle below.

1. I'm a word called a contraction. I'm similar to the word *don't.*
2. Like most other dogs, I like to do this with sticks, balls, and other things people throw.
3. I'm a word you might use to describe anything great.
4. I'm a word similar in meaning to *think, trust,* or *suppose.*
5. You'd use this word to describe an elephant wearing a skirt.
6. You'd use this word to describe why something happened.
7. I sound exactly like the word used to describe what a pitcher did with a baseball.
8. You might use this word to describe how long you saw a shooting star.
9. I'm a word similar in meaning to *completely* or *totally.*
10. I'm a word you might use to describe what a runner might do after running twenty-six miles.

Using a *Thesaurus*

THESAURUS ENTRY If you look up the list word *because* in your Writer's Thesaurus, this is what you would find. Study the entry for *because,* and then answer the questions.

Because means for the reason mentioned. *Lyle is late tonight because he missed the bus.* (conjunction)

Since can mean because. It is used when the cause is explained before the effect. *Since Lyle missed the bus, he is late tonight.*

For means because. This meaning is used mostly in writing. *The people rejoice tonight, for the long war has ended.*

So means with the effect mentioned, or for the purpose mentioned. *Tawana washed the dishes, so you don't have to.*

As a result means with the effect mentioned. *Mickey went around the corner too fast, and as a result the bike skidded.*

1. How many synonyms for *because* are listed?
2. What part of speech are *because* and its synonyms?
3. Which two synonyms for *because* make sense in this sentence: The students were happy, ___ summer vacation was about to begin.
4. Would you most likely see the word *for* meaning "because" in a comic book or in a textbook?

17

One Consonant or Two?

Sometimes double consonants stand for one sound: **embarrassment**.

■ **STUDY**   Say each word. Then read the sentence.

1. **embarrassment**   Falling is such an **embarrassment!**
2. **unnecessary**   A uniform is **unnecessary** for practice.
3. **occasionally**   The teacher **occasionally** gives a quiz.
4. **trespass**   Don't **trespass** on the neighbors' land.
5. **dismissed**   School is **dismissed** at 3:00 P.M.
6. **challenge**   I will **challenge** her to a chess match.
7. **forbidden**   She was **forbidden** to drive the car.
8. **accompany**   He will **accompany** his dad on the trip.
9. **immediately**   Call the fire department **immediately.**
10. **exaggerate**   He did not lie, but he did **exaggerate.**

11. **possessive**   Ann is **possessive** of her clothes.
12. **aggressive**   The more **aggressive** team won.
13. **accessory**   A flash is an **accessory** for a camera.
14. **compassionate**   The nurse was **compassionate.**
15. **cancellation**   The game **cancellation** is due to rain.
16. **commemorate**   The statue will **commemorate** the war.
17. **moccasin**   Joe made a leather **moccasin** at camp.
18. **accumulate**   It takes time to **accumulate** savings.
19. **dilemma**   It is hard to choose in this **dilemma.**
20. **appropriate**   The suit is **appropriate** for the party.

CHALLENGE!

preoccupation
saccharin
insufficient
constellation
commiserate

■ **PRACTICE**   Sort the words by writing
- six words with two sets of double consonants
- five other words with double **s** or **l**
- six other words with double **c** or **m**
- three words with double **g, p,** or **d**

■ **WRITE**   Choose four sentences to rewrite as questions.

ANTONYMS Write a list word that means the opposite of the underlined word in each sentence.

1. We stocked our first-aid kit with <u>essential</u> supplies.
2. Of course you'll be <u>permitted</u> to attend the carnival.
3. That lifeguard is not as <u>unfeeling</u> as he seems to be.
4. Our new kitten has a <u>passive</u> personality.
5. It is considered <u>improper</u> behavior to interrupt the speaker.
6. Will you get me that new software <u>sometime</u>?
7. I <u>generally</u> lock the front door when I leave the house.
8. I hope you didn't <u>lose</u> all your money playing video games.
9. The <u>solution</u> is simple; invite both of your friends over.
10. The hero was modest and tended to <u>understate</u> his actions.

CONTEXT Write the list word that completes each sentence.

11. No, I didn't lose a gray sandal; it was a gray ____.
12. We are ____ from class for lunch at 11:45 every day.
13. Pouring rain forced the ____ of our picnic.
14. I fell in front of the audience. What an ____!
15. My sister gets ____ and won't let me borrow her clothes.
16. Some people consider a watch an ____, but I think it's a necessity.
17. I hope you didn't ____ on our neighbor's land.
18. Would you like me to ____ you to your appointment?
19. I'd like to see a new stamp to ____ the end of the war in Vietnam.
20. I ____ you to a game of chess.

Using the Problem Parts Strategy

21–24. Double letters are often the problem parts of words. Write *embarrassment, commemorate, occasionally,* and *aggressive.* Mark the double letters in each word to help you remember them.

Did You Know?
Compassionate comes from a Latin prefix that means "with" and a root that means "suffer"; so the literal meaning of **compassionate** is "to suffer with your friend."

≡	Make a capital.
/	Make a small letter.
∧	Add something.
ℯ	Take out something.
⊙	Add a period.
⁋	New paragraph

PROOFREAD FOR USAGE To fix a run-on sentence, end the first one with a period and start the second one with a capital letter.

I had to make a police report, those kids were in the wrong place.

Check for Run-on Sentences Read this paragraph. If a sentence is a run-on, write "RO." If it is correct, write "Correct."

(1) Kids trespassed on my neighbor's land, I saw them and called the police. (2) The police challenged the kids' story and called their parents. (3) They called my neighbor too, he had the charges dismissed. (4) He's really very nice.

PROOFREAD A POLICE REPORT Find six misspelled words in this shoplifting report and write them correctly. Some may be words you learned before. Fix two run-on sentences.

> I hate to cause any embarassment, but I'm sure I saw that man shoplift. I was in the accessory area. I caught a glimspe of him taking a mocassin from a display, I saw him take earrings from the jewelry counter. I imediately reported it to the manager, he tried not to bring any uneccessary attention to him.

WRITE A POLICE REPORT Describe an incident you witnessed. Use three list words and a personal word.

Word List

dilemma	moccasin	challenge	accumulate
compassionate	unnecessary	possessive	occasionally
commemorate	accompany	trespass	immediately
aggressive	exaggerate	dismissed	appropriate
cancellation	embarrassment	forbidden	accessory

Personal Words 1.___ 2.___

SYNONYMS Write the list word in the box that is suggested by the underlined word or words in each sentence.

embarrassment	**5**
unnecessary	*6*
occasionally	*3*
trespass	*2*
dismissed	*8*
challenge	**7**
forbidden	*10*
accompany	*9*
immediately	*4*
exaggerate	*1*

1. Don't <u>overstate</u> the number of books you read over the summer.
2. The campers honored the "Do Not <u>Intrude</u>" signs on the farmer's property.
3. <u>Once in a while</u> I'll clean my room.
4. If the sirens go off, head for shelter <u>right away</u>.
5. After forgetting my lines while on stage, I'm red-faced with <u>shame</u>.
6. Bringing fifteen pencils to the test was <u>not needed</u>.
7. Loretta fought an <u>uphill battle</u> to win the state track meet.
8. Classes for the summer were <u>let out</u> when the last diploma was given.
9. Dad will <u>go along with</u> Sherise when she applies for her driver's license.
10. Smoking is <u>not allowed</u> in any public building.

Multicultural *Connection*

LANGUAGES The Europeans who came to America in the 1500s and 1600s owed a great deal to the North American Indians. These Europeans had no names for the many new plants, animals, and tools they encountered. But the Indians did. Here are just a few:

moccasin	hogan	muskrat
hickory	pecan	hominy

Write the word from the list that each sentence describes. Use your Spelling Dictionary if you need help.

1. The fur of this water rodent was valuable in trade.
2. This nut is the most valuable edible nut in North America.
3. This soft leather shoe protected Indians' feet.
4. This is a Navajo house made of logs covered with earth.
5. This hulled corn is usually eaten boiled.
6. This tree with edible nuts has tough, hard wood.

Words with Digraphs

SPELLING FOCUS

The digraphs **tu** and **ti** can stand for the sound /ch/. The digraphs **ci, ss,** and **ti** can stand for the sound /sh/.

■ **STUDY** Say each word. Then read the sentence.

1.	**adventurous**	Mountain climbers are **adventurous.**
2.	**unnatural**	The dark sky looked **unnatural.**
3.	**capture**	The police will **capture** the suspect.
4.	**questionable**	The student's excuse was **questionable.**
5.	**beneficial**	The medicine had **beneficial** effects.
6.	**efficient**	The **efficient** worker didn't waste time.
7.	**impression**	The speaker made a good **impression.**
8.	**expression**	The judge wore a solemn **expression.**
9.	**emotional**	The **emotional** film made me cry.
10.	**negotiate**	The athlete will **negotiate** a contract.
11.	**posture**	Exercise will improve your **posture.**
12.	**punctual**	I was late, but I am usually **punctual.**
13.	**cultural**	Our country has **cultural** diversity.
14.	**congestion**	Her cold caused nasal **congestion.**
15.	**sufficient**	Crops must get **sufficient** rain.
16.	**ancient**	Homer was an **ancient** Greek poet.
17.	**spacious**	The large school had **spacious** rooms.
18.	**reassure**	The police will **reassure** the citizens.
19.	**intermission**	The play has a brief **intermission.**
20.	**initiation**	The new members underwent **initiation.**

CHALLENGE!

picturesque
auspicious
repercussion
minutia
caricature

■ **PRACTICE** Sort the list words by writing
- five words with **ci**
- four words with **ss**
- five words with **ti**
- six words with **tu**

■ **WRITE** Choose ten words to write in sentences.

WORD FORMS   Write the list word that contains each base word below.

1. assure
2. emotion
3. express
4. adventure
5. nature

6. congest
7. initiate
8. culture
9. question
10. impress

RELATIONSHIPS   Write the list word that completes each analogy.

11. Modern is to new as ____ is to old.
12. Half time is to a football game as ____ is to a play.
13. Small is to crowded as large is to ____.
14. Terrible is to awful as ____ is to good.
15. Satisfactory is to adequate as enough is to ____.
16. Release is to free as ____ is to grab.
17. Slouching is to curved back as good ____ is to straight back.
18. Delayed is to late as ____ is to on time.
19. Compromise is to meet halfway as ____ is to talk over.
20. Incompetent is to unable as ____ is to capable.

Seeing Meaning Connections

nature
natural
naturalist
unnatural

The words in the box, including the list word **unnatural,** are related in spelling and meaning. Complete the sentences with these words.

My friends and I went on a _(21)_ walk in a nearby forest preserve. We were guided by a _(22)_ who works there. Our guide was able to point out plants, animals, and birds that are native to our region. It's great to see them in their _(23)_ habitat. What wasn't great, though, was seeing the litter that people had left. It looked so _(24)_ .

> **Did You Know?**
> **Ancient**, which means "very old," actually comes from a Latin word meaning "before"; so something that is **ancient** certainly came before now.

≡	Make a capital.
/	Make a small letter.
∧	Add something.
ℯ	Take out something.
⊙	Add a period.
⨍	New paragraph

PROOFREAD FOR CAPITALIZATION

Capitalize the names of countries, cities, states, and nationalities. For example:

How many people left mexico with you?

Check Capitalization Read each interview question. Correct any capitalization errors. If it's correct, write "Correct."

1. What do you like most about chicago?
2. What has been most exciting for you since coming to Illinois?
3. Is there more traffic congestion in guadalajara than here?
4. What are the ancient Mayan ruins in your country like?
5. Do we use english expressions that you don't understand?

PROOFREAD INTERVIEW QUESTIONS Find the five

misspelled words in Marcia's questions. Write them correctly. They may be list words or words you have learned before. Fix three capitalization errors too.

> 1. What was your first impreshin of fairfield?
>
> 2. What advencherous things have you done since coming to the United states?
>
> 3. What cultoral differences have you seen?
>
> 4. Were you emoshinal when you arrived?
>
> 5. Wich american TV shows do you like?

WRITE INTERVIEW QUESTIONS Write a list of questions

that you would like to ask someone who just moved to this country. Try to use three list words and a personal word.

Word List

adventurous	posture	expression	capture
impression	sufficient	negotiate	congestion
emotional	reassure	efficient	punctual
unnatural	intermission	spacious	cultural
beneficial	ancient	questionable	initiation

Personal Words 1.____ 2.____

CONTEXT CLUES   Use the context clues given in each sentence to write the correct list word from the box.

adventurous
unnatural
capture
questionable
beneficial
efficient
impression
expression
emotional
negotiate

1. I named the fifty state capitals so I could make an ___ on my teacher.
2. Felipe wasn't sure he was ___ enough to go into the cave.
3. The athlete wanted to ___ with the owners for more money.
4. Exercise and a good diet are ___ to your health.
5. The police and our neighbors worked to ___ the car thief.
6. That giraffe walking down the street was a most ___ event!
7. To make studying more ___, find a quiet room.
8. You should have seen the ___ on her face when Marissa heard she got an A!
9. When the patient finally woke up, all felt very ___.
10. Keeping the money you found is an act that's quite ___.

Word *Study*

LATIN ROOTS: *bene*   The list word *beneficial* contains the Latin root *bene,* which means "good" or "well." All the words in the box contain the root *bene.*

beneficial
benign
beneficiary
benefit
benevolent

Complete the word web below with the *bene* words in the box. Use your Spelling Dictionary if you need help.

1. "an advantage, a help"

2. "a person who receives a benefit"

***bene*—"good or well"**

3. "promoting the happiness of others; charitable"

5. "advantageous, helpful"

4. "harmless, gentle"

Now that you know their meanings, use one of the *bene* words to complete each sentence.

6. Brushing and flossing are ___ to your dental health.
7. Their ___ donations brought much joy to those in need.
8. The best ___ from studying hard is getting good grades.
9. Who is the ___ on your insurance policy?
10. We were thankful when we learned that the tumor was ___.

Greek Word Parts

Many words are made up of Greek word parts. **Hydro** means "water," **chronos** means "time," **thermo** means "heat," and **meter** means "device for measuring."

■ **STUDY** Say each word. Then read the sentence.

1.	**hydrant**	Firefighters get water from a **hydrant.**
2.	**hydrogen**	One element of water is **hydrogen.**
3.	**dehydrated**	To eat **dehydrated** foods, add water.
4.	**chronic**	Lu has a constant, **chronic** backache.
5.	**synchronize**	Let's **synchronize** our watches.
6.	**thermos**	The **thermos** kept the soup hot.
7.	**thermometer**	A **thermometer** measures temperature.
8.	**diameter**	The plate has a ten-inch **diameter.**
9.	**speedometer**	The car's **speedometer** read 45 mph.
10.	**centimeter**	The insect measured one **centimeter.**

11.	**hydrophobia**	He won't swim; he has **hydrophobia.**
12.	**hydraulic**	The mechanics used a **hydraulic** lift.
13.	**hydroelectric**	The dam produces **hydroelectric** power.
14.	**chronicle**	He wrote a **chronicle** of the war.
15.	**chronological**	Tell the story in **chronological** order.
16.	**thermostat**	Adjust the **thermostat** for more heat.
17.	**thermal**	The skier wore **thermal** underwear.
18.	**geometry**	We measured angles in **geometry.**
19.	**barometer**	Weather forecasters use a **barometer.**
20.	**symmetry**	The two sides showed perfect **symmetry.**

CHALLENGE!

chronograph
thermodynamic
thermonuclear
metronome
asymmetrical

■ **PRACTICE**
- Write four words with **chronos.**
- Write six words with **hydro.**
- Write one word with both **thermo** and **meter.**
- Write three more words with **thermo.**
- Write six more words with **meter.**

■ **WRITE** Choose two sentences to write a rhyme or riddle.

MAKING CONNECTIONS   Write the list word that matches each clue.

1. This is where you would get water to put out a fire.
2. This electricity is generated using water power.
3. It's a gas that combines with oxygen to form water.
4. This describes a machine that is powered by water pressure.
5. This is the fear of water.
6. The water has been taken out.
7. This is another word for time order.
8. When something lasts a long time, it is this.
9. This is to arrange for two things to happen at the same time.
10. This is a history of events based on their time order.

DEFINITIONS   Write the list word that matches each clue.

11. I'm a line segment that goes from one side to the other through the center of a circle.
12. Use me when you want to know how fast a car is going.
13. I'll keep your soup hot and your lemonade cold.
14. You use me to find out if you have a fever.
15. When something is the same on both sides, it has this.
16. When you want to see if the weather will change, I'm there.
17. Wool-lined gloves like me can be described as this.
18. I am one-hundredth of a meter.
19. When it gets too cold, I tell the furnace to get to work.
20. In math, I'm the study of circles, squares, and other shapes.

Seeing Meaning Connections

These words come from **phobia,** meaning "fear." Write the word that fits each definition. One is from your word list. *Hint:* **pyro** means "fire" and **arachnē** means "spider."

hydrophobia
arachnophobia
pyrophobia

21. fear of water
22. fear of fire
23. fear of spiders

Did You Know?
When the Thermos bottle was patented in 1904, **Thermos** was a trademark. Since then it's been used so much it's no longer considered a trademark and is not capitalized.

■ PROOFREADING AND WRITING

≡	Make a capital.
/	Make a small letter.
∧	Add something.
ℯ	Take out something.
⊙	Add a period.
⨏	New paragraph

PROOFREAD FOR CARELESS ERRORS

Adding and dropping letters are usually careless errors. For example:

You have to find ever~~y~~ item on th~e~ list.

Check for Careless Errors Read each sentence. Correct any words with added or dropped letters.

1. Pleas remain in our immediate neighborhood.
2. Try to find all of you items in your assigned area.
3. Do note go beyond the fire hydrant on South Street.
4. Smile for they photographer from *The Daily Chronicle.*
5. Hurry, because there is and time limit.

PROOFREAD DIRECTIONS

Find the eight misspelled words in the rest of the directions and write them correctly. Three are careless errors. Some may be words you learned before.

You have exactly thirty minutes to find everything. Let's synkronize our watches and go! You need too find the following: a thermometer, a measuring cup, a pair off thermle underwear, a mocassin, a ruler with centameter marks, a thimble, tree safety pins, a wooden coat hanger, a thermus jug, and a compass.

WRITE DIRECTIONS

Plan your own scavenger hunt. Write directions and brainstorm a list of items that you want your friends to find. Try to use three list words and a personal word.

Word List

hydrant	speedometer	hydroelectric	symmetry
hydrophobia	thermos	chronic	dehydrated
chronicle	hydrogen	thermometer	thermal
diameter	synchronize	geometry	centimeter
thermostat	barometer	hydraulic	chronological

Personal Words 1.____ 2.____

hydrant
hydrogen
dehydrated
chronic
synchronize
thermos
thermometer
diameter
speedometer
centimeter

WHO SAID THAT?   Write the list word from the box
suggested by each quotation.

1. "I need this to put out that fire," the firefighter said.
2. "If you had looked at this, you wouldn't get a ticket," the police officer said.
3. "Combine this and oxygen to make water," the scientist said.
4. "For long-term pain, take aspirin every day," said the doctor.
5. "Let's make sure our watches match," said the sergeant.
6. "Two weeks in the desert did this to me," the prospector said.
7. "The earth's is about 8,000 miles," said the astronaut.
8. "Keep your soup hot in this," the father said.
9. "Hold this under your tongue," the nurse said.
10. "A hundred germs measure this long," the biologist said.

Using a *Dictionary*

DICTIONARY: PARTS OF AN ENTRY   A dictionary
gives you all sorts of interesting information about a word. Look
at this dictionary entry for *synchronize.*

entry word ┐ pronunciation ┐ inflected forms ┐   ┌ part-of-speech label

syn chro nize (sing′krə nīz), *v.,* **-nized, -nizing.**—*v.i.* **1** occur at the same ——— definition
time; agree in time. **2** move or take place at the same rate and exactly
together. —*v.t.* **1** make agree in time: *synchronize all the clocks in a* ——— illustrative
building. **2** assign to the same time or period. [< Greek *synchronizein*   sentence or
< *synchronos* < *syn*- together + *chronos* time] —**syn′chro ni za′tion,** *n.*   phrase
—**syn′chro ni′zer,** *n.*
       └ etymology   └ run-on entry

Answer these questions using the entry for *synchronize.*

1. How many syllables are there in *synchronize?*
2. What part of speech is *synchronize?*
3. How do you spell the past tense of *synchronize?*
4. How many definitions are given for *synchronize?*
5. From what language does *synchronize* come?

Irregular Plurals

Most plurals are formed by adding **-s** or **-es.** Irregular plurals are formed in different ways.

■ **STUDY** Say each word on the left. Then read its plural form.

wife	1.	**wives**
giraffe	2.	**giraffes**
tariff	3.	**tariffs**
great-aunt	4.	**great-aunts**
memento	5.	**mementos**
mosquito	6.	**mosquitoes**
crisis	7.	**crises**
analysis	8.	**analyses**
criterion	9.	**criteria**
species	10.	**species**

wharf	11.	**wharves**
ghetto	12.	**ghettos**
pistachio	13.	**pistachios**
veto	14.	**vetoes**
embargo	15.	**embargoes**
sister-in-law	16.	**sisters-in-law**
diagnosis	17.	**diagnoses**
stimulus	18.	**stimuli**
phenomenon	19.	**phenomena**
Sioux	20.	**Sioux**

CHALLENGE!

armadillos
supercargoes
memoranda
radii
commandos

■ **PRACTICE** Sort the words by writing
- two plurals identical to their singular form
- three plurals in which **is** becomes **es**
- three plurals that aren't formed with **-s** or **-es**
- five plurals to which **-es** was added
- seven plurals to which **-s** was added

■ **WRITE** Choose ten words to write in sentences.

WORD FORMS Write the plural forms of the words in parentheses.

1. We had (analysis) of the problem done by three scientists.
2. I bought (memento) of our trip to the Smoky Mountains for my traveling companions.
3. The (tariff) on some imports are high.
4. A set of (criterion) had to be met before it was accepted.
5. The (stimulus) for achievement are punishment and reward.
6. A series of (crisis) cause a lot of stress in our lives.
7. The President's (veto) kept several bills from becoming laws.
8. The (diagnosis) of the two diseases were quite similar.
9. Will their government lift the (embargo) on our ships?

CLASSIFYING Write the list word that belongs in each group.

10. macadamias, pecans, cashews
11. happenings, events, occurrences
12. Navajo, Iroquois, Cheyenne
13. mothers-in-law, fathers-in-law, brothers-in-law
14. neighborhoods, areas, districts
15. great-uncles, great-grandmothers, great-grandfathers
16. grasshoppers, bees, flies
17. piers, docks, platforms
18. sisters, brothers, husbands
19. kingdoms, phylums, genuses
20. elephants, aardvarks, lions

Strategic Spelling

Building New Words

Form the plurals of these words: *portfolio, volcano, motto, handcuff.* Use your Spelling Dictionary if you need to.

Plurals with -s
21.____
22.____

Plurals with -es
23.____
24.____

Take a Hint
Need help spelling **mementos?**
Remember that <u>memen</u>tos are to
preserve <u>memo</u>ries.

≡	Make a capital.
/	Make a small letter.
∧	Add something.
ℓ	Take out something.
⊙	Add a period.
¶	New paragraph

PROOFREAD FOR USAGE Having verb tenses consistent keeps your writing from being confusing. For example:

traveled

We went to South Dakota first. Then we ∧ t̶r̶a̶v̶e̶l̶ to Montana.

Check Verb Tense Read each sentence. If the underlined verb is correct, write "Correct." If not, write it correctly.

1. First we were in Iowa, and then we <u>go</u> to South Dakota.
2. The Badlands were beautiful. We <u>explore</u> them.
3. We found a campground that <u>had</u> a fantastic view.
4. I was amazed at how cold it got. I <u>needed</u> a heavy sweater.
5. We left early the next morning and <u>drive</u> to the Black Hills.

PROOFREAD A TRAVEL DIARY Find five misspelled words in this travel diary. Write them correctly. Some may be words you have learned before. Fix three errors with verb tense too.

> We spent the morning at Mt. Rushmore. I buy mementos their. I bought gifts for my great-aunts and sister-in-laws too. We left for Montana at noon. We didn't stop for lunch but munch on pistachioes in the car and tried to find as many animal speces as we could. We also go to where the Sioux defeated Custer,

WRITE A TRAVEL DIARY Write a travel diary about a trip that you enjoyed. Use three list words and a personal word.

Word List

wharves	ghettos	sisters-in-law	crises
wives	mementos	great-aunts	diagnoses
giraffes	vetoes	criteria	analyses
tariffs	mosquitoes	stimuli	Sioux
pistachios	embargoes	phenomena	species

Personal Words 1.___ 2.___

Review

DEFINITIONS   Write the list word that fits each definition.

1. systems of duties or taxes on imports and exports
2. the breaking up of something complex into simpler elements
3. rules or standards for making judgments
4. the aunts of one's father or mother
5. states of danger or anxious waiting
6. large African mammals with very long necks
7. groups of related organisms
8. married women
9. things that serve as reminders of the past
10. small, slender insects with two wings

wives
giraffes
tariffs
great-aunts
mementos
mosquitoes
crises
analyses
criteria
species

Word *Study*

ANALOGIES   An **analogy** shows how two pairs of words are related. In the analogy **mammal : giraffes :: insect : mosquitoes,** the first word is a *class* and the second is a *member* of that class. The analogy is read "mammal is to giraffes as insect is to mosquitoes." Some other types of analogies, besides *Class and Member,* are *Worker and Tool* **(painter : brush :: golfer : club)** and *Part to Whole* **(finger : hand :: letter : alphabet).**

Label each analogy below as *Class and Member, Worker and Tool,* or *Part to Whole.*

1. furniture : sofa :: tree : maple
2. doctor : stethoscope :: carpenter : hammer
3. leaf : tree :: petal : flower
4. poem : limerick :: song : ballad
5. pilot : airplane :: artist : easel

Now that you know some types of analogies, use these words to complete the following analogies: *whale, pistachio, tractor, stove,* and *team.*

6. vegetable : carrot :: nut : ____
7. page : book :: player : ____
8. judge : gavel :: farmer : ____
9. fish : trout :: mammal : ____
10. conductor : baton :: chef : ____

Review

Lesson 1: Getting Letters in Correct Order
Lesson 2: One Consonant or Two?
Lesson 3: Words with Digraphs
Lesson 4: Greek Word Parts
Lesson 5: Irregular Plurals

REVIEW WORD LIST

1. because
2. believe
3. doesn't
4. glimpse
5. mediocre
6. naive
7. perceive
8. perception
9. preferable
10. thoroughly
11. tremendous
12. weird
13. accumulate
14. aggressive
15. appropriate
16. challenge
17. commemorate
18. dismissed
19. embarrassment
20. immediately
21. moccasin
22. occasionally
23. trespass
24. unnecessary
25. adventurous
26. ancient
27. capture
28. congestion
29. expression
30. punctual
31. questionable
32. spacious
33. sufficient
34. barometer
35. dehydrated
36. diameter
37. hydrogen
38. thermal
39. thermometer
40. thermos
41. analyses
42. criteria
43. giraffes
44. great-aunts
45. mementos
46. mosquitoes
47. phenomena
48. Sioux
49. sisters-in-law
50. species

■ PROOFREADING

Find the spelling errors in each passage and write the words correctly. All passages have seven errors except the last one, which has eight.

PROOFREAD A MOVIE REVIEW

The Gnat
The movie *The Gnat* is an embarassment by any ordinary critearia for judging films. When a niave scientist accidentally injects a pair of gnats with a chemical, they grow to the size of girraffes and immediatly start eating Washington, D.C. The mutant specis manages to cause conjestion on Constitution Avenue and panic in the Pentagon. You can fly away from this one.

PROOFREAD A REPORT

Origins of State Names

Many states take their names from Native American or Spanish words. Others comemorate a person or place. Kansas is a Suoix word meaning "south wind people." The origin of Mississippi is questionible. It may come from a Chippewa or an Algonquin word. New Hampshire was named by Capt. John Mason becuse his home was originally in the county of Hampshire in England. Louisiana was named by the adventurus explorer Sieur de La Salle for Louis XIV, a French king. Nevada is a Spanish word meaning "covered with snow," certainly approppriate for northern Nevada. Washington State was originally the Territory of Columbia, but Congress thought Washington perferable because of the already-named District of Columbia.

PROOFREAD A CHARACTER SKETCH

My Granddad

My granddad is an amateur weatherman. Not only does he have a thermometre, but he also has a barmeter, a rain gauge, and a device for measuring wind speed. He records all the data measured by his instruments three times a day. He also studies the clouds. From his analises of all this information, he can forecast local weather. He has predicted all kinds of fenomena, including a ten-inch snowfall when school was dismised. He says his methods are based on a close preception of nature and a tremedous intellect.

PROOFREAD A FRIENDLY LETTER

November 19, 20_ _

Dear Karen,

In looking through a box of momentoes and photographs, I found the enclosed picture of three of our great-ants taken when they were young women. They are all wearing rather wierd clothes, and Emily seems to be holding up a mocassin! The house in the background looks very spacouis. There is a mystery, however. Who is the fourth woman in the photo with the amused exspression? Is she one of your sister-in-laws?

Love from your cousin,

Felicia

PROOFREAD A SCIENCE REPORT

The Planet Mercury

Mercury is the nearest planet to the sun. With a diamter of 3100 miles, it is the second smallest of the planets. Scientists now belive that Mercury has an atmosphere, probably made up of hydragen and helium. In Roman mythology, Mercury was a messenger to the gods. Like the anchant Roman god for whom it is named, the planet Mercury moves quickly. It completes its journey around the sun in 88 days. It dosen't have a great climate, however. The temperature probably

reaches 800 degrees Fahrenheit. We can often glipse the planet during early morning or early evening hours, but we cannot percieve it from Earth against a night sky, for it is too much in line with the sun.

PROOFREAD AN INSTRUCTION SHEET

Instructions for Minnesota Expedition

Please read these instructions. They tell you about the Minnesota Expedition in October.

In addition to your usual hiking gear, please remember to bring these items:

thermel jacket
sleeping bag
something to repel mosquitos

flashlight
thermus or canteen

We will supply these items:

dehidrated food

cooking equipment

The bus leaves October 1 at 6:00 A.M. from Sharp School. Please be punchual! Do not bring uneccessary items. Hikers are not to tresspass on private property.

PROOFREAD A SPORTS STORY

Cougars Win

The Cougars throughly trounced the Tigers last Friday in a 43-38 victory in the first home game of the season. After a medioakre first quarter, the Cougars caught fire when Charles Green scored six baskets, and they led 25-17 at the half. The Tigers mounted an agressive challange in the third quarter but couldn't acumulate sufficent points to win. With three lay-up shots by the Tigers' Joseph Porter and Jose Rico's spirited attempts to capshure the ball in the fourth quarter, the Tigers occaisonally showed some of last year's spunk, but missed free throws finally told the story.

STRATEGY WORKSHOP

Pronouncing for Spelling

DISCOVER THE STRATEGY 1 Annie misspells the middle part of *probably* because she mispronounces it. She needs to try this correct pronunciation strategy:

1. Read the word aloud carefully and correctly. Listen to the sound of each letter.
2. Pronounce the word again as you write it.

TRY IT OUT Now practice this strategy. Pronounce the words in dark type slowly and correctly. As you do, listen carefully to the sounds of the underlined letters. Pronounce each word again as you write it.

1. **finally** (not "fin▪ly")
2. **medicine** (not "med▪cine")
3. **candidate** (not "can▪i▪date")
4. **accidentally** (not "ac▪ci▪dent▪ly")
5. **memory** (not "mem▪ry")

DISCOVER THE STRATEGY 2 It wouldn't—but making up
a secret pronunciation might help.

- Pronounce the silent letters in the word as you write it. For
  example, say the sound of the **h** in *vehicle*: "ve-**hi**-cle."
- Or change the way you say a tricky sound in the word. For
  example, to remember the **o** at the end of *conductor*, say it to
  yourself like the word *or*: "con-duct-**or**." To remember the **i** in
  gratitude, say it like the letter **i**: grat-**i**-tude.

TRY IT OUT Practice this secret pronunciation strategy on
words that aren't spelled the way they're spoken. Make up secret
pronunciations for these words. Concentrate on the underlined
letters. Write each word as you say its secret pronunciation.

6. shepherd   9. asthma
7. unique   10. victim
8. calves

LOOK AHEAD Look ahead at the next five lessons. Write
three list words that you could use the strategy with. Mark the
part of each word that you'll pay special attention to when you
pronounce it.

Words with No Sound Clues

SPELLING FOCUS

Vowel sounds you hear in some words give no clue to spelling: **luck_ily, favo̲rite.** Pronounce each syllable carefully.

■ **STUDY** Say each word. Then read the sentence.

WATCH OUT FOR FREQUENTLY MISSPELLED WORDS!

1.	**identify**	Use a passport to **identify** yourself.
2.	**government**	The mayor heads the city **government.**
3.	**everything** ✳	Alex put **everything** in his backpack.
4.	**environment**	Automobiles pollute the **environment.**
5.	**probably** ✳	Jim will **probably** play quarterback.
6.	**really** ✳	The drought is **really** severe.
7.	**semester**	Lee got good grades this **semester.**
8.	**luckily**	Jill **luckily** found her wallet.
9.	**favorite** ✳	Peaches are my **favorite** fruit.
10.	**delicate**	The old lace dress is very **delicate.**

11.	**automatically**	The door opens **automatically.**
12.	**mortgage**	A **mortgage** must be paid each month.
13.	**temperamental**	The **temperamental** child cried loudly.
14.	**consequences**	The war had tragic **consequences.**
15.	**trampoline**	The gymnast jumped on a **trampoline.**
16.	**therapy**	The athlete had **therapy** for her knee.
17.	**catastrophe**	The flood was a major **catastrophe.**
18.	**distribute**	The coach will **distribute** uniforms.
19.	**criticism**	Try to accept **criticism** gracefully.
20.	**hideous**	That dinosaur looked **hideous.**

CHALLENGE!

| mannequin |
| annihilate |
| aesthetic |
| apropos |
| aerobics |

■ **PRACTICE** Look over the list words carefully. First, write the words that are the most difficult for you to spell. Then write the rest of the words. Underline any letters that cause you a particular problem.

■ **WRITE** Choose four sentences to rewrite as questions.

SEEING RELATIONSHIPS Write the list word that completes each sentence.

1. I'm absolutely, positively certain. I'm ____ certain.
2. Physical and occupational are two kinds of me. I'm ____.
3. Two of me together make a school year. I'm a ____.
4. I'm made up of the executive, judicial, and legislative branches. I'm your ____.
5. You lost a ring and want to claim it. You must ____ it first.
6. I include everything around you. I'm your ____.
7. A volcano, hurricane, or tornado is an example of me. I'm a natural ____.
8. Acrobatically speaking, I'm "hopping" fun. I'm a ____.
9. Follow directions exactly or you will suffer me. I'm the ____.
10. You want everyone to have the same amount. You need to ____ the money evenly.
11. You borrow money to buy a house, but the bank gets the house if you can't pay. That's a ____.

ANTONYMS Write the list word that completes each phrase.

12. not nothing, but ____
13. not manually, but ____
14. not easy to get along with, but ____
15. not beautiful, but ____
16. not unfortunately, but ____
17. not approval, but ____
18. not strong, but ____
19. not the least-liked, but the ____
20. not unlikely, but ____

> **Did You Know?**
> **Trampoline** comes from a German word that means "to trample." When you bounce on a trampoline, are you trampling, or "walking heavily," on it?

21.–24. We sometimes spell words wrong because we say them wrong. Write *identify, government, temperamental,* and *automatically.* Now say each word carefully. Be sure to pronounce the sounds of the underlined letters.

■ PROOFREADING AND WRITING

≡	Make a capital.
/	Make a small letter.
∧	Add something.
ℓ	Take out something.
⊙	Add a period.
⌐F	New paragraph

PROOFREAD FOR CARELESS ERRORS

Proofread carefully so you don't carelessly leave out words when you write. For example:

We need ⟨to⟩ start a recycling program at Hillside Middle School.

Check for Careless Errors Read more of this editorial. Write any words that were left out. Write "Correct" if the sentence is correct.

1. It going to be up to us to save our environment.
2. If we don't, we'll have face future consequences.
3. Luckily for us, it's not too late.
4. There are lot of things we can do around our school.
5. To start, we will distribute recycling bins around the school.

PROOFREAD AN EDITORIAL Find the six misspelled words in the rest of this editorial and write them correctly. Some may be words you learned before. Write three missing words too.

> We'll idenify the bins by color. Orange is for cans and green is for paper. Are world doesn't seem delacate, but it. It probably take awhile get used to recycling. We hope that by next smester, recycling will come automaticly to you. We're trying realy hard to make a difference.

WRITE AN EDITORIAL Identify a situation in your school that you think needs to change. Write an editorial calling for action. Try to use three list words and a personal word.

Word List

identify	mortgage	really	distribute
government	temperamental	therapy	favorite
everything	probably	semester	delicate
environment	consequences	catastrophe	criticism
automatically	trampoline	luckily	hideous

Personal Words 1.___ 2.___

42

Review

WORD CLUES Write the word from the box suggested by each group of words.

1. surroundings, ecology, Earth
2. all, each and every one
3. term, part of school year
4. fragile, dainty, pleasing
5. likely to happen, likely to be true
6. President, Cabinet, Congress
7. actually, truly, in fact
8. preferred over others, best chance
9. fortunately, by good luck
10. recognize, point to

identify
government
everything
environment
probably
really
semester
luckily
favorite
delicate

Multicultural *Connection*

LANGUAGES Know what a tidal wave is? It's a catastrophe that can happen after an underwater earthquake. But a tidal wave has nothing to do with tides. That's why we now use the more accurate Japanese word *tsunami*. In the box are other words from Asian languages that have become part of American English.

tsunami
bamboo
kumquat
sukiyaki
tycoon
tatami
orangutan
chop suey

Write the word from the box that best fits each clue. Use your Spelling Dictionary if you need help.

1. From the Japanese *tai kiun,* it now means "a business person with wealth and power."
2. From the Chinese word *kamkwat,* it is a yellow fruit.
3. From a Malay word, it is a treelike, woody grass.
4. This combines the Japanese words meaning "harbor" and "wave."
5. This word from Malay for a large ape literally translates as "man of the woods."
6. This dish of meats and vegetables comes from the Chinese word *tsap sui,* meaning "odds and ends."
7. This is a Japanese dish of strips of meat with vegetables.
8. This is a straw floor mat used in Japanese homes.

Related Words 1

SPELLING FOCUS

Related words often have parts that are spelled the same but pronounced differently: **st_a_ble, st_a_bility.**

■ **STUDY**   Say each word. Then read the sentence.

1.	**define**	A French teacher can **define** that word.
2.	**definition**	The word has more than one **definition.**
3.	**protect**	A hat will **protect** you from the sun.
4.	**protection**	A tent gives **protection** from the rain.
5.	**stable**	Three legs make the stool **stable.**
6.	**stability**	The rickety stairs lacked **stability.**
7.	**victory**	The tennis player enjoyed his **victory.**
8.	**victorious**	The fans cheered the **victorious** team.
9.	**politics**	The senator understands state **politics.**
10.	**political**	We have two main **political** parties.
11.	**congratulate**	We will **congratulate** the winners.
12.	**congratulations**	The winner accepted **congratulations.**
13.	**graduate**	Her goal is to **graduate** from college.
14.	**graduation**	A top student spoke at **graduation.**
15.	**inspect**	Officials will **inspect** the fruit.
16.	**inspection**	The school passed its fire **inspection.**
17.	**narrate**	The author will **narrate** a scary story.
18.	**narrative**	We read a **narrative** about the journey.
19.	**strategy**	The coach has a **strategy** for the game.
20.	**strategic**	The army was in a **strategic** location.

CHALLENGE!

immune
immunize
tranquil
tranquillity
intuitive
intuition

■ **PRACTICE**   Sort the words by writing
- five pairs of words in which the suffix **-ion** or **-tion** is added
- two pairs of words in which the suffix **-ity** or **-ive** is added
- two pairs of words in which the suffix **-al** or **-ous** is added
- one pair of words in which the suffix **-ic** is added

■ **WRITE**   Choose two sentences to include in a paragraph about an election.

WORD RELATIONSHIPS   Write the list word that matches each clue. Then write the list word that is related to it.

1.–2.   to tell a story about
3.–4.   to give the meaning of
5.–6.   not likely to fall
7.–8.   to shield from harm
9.–10.   to look closely at

DRAWING CONCLUSIONS   Write the list word that answers each question.

11. If your dog finishes its training class, it will what?
12. What do you call a win?
13. What would you say to someone who just won an award?
14. What is another name for a plan of attack?
15. What word would you use to describe the winning team?
16. What do you call the science and art of government?
17. What is the ceremony for when you finish high school?
18. What would you call the methods of a politician?
19. If you set yourself up in exactly the right spot, what word would you use to describe your location?
20. If you were really happy for the bride and groom, what would you do to them?

STRATEGIC SPELLING
Building New Words

Add the suffix **-ic** to make new words. Circle the words that have spelling changes. Use your Spelling Dictionary if you need help.

21. strategy
22. telescope
23. hero
24. scene
25. economy

Take a Hint
Exaggerating the pronunciation of **congratulations** can help you spell it correctly. Try to emphasize the first **t.**

≡	Make a capital.
/	Make a small letter.
∧	Add something.
ℯ	Take out something.
⊙	Add a period.
⨍	New paragraph

PROOFREAD FOR PUNCTUATION

Most abbreviations that are the initials of words need periods. For example:

When: Saturday, August 4, at 10:00 A̲M̲
⊙⊙

Check Abbreviations Write these abbreviations from party invitations correctly. If they are correct, write "Correct."

1. DJ Johnson has just completed college.
2. Let's congratulate D.J. on completing his BA in business.
3. Where: at the Lincoln Memorial, Washington, DC
4. Please send all replies to PO Box 348.
5. When: 4:00 P.M. on Sunday

PROOFREAD AN INVITATION   Find the five misspelled

words in this party invitation and write them correctly. Some may be words you learned before. Find two abbreviation errors too.

Its a surprise graduation party!

Help us congradulate Shawn.

When: Sunday, June 6

2:00 PM (Please be prompt.)

Where: 1453 Madison Ave.

Please write a short narritive about the graduite to share. Anything that will cause embarasment is preferred! RSVP by June 4.

WRITE AN INVITATION   Write an invitation to a party

you might like to give. Be sure to write the dates and addresses correctly. Use three list words and a personal word.

Word List

stable	graduation	define	victorious
stability	narrate	definition	politics
congratulate	narrative	inspect	political
congratulations	strategy	inspection	protect
graduate	strategic	victory	protection

Personal Words 1.___ 2.___

Review

WORD CLUES   Write the words from the box suggested by each set of clues.

define
definition
protect
protection
stable
stability
victory
victorious
politics
political

1. steady, firm
2. defeat of an enemy, success in a contest
3. shield, shelter, defend
4. make clear, explain, characterize
5. of politics, of government
6. conquering, ending in victory
7. firmness, permanence
8. statement of meaning
9. the science of government, political methods
10. thing that prevents damage, defense

Word *Study*

LATIN ROOTS: MILITARY WORDS   The words *victory, convict, convince,* and *invincible* come from the Latin root *vict,* meaning "to conquer." Answer the questions below with one of these military words. Use your Spelling Dictionary if you need help.

1. What are you if you can't be conquered?
2. What do you call a person who is serving a prison sentence?
3. What can you claim when you conquer an opponent?
4. What do you do when you persuade a person to change his or her mind?

The words *command, demanding, mandates,* and *commander* come from another Latin root, *mand,* which means "to order." Complete each of these sentences with one of these military words. Use your Spelling Dictionary if you need help.

5. The ___ ordered the troops to march.
6. George Washington was in ___ during the Revolutionary War.
7. The military is ___ that we follow all of the rules and regulations.
8. The Pentagon passed down new ___ about training and educational levels for recruits.

Latin Roots 1

■ **SPELLING FOCUS**

Many words are made up of Latin roots. The root **fer** means "carry," **struct** means "build," and **sens** or **sent** means "feel."

■ **STUDY**   Say each word. Then read the sentence.

1. **transfer**   Ann will **transfer** to another school.
2. **different**   The land and sky are **different** colors.
3. **conference**   Ty had a **conference** with the teacher.
4. **construction**   The house **construction** took six weeks.
5. **instructor**   The math **instructor** teaches algebra.
6. **reconstruct**   We had to **reconstruct** the tree house.
7. **sensational**   The athlete's feat was **sensational.**
8. **resentment**   He felt **resentment** after being fired.
9. **sensitivity**   Kay has a **sensitivity** to poison ivy.
10. **consent**   Lea got her dad's **consent** for the trip.

11. **fertilize**   The farmer must **fertilize** his fields.
12. **preferred**   Zoe **preferred** basketball to soccer.
13. **referral**   Mr. Van gave us a **referral** to a tutor.
14. **inference**   I made an **inference** from the facts.
15. **destructive**   That weapon is very **destructive.**
16. **obstruction**   We came to an **obstruction** on the road.
17. **structural**   A house fire caused **structural** damage.
18. **sensibility**   A painter has artistic **sensibility.**
19. **consensus**   The committee reached a **consensus.**
20. **sensitize**   The disease may **sensitize** your skin.

*
WATCH OUT FOR FREQUENTLY MISSPELLED WORDS!

■ **PRACTICE**   Sort the words by writing
- seven words with **fer**
- six words with **struct**
- seven words with **sens** or **sent**

■ **WRITE**   Choose ten words to write in sentences.

CHALLENGE!

preferential
differentiate
indestructible
insensitive
sentimental

WORD ENDINGS   Write the list words that end with each of these suffixes.

1.–2.   -ion
3.–4.   -ence
5.–6.   -ize
7.–8.   -ity

CONTEXT   Write the list word that completes each sentence.

9. We faced a new challenge every week because we played a ____ team.
10. We were amazed at how ____ a tornado can be.
11. The swimming ____ had to cancel class this week.
12. When you think you are being treated unfairly, you build up a lot of ____.
13. My mom found a piano teacher on a ____ from your mom.
14. We were unable to reach a ____, so no decision was made.
15. The fire caused smoke damage, but fortunately there was no ____ damage to the house.
16. My parents gave their ____ for me to go on the field trip.
17. My toothpick model of the bridge collapsed on the way to school, so I had to ____ it when I got there.
18. I would have ____ seeing the other movie.
19. Because we moved, I have to ____ to a new school.
20. The outfielder made a ____ catch and threw the runner out at home plate.

STRATEGIC SPELLING
Building New Words

Add the suffix **-al** to make new words. Use your Spelling Dictionary if you need help.

21. transfer
22. instruction
23. environment
24. exception

FREQUENTLY MISSPELLED WORDS ✳ FREQUENTLY MISSPELLED WORDS ✳ FREQUENTLY MISSPELLED WORDS

When you say **different**, make sure to say three syllables: dif•fer•ent. This will help you include all the letters when you write it.

≡	Make a capital.
/	Make a small letter.
∧	Add something.
ℓ	Take out something.
⊙	Add a period.
⫪	New paragraph

PROOFREAD FOR CAPITALIZATION

Capitalize proper names, the first word of a sentence, and the pronoun *I*. For example:

My parents think gary is a bad influence.
                    ≡

Check Capitalization Correct capitalization errors in these sentences from a letter. If there are no errors, write "Correct."

1. If Mom sees me with Gary, she thinks we're causing trouble.
2. We really aren't doing anything wrong. we're just laughing.
3. One time we took some flowers out of Mrs. steen's garden.
4. He and i have been in trouble because of that ever since.

PROOFREAD A LETTER Find five misspelled words in this letter to an advice columnist and write them correctly. Some may be words you learned before. Fix three capitalization errors.

> November 1, 20_ _
>
> Dear Mr. Fix-it,
>
> My parents had a confrence with Mr. strong, my language arts instructer. He wanted me to move to a diffrent class because i'm a good writer. I asked my parents not to make me transfer until next smester, but there making me go now. I don't want to. what should I do?
>
> LeRoy

WRITE A RESPONSE Write a response, giving LeRoy your best advice. Use three list words and a personal word.

Word List

sensational	consensus	referral	inference
construction	destructive	obstruction	sensitivity
preferred	fertilize	transfer	conference
sensibility	instructor	resentment	consent
different	sensitize	structural	reconstruct

Personal Words 1._____ 2._____

Review

transfer
different
conference
construction
instructor
reconstruct
sensational
resentment
sensitivity
consent

WHO SAID THAT? Write the list word that best completes each quotation.

1. "You must have your parents' ___ to go on the field trip," the principal said.
2. "That was a ___ catch you made today," said the coach.
3. "We're trying to ___ the accident to find out how it happened," the police officer said.
4. "Because we're moving, I'll need to ___ to a new school," the eighth-grader said.
5. "Welcome to judo class. I'm your ___," Ms. Nakamoto said.
6. "You don't have to feel ___ because you weren't chosen to be in the play," the director said.
7. "The road is under ___, so we took a detour," the driver said.
8. "A parent-teacher ___ will be held today," said the dean.
9. "You should try a ___ hair style," the beautician suggested.
10. "I can't drink cold liquids because of my teeth's ___," the patient said.

Word *Study*

IDIOMS An **idiom** is an expression whose meaning can't be understood from the ordinary meanings of the words in it. For example, the idiom *sing a different tune* doesn't mean you're singing "Happy Birthday" while everyone else is singing "America, the Beautiful." It means that you have changed your mind about something.

off the record
hit the roof
chew the fat
take the cake
out of line

Write the idiom from the box that matches each definition. Use your Spelling Dictionary if you need help. Look up idioms under the most important word in the phrase. For example, look up *off the record* under the entry for *record*.

1. win the first prize
2. become angry or excited
3. uncalled-for, improper
4. friendly talk or chatting
5. not to be quoted

Suffixes -age, -ism, -ure

The suffixes **-age, -ism,** and **-ure** form nouns when added to words. Sometimes the spelling of the base word changes.

■ **STUDY**   Say each word. Notice if the base word changes.

mile + -age	=	1.	**mileage**
post + -age	=	2.	**postage**
pass + -age	=	3.	**passage**
bag + -age	=	4.	**baggage**
real + -ism	=	5.	**realism**
capital + -ism	=	6.	**capitalism**
journal + -ism	=	7.	**journalism**
please + -ure	=	8.	**pleasure**
moist + -ure	=	9.	**moisture**
press + -ure	=	10.	**pressure**

store + -age	=	11.	**storage**
wreck + -age	=	12.	**wreckage**
vandal + -ism	=	13.	**vandalism**
manner + -ism	=	14.	**mannerism**
hero + -ism	=	15.	**heroism**
optimist + -ism	=	16.	**optimism**
compose + -ure	=	17.	**composure**
legislate + -ure	=	18.	**legislature**
sculpt + -ure	=	19.	**sculpture**
fail + -ure	=	20.	**failure**

CHALLENGE!

acreage
metabolism
materialism
architecture
enclosure

■ **PRACTICE**   Sort the words by writing
- seven words with **-ure**
- six words with **-age**
- seven words with **-ism**

■ **WRITE**   Choose three words to write a paragraph about a car trip you've taken.

DEFINITIONS Write the list word that fits the definition.

1. tendency to look on the bright side of things
2. amount paid on anything sent by mail
3. the work of writing for a newspaper or magazine
4. put a lot of stress or strain in one spot
5. an economic system in which individual people own businesses and compete with others for profit
6. calmness; quietness; self-control
7. an odd habit or behavior
8. a way through or between parts of a building
9. a feeling of enjoyment or delight
10. a place for storing goods

WORD FORMS Write the list word that has each meaning and ending indicated below.

11. the art of making figures + ure
12. actual + ism
13. a sack + age
14. to make or enact laws + ure
15. to not succeed + ure
16. a person admired for bravery + ism
17. slightly wet + ure
18. the partial or total destruction of a vehicle + age
19. a person who destroys or damages valuable things + ism
20. five thousand two hundred and eighty feet + age

STRATEGIC SPELLING
Seeing Meaning Connections

Write the words from the box that fit the definitions. One is a list word.

Words with *real*

realism
realize
unreal
real estate

21. picturing life as it is
22. imaginary
23. to understand clearly
24. land you can own

Did You Know?
The Vandals were early Europeans who earned a destructive reputation as they invaded parts of Spain and North Africa. Do you see the connection with the current meaning of **vandalism?**

■ PROOFREADING AND WRITING

☰	Make a capital.
/	Make a small letter.
∧	Add something.
ℓ	Take out something.
⊙	Add a period.
⁋	New paragraph

PROOFREAD FOR PUNCTUATION

Be sure to use commas and capital letters correctly in the heading, greeting, and closing of a personal letter. For example:

October 20 20_ _

dear Hong

Check Commas and Capitals Fix comma and capitalization errors in these headings, greetings, and closings from letters.

1. march 11, 20_ _   3. June 23 20_ _   5. Yours truly
2. Dear Felicia   4. Dear Mrs. Lopez   6. sincerely,

PROOFREAD AN APOLOGY LETTER
Find five misspelled words in the letter and write them correctly. Fix three errors with commas and capital letters too.

> August 25 20_ _
>
> Dear Sophie
>
> I'm sorry for my faliure to put postige on your birthday gift. I didint mean for you to pay. The preshure of getting it to you on time got to me. I hope you enjoy the sculpsure. To apologize, may I treat you to dinner?
>
> sincerely,
> Melissa

WRITE AN APOLOGY LETTER
Write a letter of apology to a friend. Use three list words and a personal word.

Word List

mileage	passage	vandalism	legislature
storage	journalism	capitalism	sculpture
postage	realism	optimism	moisture
baggage	mannerism	pleasure	failure
wreckage	heroism	composure	pressure

Personal Words 1.___ 2.___

Review

WORD GROUPS Write the list word suggested by each group of words.

1. weight, force
2. actual, based on realities
3. economic system, not communism
4. luggage, suitcases, duffel bags
5. way through, hallway, tunnel
6. stamps, air mail, first class
7. enjoyment, delight, joy
8. dampness, wet, rain
9. distance, speedometer
10. newspapers, reporters, headlines

mileage
postage
passage
baggage
realism
capitalism
journalism
pleasure
moisture
pressure

Word *Study*

CONTEXT: EXAMPLES Often you can guess the meaning of an unfamiliar word by its **context**—the words around it. Sometimes this context comes in the form of an example. Read this sentence: "She showed us her *composure* by not panicking during the tornado." The word *composure* may be unfamiliar to you, but the example, "by not panicking during the tornado," gives you a clue that *composure* means "calmness and self-control."

Write the example in each sentence that gives you a clue to the meaning of each underlined word.

1. The two teams displayed sportsmanship by shaking hands after the game.
2. Amphibians, such as frogs, spend part of their life cycle in water.
3. In my floriculture class, we arranged roses and ferns.
4. Theropods, such as tyrannosaurus, walked on two legs.

Now write the word or words in each sentence that the underlined examples give you clues about.

5. Kangaroos and koalas live in Australia, but the only marsupial in North America is the opossum.
6. Some archipelagos, such as the Hawaiian Islands, have become heavily populated.
7. Woodwind instruments, like the clarinet and flute, are an important part of an orchestra.
8. Mark Twain was the nom de plume of Samuel Clemens.

Compound Words

Some compounds are written as one word, **outside;** with hyphens, **well-known;** or as two separate words, **no one.**

■ **STUDY** Say each word. Then read the sentence.

**WATCH OUT FOR
FREQUENTLY
MISSPELLED
WORDS!**

1.	**underground**	Subways are in **underground** stations.
2.	**halfway**	Sara walked Tina **halfway** home.
3.	**outside** ✻	The dog stood **outside** the door.
4.	**granddaughter**	Al took his **granddaughter** to the zoo.
5.	**daydream**	He tends to **daydream** in class.
6.	**seventy-two**	The house is **seventy-two** years old.
7.	**self-esteem**	Praise increases **self-esteem.**
8.	**well-known**	A **well-known** author came to class.
9.	**life jacket**	Each sailor had a **life jacket.**
10.	**shopping center**	The bookstore is in a **shopping center.**

11.	**thunderstorm**	A **thunderstorm** brings heavy rains.
12.	**throughout**	It snowed **throughout** the day.
13.	**bookkeeper**	A **bookkeeper** checked the receipts.
14.	**wheelchair**	This ramp is used for a **wheelchair.**
15.	**underrated**	The film was **underrated** by critics.
16.	**vice-president**	The **vice-president** has many duties.
17.	**great-grandmother**	My **great-grandmother** is very active.
18.	**no one** ✻	I told the secret to **no one.**
19.	**remote control**	He has a **remote control** toy car.
20.	**role model**	The teacher was a good **role model.**

CHALLENGE!

straightforward
straight-faced
daylight-saving
time
stage fright
report card

■ **PRACTICE** Sort the words by writing
- five open compound words
- five hyphenated compound words
- ten closed compound words

■ **WRITE** Choose two sentences to write a poster about someone you admire.

JOINING WORDS Find two words in each sentence that make up a compound word from the list and write the word.

1. Did you go shopping at the center near your home?
2. I won't be through until I'm out of time.
3. It's great that your grandmother could come for a visit.
4. We split the sandwich in half and ate it on our way to school.
5. The thunder told us that there was a storm approaching.
6. No, you may have only one cookie.
7. There were seventy pieces to the puzzle, but we lost two.
8. She has never in her life owned a jacket like that.
9. The possibility is remote, but can you control your dog?
10. Take that out and put it by the side of the house.

COMPOUND COMBINATIONS Write the list word that includes the underlined part of each of these compound words.

11. <u>daughter</u>-in-law
12. <u>day</u>break
13. over<u>rated</u>
14. role-<u>play</u>
15. play<u>ground</u>
16. <u>shop</u>keeper
17. <u>president</u>-elect
18. my<u>self</u>
19. <u>wheel</u>barrow
20. <u>well</u>-meaning

STRATEGIC SPELLING
Seeing Meaning Connections

Words with *life*

life jacket
life expectancy
life insurance
lifeguard
life-size

Write the word from the box that fits each definition. One is a list word.

21. I keep a watchful vigil over the beach and water.
22. I'll help support your loved ones after you die.
23. I am equal to the size of the original.
24. I'll keep you afloat if you fall overboard.
25. I'm how long you will probably live.

FREQUENTLY MISSPELLED WORDS ❋ FREQUENTLY MISSPELLED WORDS

To remember that **no one** is two words, think about how you say it. Two **o**'s written together are rarely pronounced separately as they are in **no one.**

■ PROOFREADING AND WRITING

≡	Make a capital.
/	Make a small letter.
∧	Add something.
ℰ	Take out something.
⊙	Add a period.
⁋	New paragraph

PROOFREAD FOR USAGE The pronouns *me, him, her, us,* and *them* are used as the object of a preposition or the direct object.

Between you and ~~I~~ me, Great-grandmother allows ~~he~~ him and ~~I~~ me to get away with a lot.

Check Pronouns Read each sentence. Correct any pronoun errors. Write "Correct" if all the pronouns are correct.

1. Great-grandmother is a good role model for my mom and I.
2. She gives Mom and I a care package to take home with us.
3. I try to help her do things around the house when I can.
4. No one is as nice to Mom and me as Great-grandmother is.

PROOFREAD A DESCRIPTION Find six misspelled words in this description and write them correctly. Some may be words you learned before. Fix three pronoun errors too.

> My great-grandmother's house is neat. She is seventytwo and in a wheel chair, so she has ramps througout her house. She lets my freinds and I ride our bikes on the one outside. There's an under ground tunnel that connects the house to a cellar. My friend and I went down it but got scared because noone was with he and I.

WRITE A DESCRIPTION Do any of your friends or relatives live in an interesting place? Write a description of a house you think is neat. Try to use three list words and a personal word.

Word List

thunderstorm	vice-president	halfway	throughout
granddaughter	wheelchair	outside	well-known
remote control	great-grandmother	underground	role model
no one	shopping center	life jacket	underrated
bookkeeper	seventy-two	self-esteem	daydream

Personal Words 1.___ 2.___

ANSWER THE QUESTIONS Write the word from the box that answers each question.

life jacket
shopping center
seventy-two
self-esteem
well-known
halfway
outside
underground
granddaughter
daydream

1. What word would you use to describe a tunnel below the earth?
2. Where would you find all kinds of stores?
3. What might you find in a boat?
4. If someone is famous, what do call that person?
5. What might you do when you stare out the window awhile?
6. What do you call it when you feel good about yourself?
7. Where should you do things such as playing baseball?
8. If you're a girl, what does your grandmother call you?
9. What do you get when you multiply thirty-six by two?
10. What word might you use to describe a job not completely done?

Word *Study*

EXPLORING LANGUAGE: JARGON A life jacket is a basic piece of equipment for sailing, and almost everyone knows what one is. However, sailing also has its own special language, or **jargon,** that is mostly known only by those who actually sail. Look at these parts of a sailboat:

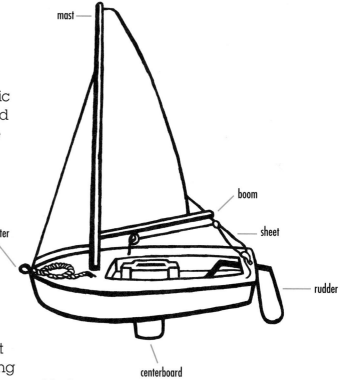

Some of these words, such as *boom* and *painter,* have familiar meanings, but they have their own special meanings in sailing jargon. Write the sailing word that fits each definition. Use the drawing and your Spelling Dictionary if you need help.

1. the pole that holds up the sail
2. the pole that holds the bottom edge of the sail
3. board that keeps the boat from slipping sideways in the water
4. the piece at the back of the boat used to steer it
5. line used for controlling the sail
6. rope for tying the boat to a pier

Review

Lesson 7: Words with No Sound Clues

Lesson 8: Related Words 1

Lesson 9: Latin Roots 1

Lesson 10: Suffixes -age, -ism, -ure

Lesson 11: Compound Words

REVIEW WORD LIST

1. automatically
2. catastrophe
3. consequences
4. criticism
5. delicate
6. distribute
7. environment
8. everything
9. favorite
10. government
11. identify
12. luckily
13. probably
14. really
15. semester
16. temperamental
17. congratulate
18. congratulations
19. graduation
20. inspect
21. narrative
22. political
23. politics
24. protection
25. stable
26. strategic
27. construction
28. destructive
29. different
30. instructor
31. obstruction
32. preferred
33. reconstruct
34. sensational
35. structural
36. composure
37. heroism
38. journalism
39. postage
40. sculpture
41. vandalism
42. wreckage
43. great-grandmother
44. life jacket
45. no one
46. outside
47. remote control
48. throughout
49. thunderstorm
50. well-known

■ PROOFREADING

Find the spelling errors in each passage and write the words correctly. All passages have seven errors except the last one, which has eight.

PROOFREAD A NOTICE

Several articles are in the lost-and-found boxes in the main office. If you have lost something, you may insect or idenify the articles from noon until 3:00 today. We will distribyute every thing not picked up to the children's home. Items in the boxes include a book of postige stamps, a remotcontrol car, four sweaters, a black notebook, a softball, a tape by a wellnown rock group, and two mismatched athletic socks.

PROOFREAD BABY-SITTER INSTRUCTIONS

Angela,

Please put the baby to bed. She has been fed, but she was rather tempramental today, so she may not go to sleep right away.

Dinner for you and the twins is in the oven, which will automaticly turn off at 6:30. Each of you may have a diffrent fruit for dessert. Tim's favorit is in the bowl out side the refrigerator. Luckly, I shopped today.

The twins are to be in bed by 8:00. They know the consiquences if they are not. I'll be home by 9:30.

Mrs. Fitzgerald

PROOFREAD A NEWS STORY

Vandals at Work

Several exhibits in the indoor sculpsure garden were damaged by vandalsm last week. Art instructer Tad Morelli said that students can reconstrut some of the work, but that the most delecate pieces are probly not replaceable. The exhibit was completed last smester by students from three middle schools, and several of the pieces won awards. One of the works damaged was a sea gull made from clay, which won a blue ribbon. It was sculpted by Blaine Newsome.

PROOFREAD A JOURNAL ENTRY

We had a hard time getting to Grategrandmother Rosa's house today. In fact, Mom lost her composer. We were driving on the expressway when we saw the reckage from an accident. Then there was an abstruction on a bridge. After that we hit a sentsational storm with thunder and lightning. I was about to congradulate Mom on her driving when we had a flat tire. Mom says she would have prefered to have stayed home.

PROOFREAD A SOCIAL STUDIES REPORT

Benjamin Franklin

Benjamin Franklin (1706-1790) was active and influential in journlism, science, and politicks. He started his career as a printer's apprentice and went on to become owner of his own newspaper in Philadelphia. There he helped establish the first public library in the colonies and became postmaster of Philadelphia. In his famous kite experiment, he made a kite of silk, strips of cedar, and a wire and attached a key to the string. When he flew the kite in a thunderstrom, he drew down lightning. He developed important ideas about electricity and also invented the lightning rod. He was a signer of the Declaration of Independence and was sent by the goverment to France as a diplomat. He remained active in politickal affairs threwout his career. His famous autobiography is a narritive of his unusual life.

PROOFREAD A FRIENDLY LETTER

> November 3, 20_ _
>
> Dear Uncle Ignacio,
>
> Congradulations on winning an award for heroizm. We read about your rescue of the boy in the river. It's a good thing that you were wearing a lifejacket. That swimmer was realy lucky that you were in a stategic spot when he fell in. The newspaper reported that he is in stabel condition. We hope you are too.
>
> Will you be able to come to my graduatetion in June? It would be great to see you again.
>
> Your nephew,
>
> Roberto

PROOFREAD A FEATURE STORY

Hurricanes: Costly and Cruel

Hurricanes usually start over tropical ocean waters and can do much strutural damage to buildings as well as damage to the enviroment. Often high waves are as distructive as the wind. Offshore islands, which extend from New England to Texas, have been seriously eroded over the years, and there has been critisim of the construcshin that has taken place on coastal areas. Mobile homes in particular offer little pertection from hurricane winds.

Hurricane winds rotate in a circle or oval that may be as big as 500 miles in diameter. In 1993, Hurricane Emily's winds reached 115 miles per hour. Since knowone can predict exactly which direction a hurricane will take, a catastrope can occur with very little warning.

STRATEGY WORKSHOP

Divide and Conquer

DISCOVER THE STRATEGY Here's a strategy for studying extra-long words that you keep having trouble with. Cut them down to size by cutting them up. Then study them piece by piece. How do you divide these words for study? That depends on the kind of word you're working with.

Compounds: divide between base words	Words with Affixes: divide between affix and base word	Other Words: divide between syllables
grand/daughter through/out under/ground	re/construct/ion fertil/ize compos/ure	tram/po/line ca/tas/tro/phe i/den/ti/fy

TRY IT OUT Now try this divide and conquer strategy.

Compounds Write these compounds:

> thunderstorm   bookkeeper   underrated   wheelchair   daydream

1.–5. Draw a line between the two base words that make up each compound. *Note:* This will show you that two words have been put together with no letters lost.

Affixes Write these words:

> subdivision   structural   pleasure   failure   mileage

6.–10. Draw lines between each base word and any prefixes or suffixes. *Note:* This will show you whether adding a suffix changes the spelling of the base word.

Now look back at the words you wrote. Three base words changed spelling when the suffix was added. Underline the base words that changed spelling.

Syllables Write these words:

> consequences   pistachios   temperamental
> diagnoses   thermostat

11.–15. Say each word. Listen carefully for the syllables and draw lines between them. Check a dictionary for how to divide any words that you're not sure of.

LOOK AHEAD Look ahead at the next five lessons. Write six list words that you could use these strategies with. Say each word to yourself and divide it into smaller pieces. Divide each word the way that works best for you.

Directional Prefixes

SPELLING FOCUS

The prefixes **sub-, trans-,** and **super-** indicate direction or degree. **Sub-** means "below," **trans-** means "across," and **super-** means "greater than."

■ **STUDY** Say each word. Then read the sentence.

1.	**submarine**	A **submarine** located the sunken ship.
2.	**subtraction**	I'm better at addition than **subtraction.**
3.	**subheading**	Each outline heading has a **subheading.**
4.	**transparent**	We saw through a **transparent** curtain.
5.	**translate**	I can **translate** the poem into English.
6.	**transcript**	To apply, send your school **transcript.**
7.	**transmit**	The radio can **transmit** messages.
8.	**supermarket**	We bought apples at the **supermarket.**
9.	**supersonic**	The **supersonic** jet flies overseas.
10.	**superstition**	I don't believe in that **superstition.**
11.	**submerge**	To swim, **submerge** your head in water.
12.	**subcommittee**	The **subcommittee** studied health care.
13.	**subsection**	Eva wrote a **subsection** of the report.
14.	**subdivision**	The new **subdivision** has large houses.
15.	**transfusion**	The patient had a blood **transfusion.**
16.	**transaction**	A bank teller handled the **transaction.**
17.	**transportation**	Buses provide public **transportation.**
18.	**supernatural**	The **supernatural** tale scared everyone.
19.	**supersede**	This law will **supersede** an earlier one.
20.	**superficial**	The twins' likenesses are **superficial.**

CHALLENGE!

subterranean
subordinate
translucent
transoceanic
superimpose

■ **PRACTICE** Sort the list words by writing
- seven words with **sub-**
- six words with **super-**
- seven words with **trans-**

■ **WRITE** Choose four sentences to rewrite as questions.

MAKING CONNECTIONS   Write the list word that matches each clue.

1. I am a boat found below the surface of the water.
2. You can see through me.
3. I am not deep.
4. I am a part of a section.
5. I travel faster than the speed of sound.
6. I am the transfer of blood from one person to another.
7. I am above or beyond what is natural.
8. I mean "to put under water."
9. I am a piece of land divided into smaller parts.
10. I mean "to be greater than something that came earlier."

CONTEXT CLUES   Write the list word that completes each sentence.

11. My grandmother had a ___ about walking under ladders.
12. A ___ of the chapter titled "Ecology" is "Saving Our Environment."
13. Some members of the dance committee formed a ___ to choose songs.
14. Could you ___ this Spanish song into English for me?
15. An airplane is usually the fastest mode of ___.
16. I find it easier to do ___ than multiplication.
17. The college will want a ___ of your high school grades before it will consider accepting you as a student.
18. I'm on my way to the ___ to buy some milk.
19. This ___ won't be on your bill until next month.
20. We ___ documents over the phone lines now.

The Divide and Conquer Strategy

21.–24. It often helps to study longer words piece by piece. Write *transportation, supernatural, subheading,* and *subtraction.* Draw lines to break them into smaller parts. Study the parts.

> **Did You Know?**
> **Supersede** is the only word in English that ends in *sede.*

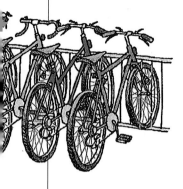

≡	Make a capital.
/	Make a small letter.
∧	Add something.
ℯ	Take out something.
⊙	Add a period.
¶	New paragraph

PROOFREAD FOR USAGE Some indefinite pronouns, such as *each, either, everyone, neither, no one, somebody*, and *one*, are singular and need singular verbs.

Each one of the committee members looking into the bike rack situation ~~have~~ come up with a plan.
(with *has* inserted above)

Check Subjects and Verbs Read each sentence. Correct the verbs that do not fit subjects. If a verb is correct, write "Correct."

1. Somebody on the committee objects to the investigation.
2. No one on the council really have an opinion.
3. Everyone at school uses bicycles as a form of transportation.
4. Each of the teachers have voiced an opinion on the subject.
5. Neither of the advisers feel this issue supersedes all others.

PROOFREAD MEETING MINUTES Find five misspelled words in the rest of the student council minutes and write them correctly. Some may be words you learned before. Correct three incorrect verbs following indefinite pronouns too.

> The subcommitee looking into the cost of new bike racks reported that every one of the existing racks are in terrible condition. Each have been partly submerjed in water and are rusting. Racks range in price, but the differences among them are superfishal. Were hoping to complete a transackton for four new racks soon.

WRITE MEETING MINUTES Write the minutes of a meeting concerning plans for a community clean-up project. Use three list words and a personal word.

Word List

submarine	subtraction	superficial	submerge
transportation	translate	transaction	supersonic
supernatural	supermarket	superstition	transcript
subheading	subcommittee	transparent	subdivision
transfusion	subsection	supersede	transmit

Personal Words 1.___ 2.___

Review

DEFINITIONS   Write the word from the box that fits each definition.

1. change from one language into another
2. a large grocery store
3. a boat that can operate under water
4. send over or pass on
5. greater than the speed of sound
6. a written or typewritten copy
7. an unreasoning fear of what is unknown
8. easily seen through
9. finding the difference between two numbers
10. a subordinate heading or title

submarine
subtraction
subheading
transparent
translate
transcript
transmit
supermarket
supersonic
superstition

Word *Study*

LATIN ROOTS: *fundere*   *Transfusion* comes from the Latin root *fundere*, which means "melt or pour." The rest of the words in the box also have something to do with melting or pouring because they also come from *fundere*. Write the word from the box that fits each definition in the word web. Use your Spelling Dictionary if you need help.

refund
fuse
funnel
transfusion
foundry

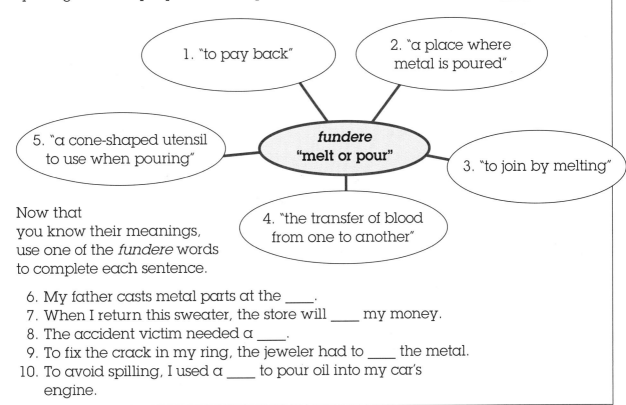

1. "to pay back"
2. "a place where metal is poured"
5. "a cone-shaped utensil to use when pouring"
fundere **"melt or pour"**
3. "to join by melting"
4. "the transfer of blood from one to another"

Now that you know their meanings, use one of the *fundere* words to complete each sentence.

6. My father casts metal parts at the ____.
7. When I return this sweater, the store will ____ my money.
8. The accident victim needed a ____.
9. To fix the crack in my ring, the jeweler had to ____ the metal.
10. To avoid spilling, I used a ____ to pour oil into my car's engine.

Related Words 2

SPELLING FOCUS

Sometimes a letter is dropped or changed in related words: **exclaim, exclamation; intrude, intrusion.**

■ **STUDY** Say each word. Then read the sentence.

1. **exclaim**   We heard him **exclaim** excitedly.
2. **exclamation**   She gave a surprised **exclamation.**
3. **detain**   The officers will **detain** the suspect.
4. **detention**   He has a **detention** period after school.
5. **comprehend**   Steve didn't **comprehend** the lecture.
6. **comprehension** She has good **comprehension** of math.
7. **intrude**   I didn't want to **intrude** on the party.
8. **intrusion**   A robbery is a disturbing **intrusion.**
9. **ferocious**   A hungry bear can be quite **ferocious.**
10. **ferocity**   The dog's **ferocity** was frightening.

11. **sustain**   The pitcher did not **sustain** his power.
12. **sustenance**   Bread and water serve as **sustenance.**
13. **pertain**   These facts **pertain** to the subject.
14. **pertinent**   The judge asked for **pertinent** details.
15. **commit**   A witness saw her **commit** the crime.
16. **commission**   The salesperson receives a **commission.**
17. **recede**   The waves **recede** as the storm weakens.
18. **recession**   The economy experienced a **recession.**
19. **invade**   The ants will **invade** your picnic.
20. **invasion**   The soldiers prepared for an **invasion.**

CHALLENGE!

atrocious
atrocity
abstain
abstention
apprehend
apprehension

■ **PRACTICE** Sort the words by writing
- four pairs of words in which **ai** changes to **a**, **e**, or **i**
- five pairs of words in which **d** or **t** changes to **s** or **ss**
- one pair of words in which **ous** disappears

■ **WRITE** Choose two sentences to write a rhyme.

SYNONYMS Write the list word that means the same as the underlined word or phrase in each sentence.

1. How long can you <u>hold</u> that high note?
2. Let's limit ourselves to facts that <u>relate</u> to the problem.
3. Is our economy starting to recover from the latest <u>slump</u>?
4. Ann led the midnight <u>raid</u> of the kitchen.
5. Please pardon our <u>barging in</u> on your quiet time.
6. I know you're in a hurry, so I won't <u>delay</u> you any longer.
7. I heard him <u>yell</u> with pain when he hit his thumb with the hammer.
8. Did you <u>promise</u> your time to picking up litter this Saturday?
9. You shouldn't <u>meddle</u> in your friend's private affairs.
10. Do you receive a <u>portion of the profit</u> on each sale?
11. The prisoner was placed in a small <u>confinement</u> room before she was moved to her cell.
12. The Blue Team will attempt to <u>enter</u> the Orange Team's territory in the game of military strategy.

SYLLABLES Write the list word that matches the number of syllables shown. The last syllable has been given.

13. ___ ▪ ___ ▪ ___ ▪ sion
14. ___ ▪ ___ ▪ ___ ▪ ty
15. ___ ▪ ___ ▪ nent
16. ___ ▪ ___ ▪ nance
17. ___ ▪ ___ ▪ ___ ▪ tion
18. ___ ▪ ___ ▪ cious
19. ___ ▪ ___ ▪ hend
20. ___ ▪ cede

Building New Words

Add the suffix **-ent** to make new words. Circle the words with spelling changes. One is a list word. Use your Spelling Dictionary if you need help.

21. pertain
22. depend
23. precede
24. excel
25. persist

Did You Know?
Not only can an army **invade** a country, but tourists can **invade** a city and ants can **invade** a picnic.

■ PROOFREADING AND WRITING

≡	Make a capital.
/	Make a small letter.
∧	Add something.
ℯ	Take out something.
⊙	Add a period.
⁋	New paragraph

PROOFREAD FOR USAGE Use only one negative word, such as *no, never, not* (or its contraction *n't*), *nothing, nobody,* or *neither,* when you mean "no." For example:

Serving time in detention isn't ~~no~~ ^any^ fun.

Check for Double Negatives Write the word from the parentheses that correctly completes each sentence.

1. I don't like (any, none) of the rules in detention.
2. You can do (anything, nothing) but schoolwork there.
3. I have had (any, no) pertinent schoolwork all week.
4. The detention teacher makes sure you're not doing (anything, nothing) that you're not supposed to do.
5. I can't take (any, no) more invasion of my privacy.

PROOFREAD A COMPLAINT Find five misspelled words in the rest of this complaint. Write them correctly. Some may be words you learned before. Fix two double negatives too.

> For one thing, you're supposed to work on pertnent schoolwork, but you can't do that if you don't have nothing that day. Also, if you comit a second offense while your in detension, you should get a diffrent punishment pertaining to the new violation. You shouldn't never have the same punishment for different crimes.

WRITE A COMPLAINT What rule around your school would you like to change? Write a complaint to your principal, making sure to give reasons. Use three list words and a personal word.

Word List

exclaim	detention	pertain	recession
exclamation	ferocious	pertinent	sustain
commit	ferocity	intrude	sustenance
commission	comprehend	intrusion	invade
detain	comprehension	recede	invasion

Personal Words 1.___ 2.___

Review

QUOTES Write the word from the box that goes with each quotation.

1. "I have to serve a ___ for spraying graffiti," the student said.
2. "Please don't ___ on me while I grade papers," the teacher said.
3. "That wild boar is a ___ looking beast," the zoo visitor cried.
4. "This test will show your ___ of the book," the professor said.
5. "We must ___ you for further questioning," the officer said.
6. "A lion's roar shows you the ___ of this animal," the keeper said.
7. "Coming into my room without knocking is an ___," the mother said.
8. "Can you ___ how seriously wrong stealing is?" the father asked.
9. "The First Amendment does not allow you to ___ 'Fire' in a crowded room," the judge admonished.
10. "You should end this sentence with an ___ mark," my friend suggested.

exclaim
exclamation
detain
detention
comprehend
comprehension
intrude
intrusion
ferocious
ferocity

Using a *Dictionary*

MULTIPLE MEANINGS Some words have more than one meaning. To help you choose the right one, use the part-of-speech label and the sample sentences or phrases in a dictionary entry. Look at all the different meanings in this entry for *commit*.

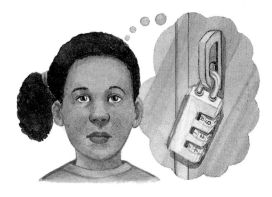

com mit (kə mit′), *v.t.,* **-mit ted, -mit ting. 1** to do or perform (usually something wrong): *commit a crime.* **2** to hand over for safekeeping; deliver. **3** to send to prison or an asylum. **4** to give over; carry over; transfer: *commit a poem to memory.* **5** to reveal (one's opinion). **6** to involve; pledge: *I would not commit myself in any way.* [< Latin *committere* < *com-* with + *mittere* send, put]—**committable,** *adj.*

Write the number of the definition of *commit* that fits each sentence. Use your Spelling Dictionary if you need help.

1. Did you commit your new locker combination to memory?
2. We are committed to working to save our environment.
3. A person who steals is committing a crime.
4. I commit my child to your care until I return.
5. When asked if he was a candidate for president, he refused to commit.
6. The convicted thief was committed to the state prison.
7. He received a five-year sentence for committing bribery.
8. I have committed to going and will not change my mind.

Latin and Greek Word Parts 1

SPELLING FOCUS

Many words are made up of Greek and Latin word parts.
Scrib, script, and **graph** mean "write." **Voc** and **vok** mean
"call." **Loq** means "speak."

■ **STUDY** Say each word. Then read the sentence.

1.	**scribble**	A child can **scribble** with a crayon.
2.	**describe**	My poem will **describe** the sunset.
3.	**manuscript**	The writer completed her **manuscript.**
4.	**graphic**	The book has **graphic** details on war.
5.	**paragraph**	Each **paragraph** was well-written.
6.	**photography**	The **photography** class took pictures.
7.	**geography**	We studied the **geography** of Asia.
8.	**revoke**	The teacher may **revoke** our privileges.
9.	**vocalize**	Students can **vocalize** their opinions.
10.	**eloquent**	He gave an **eloquent** speech on ecology.

11.	**subscribe**	I will **subscribe** to the magazine.
12.	**postscript**	Mary added a **postscript** to the letter.
13.	**inscription**	She wrote an **inscription** in the book.
14.	**biography**	We read a **biography** of Roosevelt.
15.	**vocation**	His choice of a **vocation** was teaching.
16.	**advocate**	She is an **advocate** for education.
17.	**invoke**	The state will **invoke** federal aid.
18.	**soliloquy**	The actor must perform a **soliloquy.**
19.	**loquacious**	Many **loquacious** pupils spoke at once.
20.	**colloquial**	The author used **colloquial** phrases.

CHALLENGE!

circumscribe
cartographer
choreograph
irrevocable
circumlocution

■ **PRACTICE**
- Write six words with **scrib** or **script.**
- Write five words with **graph.**
- Write five words with **voc** or **vok.**
- Write four words with **loq.**

■ **WRITE** Choose two sentences to include in a short friendly
letter.

WORD PARTS Write the list word that includes the underlined part of each word.

1. <u>bio</u>degradable
2. <u>manu</u>facture
3. <u>soli</u>tary
4. photo<u>co</u>py
5. <u>post</u>humous
6. <u>para</u>phrase
7. <u>re</u>peal
8. <u>geo</u>metry

ROOTS AND MEANING Write the word that fits the Latin or Greek word and the definition. Use your Spelling Dictionary.

9. From *loqui,* this means "talkative."
10. From *scribere,* this means "to write carelessly."
11. From *graphein,* this means "shown with a picture."
12. From *scribere,* this is your promise that you'll pay for the daily newspaper that is delivered every morning.
13. From *vocare,* this is "an occupation or profession."
14. From *scribere,* this is "something engraved on a plaque."
15. From *vocare,* this means "to support or promote."
16. From *loqui,* this describes "everyday, informal conversation."
17. From *vocare,* this means "to use your voice."
18. From *loqui,* this is "speech that is expressive and graceful."
19. From *vocare,* this means "to appeal for help."
20. From *scribere,* this is "to tell about something in detail."

STRATEGIC SPELLING

Seeing Meaning Connections

Words with *bio*
biology
biochemist
biographer

The root **bio** means "life." Write the words from the box that fit the definitions. Use your Spelling Dictionary if you need help.

21. scientist who studies the chemical processes of life
22. the scientific study of life
23. one who writes about someone else's life

Did You Know?
Before printing was invented, all books were written by hand, a long and laborious task. Combine the Latin words for "hand" and "write" and you get **manuscript.**

75

☰	Make a capital.
/	Make a small letter.
∧	Add something.
℮	Take out something.
⊙	Add a period.
⁊	New paragraph

PROOFREAD FOR PUNCTUATION

Add an apostrophe and **s ('s)** to form the possessive of singular nouns. Add an apostrophe to form the possessive of most plural nouns. For example:

All classes' plays are about a time in America's history.

Check Apostrophes Add apostrophes to possessives that need them. If a possessive is correct, write "Correct."

1. Each class's play will be performed Saturday.
2. The seventh-graders performance will be first.
3. Their play is based on Helen Kellers autobiography.
4. Their teachers husband designed a set for them.
5. He used photography to show Helen's house in the background.

PROOFREAD A REVIEW

Find the five misspelled words in this review of a school play. Write them correctly. Some may be words you learned before. Fix three possessive errors too.

> The eighth-graders play, <u>Huckleberry Finn</u>, was about two friends on a river. It also told about the river's geagraphy. Hucks soliloqwey helped to discribe the scenery. Coloquial language added to the charm. The actors costumes were neat. They had to where them to school the day before the play for publicity.

WRITE A REVIEW

Choose a movie or play you've seen recently and write a review of it. Describe the sets, costumes, and acting. Try to use three list words and a personal word.

Word List

subscribe	loquacious	advocate	invoke
eloquent	scribble	colloquial	soliloquy
biography	geography	manuscript	vocalize
revoke	vocation	paragraph	photography
graphic	postscript	describe	inscription

Personal Words 1.____ 2.____

Review

scribble
describe
manuscript
graphic
paragraph
photography
geography
revoke
vocalize
eloquent

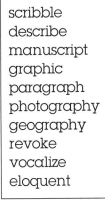

RIDDLES   Write the word from the box that best answers each riddle.

1. The police can do this to someone's driver's license.
2. You do this when you write someone to tell what you look like.
3. This is a word you'd use to describe a really fine speech.
4. If you like studying mountains, you might take a class in this.
5. If you like using a camera, you might take a class in this.
6. When you do this, your writing is hard to read.
7. A report you wrote probably had more than one of these.
8. A graph, chart, or drawing is an example of this.
9. When you tell your idea at a meeting, you do this.
10. This might be a collection of poems you wrote that you want to send to a publisher.

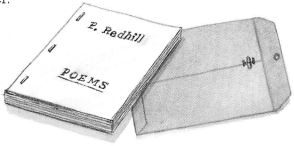

Word *Study*

INITIALS AND ACRONYMS   Have you ever added *PS* to a letter? These are the **initials** for *postscript.* When you address the envelope for that letter, you should add a ZIP code. *ZIP* is an **acronym** for *Zone Improvement Plan.* What's the difference between initials and acronyms? Each letter of an initial is pronounced, but acronyms are pronounced as single words. The box lists other initials and acronyms.

laser	snafu	D.J.	NATO	SWAT
IQ	NASA	VISTA	UNICEF	RV

Write the initials or acronyms that stand for these phrases.

1. situation normal—all fouled up
2. North Atlantic Treaty Organization
3. United Nations International Children's Emergency Fund
4. recreational vehicle
5. light amplification by stimulated emission of radiation
6. Special Weapons and Tactics
7. Volunteers in Service to America
8. National Aeronautics and Space Administration
9. disc jockey
10. intelligence quotient

Easily Confused Words

Some words are easily confused because they have similar pronunciations and spellings: **collage, college.**

■ **STUDY** Say each word. Then read the sentence.

WATCH OUT FOR FREQUENTLY MISSPELLED WORDS!

1.	**collage**	The art student created a **collage.**
2.	**college** ✳	He will study journalism in **college.**
3.	**emigrants**	Many **emigrants** left China.
4.	**immigrants**	Some Chinese **immigrants** came here.
5.	**hardy**	This **hardy** plant will withstand cold.
6.	**hearty**	I had a **hearty** appetite at breakfast.
7.	**envelop**	This huge blanket will **envelop** you.
8.	**envelope**	She put the letter in an **envelope.**
9.	**magnet**	The **magnet** will attract paper clips.
10.	**magnate**	The **magnate** owns many companies.

11.	**liable**	My dog is **liable** to bark at strangers.
12.	**libel**	The actor sued the reporter for **libel.**
13.	**allude**	The report may **allude** to the meeting.
14.	**elude**	The robber tried to **elude** the police.
15.	**rational**	His decision to leave was **rational.**
16.	**rationale**	She gave a **rationale** for her behavior.
17.	**persecute**	The king used to **persecute** opponents.
18.	**prosecute**	The court will **prosecute** criminals.
19.	**imply**	Did I **imply** that I disagreed?
20.	**infer**	I **infer** that you didn't like the book.

CHALLENGE!

affective
effective
eminent
imminent
perpetrate
perpetuate

■ **PRACTICE** Some of these word pairs are more confusing than others. Write the word pairs that you use correctly. Then write the pairs you aren't sure of.

■ **WRITE** Choose ten words to write in sentences.

DEFINITIONS Write the list word that matches each clue.

1. people who move into a country
2. people who move out of a country
3. to refer to or mention in passing
4. to cleverly avoid or escape
5. to draw conclusions from hints
6. to mean something without saying it directly
7. to cause to suffer
8. to bring before a court of law

CLASSIFYING Write the list word that relates to each group.

9. durable, robust, lasting
10. stationery, stamp, address
11. attract, pull, polar
12. university, school, institution
13. warm, friendly, strong
14. explanation, justification, reason
15. mosaic, mural, montage
16. likely, possible, probable
17. businessperson, tycoon, entrepreneur
18. sensible, reasonable, logical
19. cover, enfold, conceal
20. falsehood, slander, lie

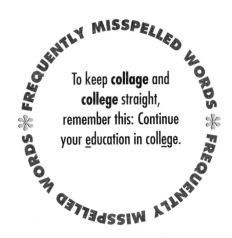

FREQUENTLY MISSPELLED WORDS * FREQUENTLY MISSPELLED WORDS *

To keep **collage** and **college** straight, remember this: Continue your <u>e</u>ducation in coll<u>e</u>ge.

STRATEGIC SPELLING

Seeing Meaning Connections

immigrants
emigrated
immigrating
immigration

Complete the sentences in this passage with words from the box. One is a list word.

Between 1892 and 1943, Ellis Island in Upper New York Bay was the main (21) center in the United States. As many as one million (22) were processed there in a year. People (23) from their native countries for various reasons, such as fleeing persecution. They hoped to get a better life by (24) to the U.S.

≡	Make a capital.
/	Make a small letter.
∧	Add something.
ℯ	Take out something.
⊙	Add a period.
⌗	New paragraph

PROOFREAD FOR CARELESS ERRORS

Capitalize nouns only if they name a specific person, place, or thing. For example:

> Fourteen-year-old Tex lives with his seventeen-year-old B̶rother, Mason.

Check for Capital Letters Write correctly the five incorrectly capitalized words in the rest of this blurb for *Tex,* by S.E. Hinton.

> The two Brothers are often in conflict. No one has seen their Father for months. Mason has dreams of going to College, while Tex has a hard time just keeping out of Trouble. A terrifying Experience forces them together.

PROOFREAD A BLURB

Find five spelling errors in this blurb for *I Am the Cheese,* by Robert Cormier. Write them correctly. Some may be words you learned before. Fix three words that shouldn't be capitalized too.

> The goverment and a Criminal organization envelope Adam's family in danger. His father gave testimony to help persecute the Organization, but Adam has blanked it out. The Family has been in witness protection, but the are no longer able to allude the organization. Adam is finally let in on the horrible secret.

WRITE A BLURB

Choose a book or story that you have recently read and write a blurb for it. Try to use three list words and a personal word.

Word List

collage	immigrants	persecute	envelope
college	allude	prosecute	imply
liable	elude	hardy	infer
libel	rational	hearty	magnet
emigrants	rationale	envelop	magnate

Personal Words 1.____ 2.____

Review

WORD PAIRS Write the word from the box that best completes each sentence pair.

collage
college
emigrants
immigrants
hardy
hearty
envelop
envelope
magnet
magnate

1. If you want to head your own business, you can be a (a). If you want to attract a piece of metal, use a (b).
2. People who leave their country are (a), but people who move into a new country are (b).
3. To describe a settler of the West, use the word (a). To describe nourishing food, use the word (b).
4. Fog can (a) the tops of skyscrapers. An (b) can hold a friendly letter.
5. You would go to (a) to get a higher education. You'd make a (b) to express something artistic.

Multicultural Connection

ART The collage is a relatively new art form, really only begun in the last one hundred years. **Mosaics**—pictures made of pieces of stone, glass, or wood—have been around for thousands of years. Mosaics found in the Middle East were completed as long as five thousand years ago.

Look at these mosaics from various times and places. Use the information at the right to help you label each with its country of origin.

Israel Thousands of years ago, Middle Eastern people used mosaics in geometric patterns to decorate buildings.

Mexico In the 7th or 8th century, the Maya often used mosaics to decorate ceremonial masks.

Italy The mosaics of Italy, dating from the 1st century to the present, often resemble paintings.

Spain In the 20th century, mosaics were revived to decorate the outside of modern buildings, often made of tiles of assorted shapes and sizes.

1.

3.

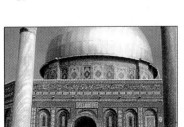
2.

4.

Words from Many Cultures 1

SPELLING FOCUS

Many words in English come from other languages and may have unexpected spellings: **amateur.**

■ **STUDY**   Say each word. Then read the sentence.

1. **amateur**   An unpaid athlete is an **amateur.**
2. **calligraphy** The notes were written in **calligraphy.**
3. **batik**   Lisa used **batik** to dye the shirt.
4. **rodeo**   A cowboy roped a calf at the **rodeo.**
5. **snorkel**   The diver used a **snorkel.**
6. **karate**   Learn **karate** for self-defense.
7. **banjo**   The musician strummed a **banjo.**
8. **jukebox**   The **jukebox** played our favorite song.
9. **luggage**   Are you taking **luggage** on the trip?
10. **umbrella**   I took an **umbrella** in case of rain.

11. **origami**   Fold paper to make **origami** designs.
12. **macramé**   I tied knots for a **macramé** vest.
13. **toboggan**   We sped down the hill on a **toboggan.**
14. **slalom**   The skier won the **slalom** event.
15. **safari**   People on a **safari** see wild animals.
16. **tambourine** The drummer tapped a **tambourine.**
17. **ukulele**   The Hawaiian singer played a **ukulele.**
18. **encore**   I hope the band will play an **encore.**
19. **hammock**   We hung a **hammock** between two trees.
20. **machete**   He needs a **machete** to cut those weeds.

CHALLENGE!

mah-jongg
jai alai
boccie
croquet
canasta

■ **PRACTICE**   Sort the list words by writing
- four words that have to do with arts or crafts
- six words that have to do with sports or adventure
- six words that have to do with music or performing
- four words that name tools or things we use

■ **WRITE**   Choose two sentences to write an advertisement.

RIDDLES   Write the list word that answers each riddle.

1. I am a hanging bed from the Spanish word *hamaca*.
2. From the German *schnorchel*, I am a tube you can breathe through while underwater.
3. From a Swahili word, I am an expedition in Africa.
4. I'm a Javanese word describing a method of dyeing fabric.
5. I am from a Greek word meaning "beautiful handwriting."
6. I am the Japanese art of paper folding.
7. I am the French word you shout when you have especially enjoyed a performance.
8. From a Norwegian word, I am a zigzag race downhill.
9. I am baggage, from a Swedish word for pull.
10. I am a small guitar of Hawaiian origin.

DEFINITIONS   Write the list word that fits each definition.

11. From the French word meaning "to love," this describes a person who does a sport for love, not money.
12. From Arabic, this instrument can be shaken and drummed.
13. An automatic record machine, part of its name is from Bantu.
14. This French word describes lace made from knotting patterns with thread or cord.
15. This tool to protect you from the rain is from an Italian word.
16. From Spanish, it is a contest in roping cattle and riding horses.
17. Of Algonquin origin, this is a sled without runners.
18. This is a Spanish word for a large knife used for cutting brush and sugar cane.
19. This stringed musical instrument is from the Bantu language.
20. This is a Japanese style of fighting without weapons.

STRATEGIC SPELLING

Building New Words

21.–24. Write the plural form of each of these list words: *rodeo, banjo, jukebox, safari.*

> ### Did You Know?
> **Ukulele** combines two Hawaiian words: **uku** and **lele.** Literally, ukulele means "the jumping flea," probably because of the quick way the player's fingers move over the strings.

■ PROOFREADING AND WRITING

≡	Make a capital.
/	Make a small letter.
∧	Add something.
ℯ	Take out something.
⊙	Add a period.
⌗	New paragraph

PROOFREAD FOR PUNCTUATION

Items in a series should be separated by commas. For example:

The International Day program will
include arts and crafts food, and a parade of world flags.
∧

Check Commas Read this passage. Write the four words that should have commas after them.

Mrs. Osawa will make origami cranes fish, and flowers. Then Mr. Osawa will demonstrate karate. For lunch we will serve foods from Sweden China Turkey, and Brazil. In the afternoon we will explore holidays in Korea Mexico, and Poland. At the end of the day, we will see many flags from around the world.

PROOFREAD A PROGRAM Find five spelling errors in this program for International Day and write them correctly. Some may be words you learned before. Fix three comma errors too.

8:00	The Arts: Chinese caligraphy macramé plant hangers, and photografhy
10:00	Music: uklele drum banjoe, and accordion
12:00	International Lunch
1:00	Presentation: Chrismas Around the World

WRITE A PROGRAM Plan a program for a special day at your school. It could be an International Day or some other occasion. Write the program and decorate a cover for it. Try to use three list words and a personal word.

Word List

calligraphy	rodeo	jukebox	macramé
hammock	snorkel	luggage	umbrella
toboggan	banjo	ukulele	safari
tambourine	amateur	batik	encore
slalom	origami	machete	karate

Personal Words 1.___ 2.___

Review

WHAT IS IT?   Write the word from the box that fits each item below.

1. If you wanted to see cowboys perform, you'd attend this.
2. If you wanted to swim underwater, you would need this.
3. If you didn't want to hire a professional, you'd look for this.
4. If you got caught in a thunderstorm, you'd really want this.
5. If you wanted some beautiful stationery, you'd ask someone to use this.
6. If you wanted to pluck a country tune, you'd play this.
7. If you went on a long vacation, you'd carry this.
8. If you went to a diner, you'd put money in this to hear music.
9. If you wanted to learn self-defense, you'd take this class.
10. If you wanted to make a pretty fabric for curtains, you'd use this technique.

amateur
calligraphy
batik
rodeo
snorkel
karate
banjo
jukebox
luggage
umbrella

Word *Study*

PERSONIFICATION   "The hammock groaned from the weight of the three sisters." Of course, a hammock can't really groan. The writer is using **personification**—giving human qualities to nonhuman things. Personification helps make descriptions in your writing come alive. The writer could have said "The hammock stretched under the weight of the sisters." But doesn't the first sentence give you a more vivid picture?

1.–4. Read this passage and find four examples of personification. First, write the thing being given human qualities. Then write the human quality given it.

It was a lovely summer day. As a cool breeze whispered through the trees, the sun teased the flowers growing on the forest floor. A young maple tree off in the distance wrapped its arms around a mature oak. The maple sighed to have such a strong tree to grow next to. This was one of my favorite places to be.

Now try your hand at writing personification. For each of the following, write a phrase that gives it a human quality.

5. chair ___

6. doorbell ___

7. coffeepot ___

8. thunderstorm ___

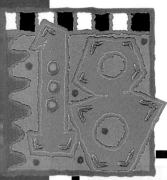

Review

Lesson 13: Directional Prefixes

Lesson 16: Easily Confused Words

Lesson 14: Related Words 2

Lesson 17: Words from Many Cultures 1

Lesson 15: Latin and Greek Word Parts 1

REVIEW WORD LIST

1. subcommittee
2. subdivision
3. supernatural
4. superstition
5. translate
6. transmit
7. transportation
8. commission
9. commit
10. comprehend
11. comprehension
12. exclaim
13. ferocity
14. invasion
15. pertinent
16. sustain
17. sustenance
18. advocate
19. biography
20. colloquial
21. eloquent
22. geography
23. graphic
24. inscription
25. loquacious
26. manuscript
27. photography
28. scribble
29. vocation
30. collage
31. elude
32. envelope
33. hardy
34. immigrants
35. imply
36. infer
37. magnate
38. rationale
39. amateur
40. banjo
41. batik
42. calligraphy
43. hammock
44. karate
45. luggage
46. macramé
47. origami
48. toboggan
49. ukulele
50. umbrella

■ PROOFREADING

Find the spelling errors in each passage and write the words correctly. All passages have seven errors except the first one, which has eight.

PROOFREAD A NEWSLETTER

Main Street Messenger

Fall classes at the Main Street Center begin September 22. New offerings this year include classes in caligraphy, oragami, photogaphy, knitting, and macramay. Guitar, banjoe, and uklele classes will start October 5. Classes in krate have been postponed until January. You may transmitt your enrollment form by mail or fax.

PROOFREAD A SOCIAL STUDIES REPORT

At the start of the War for Independence, the American militia was poorly trained, poorly armed, and inexperienced, but these emigrants to America were hearty, and they fought with a feriocity and skill that amazed the British. The Americans attacked from behind barns and bushes at any time of the day or night, warfare the British could not at first comprahend. Americans had geagraphy on their side too and could quickly allude their enemies, who were often unfamiliar with the landscape. The winter at Valley Forge tested even the strongest, however. Hundreds of Americans died while the British were able to sustane themselves only a few miles away in Philadelphia.

PROOFREAD A DESCRIPTIVE PARAGRAPH

The Welles Mansion was built by Ashton Welles, a steel magnet. Visitors often exclaime when they see the beautiful curving staircase that rises from the entrance hall. Over the dining room fireplace is a Latin enscription that may refer to Welles. Left of the entrance hall is a parlor with several oil paintings, a small college over a mahogany desk, and a framed batick print over a sofa. There is a supersition about this house: Annabelle Welles considered herself an expert on the super-natural, and she believed the mansion was haunted.

PROOFREAD A LETTER TO THE EDITOR

Help us clean up our neighborhood

For a number of years a large vacant lot next to the Sheffield sub division has been a dumping ground. Now an eloqent advacate for a cleaner neighborhood, whose vacation is landscape design, wants to buy this lot and transform it into a park. Although she is ready to spend her own money, the owners are unwilling to sell, which is beyond my comprehenshon. I can only inferr the rational behind this refusal, but surely something should be done to clean up this lot.

PROOFREAD A BOOK REVIEW

The Jericho Scroll is part thriller, part detective story set in the Middle East. A valuable manusript is stolen from a library by a scholar given permission to tranlate the work. After gaining the confidence of a commision on antiquities, he rolls up the manuscript, places it in his umberella, walks out of the library, and vanishes. The chief librarian becomes an amature sleuth and sets out to track down the scholar. His only clues are a torn piece of paper with a mysterious scribbel and a biografy of the thief taken from a reference work.

PROOFREAD A REPORT

Over 3,000 miles of canals, in combination with roads and rivers, created a vast transpertation network north of the Ohio River by 1840. Writer Charles Dickens told of his experiences on a canal boat in _American Notes_. Passengers' lugage was heaped in the middle of the deck and passengers had to lie down nearly flat when the helmsman shouted, "Low bridge!" Dickens also wrote of a loquacious fellow passenger and remarked on the coloquial speech of Americans. The usual sustanance was plain but ample, and passengers slept in a sort of wooden hamock, which Dickens described in a grafic way as a "hanging bookshelf" with a "microscopic blanket."

PROOFREAD THE MINUTES OF A MEETING

Forty student council members were present at the October 21 meeting when several pertnent matters were discussed. Eugene Slater asked if the council could send a letter to the school board about locker searches, which he said seemed to immply distrust of students and were an envasion of privacy. Members also voted to comit volunteer time to helping at the Walkathon. A subcommitee was appointed to explore locations and cost of a tobbogan party in December. Tiffany Baker passed an envelop around for contributions for flowers for Mr. Adkins, who is in the hospital. The next meeting is in November.

STRATEGY WORKSHOP

Creating Memory Tricks

DISCOVER THE STRATEGY We all have words that give us trouble. Outwit these tricky words with tricks of your own. Give this strategy a try.

First, mark the letters that give you problems.

~~mosquetoes~~   mosqui̲toes

Then think of memory helpers—words or phrases you already can spell—that have the same letters.

qui̲ck   qui̲te   qui̲t

Now you're ready to create your memory trick. Link your word with a memory helper that helps you remember it.

Tell these mosqui̲toes to qui̲t biting!

Tips: It helps to **visualize** the scene as you say the trick. Also, your trick doesn't have to be serious, nor does it have to make sense. It only has to help you remember how to spell the word.

TRY IT OUT Now try this memory tricks strategy with a partner.

crew	hideout	quacks	cute, cozy shoes

Write a helper from the box to complete each memory trick. Underline the matching letters. *Note:* A helper could be one word or more. A memory trick could be a phrase **(the eloquent queen)** or a sentence **(Al always acts)**.

1. a hideous ___
2. a mediocre ___
3. My moccasins are ___.
4. The loquacious duck ___ often.

Pick a helper from the box and create a memory trick for each word below. Underline the matching letters in the word and helper. Draw any tricks you can visualize.

rough	brain	comma	Mort

5. mortgage
6. dilemma
7. naive
8. thoroughly

LOOK AHEAD Look ahead at the next five lessons for list words that might give you problems. Create memory tricks for two of them. Share your results with the class.

Unusual Letter Combinations

Some words have sounds represented by unusual letter combinations: /ā/ spelled **ee—matinee**; /ü/spelled **eu—sleuth**.

■ **STUDY**   Say each word. Then read the sentence.

1.	**matinee**	We went to a **matinee** after lunch.
2.	**sleuth**	A **sleuth** solved the crime.
3.	**forfeit**	The ill player must **forfeit** the match.
4.	**porcelain**	Tea was served in **porcelain** cups.
5.	**limousine**	We rode to the wedding in a **limousine**.
6.	**guarantee**	My watch has a money-back **guarantee**.
7.	**camouflage**	Soldiers wear **camouflage** face paint.
8.	**cantaloupe**	We ate juicy **cantaloupe** for breakfast.
9.	**parliament**	British laws are made by a **parliament**.
10.	**pageant**	We all sang in the holiday **pageant**.

11.	**turquoise**	The **turquoise** stones are bluish green.
12.	**nuisance**	The barking dog was a **nuisance**.
13.	**sergeant**	The **sergeant** trained the soldiers.
14.	**counterfeit**	The thieves had **counterfeit** money.
15.	**connoisseur**	An art **connoisseur** liked my painting.
16.	**silhouette**	She drew a **silhouette** of a reindeer.
17.	**archaeology**	I went on an **archaeology** dig in Egypt.
18.	**ricochet**	I was hit by the ball's **ricochet**.
19.	**liaison**	He is our **liaison** with the community.
20.	**aerial**	The **aerial** view of the city was great.

CHALLENGE!

hors d'oeuvre
bureaucrat
reveille
entrepreneur
reconnaissance

■ **PRACTICE**   Sort the words by writing
- one word that has one syllable
- five words that have two syllables
- thirteen words that have three syllables
- one word that has five syllables

■ **WRITE**   Choose ten words to write in sentences.

ANALOGIES   Write the list word that completes each analogy.

1. Orange is to citrus as ___ is to melon.
2. Congress is to United States as ___ is to England.
3. Pilot is to airplane as chauffeur is to ___ .
4. Superman is to superhero as Sherlock Holmes is to ___ .
5. Victory is to win as give up is to ___ .
6. Corporal is to private as lieutenant is to ___ .
7. Biology is to living things as ___ is to ancient life.
8. Evening is to late show as afternoon is to ___ .
9. Real is to genuine as fake is to ___ .
10. Silver is to metal as ___ is to stone.

WORD ASSOCIATIONS   Write the list word that is associated with each group.

11. disguise, conceal, hide
12. china, pottery
13. form, outline, shadow
14. money-back, warranty, promise
15. pesky, annoying
16. go-between, middleman, mediator
17. bounce, spring, boomerang
18. beauty contest, spectacle
19. aeronautic, aerospace
20. expert, professional

STRATEGIC SPELLING

Using the Memory Tricks Strategy

Use memory tricks to help you spell. Create memory tricks using the list words and helpers below. Underline the matching letters.

21. camouflage—amount
22. pageant—age

> **Did You Know?**
> The French word that **turquoise** comes from means "Turkish stone."

≡	Make a capital.
/	Make a small letter.
∧	Add something.
ℓ	Take out something.
⊙	Add a period.
¶	New paragraph

PROOFREAD FOR USAGE Most nouns are made plural by adding **-s** or **-es.** Some words change spelling and others remain the same word. For example

Clarke's makes fine porcelain figures that won't just sit on your ~~shelfs.~~ shelves

Check Plurals Correct the mistakes in this advertisement by writing the five misspelled plurals correctly.

Clarke's new line of dishs and utensils is a sight to behold. The knifes, forks, and spoons have lovely porcelain handles. The first two serieses of patterns are decorated with delicate, hand-painted summer daisies and winter berrys. A new pattern, available this October, will use autumn leafs.

PROOFREAD AN ADVERTISEMENT Find the eight misspelled words in this advertisement and write them correctly. Some may be words you learned before. Three of the misspellings are incorrect plurals.

Are you a connoseur of modern art? If so, you'll love our new turqiuose jewelry designes. Furthermore, you won't have to forfit other luxurys to afford them. We garenty you'll wear these unique creationes know and for years to come.

WRITE AN ADVERTISEMENT Plan and write an advertisement for a product you like. Try to use three list words and a personal word.

Word List

limousine	connoisseur	porcelain	sleuth
guarantee	cantaloupe	nuisance	liaison
counterfeit	turquoise	ricochet	pageant
archaeology	parliament	sergeant	aerial
camouflage	silhouette	matinee	forfeit

Personal Words 1.____ 2.____

Review

WORDS IN CONTEXT   Use the underlined words in each sentence to help you write the correct list word from the box.

1. "I'm a super <u>detective</u>," said Sherlock Holmes.
2. I couldn't decide between the green melon or the <u>orange melon</u>.
3. The members of the <u>lawmaking body</u> cast their final votes.
4. "Jeeves, let's take the <u>luxurious car</u> today," said Ms. Daisy.
5. We tried to go to the <u>afternoon show</u>, but it was sold out.
6. White fur was a perfect <u>disguise</u> for the polar bear in the snow.
7. "We <u>promise to replace</u> your radio," the announcer said.
8. Our homecoming parade was quite an <u>elaborate show</u>.
9. The team had to <u>give up</u> the game when the pitcher got sick.
10. This <u>china</u> collection looks lovely on the table.

matinee
sleuth
forfeit
porcelain
limousine
guarantee
camouflage
cantaloupe
parliament
pageant

Word *Study*

WORDS FROM NAMES AND PLACES   Did you know that the word **cantaloupe** comes from Cantalupo, an area near Rome where the melons were originally grown? Many English words come from the names of places and people. Write the words from the box that are from the names of the people and places described. Use your Spelling Dictionary if you need help.

leotard	graham crackers	tangerine
teddy bear	Ferris wheel	zeppelin

1. Sylvester Graham invented this healthful snack.
2. This orange citrus fruit came by way of Tangier, Morocco.
3. Count Ferdinand von Zeppelin invented this airship.
4. This toy was named after President Theodore Roosevelt.
5. George Ferris designed this amusement park ride that was a big attraction at the 1893 World's Fair in Chicago.
6. Jules Léotard, a nineteenth-century circus performer, designed his own stretch, tight-fitting costume.

Latin and Greek Word Parts 2

Many words contain Greek and Latin word parts. **Jud, jur,** and **jus** mean "law" or "judge." **Crit** and **reg** mean "to judge" or "to guide." **Pol** and **dem** mean "people" or "city."

■ **STUDY**   Say each word. Then read the sentence.

1.	**justify**	The judge must **justify** her decision.
2.	**jury**	The **jury** listened to the witnesses.
3.	**judicial**	Lawyers work in the **judicial** system.
4.	**critical**	The reviewer was **critical** of the film.
5.	**regular**	Doctors recommend **regular** exercise.
6.	**regal**	The princess had **regal** manners.
7.	**regional**	The senator held **regional** meetings.
8.	**democracy**	Voters choose leaders in a **democracy**.
9.	**policy**	The coach has a strict absence **policy**.
10.	**metropolis**	New York City is a great **metropolis**.
11.	**perjury**	He lied in court, committing **perjury**.
12.	**jurisdiction**	The police are under his **jurisdiction**.
13.	**judicious**	Her choice of speakers was **judicious**.
14.	**critique**	I wrote a **critique** of the new book.
15.	**hypocrite**	A **hypocrite** only pretends to be kind.
16.	**regiment**	A **regiment** of soldiers marched to war.
17.	**regime**	The king had a peaceful **regime**.
18.	**cosmopolitan**	She is sophisticated and **cosmopolitan**.
19.	**demographic**	The census includes **demographic** data.
20.	**epidemic**	He became ill during the flu **epidemic**.

CHALLENGE!

prejudicial
hypercritical
regalia
acropolis
megalopolis

■ **PRACTICE**   Sort the words by writing
- six words with **jud, jur,** or **jus**
- three words with **crit**
- five words with **reg**
- six words with **pol** or **dem**

■ **WRITE**   Choose two sentences to include in a paragraph.

SYNONYMS Write the list word that means the same as each word or phrase below.

1. royal
2. false testimony
3. big city
4. sophisticated
5. evaluation

6. ordinary
7. phony
8. disapproving
9. plan of action
10. military unit

CONTEXT CLUES Write the list word that matches each clue.

11. Our school was struck with an ___ of chicken pox.
12. The ___ delivered a verdict of "not guilty."
13. In the ___ study, the scientists studied changes in where people of different backgrounds live.
14. In a ___, the people have a say in their government.
15. The Supreme Court is the ___ branch of our government.
16. The old government was overthrown, and the country is now ruled by a new ___.
17. Lee tried to ___ her mistake by saying it was Jim's fault.
18. The ___ teacher thought carefully before deciding.
19. The local police could not arrest the speeder because he was out of their ____.
20. A ___ agency handles all calls in our region.

STRATEGIC SPELLING

Seeing Meaning Connections

regulate
regularly
regular
irregular

The words in the box, including the list word **regular,** are related in spelling and meaning. Complete the sentences with these words.

A (21), healthy pulse rate is between 50 and 100 steady beats per minute. An (22) heartbeat can be dangerous, but there are some things a doctor can do to (23) the rhythm and pace of the heart so that it is beating (24) again.

Did You Know?
An **epidemic** of plague, known as the *Black Death,* killed about a fourth of the European population in the mid-1300s.

Make a capital. =
Make a small letter. /
Add something. ∧
Take out something. ℯ
Add a period. ⊙
New paragraph ⸿

PROOFREAD FOR CARELESS ERRORS

Proofread carefully so you don't repeat or drop words when you write. For example:

Fasten your seat belt to ~~to~~ prepare ^for^ takeoff.

Check for Repeated and Dropped Words Write any repeated or dropped words. Write "Correct" if the sentence is correct.

1. Keep luggage under seats or in overhead compartments.
2. Keep your belt fastened until the light on the panel goes off.
3. Let flight attendants know if you ordered a a special meal.
4. Ask flight attendants for magazines or or newspapers.
5. After landing, stay seated until the plane is the gate.

PROOFREAD A SIGN   Find the five misspelled words in this sign and write them correctly. Some may be words you learned before. Fix three repeated or dropped words too.

Store Hours and Policies
- Our reguler weekday hours are 9–6; Saturday hours 10–5.
- It store policie to refund money for returned items only if the customer can can justafy the return.
- Exchanges are allways possible.
- We will prasecute shoplifters.

WRITE A SIGN   Write a sign about a school policy that might be posted in a hallway at your school. Try to use three list words and a personal word.

Word List

judicial	cosmopolitan	regiment	perjury
democracy	jurisdiction	judicious	regal
regular	demographic	critical	epidemic
justify	critique	jury	regional
policy	metropolis	regime	hypocrite

Personal Words 1.___ 2.___

Review

QUOTABLES   Write the word from the box that best completes each quotation.

1. "You're looking quite ___ in your tuxedo," the hostess said.
2. "Has the ___ reached a verdict?" the judge asked.
3. "Crime is down in our ___," the New York newspaper said.
4. "Don't be so ___ of my acting," the actor said to the critic.
5. "The U.S. is the world's oldest, continuous ___," the history teacher said.
6. "Our school has a zero-tolerance ___," the principal stated.
7. "The storm is ___, confined to our area," the announcer said.
8. "How can you ___ spending all your money on video games?" the parents asked.
9. "The ___ system will decide if they are guilty," lawyers said.
10. "Good food and ___ exercise will keep you fit," the doctor said.

justify
jury
judicial
critical
regular
regal
regional
democracy
policy
metropolis

Word *Study*

CONTEXT: DEFINITIONS AND EXPLANATIONS   Suppose you read: "For a metropolis to thrive, both the central city and its surrounding communities must work together to provide housing and jobs." You can get the meaning of *metropolis* from the **context,** or words around it. The words "central city and surrounding communities" explain what a metropolis is.

Use context to write what the underlined words mean. The context may not be in the same sentence as the word.

<u>Suburbanization</u> contributed to the development of metropolitan areas by expanding cities beyond their boundaries and thus creating suburbs. Many suburbs were almost completely <u>residential</u>. However, the <u>urbanity</u>, or easy and refined living, of the suburbs had a price. Since most people resided but did not work there, they had to <u>commute</u>, or travel by train, car, or bus to their jobs in the cities.

1. suburbanization
2. residential
3. urbanity
4. commute

Suffixes -able, -ible, -ance, -ence

When adding the suffix **-able**, **-ible**, **-ance**, or **-ence**, there is no sound clue to help you decide which form to use.

STUDY Say each word. Then read the sentence.

1. **flammable** — The **flammable** rags could start a fire.
2. **noticeable** — The spot on my shirt is not **noticeable**.
3. **available** — Many good seats are still **available**.
4. **collectible** — The shop sold **collectible** dolls.
5. **divisible** — Twelve is **divisible** by two and four.
6. **edible** — The potato salad is still **edible**.
7. **endurance** — A runner must have **endurance**.
8. **attendance** — Daily school **attendance** is essential.
9. **reference** — An atlas is a useful **reference** book.
10. **intelligence** — Einstein had great **intelligence**.

11. **knowledgeable** — I am **knowledgeable** about dinosaurs.
12. **charitable** — He is **charitable** to unfortunate people.
13. **deductible** — Taxes are **deductible** from your salary.
14. **compatible** — She and her roommate are **compatible**.
15. **resemblance** — The sisters have a close **resemblance**.
16. **vengeance** — The enemies fought with a **vengeance**.
17. **elegance** — The stately mansion had **elegance**.
18. **occurrence** — Today there was a strange **occurrence**.
19. **convenience** — A microwave oven offers **convenience**.
20. **competence** — He did the job with **competence**.

CHALLENGE!

foreseeable
unpronounceable
imperceptible
perseverance
effervescence

PRACTICE Sort the words by writing
- five words with **-able**
- five words with **-ible**
- five words with **-ance**
- five words with **-ence**

WRITE Choose four sentences to rewrite as questions.

WORD FORMS   Write the list words that come from these base words.

1. flame
2. eat
3. divide
4. attend
5. endure
6. collect

7. charity
8. occur
9. resemble
10. refer
11. deduct
12. knowledge

CONTEXT CLUES   Write the list word that completes each sentence.

13. The mansion's ___ was due as much to the rich and tasteful furnishings as it was to the marble floors.
14. That style of purse is no longer ___, so please choose another.
15. Martin showed some ___ in leading the group but not in solving problems.
16. Even though Charisse and Sylvia get along well now, they aren't sure if they would be ___ as roommates.
17. Knowledge and good judgment are signs of ___.
18. Andrew vowed ___ for the wrong that was done to him.
19. If I move, I will miss the ___ of having a grocery store only one block away.
20. That old ink stain on the tablecloth is barely ___ now.

Building New Words

Add the suffix **-able** or **-ible** to the following base words: *rely, sense, resist, manage, envy, corrupt.* Use your Spelling Dictionary if you need help.

Add -able

21.___

22.___

23.___

Add -ible

24.___

25.___

26.___

Take a Hint
You can spell **reference** with ease. Spell it with **e's:**
r<u>e</u>fer<u>e</u>nc<u>e</u>.

☰	Make a capital.
/	Make a small letter.
∧	Add something.
℮	Take out something.
⊙	Add a period.
¶	New paragraph

PROOFREAD FOR PUNCTUATION Put quotation marks around direct quotations and capitalize the first word of the quotation.

Before operating, Dr. Ornaf explained, "this is a new surgical procedure."

Check for Quotation Marks and Capitals Correct the mistakes in these sentences from a news item by writing the word and the quotation mark that should come before or after it. Make sure all words are correctly capitalized.

Mrs. Flores replied, we're thrilled that this new procedure is available. She also noted, "Willy never gave up hope; his courage kept us going. Her husband quickly added, our friends and neighbors have been very supportive.

PROOFREAD A NEWS ITEM Find the five misspelled words and write them correctly. Some may be words you learned before. Also fix the mistakes in the direct quotations.

Teenager Luz Ruiz organized a neighborhood fund-raiser to help pay for Willy Flores's operation. Luz said, "I no I cant do much myself, but all of us together can. One of Ruiz's neighbors remarked, that girl's compatance, endurence, and charitible heart inspired us all.

WRITE A NEWS ITEM Plan and write a news item about a recent school event. Use three list words and a personal word.

Word List

occurrence	resemblance	noticeable	charitable
endurance	reference	intelligence	edible
deductible	knowledgeable	collectible	attendance
convenience	compatible	elegance	available
flammable	vengeance	divisible	competence

Personal Words 1.____ 2.____

Review

WHAT CAN IT BE? Write the list word from the box that is suggested by each sentence.

1. I'm a book you use over and over, such as a dictionary.
2. I'm something people like to collect, such as dolls or coins.
3. I'm easily set on fire, like paper.
4. I'm something that's okay to eat.
5. I'm the ability to learn and to know.
6. I'm something that catches your eye, like a bright color.
7. I'm the number of people who attend an event, like a game.
8. I'm able to be divided, like a pie.
9. I'm able to last and last, such as in a race.
10. I'm usually there when you need me, like electricity.

flammable
noticeable
available
collectible
divisible
edible
endurance
attendance
reference
intelligence

Word *Study*

LATIN ROOTS: *vindicare* The list word **vengeance** comes from the Latin root *vindicare*, which means "avenge." The words in the box below have different meanings, but because they all come from *vindicare*, their meanings have something to do with revenge.

vengeance	vendetta	avenger	vindictive	avenge

Write the "revenge" word from the box for each definition below. Use your Spelling Dictionary if you need help.

1. one who takes revenge
2. a bitter feud based on getting revenge
3. take revenge for or on behalf of
4. punishment in return for a wrong; great force or violence
5. feeling a strong tendency for revenge

One Word or Two?

Some words often used together are never written as one word: **kind of, have to.** For other words, you have to think about their meanings to spell them: **maybe, may be.**

■ **STUDY**   Say each word. Then read the sentence.

WATCH OUT FOR FREQUENTLY MISSPELLED WORDS!

1.	**kind of**	She was **kind of** tired after the game.
2.	**have to**	Do I **have to** do the dishes?
3.	**all ready**	He was **all ready** for school at 7:00.
4.	**already**	We have **already** seen that movie.
5.	**a lot** ✳	They had **a lot** of food at the party.
6.	**allot**	We will **allot** two tickets per student.
7.	**every day**	We have math homework **every day.**
8.	**everyday**	These dishes are for **everyday** use.
9.	**may be**	You **may be** surprised at the results.
10.	**maybe** ✳	Today, **maybe** the team will win.
11.	**supposed to**	He is **supposed to** ride the bus home.
12.	**going to** ✳	We are **going to** put on a play.
13.	**any way**	You can dress **any way** you like.
14.	**anyway**	She had a sore foot but won **anyway.**
15.	**a part**	I painted **a part** of the mural.
16.	**apart**	The mechanic took the engine **apart.**
17.	**all together**	The boys sang the song **all together.**
18.	**altogether**	My situation is **altogether** different.
19.	**any more**	There isn't **any more** chocolate cake.
20.	**anymore**	We never play tennis **anymore.**

■ **PRACTICE**   Sort the words by writing
- those that are two words
- those that are one word

■ **WRITE**   Choose two sentences to write a rhyme or riddle.

CHALLENGE!

à la carte
all-American
breathtaking
foreword
afterwards

SYNONYMS Write the list word that means the same as the words in each group below.

1. sort of, in a way, ___
2. intending to, planning to, ___
3. ought to, expected to, ___
4. must, required to, ___

CONTEXT CLUES Write the list words that complete the sentences. Choose from the words in parentheses.

5. I don't want (anymore, any more) peas.
6. Lenka doesn't live here (anymore, any more).
7. Well, (maybe, may be) you can go next time.
8. It (maybe, may be) a long time before we're through.
9. I saw a movie (everyday, every day) this week.
10. These are my (everyday, every day) clothes.
11. Rami has (allot, a lot) of spare time these days.
12. How much did you (allot, a lot) for each person?
13. That is (altogether, all together) too difficult for my little sister.
14. We were (altogether, all together) when Mom found us.
15. I (already, all ready) finished cleaning my room.
16. The others were (already, all ready) to go when I arrived.
17. Were you able to get (apart, a part) to fix your bike?
18. Ali likes to take things (apart, a part) so she can put them back together.
19. Why don't I go to the park (anyway, any way)?
20. I can't find (anyway, any way) to finish before the deadline.

Seeing Meaning Connections

Words with _part_
apart
apartheid
partake
partnership

Write the words from the box that fit the definitions. One is a list word.

21. take or have a share
22. in separate parts
23. joint association
24. racial segregation

FREQUENTLY MISSPELLED WORDS

Regardless of how you say it, **going to** is always written as two words.

≡	Make a capital.
/	Make a small letter.
∧	Add something.
ℓ	Take out something.
⊙	Add a period.
⁋	New paragraph

PROOFREAD FOR USAGE Avoid sentence fragments. Make sure each sentence has a subject and verb and makes sense.

I love sports. Because I'm from a family of athletes.

Check for Sentence Fragments Read each item below. If it is a fragment, write "F." If it is a complete sentence, write "Correct."

1. My favorite thing to watch on TV is sports.
2. Especially football and hockey.
3. Because they're action-packed.
4. Basketball is kind of fun to watch too.
5. During the playoffs.

PROOFREAD A PERSONAL NARRATIVE Find the five misspelled words in Alex's personal narrative. Some may be words you learned before. Also correct three sentence fragments.

> My day begins at 7:00. I eat a lot at breakfast everyday. I often hafta run for the bus. Because I'm late. My buddies and I all ways tell jokes at lunch. Play football out side after school. In the evening, I do my homework. See if there's anyway to bug my sister.

WRITE A PERSONAL NARRATIVE Write a personal narrative describing a really good day for you. Try to use three list words and a personal word. Proofread your paragraph.

Word List

kind of	altogether	a lot	maybe
supposed to	all ready	allot	any more
going to	already	every day	anymore
have to	a part	everyday	any way
all together	apart	may be	anyway

Personal Words 1.___ 2.___

Review

DEFINITIONS Write the words from the box that mean the same as the underlined words in each sentence.

1. This is the breakfast I have <u>each day</u>.
2. Today <u>might be</u> the last day to sign up.
3. My <u>daily</u> routine includes exercise and meditation.
4. Are you <u>completely prepared</u> to take your spelling test?
5. The boys <u>are required to</u> see their dentist monthly.
6. The guards will <u>distribute</u> one cup of rice to each prisoner.
7. <u>Perhaps</u> it's time to get new sneakers.
8. We got there at noon, but you had left <u>before that time</u>.
9. That new hat looks <u>sort of</u> interesting on you.
10. I like to read books of historical fiction <u>very much</u>.

kind of
have to
all ready
already
a lot
allot
every day
everyday
may be
maybe

Using a *Thesaurus*

SYNONYMS If you say *a lot of,* you are using a synonym for the word *many.* Words that have the same or similar meanings are called **synonyms.** When you look up *many* in your Writer's Thesaurus, you will find these synonyms: *numerous, multitudinous, countless, innumerable, umpteen, a lot of, lots of,* and *quite a few.* Synonyms make your writing more interesting.

Synonyms are often very close in meaning, though sometimes one synonym is clearly better in a sentence than others. At other times, synonyms can be used interchangeably: *countless* and *innumerable* both mean "too many to count," while *a lot of, lots of,* and *quite a few* mean "many."

In the paragraph below, replace each use of *a lot of* with the synonym from the box that you think works best. HINT: There aren't any right or wrong answers to this. However, one use of <u>a lot of</u> is okay. Mark that one "Do not change."

many	**numerous**	**countless**	**innumerable**	**quite a few**

There are (1) <u>a lot of</u> things to see at the zoo. Last time I went, I saw (2) <u>a lot of</u> flamingoes, with their fiery-pink feathers and skinny legs. (3) <u>A lot of</u> people think they're weird birds, but I don't agree. Another time I saw (4) <u>a lot of</u> seals in the pool. They like to swim (5) <u>a lot of</u> the time. (6) <u>A lot of</u> seals were sunning themselves on rocks. I love the zoo!

Homophones

A homophone is a word that sounds exactly like another word but has a different spelling and meaning: **aloud, allowed.**

■ **STUDY** Say each word. Then read the sentence.

WATCH OUT FOR FREQUENTLY MISSPELLED WORDS!

1.	**aloud**	Jan read a story **aloud** to her sister.
2.	**allowed** ✳	Picnics are not **allowed** on the field.
3.	**assistance**	A nurse gave **assistance** to a patient.
4.	**assistants**	The lawyer has two **assistants.**
5.	**suite**	The family stayed in a hotel **suite.**
6.	**sweet**	This syrup tastes very **sweet.**
7.	**symbol**	A red rose is a **symbol** of love.
8.	**cymbal**	The drummer banged on a **cymbal.**
9.	**overdue**	I had to pay for an **overdue** videotape.
10.	**overdo**	Don't **overdo** exercising the first day.
11.	**aisle**	We sat near the **aisle** in the theater.
12.	**isle**	The family relaxed on a tropical **isle.**
13.	**bizarre**	The movie featured a **bizarre** monster.
14.	**bazaar**	I found a cool hat at a church **bazaar.**
15.	**ascent**	A climber made an **ascent** up the hill.
16.	**assent**	Dad gave his **assent** to our plan.
17.	**canvas**	The tent was made of heavy **canvas.**
18.	**canvass**	I will **canvass** the area for clues.
19.	**colonel**	A **colonel** led the regiment of soldiers.
20.	**kernel**	Each **kernel** of corn is tasty.

CHALLENGE!

bouillon
bullion
cue
queue
callous
callus

■ **PRACTICE** First write the homophone groups that are most confusing for you. Then write the rest of the homophones.

■ **WRITE** Choose two sentences to write a want ad.

HOMOPHONE SENTENCES   Write the homophone pairs that complete each sentence.

You are not (1) to read (2) in the library.

Let my two (3) know if you need (4) .

The army (5) broke a tooth on a (6) of popcorn.

They were selling many (7) items at the neighborhood (8) .

It was (9) of you to let us use your (10) of rooms for our meeting.

WORD CHOICE   Write the correct list word for each sentence.

11. This book is (overdue, overdo) at the library.
12. Try not to (overdue, overdo) running games on a hot day.
13. Please keep the center (aisle, isle) clear so people can leave.
14. We took a rowboat to the (aisle, isle) in the middle of the lake.
15. The handle on my (symbol, cymbal) broke, and I had to get it fixed before the concert.
16. The memorial is a (symbol, cymbal) of military service.
17. Drew will (canvas, canvass) the area before the election.
18. The oil painting on (canvas, canvass) was beautiful.
19. Yvette will (ascent, assent) to the plan if you do.
20. The (ascent, assent) of the balloons was a colorful sight.

STRATEGIC SPELLING
Using the Memory Tricks Strategy

Use memory tricks to help you use homophones correctly. Create homophone sentences for each of the pairs below.

21. ascent—assent
22. overdue—overdo
23. symbol—cymbal

FREQUENTLY MISSPELLED WORDS * FREQUENTLY MISSPELLED WORDS *

Think of this sentence when spelling **allowed:** Mom <u>owed</u> me a favor, so I was all<u>owed</u> to go.

≡	Make a capital.
/	Make a small letter.
∧	Add something.
ℓ	Take out something.
⊙	Add a period.
¶	New paragraph

PROOFREAD FOR CAPITALIZATION

Use capitals correctly in the heading, inside address, greeting, and closing of a business letter. For example:

2855 rockdale road

Virginia Beach, VA 23452

april 18, 19--

Check Capitalization Fix the capitalization errors in these parts of an inside address and greeting. Write the words correctly.

1. Ms. akemi Shigota
2. York Conference center
3. 986 Washington boulevard
4. scottsdale, AZ 85245
5. Dear Ms. shigota:

PROOFREAD A BUSINESS LETTER   Find five misspelled words in the body of the letter and write them correctly. Some may be words you learned before. Fix three capitalization errors.

> I'd appreciate assistence in obtaining a sweet for our regionel conference. I'll also need a lectern and chairs set up with an aile in the center. Please let me know if thats possible for November 28–30.
>
> very truly yours,
> donald rourke

WRITE A BUSINESS LETTER   Write to a company requesting information about their products. Use three list words and a personal word. For correct letter form, see page 245.

Word List

aisle	bazaar	allowed	assent
isle	assistance	aloud	canvas
symbol	assistants	overdue	canvass
cymbal	suite	overdo	colonel
bizarre	sweet	ascent	kernel

Personal Words 1.___ 2.___

Review

DRAWING CONCLUSIONS Write the word from the box suggested by each group.

1. helpers, aides, ___
2. library book, late, ___
3. sugar, honey, ___
4. permitted, okay, ___
5. &, %, $, ___
6. too much, exaggerate, ___
7. rooms, hotel, ___
8. vocally, orally, ___
9. help, aid, ___
10. crash, metal, orchestra, ___

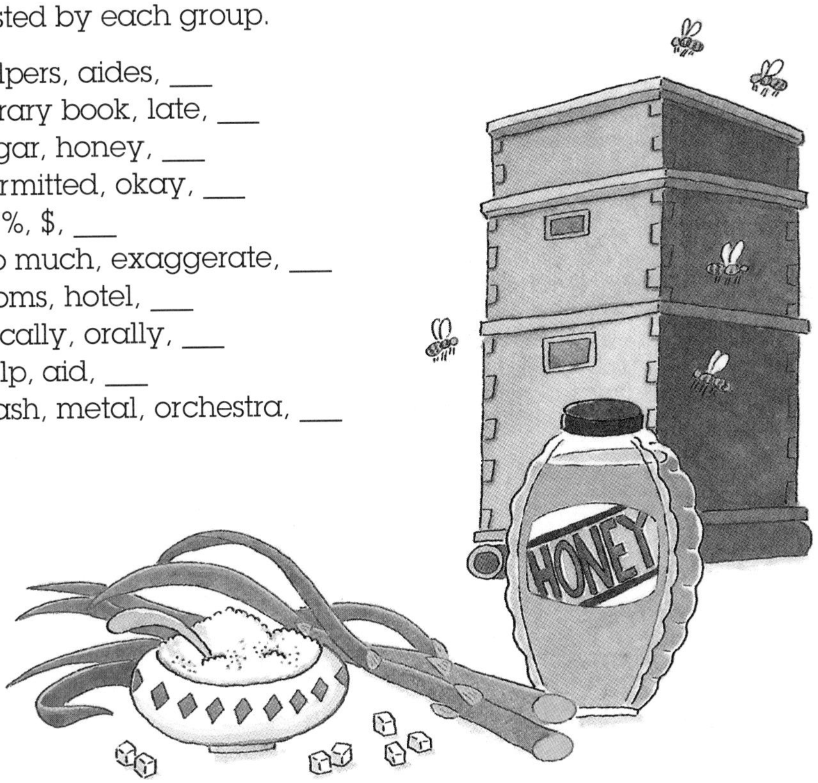

aloud
allowed
assistance
assistants
suite
sweet
symbol
cymbal
overdue
overdo

Multicultural *Connection*

FOODS We can buy fresh herbs and spices at supermarkets, farmer's markets, and roadside stands. People in other countries can also buy such things at **bazaars.** A few herbs and spices you might find at bazaars are listed in the box.

Write the word from the box that fits each definition. Use your Spelling Dictionary if you need help.

thyme	saffron	caraway	cinnamon

1. from the Arabic *za'faran,* an orange-yellow coloring and flavoring that comes from the dried stigmas of a crocus flower
2. from the Greek *kinnamon,* a spice made from the dried, reddish-brown inner bark of a laurel tree of the East Indies
3. a spicy seed used to flavor bread, rolls, and cakes, from a plant whose name comes from the Arabic *karawyā*
4. leaves used for seasoning from a variety of plants in the mint family, from the Greek *thymon*

Review

Lesson 19: Unusual Letter Combinations
Lesson 20: Latin and Greek Word Parts 2
Lesson 21: Suffixes -able, -ible, -ance, -ence
Lesson 22: One Word or Two?
Lesson 23: Homophones

REVIEW WORD LIST

1. archaeology
2. cantaloupe
3. connoisseur
4. forfeit
5. guarantee
6. limousine
7. matinee
8. nuisance
9. pageant
10. porcelain
11. sleuth
12. turquoise
13. critical
14. critique
15. democracy
16. epidemic
17. judicial
18. jury
19. perjury
20. policy
21. regal
22. regime
23. regiment
24. regional
25. regular
26. assistance
27. attendance
28. available
29. charitable
30. compatible
31. convenience
32. elegance
33. endurance
34. intelligence
35. knowledgeable
36. occurrence
37. reference
38. resemblance
39. a lot
40. already
41. every day
42. everyday
43. going to
44. may be
45. allowed
46. ascent
47. bizarre
48. canvas
49. overdue
50. sweet

PROOFREADING

Find the spelling errors in each passage and write the words correctly. All passages have seven errors except the last one, which has eight.

PROOFREAD A NOTICE

For the convence of our riders, the Safety Transit Company is gonna follow a new policie beginning November 1. Passengers asking for charitible contributions on the buses or trains will forfit their right to ride. Such requests have become a nusence to other riders and are not compatable with our pledge to provide safe and comfortable service to all. This ruling will be enforced.

PROOFREAD A REVIEW OF A PLAY

Art Attack

Mystery fans will enjoy *Art Attack,* in which a museum is robbed of priceless porcelin, paintings, and precious jewels, including a turkose necklace dating from ancient times. An archaeloge student (Ruth Harris) is a suspect and so is an aging connoissur of art (Werner Schatz), a daily visitor to the museum. The slueth who solves the case is played by Dirk Hamilton, and in one funny scene he discovers a jewel in his breakfast cantalope. Performances are nightly at 7:20 at the Rialto. There is a Sunday matinae at 3:00.

PROOFREAD A FEATURE STORY

At the regionel football games last weekend, attendence was high, partly because of the games, but also because of other attractions, such as the regimant of bagpipers. The Octoberfest pagent with regel Queen Lara and her court was also a popular event. This reporter spotted a gentleman who bore a remarkable resemblence to a famous pro star. When he climbed out of a white limosine, we were certain it was Monte Ranger, who graduated from Central in 1985.

PROOFREAD A CLASSIFIED AD

I need a job. Do you need assisstence with long over due lawn work this fall? I am knowlagable and avalable and can work everyday after school. I will rake, bag, and do general cleanup. I garenty all work and can provide a referance. Call Steve at 555-1102 and leave a message.

PROOFREAD A BOOK REVIEW

Going Home by Boris Gorchoff is about the experiences of a young Russian boy during the breakup of the Soviet regeem and the criticle events that led to attempts to establish damocracy through the former Soviet Union. The author writes of the every day hardships and the endurence of Moscow citizens who had all ready known food shortages. Gorchoff had not been aloud to emigrate but is now in the United States. This book gives an insider's view of the turmoil the Russians faced during those fateful days.

PROOFREAD A LETTER TO THE EDITOR

The right to a speedy trial

Your editorial about the jurey who convicted a former official of perjary was a good criteke of what's wrong with the judishal system. The intelligance of the jurors should not be questioned, however. What should be questioned is the epedemic of lawsuits that prevent citizens from getting a speedy trial. Although the former official maybe guilty, it shouldn't have taken three years to convict her.

Dallas Young

PROOFREAD A DESCRIPTIVE PARAGRAPH

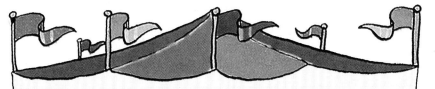

Before television, movies, or radio, the arrival of the circus was an eagerly awaited occurance. When the huge canvass tent was unloaded from the circus train, life seemed alot more interesting than it had the day before. Going to the circus meant the thrill of watching the assent of the trapeze artists and admiring the elagence of the bareback riders. It meant the sweat smell of cotton candy. It meant hearing the reguler beat of a circus band and the calls of the barkers in front of the bizaare sideshows outside the big top.

Using Meaning Helpers

DISCOVER THE STRATEGY Word pairs like *attend* and *attendance* are related in spelling and meaning. You can use the shorter word as a **meaning helper**—a reminder of how to spell the longer word. For example:

Longer Word	Helper	Clue
attendance	attend	attend + ance
charitable	charity	charity - y + able

TRY IT OUT Now try this meaning helpers strategy. Tell how the helper reminds you of how to spell the longer word. Don't forget to note any spelling changes that take place between the two words.

Longer Word	Helper	Clue
1. luckily	lucky	____
2. vocalize	vocal	____
3. noticeable	notice	____
4. resemblance	resemble	____
5. commission	commit	____
6. invasion	invade	____

Some meaning helpers give you extra help by reminding you of how a tricky sound is spelled in the longer word. For example:

Longer Word	Helper	Clue
moisture	moist	The sound of the **t** in *moist* reminds me that *moisture* is also spelled with a **t**.
narrative	narrate	The long **a** in *narrate* reminds me that the second vowel sound in *narrative* is spelled with an **a**.

Tell how the helper gives a sound clue for the longer word.
Be sure to note any spelling changes.

Longer Word	Helper	Clue
7. expression	express	____
8. spacious	space	____
9. protection	protect	____
10. pressure	press	____

LOOK AHEAD Look ahead at the next five lessons for list words that you might use this strategy with. Find two words and write them down. Then write a meaning helper for each word. Use this strategy when you study those words.

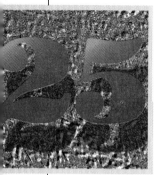

Suffixes -ous, -ment, -ness

SPELLING FOCUS

Sometimes when **-ous, -ment,** or **-ness** is added to a word ending in a consonant or an **e,** the spelling of the base word doesn't change: **courage, courageous.** Other times, it does change: **ridicule, ridiculous; sleepy, sleepiness.**

■ **STUDY** Say each word. Notice if the base word changes.

courage + -ous	=	1. **courageous**
ridicule + -ous	=	2. **ridiculous**
hazard + -ous	=	3. **hazardous**
argue + -ment	=	4. **argument**
excite + -ment	=	5. **excitement**
improve + -ment	=	6. **improvement**
refresh + -ment	=	7. **refreshment**
gentle + -ness	=	8. **gentleness**
sleepy + -ness	=	9. **sleepiness**
open + -ness	=	10. **openness**

outrage + -ous	=	11. **outrageous**
suspicion + -ous	=	12. **suspicious**
miscellany + -ous	=	13. **miscellaneous**
acknowledge + -ment	=	14. **acknowledgment**
judge + -ment	=	15. **judgment**
engage + -ment	=	16. **engagement**
arrange + -ment	=	17. **arrangement**
stubborn + -ness	=	18. **stubbornness**
cleanly + -ness	=	19. **cleanliness**
even + -ness	=	20. **evenness**

CHALLENGE!

advantageous
conscientious
encouragement
achievement
outspokenness

■ **PRACTICE** • Alphabetize the six words with **-ous.**
  • Alphabetize the eight words with **-ment.**
  • Alphabetize the six words with **-ness.**

■ **WRITE** Choose ten words to write in sentences.

WORD FORMS   Write the list word that has each meaning and ending indicated below.

1. flat + ness =
2. to decide + ment =
3. not shut + ness =
4. make better + ment =
5. make fun of + ous =
6. not harsh + ness =
7. a mixed selection + ous =
8. to admit you know + ment =
9. hard to deal with + ness =
10. promise to marry + ment =
11. freshen + ment =
12. organize + ment =
13. disagree + ment =

ANTONYMS   Write the list word that completes each phrase.

14. not wakefulness, but ___
15. not inoffensive, but ___
16. not cowardly, but ___
17. not dirtiness, but ___
18. not trusting, but ___
19. not boredom, but ___
20. not safe, but ___

Using the Meaning Helpers Strategy

21.–24. Write four list words that are hard for you. Write a meaning helper below each one and underline the matching letters. Notice any spelling changes between each pair of words.

> **Did You Know?**
> The word **miscellaneous** comes from a Latin word that means "to mix." Then why isn't it *mixcellaneous*?

☰	Make a capital.
/	Make a small letter.
∧	Add something.
ℓ	Take out something.
⊙	Add a period.
¶	New paragraph

PROOFREAD FOR CARELESS ERRORS

Proofread carefully so you don't misspell words by reversing letters. For example:

There are no ~~mediocer~~ *mediocre* players on this team.

Check for Reversed Letters Write correctly any words with reversed letters. Write "Correct" if the sentence is correct.

1. Never before has our team gotten this close to a pennant.
2. The team's termendous strength has been its pitching.
3. Tickets to the playoff games are available thourgh Friday.
4. Stores are selling out of T-shirts and caps.
5. Fans are ready to cheer thier team to victory.

PROOFREAD A SPORTS REPORT

Find the eight misspelled words in this sports report and write them correctly. Some may be words you learned before. Three of the misspellings are with reversed letters.

> *Pennant Fever Hits*
>
> Be perpared for the wierd and wild excitment of the pennant race. Count on rediculous behavior and outragues outfits in the stands. Watch out for hazordous leaping as fans try to catch foul balls. Dont expect good judgment to reign becuase fans are catching pennant fever.

WRITE A SPORTS REPORT

Write a sports report about a game you've seen or a team you follow. Use three list words and a personal word.

Word List

courageous	hazardous	excitement	stubbornness
outrageous	acknowledgment	improvement	openness
suspicious	argument	arrangement	cleanliness
ridiculous	judgment	refreshment	sleepiness
miscellaneous	engagement	evenness	gentleness

Personal Words 1.___ 2.___

Review

BOOK TITLES   Write the word from the box that best completes each book title. Use the underlined words as clues.

1. *Cure ___ and Stay Awake* by I. Snore
2. *Find ___ and Adventure in Travel* by Otto Mobile
3. *Solving an ___ or Dispute* by A. Turney
4. *___ and Kindness with Pets* by Ellie Fant
5. *Twenty Harmful and ___ Things Around the House* by O. Zone
6. *The ___ and Heroic Lives of Firefighters* by Smokey Pit
7. *One Hundred Silly and ___ Jokes* by T. Zer
8. *Meditating, Getting Better, and Making ___ in Yourself* by Sy Kyatrist
9. *Find Renewed Energy and ___ in Walking* by N. Stride
10. *___ and the Wide, Great Plains* by O. Klahoma

courageous
ridiculous
hazardous
argument
excitement
improvement
refreshment
gentleness
sleepiness
openness

Multicultural *Connection*

LANGUAGES   There are more than 800 African languages. Some English words come from words used by speakers of African languages. One of those words names the carrier of a disease causing sleepiness: the tsetse fly. Other English words originating from African languages are listed in the box.

tsetse fly	impala	gumbo	okra	yam	jazz	gnu

Write the word from the box that fits each definition below. Use your Spelling Dictionary if you need help.

1. a large African antelope, also called a wildebeest
2. soup often made with chicken, rice, and okra
3. a root, like a sweet potato
4. pods of a tall plant, used as a vegetable in gumbo
5. a medium-sized African antelope with long pointed horns
6. music developed from African American spirituals
7. an African fly that transmits certain diseases

Latin Roots 2

Many words have the Latin roots **corpus** meaning "body," **ped** or **pedem** meaning "foot," **manus** meaning "hands," and **spirare** meaning "breathe": **corpse, pedestal, manicure, expire.**

■ **STUDY** Say each word. Then read the sentence.

1.	**corporation**	The employees work for a **corporation.**
2.	**incorporate**	The report will **incorporate** that data.
3.	**corpse**	Historians found a **corpse** in the tomb.
4.	**centipede**	I jumped when a **centipede** crawled by.
5.	**pedestal**	The sculpture rested on a **pedestal.**
6.	**manicure**	A **manicure** made my nails look pretty.
7.	**management**	A company needs good **management.**
8.	**manufacture**	The factory will **manufacture** cars.
9.	**perspiration**	The runner was damp with **perspiration.**
10.	**expire**	The license will **expire** next week.

11.	**corporal**	His brother is a **corporal** in the army.
12.	**corps**	The officer led a **corps** of soldiers.
13.	**pedigree**	The dog has an excellent **pedigree.**
14.	**pedometer**	A **pedometer** measures steps taken.
15.	**impede**	Traffic jams may **impede** our progress.
16.	**manipulate**	A child can **manipulate** the blocks.
17.	**emancipate**	Many worked to **emancipate** the slaves.
18.	**respiration**	Lungs are essential for **respiration.**
19.	**conspire**	The girls may **conspire** to surprise us.
20.	**spiritual**	The minister sent out a **spiritual** message.

CHALLENGE!

corpuscle
impediment
manacle
manipulative
conspirator

■ **PRACTICE**
- Write five words from **corpus.**
- Write five words from **ped** or **pedem.**
- Write five words from **manus.**
- Write five words from **spirare.**

■ **WRITE** Choose ten words to write in sentences.

CLASSIFYING   Write a list word that belongs in each group.

1. company, business, ___
2. barometer, speedometer, ___
3. block, hold back, ___
4. produce, make, ___
5. earthworm, caterpillar, ___
6. fingernails, pedicure, ___
7. easel, stand, ___
8. ventilation, inhalation, ___
9. body, dead, ___
10. scheme, plan, ___

CONTEXT CLUES   Write the list word that fits in each sentence.

11. My mom's driver's license will ___ on her birthday.
12. A ___ of nurses was sent to tend to those injured in the battle.
13. The pet owner used a ___ to prove the value of his dog.
14. Our apartment building's ___ company handles repairs.
15. The bank officer tried to ___ the bank's accounts to hide the fact that he had been stealing.
16. When did the owners ___ the slaves?
17. He was drenched with ___ after running five miles.
18. I will ___ your ideas with mine to come up with one proposal for the guidelines.
19. We learned a ___ at choir practice last night.
20. The ___ is hoping to be promoted to sergeant soon.

STRATEGIC SPELLING

Building New Words

The prefixes **in-** and **en-** often mean "in" or "into." Add **in-** or **en-** to each of the following base words to make new words: *born, flame, danger, put, close, vision.* Use your Spelling Dictionary if you need help.

Add in-	Add en-
21. ____	24. ____
22. ____	25. ____
23. ____	26. ____

> **Did You Know?**
> The word **centipede** literally means "one hundred feet."

≡	Make a capital.
/	Make a small letter.
∧	Add something.
ℓ	Take out something.
⊙	Add a period.
¶	New paragraph

PROOFREAD FOR USAGE Use the adjective *good* to modify a noun or pronoun. Use the adverb *well* to modify a verb.

> I'll be a *good* employee who works *well* with others.

Check for *good* and *well* Write "Incorrect" if *good* or *well* is used incorrectly. Write "Correct" if *good* or *well* is used correctly.

1. I'll do good in college.
2. Being conscientious will help me succeed good in life.
3. I'll be a good influence on others too.
4. I have always been able to set goals good.
5. That's why I predict I'll perform well in college and beyond.

PROOFREAD A PREDICTION Find five misspelled words in Bonita's prediction of her future. Some may be words you've learned before. Also fix two mistakes with *good* and *well*.

> After high school I will go to a good business college. I will join a corperation and work good enough to become part of managment. I will than be able to incorperate my ideas and show that I work good with people. I predict nothing will impede my rise to the top. My image in bronze will be placed on a pedistol in the corporate offices.

WRITE A PREDICTION Write a prediction about your own future. Use three list words and a personal word.

Word List

emancipate	perspiration	pedometer	corporal
centipede	management	respiration	expire
manipulate	incorporate	corpse	impede
corporation	pedigree	manicure	spiritual
pedestal	manufacture	conspire	corps

Personal Words 1.___ 2.___

Review

corporation
incorporate
corpse
centipede
pedestal
manicure
management
manufacture
perspiration
expire

HEADLINES   Use a word from the box to complete the following newspaper headlines.

1. Company Closes Due to Poor ___
2. Temperature to Reach 100! Expect ___ Today!
3. Many-Legged ___ Is Star of New Horror Movie
4. Statue Is a Bust As ___ Crumbles
5. Giant Television ___ to Show Only Cartoons
6. Missing ___ Found by Police After Search
7. President Says She'll ___ New Senator's Ideas
8. Get Both a Pedicure and a ___ for $15!
9. Union Contract Will ___ at Midnight Tonight
10. New Business to ___ Toys and Sporting Goods

Word *Study*

METAPHORS   Writers use metaphors to enliven their writing. A **metaphor** is a comparison that describes something by vividly saying it is another thing. For example, in this metaphor, the writer is saying a corporation is a fortress: The successful *corporation* <u>is</u> a *fortress* that protects our town's economy.

icicles
campfires
hurricane
waiters
eel

Use the words from the box to complete these metaphors.

1. The shining stars are ___ in the hot night sky.
2. When Charlie runs fast he is a ___.
3. Penguins are ___ in their tuxedoes.
4. Marcus's hands are ___ when he comes in from the cold.
5. The submarine is an ___, gliding silently through the water.

Prefixes anti-, inter-, intra-, pro-

SPELLING FOCUS

Adding prefixes changes the meaning of the base. The prefix **anti-** means "against," **inter-** means "between" or "among," **intra-** means "within," and **pro-** means "before" or "forward."

■ **STUDY**   Say each word. Then read the sentence.

1.	**antisocial**	He was **antisocial,** ignoring others.
2.	**antiseptic**	I washed the cut with **antiseptic** soap.
3.	**antibiotic**	An **antibiotic** cures some infections.
4.	**intermediate**	Sixth grade is an **intermediate** level.
5.	**international**	The plane made **international** flights.
6.	**interfere**	A referee mustn't **interfere** with play.
7.	**promote**	The firm may **promote** her to president.
8.	**progress**	They made **progress** on their report.
9.	**intramural**	Many students play **intramural** sports.
10.	**intrastate**	The truck made many **intrastate** trips.

11.	**antifreeze**	The car needs **antifreeze** in winter.
12.	**antidote**	The campers had a snakebite **antidote.**
13.	**antibody**	An **antibody** protects you from illness.
14.	**intervene**	The police must **intervene** in a fight.
15.	**intersection**	We turned left at the **intersection.**
16.	**intercept**	My sister may **intercept** your message.
17.	**prologue**	The play began with a **prologue.**
18.	**profound**	He expressed a **profound** idea in class.
19.	**proclaim**	The king will **proclaim** a celebration.
20.	**intravenous**	The patient had **intravenous** feeding.

CHALLENGE!

antihistamine
interdisciplinary
interchangeable
intramuscular
proclamation

■ **PRACTICE**
- Write six words with **anti-**.
- Write five words with **pro-**.
- Write six words with **inter-**.
- Write three words with **intra-**.

■ **WRITE**   Choose four sentences to rewrite as questions.

WORD BUILDING   Add prefixes to these words to make
list words.

1. social
2. claim
3. freeze
4. state
5. venous

6. national
7. body
8. mediate
9. septic
10. section

DEFINITIONS   Write the list word that is described by each clue.

11. Use this **pro-** word to say you're getting better and better.
12. Use this **inter-** word to describe when you catch a ball before
    it gets to the intended player.
13. Use this **pro-** word to describe deep feelings.
14. This **intra-** word describes games within the walls of a school.
15. Use this **pro-** word to say you're moving on to the next grade.
16. This **anti-** word names a substance that counteracts the
    effects of poison.
17. Use this **inter-** word to say you'll come between two sides
    and separate them, often to settle an argument.
18. This **anti-** word names a protein substance that helps our
    bodies fight infection.
19. This **pro-** word names the introduction to a play or novel.
20. This **inter-** word describes meddling or getting in the way.

Building New Words

Add the prefix **inter-** or **anti-** to the following base words
to make new words: *mingle, personal, aircraft, trust,
connect, missile.*

Add inter-	Add anti-
21. _____	24. _____
22. _____	25. _____
23. _____	26. _____

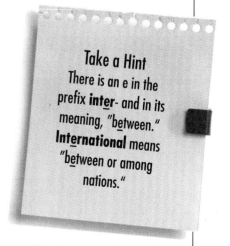

Take a Hint
There is an e in the
prefix **inter-** and in its
meaning, "b_etween."
International means
"b_etween or among
nations."

≡	Make a capital.
/	Make a small letter.
∧	Add something.
ℓ	Take out something.
⊙	Add a period.
¶	New paragraph

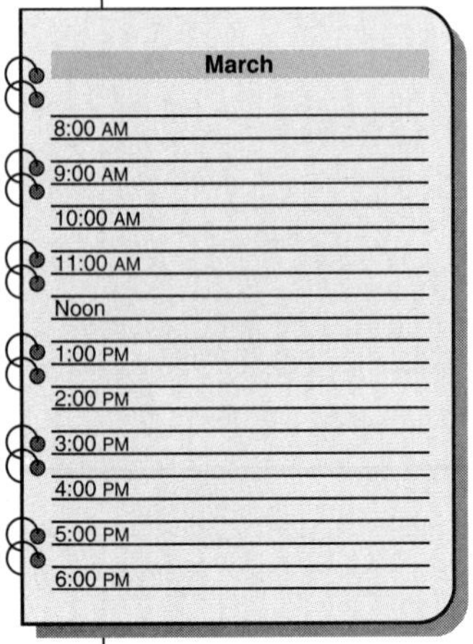

March

8:00 AM
9:00 AM
10:00 AM
11:00 AM
Noon
1:00 PM
2:00 PM
3:00 PM
4:00 PM
5:00 PM
6:00 PM

PROOFREAD FOR PUNCTUATION Use a comma or commas to set off an appositive, a word or phrase that follows a noun to identify or explain it. For example:

7:00 Make an appointment with Hal, our regional manager.

8:00 Schedule a meeting with Sue the consultant at noon.

Check for Commas Read each sentence. Write the word or words that should be followed by a comma.

1. 9:00 Fly to Cincinnati company headquarters.
2. 11:00 Interview Ms. Waters the new sales representative.
3. 2:00 Ask Ted the head custodian to fix the alarm.
4. 5:00 Watch Del Turner a company president on TV.

PROOFREAD AN APPOINTMENT CALENDAR Find five misspelled words in Mr. Eakins's appointment calendar and write them correctly. Fix three comma errors too.

9:00   Meet with Dave Eastern regional sales manager to permote Cindy.
10:00 Sales Conference—Don't interfear with there meeting.
11:00 Go over progres of ad campaign.
12:00 Lunch with Del Turner a president.
3:00   Meet with grievance committee—interveen if necessary.

WRITE AN APPOINTMENT CALENDAR Write a daily appointment calendar for a busy executive. Use three list words and a personal word.

Word List

intermediate	intersection	promote	profound
antifreeze	antiseptic	intrastate	antibody
intramural	intravenous	antidote	interfere
intervene	international	progress	proclaim
prologue	antisocial	intercept	antibiotic

Personal Words 1.___ 2.___

Review

WORD HISTORIES Use the word history in each sentence to write the correct word from the box.

1. prefix + Latin *movere* = elevate or move ahead
2. prefix + Latin *septicus* = against infection
3. prefix + Latin *medius* = middle
4. prefix + Latin *muralis* = within the walls
5. prefix + Latin *socialis* = against the principles of society
6. prefix + Latin *ferir* = get in the way of
7. prefix + Latin *gradi* = advance or grow
8. prefix + Greek *bios* = substance that attacks harmful organisms
9. prefix + Latin *nationem* = between or among nations
10. prefix + Latin *status* = within a state

> antisocial
> antiseptic
> antibiotic
> intermediate
> international
> interfere
> promote
> progress
> intramural
> intrastate

Word *Study*

GREEK AND LATIN ROOTS: SPEAKING The list word **prologue** comes from the Greek root *logos,* which can mean "word" or "speech." The Latin word *vocare* has a similar meaning, "to call." The words in the box come from these two roots.

| vocational | dialogue | provoke | eulogy | apology |

Write the word that fits each definition below. Use your Spelling Dictionary if you need help.

1. speech in praise of a deceased person
2. words of regret
3. to stir up or call to action
4. having to do with business, occupation, or calling
5. conversation between two people

Vowels in Unstressed Syllables

In some words the vowel sound you hear is a schwa, /ə/. It gives no clue to its spelling: **hesitate, memorable**. The sound /əl/ can be spelled **le** or **el**.

■ **STUDY** Say each word. Then read the sentence.

WATCH OUT FOR FREQUENTLY MISSPELLED WORDS!

1.	**hesitate**	Don't **hesitate** to ask a question.
2.	**memorable**	A wedding is a **memorable** occasion.
3.	**finally** ✳	We **finally** finished the project.
4.	**investigate**	Workers will **investigate** the problem.
5.	**usually** ✳	Dad **usually** takes the train to work.
6.	**discipline**	We had to **discipline** our dog for biting.
7.	**evidence**	The **evidence** supports the conclusion.
8.	**accuracy**	Use a calculator to check **accuracy.**
9.	**article**	I read an **article** about sports heroes.
10.	**miracle**	It is a **miracle** that you didn't drown.

11.	**irritate**	Mosquitoes really **irritate** me.
12.	**ambulance**	The injured man went in an **ambulance.**
13.	**magnificent**	The castle was **magnificent.**
14.	**extravagant**	The diamond was an **extravagant** gift.
15.	**telethon**	The **telethon** raised money for charity.
16.	**aggravate**	If I run, I will **aggravate** my injury.
17.	**marathon**	Runners dream of **marathon** wins.
18.	**gullible**	A **gullible** person may be fooled often.
19.	**versatile**	She is **versatile**, playing many parts.
20.	**inevitable**	Growing older is **inevitable.**

CHALLENGE!

belligerent
contemporary
jeopardize
predicament
justification

■ **PRACTICE** First write the words you think are easy to spell. Then write the words you think are difficult to spell. Underline any vowels in these words that give you trouble.

■ **WRITE** Choose two sentences to include in a paragraph about sports.

CLASSIFYING   Write the list word that belongs in each group.

1. at last, at the end, ___
2. footrace, 26 miles and 385 yards, ___
3. fact, clue, proof, ___
4. easily fooled, easily cheated, believing everything, ___
5. worth remembering, unforgettable, ___
6. TV program, telephones, fund-raiser, ___
7. unavoidable, has to happen, ___
8. having many talents, having a variety of uses, ___
9. control, order, punish, ___
10. luxurious, extreme, excessive, ___

CONTEXT CLUES   Write the list word that completes each sentence.

11. I can't use that strong soap because it will ___ my skin.
12. Disobeying the rules will only ___ an already tense situation.
13. Don't ___ to ask for help if you need it.
14. She was awestruck by the queen's ___ collection of jewelry.
15. He ___ does his homework before supper but couldn't tonight.
16. We called for an ___ as soon as we saw the accident.
17. According to this ___ in the newspaper, taxes will increase.
18. That secretary's typing shows a high level of ___.
19. The reporter decided to ___ the rumors of corruption.
20. They feel it's a ___ that the tornado missed their house.

STRATEGIC SPELLING

The Divide and Conquer Strategy

21.–24. Study long words piece by piece. Write four list words that are hard for you. Draw lines to break them into smaller parts. Study the parts.

FREQUENTLY MISSPELLED WORDS * FREQUENTLY MISSPELLED WORDS * FREQUENTLY

Remember to find <u>all</u> in **fin<u>all</u>y** to spell it correctly.

≡	Make a capital.
/	Make a small letter.
∧	Add something.
ℯ	Take out something.
⊙	Add a period.
¶	New paragraph

PROOFREAD FOR USAGE When you make comparisons using *good, bad, much,* or *little,* don't add **-er** or *more* to comparative forms or **-est** or *most* to superlative forms.

This is the ~~worstest~~ worst blizzard in ten years, but there is ~~more~~ better news in tomorrow's forecast.

Check Comparatives and Superlatives Read each sentence. Correct mistakes with comparisons.

1. We will have lesser snow tomorrow.
2. The bestest news is that the winds will be calm.
3. Midweek looks more better, with milder temperatures.
4. There will be plenty of sun and lesser precipitation.
5. Conditions will change and get worser at week's end.

PROOFREAD A WEATHER REPORT Find five misspelled words and write them correctly. Some may be words you learned before. Fix three incorrect comparisons too.

> The cold snap will go from bad to more worse. There's evedience of another cold front headed our way. The worstest weather usualy hits on weekends, and this front will too. Strong winds allways make temperatures seem worser, so don't hesatate to bundle up. It's better to be safe then sorry in this winter weather.

WRITE A WEATHER REPORT Report on the weather in your area. Try to use three list words and a personal word.

Word List

miracle	discipline	investigate	hesitate
irritate	gullible	article	memorable
accuracy	magnificent	versatile	inevitable
evidence	usually	telethon	aggravate
ambulance	extravagant	finally	marathon

Personal Words 1.___ 2.___

Review

QUOTATIONS   Write the word from the box that best completes what each person might say.

hesitate
memorable
finally
investigate
usually
discipline
evidence
accuracy
article
miracle

1. "My brother's birth was a ___ day for me," his sister said.
2. "Count the money twice for ___," the bank teller said.
3. "I need a news ___ on the World Series," the editor said.
4. "We need to ___ the accident scene," the officer said.
5. "I ___ eat a snack after school," the teenager said.
6. "It's a ___ you weren't hurt in the accident," the father said.
7. "I must ___ you for breaking school rules," the principal said.
8. "Is there ___ that shows he is guilty?" the judge asked.
9. "After two months I ___ finished that quilt," the artist said.
10. "Don't ___ to ask questions," the teacher said to the class.

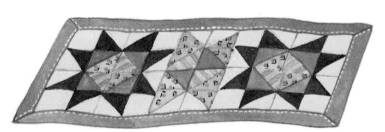

Using a *Dictionary*

SYNONYM STUDIES   Some dictionary entries include synonym studies that explain the difference between words that are closely related in meaning. Illustrative sentences show each word used in context. Below is the synonym study that appears at the end of the entry for *evidence*.

> **Syn.** *n.* **Evidence, testimony, proof** mean that which tends to demonstrate the truth or falsity of something. **Evidence** applies to facts that indicate, without fully proving, that something is so: *Running away was evidence of his guilt.* **Testimony** applies to any speech or action which serves as evidence of something: *Her testimony contradicted that of the preceding witness.* **Proof** means evidence so full and convincing as to leave no doubt or little doubt: *The signed receipt is proof that the letter was delivered.*

Write the synonyms that best complete the paragraph. Use the synonym study to help you decide which word works best.

The defense attorney planned to present (1) at the trial that she hoped would convince the jury of her client's innocence. She also expected that a character witness's (2) would help. Further (3) would be the dated receipts that showed her client to be out of town on the day of the crime.

133

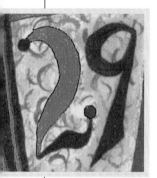

Using Just Enough Letters

SPELLING FOCUS

Pronouncing a word correctly and picturing how it looks can help you avoid writing too many letters.

■ **STUDY** Say each word. Then read the sentence.

1.	existence	It is the largest tree in **existence**.
2.	regardless	I slept **regardless** of the noise.
3.	refrigerator	Cold drinks are in the **refrigerator**.
4.	exercise	Bicycling is excellent **exercise**.
5.	allergic	She found she was **allergic** to cats.
6.	awkward	He fell in an **awkward** position.
7.	scientist	The **scientist** studied insects.
8.	drowned	A person **drowned** in the flooded town.
9.	assembly	The choir sang at the school **assembly**.
10.	especially ✳	I **especially** liked the banana bread.

WATCH OUT FOR FREQUENTLY MISSPELLED WORDS!

11.	mischievous	A **mischievous** child hid my glasses.
12.	pastime	Drawing is a relaxing **pastime**.
13.	remembrance	The statue was a **remembrance** of war.
14.	presidency	Few candidates ran for the **presidency**.
15.	disastrous	The shipwreck was **disastrous**.
16.	hindrance	The dog was a **hindrance** on the trip.
17.	monstrous	The grizzly bear looked **monstrous**.
18.	motocross	He was third in the **motocross** race.
19.	grievous	The accident caused **grievous** harm.
20.	tuxedo	The man wore a **tuxedo** to the dance.

CHALLENGE!

ambidextrous
instinctive
rambunctious
colossal
prestige

■ **PRACTICE** First, write the words that are easiest for you to spell correctly. Then, write the words that are the most difficult for you. Underline the parts of any words that cause you problems.

■ **WRITE** Choose ten words to write in sentences.

MAKING INFERENCES   Write the list word that is missing from each person's statement.

1. Athlete: "The way to stay fit is to ___ regularly."
2. Principal: "The mayor has agreed to speak at our next ___."
3. Baby-sitter: "That ___ little girl really kept me on my toes."
4. Bridegroom: "The tailor says my ___ will be ready in time."
5. Vice-president: "I plan to run for the ___ next term."
6. Student: "I plan to become a ___ who studies DNA."
7. Homeowner: "My ___ needs fixing; it's just not cold enough."
8. Shopper: "I never buy cheese because I'm ___ to milk."
9. Lifeguard: "No one has ever ___ in this pool."
10. Soldier: "I'm ___ glad to be going home for the holidays."

DEFINITIONS   Write the list word that fits each definition.

11. causing grief
12. a pleasant way of passing time
13. bringing disaster
14. not graceful
15. a keepsake or souvenir
16. being somewhere; having life
17. extremely large; enormous
18. a motorcycle race over cross-country trails
19. person or thing that gets in the way
20. without regard; in spite of what happens

> **Did You Know?**
> The **tuxedo** got its name from Tuxedo Park, New York, the site of the country club where the suit was first worn.

STRATEGIC SPELLING

Seeing Meaning Connections

Words with *time*
daytime
meantime
lifetime
pastime

The words in the box, including the list word *pastime,* are related in spelling and meaning. Complete the sentences with these words.

After a _(21)_ of work, Grandmother will retire next year. She says she enjoyed her work, but is looking forward to being outdoors in the _(22)_, so she can pursue her favorite _(23)_, gardening. In the _(24)_, we're planning a retirement party for her.

≡	Make a capital.
/	Make a small letter.
∧	Add something.
ℯ	Take out something.
⊙	Add a period.
⁋	New paragraph

PROOFREAD FOR PUNCTUATION Put quotation marks around the titles of songs, stories, poems, articles, and book chapters. Capitalize the first word, the last word, and all important words in a title. For example:

A recently published article is "Exercise for busy People."

Check for Quotation Marks and Capitals Correct the mistakes in these sentences from a want ad by writing the word and the quotation mark that should come before or after it. Also write words that need to be capitalized.

Writer needs someone to proofread his work. Topics vary widely, so you must be knowledgeable in many subject areas. For instance, two articles in progress are the best Diners in the South and Motocross Celebrities. If qualified, contact James at 555–7770.

PROOFREAD A WANT AD Find the five misspelled words. Write them correctly. Some may be words you learned before. Also fix three mistakes with quotation marks and capitals.

> Student whose pasttime is writing country songs is especialy anxious to hook up with a musician who loves country music to. Call Judd at 555–1893 to request copies of two new songs: "my Grievious Heart and Love's a Hinderance."

WRITE A WANT AD Plan and write a want ad for something you'd like to buy. Try to use three list words and a personal word.

Word List

mischievous	disastrous	motocross	tuxedo
refrigerator	existence	pastime	awkward
remembrance	hindrance	exercise	scientist
especially	monstrous	allergic	drowned
presidency	regardless	grievous	assembly

Personal Words 1.___ 2.___

Review

SENTENCE CLUES Write the word from the box that best fits each description.

1. This is how you might feel the first time you do something.
2. When you want a glass of milk, this is where you'll find it.
3. When all your classes get together, you have this in school.
4. Scientists use fossils to prove this about dinosaurs.
5. If you sneeze, you might be having this kind of reaction.
6. People do this to stay in shape and lose weight.
7. This happened to 2,000 people during the Johnstown Flood of 1889.
8. You'd use this word to describe something special.
9. This is a person who might find a cure for cancer or AIDS.
10. This word means "in spite of what happens."

existence
regardless
refrigerator
exercise
allergic
awkward
scientist
drowned
assembly
especially

Word *Study*

EXPLORING LANGUAGE: BLENDS A **blend** is a word that is made by combining, or blending, parts of two words. The list word *motocross* is a blend of *motorcycle* and *cross-country*. Motocross means "a motorcycle race run over cross-country trails rather than on a paved track." For each blend underlined in the sentences below, write the two words it came from. Use your Spelling Dictionary if you need help.

1. A <u>moped</u> can reach speeds up to thirty miles per hour.
2. My sister has learned how to <u>squiggle</u> out of her highchair.
3. The President's <u>motorcade</u> passed by our school.
4. A <u>transistor</u> is a tiny electronic device.
5. I had to <u>chortle</u> when César told me that joke.
6. <u>Gasohol</u> is a fuel used in many cars.
7. The concerts were <u>simulcast</u> on radio and TV.
8. Jeremy likes to <u>slosh</u> in the mud and slush.
9. Kendra is interested in studying <u>bionics</u> as a career.
10. The <u>sportscast</u> was interrupted by a special news report.

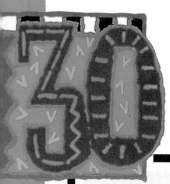

Review

Lesson 25: Suffixes -ous, -ment, -ness
Lesson 26: Latin Roots 2
Lesson 27: Prefixes anti-, inter-, intra-, pro-
Lesson 28: Vowels in Unstressed Syllables
Lesson 29: Using Just Enough Letters

REVIEW WORD LIST

1. arrangement
2. courageous
3. excitement
4. grievous
5. hazardous
6. improvement
7. judgment
8. management
9. outrageous
10. ridiculous
11. sleepiness
12. suspicious
13. conspire
14. corpse
15. impede
16. pedometer
17. perspiration
18. respiration
19. antifreeze
20. antiseptic
21. antidote
22. interfere
23. intermediate
24. intersection
25. intramural
26. intrastate
27. progress
28. ambulance
29. discipline
30. evidence
31. finally
32. hesitate
33. inevitable
34. investigate
35. magnificent
36. marathon
37. memorable
38. miracle
39. usually
40. allergic
41. assembly
42. drowned
43. especially
44. exercise
45. existence
46. hindrance
47. monstrous
48. pastime
49. refrigerator
50. regardless

■ PROOFREADING

Find the spelling errors in each passage and write the words correctly. All passages have seven errors except the last one, which has eight.

PROOFREAD A LETTER TO THE EDITOR

Collision at Fourth and Grand

Once again there has been a collision at the hazordous intrasection of Fourth and Grand Streets. It was inevitible, but it is also ridiculus that there are no stop signs on Grand. In my judgement this outragues situation should not be allowed to continue, especialy so near a playground.

PROOFREAD A FRIENDLY LETTER

April 12, 20_ _

Dear Letitia,

I wanted to tell you that last weekend we used the pedameter you gave me for my birthday. Terry and I hiked fifteen miles, and though we were drenched in persperation because of the humidity, we were determined to let nothing impeed our hike. Unfortunately, I am somewhat alergic to insect bites, but by some miricle I had my medicine with me, so the mosquitoes didn't seriously interfear with our weekend. After dinner, sleepyness quickly overcame us!

Your friend,
Martina

PROOFREAD A CHARACTER SKETCH

My older sister is planning to run in the marethon next week. She started working up to this three years ago when she began an excercise program. It wasn't long until she was able to progres to running every day. Then she started to compete in intermurial relays. Soon, running was more than a pasttime. She had the disipline to run every day and to keep pushing herself reguardless of how she felt. My whole family and I are very proud of her. You see, three years ago, she was recovering from an accident, and doctors thought she would not walk at all.

PROOFREAD A MEMO

To: Sam Tyler

From: Fred Estevez

    The following items should be stocked on the shelves: antifreez, light bulbs, antiseptick bandages, toothpaste, and film. (Film is in the refridgerator.) You made a big improvment in the arangement of hardware supplies. Thanks! Do not hesatate to ask questions of Mr. Jackson, who will be taking over managment of the store while I am away.

PROOFREAD A REPORT

Vincent Van Gogh

    Vincent van Gogh was a painter for ten years only. Before that he was a dealer in pictures, a bookseller, and an evangelist. It was not until he was twenty-seven, in 1880, that he finaly made the courages decision to become an artist. It was a decision that resulted in some magnifecent paintings and some grevious times for the artist. Lack of money was usally a hindrence to his very existance. We know of his trials from his letters to Theo, the brother who supported him. Vincent died penniless in 1890. I copied one of his self-portraits for this report.

PROOFREAD A NEWS STORY

Alicia Foster was practicing for the intarstate swim meet between the northeastern and southeastern districts of the state when she complained of dizziness last Thursday. A rumor that someone had drownded spread quickly through a school assembaly. In the excitment an ambulence was called to the itermidiate gym. Paramedics monitored her resparation and pulse but could find nothing wrong.

PROOFREAD A BROCHURE

Do you need an antedote to winter?

Why not investigat one of our Movable Mystery Tours? Participants board a train and try to solve a monstrus "crime" committed on board. Not only are there a lot of suspicous characters, but evedience at the crime scene is baffling. You won't find a real coarpse, but we will conspir to make your trip a memerable one.

CONTINENTAL RAILWAY

STRATEGY WORKSHOP

Choosing the Best Strategy

DISCOVER THE STRATEGY Remember to use this strategy to study new words:

Steps for Spelling	
1. Look at the word and say it.	4. Picture it.
2. Spell it aloud.	5. Look and write.
3. Think about it.	6. Cover, write, and check it.

For words that give you special problems, try these strategies. For each hard word, choose the strategy that works best for you.

Strategies	How to Use Them
Developing Spelling Consciousness	Dont overlook familiar words when you proofread. (Did you catch the mistake in that last sentence?)
Pronouncing for Spelling	Pronounce the word correctly, (**"fi-nal-ly"**) or make up a secret pronunciation. (**"ve-hi-cle"**)
Divide and Conquer	Divide the word into smaller parts: **grand/daughter** **re/construct/ion** **i/den/ti/fy**
Creating Memory Tricks	Link the word with a memory helper that has the same problem letters. (**Tell these mosquitoes to quit biting!**)

Strategies	How to Use Them
Using Meaning Helpers	Pair the word with a shorter, familiar word that's related in spelling and meaning: **attendance—attend** **narr<u>a</u>tive—narr<u>a</u>te**

TRY IT OUT Tell each speller which strategy you think would work best to help solve each problem.

1. I always miss the silent **t** in *mortgage*.
2. I wish I could remember how to spell the **ough** in *thoroughly*.
3. I forget the **l** in *calves* because it's silent.
4. I spell *expression* this way: **expreshion.**
5. New words give me problems. I don't know how to study them.
6. I keep spelling *moisture* with a **ch** instead of a **t.**
7. I wish I could remember the double **m** and **s** in *commission*.
8. *Chronological* is too long for me to remember.
9. I wish I could stop misspelling little words like *which* and *let's*—words I really do know how to spell.
10. *Catastrophe* is a catastrophe for me to spell. It's so long!

LOOK AHEAD Look ahead at the next five lessons for list words that might give you problems. Write four of them. Then decide which strategy you will use to help you remember how to spell each word, and write it next to the word.

Including All the Letters

Some words have more letters than you might expect.
To spell these words, pronounce each syllable carefully.
Other times, exaggerate the pronunciation of problem
letters: **adjourn.**

■ **STUDY**   Say each word. Then read the sentence.

**WATCH OUT FOR
FREQUENTLY
MISSPELLED
WORDS!**

1.	**adjourn**	The meeting will **adjourn** at 9:00.
2.	**comparable**	Mom gave the twins **comparable** gifts.
3.	**peculiar**	I noticed a **peculiar** odor in the hall.
4.	**beginning** ✳	I rewrote the **beginning** of my essay.
5.	**alcohol**	Use the **alcohol** in the first aid kit.
6.	**overrated**	I think the popular book is **overrated.**
7.	**arctic**	The temperature outside is **arctic.**
8.	**something** ✳	I read **something** funny in the paper.
9.	**veterinarian**	The **veterinarian** gave the cat a shot.
10.	**clothes** ✳	She wore new **clothes** on the trip.

11.	**acquaintance**	He said hello to the new **acquaintance.**
12.	**extraordinary**	The sight of a comet is **extraordinary.**
13.	**conscience**	My **conscience** made me tell the truth.
14.	**susceptible**	The baby is **susceptible** to colds.
15.	**respiratory**	Smoking causes **respiratory** problems.
16.	**disintegrate**	Some acids can **disintegrate** wood.
17.	**sophomore**	Tenth grade is your **sophomore** year.
18.	**basically**	The rules are **basically** simple.
19.	**liberal**	The **liberal** mayor wants many changes.
20.	**rendezvous**	The groups will **rendezvous** at the bus.

CHALLENGE!

paraphernalia
vaudeville
undoubtedly
chrysanthemum
grammatically

■ **PRACTICE**   Look over the list words carefully. First, write
the words that you are most likely to use in your writing. Then
write the rest of the words. Underline letters you might leave out.

■ **WRITE**   Choose two sentences to include in a paragraph.

144

ANALOGIES Write the list word that completes each analogy.

1. Right is to left as conservative is to ___ .
2. Junior is to senior as freshman is to ___ .
3. First is to last as ___ is to ending.
4. Pediatrician is to child as ___ is to pet.
5. South Pole is to antarctic as North Pole is to ___ .
6. Circulatory system is to heart as ___ system is to lungs.
7. Cabinet is to dishes as closet is to ___ .
8. Ordinary is to everyday as odd is to ___ .
9. Like is to love as ___ is to friend.

DEFINITIONS Write the list word that means the same as the underlined word or phrase in each sentence.

10. We used <u>an antiseptic</u> to clean the wound.
11. Let's <u>suspend</u> the meeting now and resume it later.
12. That girl is an <u>exceptionally good</u> pianist for her age.
13. He seems to have <u>a particular thing</u> on his mind.
14. People who brag a lot are often <u>sensitive</u> to flattery.
15. Our apartments are <u>approximately the same</u> in size.
16. I'd say that new movie is <u>regarded too highly</u>.
17. Please try to be on time for our <u>appointment to meet</u>.
18. My <u>sense of right and wrong</u> won't let me lie to them.
19. The final report is <u>fundamentally</u> the same as the first draft.
20. Our birdbath started to <u>break up</u> because it was exposed to rain, snow, and wind.

STRATEGIC SPELLING
Choosing the Best Strategy

21.–22. Write two list words that you find hard to spell. Which strategy could help you spell each word? Name the strategy and tell why you chose it. Then compare choices with a partner. For a list of strategies, see pages 142–143.

FREQUENTLY MISSPELLED WORDS ✳ FREQUENTLY MISSPELLED WORDS ✳ FREQUENTLY MISSPELLED WORDS

Maybe this will help you get all the letters in **beginning:** At the beg<u>inn</u>ing we stayed at the <u>inn</u>.

≡	Make a capital.
/	Make a small letter.
∧	Add something.
ℓ	Take out something.
⊙	Add a period.
⁋	New paragraph

PROOFREAD FOR USAGE Don't use *more* or *most* and don't add **-er** or **-est** when making comparisons with *less, least; better, best;* and *worse, worst.* For example:

Skipping school is the ~~most~~ worst thing I have done lately.

Check Comparisons Read this passage. Write the word that completes each comparison correctly.

I wanted the (best, most best) seats I could get. I thought I was (less, lesser) likely to get caught if I skipped school half a day than if I missed the whole day. Was I wrong! It was the (worst, worstest) day of my life. I feel (worse, more worse) about disappointing my dad than I do about missing the game.

PROOFREAD A PERSUASIVE SPEECH Find five spelling errors in this persuasive speech. Write them correctly. Some may be words you learned before. Fix three comparison errors too.

> Skipping school is overated. Tickets for the most best game of the season went on sale at 1:00. I took of right before lunch to miss the leastest amount of school. My concience bothered me too much so I told my dad. Basicly, I had to return the tickets and do a week of detention. The consaquences were worser than I thought.

WRITE A PERSUASIVE SPEECH Write a speech to persuade your classmates not to break a school rule. Try to use three list words and a personal word.

Word List

veterinarian	susceptible	peculiar	arctic
beginning	something	alcohol	basically
acquaintance	comparable	clothes	liberal
extraordinary	respiratory	sophomore	rendezvous
conscience	disintegrate	overrated	adjourn

Personal Words 1.___ 2.___

Review

SYNONYMS   Write the word from the box suggested by each group of synonyms.

adjourn
comparable
peculiar
beginning
alcohol
overrated
arctic
something
veterinarian
clothes

1. apparel, dress, attire
2. animal doctor, animal surgeon
3. strange, odd, unusual
4. start, onset, initial
5. extremely cold, frigid
6. disinfectant, flammable liquid
7. postpone, delay, recess
8. similar, alike
9. thought too highly of, idealized
10. certain thing, certain amount

Multicultural Connection

ENVIRONMENT   The tie between culture and environment is especially strong in the frigid arctic land—the northernmost region of the world. In an area where the average winter temperature is only –30°F, people's lives cannot be separated from their environment. The words in the box have come into English from the languages of people who have inhabited arctic lands for thousands of years.

parka	reindeer	mukluk	lemming	tundra	floe

Write the word from the box that fits each clue. Use your Spelling Dictionary if you need help.

1. This word of Russian origin describes the treeless plains where the ground remains frozen even in summer.
2. This word for a sheet of floating ice is of Norwegian origin.
3. This is a jacket with a hood. It comes from a Russian word.
4. The name for this deer with branching antlers originally comes from the Old Icelandic language.
5. The name for a waterproof boot often made from sealskin is the Inuit word for "large seal."
6. This rodent, whose name is of Norwegian origin, is one of the few animals that lives in the Arctic all year long.

Latin Roots 3

Many words are made up of Latin roots. The root **vertere** means "to turn"; **poser** means "to set"; **venire** means "to come"; and **facere** means "to make."

■ **STUDY**   Say each word. Then read the sentence.

1.	**advertisement**	I saw the product in an **advertisement**.
2.	**convert**	The mill will **convert** grain to flour.
3.	**introvert**	He is an **introvert** and enjoys reading.
4.	**disposable**	We used **disposable** cups at the party.
5.	**imposing**	The state is **imposing** new taxes.
6.	**advent**	I welcome the **advent** of a new year.
7.	**prevention**	Many doctors study disease **prevention**.
8.	**eventually**	Summer will be here **eventually**.
9.	**satisfaction**	Helping others gives me **satisfaction**.
10.	**artifact**	That **artifact** is from ancient Greece.
11.	**extrovert**	An **extrovert** may enjoy loud parties.
12.	**controversy**	The mayor's action caused **controversy**.
13.	**diversion**	Fishing is a nice **diversion** from work.
14.	**decompose**	Dry leaves will **decompose** on the lawn.
15.	**proposal**	She made a **proposal** for a new show.
16.	**conventional**	He led an ordinary, **conventional** life.
17.	**circumvent**	It is wrong to **circumvent** the law.
18.	**benefactor**	A **benefactor** helped pay her tuition.
19.	**faction**	One **faction** of the school voted no.
20.	**facilitate**	A computer will **facilitate** the work.

CHALLENGE!

incontrovertible
vice versa
predisposition
intervention
facsimile

■ **PRACTICE**   ▪ Write six words from **vertere**.
   ▪ Write five words from **facere**.
   ▪ Write five words from **venire**.
   ▪ Write four words from **poser**.

■ **WRITE**   Choose two sentences to write a rhyme, riddle, or dialogue.

ETYMOLOGIES   Write the list word that matches each etymology.

1. [< Latin *artem* art + *factum* made]
2. [< *extro-* outside + Latin *vertere* to turn]
3. [< Latin *adventum* < *ad-* to + *venire* come]
4. [< Latin *controversia* < *contra-* against + *versum* turned]
5. [< *intro-* within + Latin *vertere* to turn]
6. [< Latin *benefactum* befitted < *bene* well + *facere* do]
7. [< Latin *circumventum* circumvented < *circum* around + *venire* come]
8. [< Latin *convertere* < *com-* around + *vertere* to turn]

WORD MEANINGS   Write the list word that fits each definition.

9. a group of persons having a common purpose
10. usual or customary
11. able to be thrown away after use
12. to make something easier
13. a public notice recommending some product or service
14. the stopping of progress
15. a distraction from work or worry
16. a feeling of being contented or fulfilled
17. a plan, scheme, or suggestion
18. impressive because of size, appearance, or dignity
19. to break apart or decay
20. in the end

STRATEGIC SPELLING
Building New Words

Add the prefix **extra-** to these words to make new words. Remember to keep all the letters of the base word when adding a prefix.

21. curricular
22. sensory
23. terrestrial

> **Did You Know?**
> In the United States, people call **advertisements** *ads* for short, but in Great Britain the short form is *adverts*, with the accent on the first syllable.

SAVE THE EARTH

GLASS   PLASTIC

RECYCLE

≡	Make a capital.
/	Make a small letter.
∧	Add something.
ℯ	Take out something.
⊙	Add a period.
⁋	New paragraph

PROOFREAD FOR USAGE When a sentence starts with *here* or *there,* the subject often comes after the verb, but the two still need to agree. For example:

There is many things we can do to save our planet.
(correction above "is": are)

Check Subject-Verb Agreement Read each sentence. If the verb is correct, write "Correct." If not, write the correct verb.

1. Here is some ideas that we might propose.
2. There is a chance that we could use recycled paper here.
3. There are a lot of paper wasted in the office.
4. There is an attendance slip from each teacher each period.
5. There is certainly even more things we can do to help.

PROOFREAD A PROPOSAL Find six misspelled words in this proposal and write them correctly. Some may be words you learned before. Fix three errors with subject-verb agreement too.

> There is many things to improve in our school. My proposul is to convert from plastic cups to glass ones. There are proof that it is better for our enviroment. Eventualy, lets stop using disposible items. There is not enough landfills, and it takes plastic a long time to de compose.

WRITE A PROPOSAL Write a proposal suggesting a project to improve your school or community. Use three list words and a personal word.

Word List

advertisement	advent	introvert	disposable
satisfaction	eventually	prevention	faction
conventional	diversion	benefactor	proposal
facilitate	artifact	convert	extrovert
controversy	decompose	circumvent	imposing

Personal Words 1.___ 2.___

Review

RIDDLES Use the clues in each sentence to write the correct word from the box.

1. I like to be alone with my thoughts.
2. Helmets and knee and elbow pads give you this from injury.
3. I could be a bone, a stone ax, or pottery.
4. Often I'm used to announce a sale or new product.
5. I'd be this if I were eight feet tall.
6. I'm a plate or cup you can throw away.
7. I'm the feeling you have when you've done a good job.
8. I'm a word meaning "coming" or "arrival."
9. When you make ice, you do this to water.
10. I'm a word meaning "finally" or "in the end."

advertisement
convert
introvert
disposable
imposing
advent
prevention
eventually
satisfaction
artifact

Word *Study*

SYNONYMS The sentence *My father is a big man* gives a picture of the father, but the following sentence gives a better picture: *My father is an imposing man.* Why? Because **big** just means "large," but the synonym **imposing** means "impressively large." Use synonyms—words that mean almost the same—to help you express yourself more clearly in your writing.

Sort the words in the box into two groups of synonyms. Use your Spelling Dictionary if you need help.

Synonyms for *introverted* **Synonyms for *diversion***

Write the synonym from the box you think would best replace *introverted* or *diversion* in each sentence.

Because I'm so **(7) introverted,** it's hard for me to give speeches. In language arts class, I had to give a speech about my favorite **(8) diversion,** baking pies. I didn't want the class to notice my shyness, so I brought in fresh apple and blueberry pies as a **(9) diversion.** My teacher, who is usually quiet and **(10) introverted,** laughed out loud when I explained why I brought the pies.

bashful
entertainment
reserved
guarded
distraction
pastime

Prefixes ab-, ad-, co-, com-, con-

These prefixes change the meaning of the base. The prefix **ab-** or **ad-** means "to" or "toward"; **ab-** means "away from" or "off"; and **co-, com-,** or **con-** means "with" or "together."

■ **STUDY** Say each word. Then read the sentence.

1.	**abolish**	We want to **abolish** discrimination.
2.	**abnormal**	The cold summer was **abnormal.**
3.	**advantage**	Education gives you a big **advantage.**
4.	**addition**	They built an **addition** to their house.
5.	**cooperate**	The group members need to **cooperate.**
6.	**coexist**	The two sisters **coexist** happily.
7.	**compete**	She will **compete** in the tournament.
8.	**compound**	*Bookcase* is a **compound** word.
9.	**community**	Everyone wants a safe **community.**
10.	**concert**	Two bands played in the **concert.**

11.	**abbreviate**	You can **abbreviate** *doctor* as *Dr.*
12.	**absorb**	The towel will **absorb** the spilled tea.
13.	**abduct**	He tried to **abduct** someone for ransom.
14.	**adjacent**	My house is **adjacent** to the school.
15.	**adhesive**	We attached the picture with **adhesive.**
16.	**coordination**	The gymnast has great **coordination.**
17.	**cohesive**	The class became a **cohesive** unit.
18.	**confession**	The boy made a **confession** of his lie.
19.	**complicate**	My question may **complicate** the issue.
20.	**conservation**	We need water **conservation** in deserts.

CHALLENGE!

abrasive
adversity
coeducational
commendation
condemnation

■ **PRACTICE** ▪ Alphabetize five words with **ab-.**
  ▪ Alphabetize four words with **ad-.**
  ▪ Alphabetize eleven words with **co-, com-,** or **con-.**

■ **WRITE** Choose two sentences to include in a paragraph.

MAKING INFERENCES   Write the list word that fits each clue.

1. A job-seeker with skills and experience has this over a job seeker with no experience.
2. You and your neighbors are all part of this.
3. Two people may do this to get a job done faster.
4. You may attend this to hear your favorite band.
5. "Two plus two" is an example of this.
6. Faced with the evidence, a guilty person may blurt this out.
7. You do this when you participate in a race.
8. This is what kidnappers do.
9. A sponge will do this to your spilled milk.
10. People practice this when they reuse and recycle.
11. You may do this to save time when addressing envelopes.

SENTENCE COMPLETION   Write the list word that completes each sentence.

12. Water is a chemical ____ made of hydrogen and oxygen.
13. It was once considered ____ for a girl to want a career.
14. A new family moved into the apartment ____ to ours.
15. He wants to simplify his life, not ____ it.
16. The therapist suggested exercises to improve my ____.
17. You need a piece of ____ tape to hold the bandage in place.
18. We are a ____ group. We stick together through anything.
19. They want to ____ the use of animals in experiments.
20. Although they disagree politically, the nations ____ in peace.

STRATEGIC SPELLING

Seeing Meaning Connections

| adhesion |
| adhere |
| adherent |

The list word *adhesive* is related to the words in the box in spelling and meaning. Write the word from the box that fits each definition. Use your Spelling Dictionary if you need help.

21. an ____ of that religion
22. will ____ to your fingers
23. the ____ of the bandage to the skin

Take a Hint
They sound almost alike, but don't confuse **addition** with its sound-alike: *edition*. Remember that you <u>add</u> when you do <u>add</u>ition.

☰	Make a capital.
/	Make a small letter.
∧	Add something.
ℓ	Take out something.
⊙	Add a period.
¶	New paragraph

PROOFREAD FOR USAGE Be sure to use irregular verbs correctly. For example:

Many people ~~taked~~ ^took^ advantage of the free concert in the park.

Check Irregular Verbs Read each sentence. Correct any mistakes with verbs. If a sentence is correct, write "Correct."

1. The band concert brung many people to the park.
2. Selections were chose from many musical styles.
3. Not rushing, they took their time on the ballads.
4. We appreciate that people singed along with their favorites.
5. Did you notice that no one leaved early?

PROOFREAD AN ANNOUNCEMENT Find six misspelled words in this announcement and write them correctly. Some may be words you learned before. Fix two incorrect verbs too.

> A third concert by the school band was a welcome adition to the schedule. People comed from thruout the comunity and taked advantig of the chance to enjoy good music as the band prepared to compeat in a state contest. There will be a concert every Thursday untill further notice. All are invited to attend.

WRITE AN ANNOUNCEMENT Write an announcement about an upcoming event in your community or school. Try to use three list words and a personal word.

Word List

abbreviate	adjacent	cohesive	compete
absorb	advantage	cooperate	community
abduct	addition	coexist	confession
abolish	adhesive	complicate	concert
abnormal	coordination	compound	conservation

Personal Words 1.___ 2.___

Review

WORD HISTORIES Use the word histories below to write the correct word from the box.

1. *ab-* + Latin *norma* "rule" = "away from the rule or standard"
2. *co-* + Latin *operari* "to work" = "work together"
3. *con-* + Latin *certare* "strive" = "musical performance with several people"
4. from Latin *abolere* "destroy" = "put an end to"
5. from Latin *addere* "to put" = "put several numbers into one number"
6. *com-* + Latin *petere* "to seek" = "try hard to obtain something wanted by others"
7. *ab-* + Latin *ante* "before" = "a better position"
8. *com-* + Latin *munia* "duties" = "group of people living together"
9. *co-* + Latin *exsistere* "to stand forth" = "exist together"
10. *com-* + Latin *ponere* "put" = "join by putting two or more things together"

abolish
abnormal
advantage
addition
cooperate
coexist
compete
compound
community
concert

Word *Study*

LATIN ROOTS: TIME The words in the box are from the Latin root *brevis,* which means "short," and the Latin root *tempus,* which means "time." Write the word from *brevis* or *tempus* that best completes each sentence. Use your Spelling Dictionary if you need help.

| brief | brevity | abbreviate | abbreviation |
| tempo | temper | temporary | contemporary |

1. I wrote a ___ note to my mom asking her a question.
2. Wendell lost his ___ when the car splashed water on him.
3. Is the ___ for Missouri MI or MS or MO?
4. To avoid long speeches, politicians should practice ___ in their writing.
5. A conductor helps an orchestra maintain a musical ___.
6. People sometimes ___ the phrase "as soon as possible" ASAP.
7. Hannah doesn't like old music; she prefers ___ music.
8. A plastic cover is a ___ solution to a leaky roof.

155

■ INTRODUCTION

Related Words 3

SPELLING FOCUS

Sometimes a letter is dropped, changed, or added in related words: **publish, publication; prescribe, prescription; consume, consumption.**

■ **STUDY** Say each word. Then read the sentence.

1. **publish**   The company will **publish** that book.
2. **publication** The article is in that **publication.**
3. **prescribe**   The doctor can **prescribe** medication.
4. **prescription** I took a **prescription** to the pharmacy.
5. **consume**   He can **consume** four tacos for dinner.
6. **consumption** I must limit my **consumption** of sweets.
7. **conclude**   What can you **conclude** from the facts?
8. **conclusion**   I did not like the movie's **conclusion.**
9. **substance**   A sticky **substance** is on the floor.
10. **substantial** The doctor's salary was **substantial.**

11. **suspend**   I will **suspend** the flag from the roof.
12. **suspension** Rain caused a **suspension** of the game.
13. **persuade**   I will **persuade** you to see the movie.
14. **persuasive** The lawyer's argument was **persuasive.**
15. **provoke**   A rude remark may **provoke** a fight.
16. **provocative** The **provocative** comment angered her.
17. **influence**   My teachers have much **influence** on me.
18. **influential** The mayor has **influential** friends.
19. **omit**   Don't **omit** your name from your paper.
20. **omission**   I corrected an **omission** in the report.

CHALLENGE!

presume
reprehend
circumstance
presumption
reprehension
circumstantial

■ **PRACTICE** Sort the list words.
- Write three pairs of words in which **d** changes to **s.**
- Write two pairs of words in which **c** changes to **t.**
- Write two pairs of words in which **sh** or **k** changes to **c.**
- Write two pairs of words in which **t** or **b** changes to **ss** or **p.**
- Write one pair of words in which a **p** is added.

■ **WRITE** Choose ten words to write in sentences.

156

MAKING CONNECTIONS Write the list word that completes each unfinished sentence in the letter.

Dear Aspiring Author,

We are pleased to inform you that we plan to (1) your article, "How to Survive Junior High," in the spring issue of our (2) , *American Teen*. We found the article (3) and humorous, and we think it will (4) a strong response in our readers as well. However, we want to suggest a few changes to shorten and improve it. First, we'd like you to (5) the introduction; readers will never notice the (6) . We'd also like you to edit the (7) to make the article (8) on a more upbeat note. Most importantly, we want to (9) you to rewrite the entire article in the first person. To be (10) , we are offering an additional fee of ten percent. Please respond to this proposal as soon as possible. Thank you.

Sincerely,

The Editors of *American Teen*

WORD RELATIONSHIPS Write the list word that matches each clue. Then write the list word that is related to it.

11.–12. to order or direct
13.–14. having great prestige or importance
15.–16. to hang down from something high
17.–18. what something is made up of
19.–20. to use up or expend

STRATEGIC SPELLING

Building New Words

Add the suffix **-ive** to each base word from the list to make a new word. Circle any words with spelling changes. Use your Spelling Dictionary if you need help.

21. persuade
22. conclude
23. permit
24. destroy

Did You Know?
Rx, the symbol for medical **prescription,** is an abbreviation of the Latin word *recipe*, which means "take."

≡	Make a capital.
/	Make a small letter.
∧	Add something.
ℯ	Take out something.
⊙	Add a period.
⸿	New paragraph

PROOFREAD FOR CARELESS ERRORS

If you divide a word at the end of a line, divide between syllables. For example:

For people new in town, I'd like to ~~reco~~ recom-
~~mend~~
~~mmend~~ a fantastic restaurant.

Check Hyphenation Write three words that are incorrectly divided and draw a line to show where the hyphen should be. Use your Spelling Dictionary if you need help.

I don't mean to influence you too much, but I'd like to tell you about my favorite restaurant, Si's Roost. If knowing that ev-erything is made fresh daily doesn't persuade you, the ta-ntalizing aroma of his apple pie will. Si's Roost is the best resta-urant in town.

PROOFREAD A RECOMMENDATION Find the five

misspelled words and write them correctly. Some may be words you learned before. Fix three incorrectly hyphenated words too.

Don't hesatate to stop for the most subst-antial meal in town at Si's Roost. First, concume as much chicken as you can. Then let the ow-ner, Si, persuiade you to try his homemade pie. Theres also Si's world famous potato salad that you must try. Si's waitresses even pubulish a we-ekly newsletter about the specials.

WRITE A RECOMMENDATION Write a recommendation

for a restaurant. Use three list words and a personal word.

Word List

suspend	consumption	prescribe	conclusion
suspension	omit	prescription	influence
publish	omission	provoke	influential
publication	substance	provocative	persuade
consume	substantial	conclude	persuasive

Personal Words 1.____ 2.____

Review

publish
publication
prescribe
prescription
consume
consumption
conclude
conclusion
substance
substantial

QUOTATIONS Write the word from the box that best completes each quotation.

1. "At the ___ of the dance, we'll have a raffle," the chaperone said.
2. "I'll give you a ___ for your fever," the doctor said.
3. "Submit your story so the newspaper can ___ it," Dad said.
4. "An odd ___ is oozing from the lab," the scientist screamed.
5. "After looking at the clues, I ___ that the butler did it," said the detective.
6. "Try reducing your ___ of sugar," the dentist said.
7. "What do you ___ for a headache?" he asked the doctor.
8. "I'm so hungry I could ___ a bear," the hiker said.
9. "Our ___ is printed bi-monthly," the editor said.
10. "The building is ___ enough to withstand a tornado," said the builder.

Using a *Thesaurus*

USING EXACT WORDS How many "ways" can you *persuade* someone? If you look up *persuade* in your Writer's Thesaurus, you'll find out that you can also *convince, talk into, sell on, win over,* or *prevail upon.* Some synonyms, such as *prevail upon,* are formal and can only be used in certain situations. Others, such as *convince* and *persuade,* are pretty much interchangeable.

Use *persuade* or one of its synonyms in each of the following sentences. Use whichever one sounds best to you.

1. "Can I ___ you ___ lending me five dollars?" my brother asked.
2. At first, Keisha's parents said no to a new bike, but she eventually ___ them ___ with good reasons.
3. The candidate tried to ___ the voters to elect her.
4. The clerk tried to ___ me to buy the more expensive TV.
5. Aunt Opal ___ ___ us to stay another few days.
6. Connor is trying to ___ his parents ___ the idea of a vacation in Florida.

159

Words from Many Cultures 2

SPELLING FOCUS

Many words in English come from other languages and may have unexpected spellings: **ka̲ya̲k.**

■ **STUDY** Say each word. Then read the sentence.

1. **kayak**   We paddled a **kayak** down the river.
2. **admiral**   The **admiral** commanded the navy.
3. **anchor**   The ship dropped **anchor** in the harbor.
4. **kimono**   She wore a pretty **kimono** to the party.
5. **pajamas**   I wore my warmest **pajamas** to bed.
6. **poncho**   A **poncho** keeps you dry in the rain.
7. **indigo**   They used a blue dye called **indigo**.
8. **cafeteria** We ate good pizza in the **cafeteria**.
9. **mattress**   Dad bought a firm **mattress** for my bed.
10. **estate**   There is a lovely garden on the **estate**.

11. **catamaran** We sailed by the coast in a **catamaran**.
12. **gondola**   In Italy, I rode a **gondola** in a canal.
13. **gingham**   I wore a blue and white **gingham** shirt.
14. **suede**   The **suede** shoes are soft to touch.
15. **sequin**   She sewed a **sequin** on the costume.
16. **khaki**   The pants are made of cloth called **khaki**.
17. **bungalow**   We stayed in a **bungalow** near the lake.
18. **pueblo**   I visited a Hopi **pueblo** in New Mexico.
19. **bureau**   He put his clothes away in the **bureau**.
20. **yacht**   They cruised on a luxurious **yacht**.

CHALLENGE!

marimba
maraca
accordion
castanet
timpani

■ **PRACTICE** Sort the words by writing
- six words about boats and the sea
- eight words about textiles and clothing
- six words about buildings and their contents

■ **WRITE** Choose two sentences to write a rhyme, riddle, or dialogue.

CONCLUSIONS   Write the list word that fits each clue.

1. I am from a Mexican Spanish word for coffee shop.
2. I'm a loose Japanese garment.
3. I am a Hindustani word for a small house.
4. I am from a Greek word; I hold your boat in one place.
5. From an Arabic word for "the cushion," I am used on a bed.
6. From a Spanish word, I'm a coat that slips over your head.
7. I am from a French word for a large piece of land.
8. From an Arabic word meaning "the chief," I am the commander of a ship.
9. I'm a dull brown fabric from a Persian word for dust.
10. I am a boat with two hulls, from a Tamil word for tied tree. (Tamil is a language of the people of India and Sri Lanka.)
11. I am an Italian boat found in the canals of Venice.

DEFINITIONS   Write the list word that fits each definition.

12. a cotton cloth of colored threads, from a Malay word for striped
13. an Inuit canoe made of skins stretched over a frame with an opening in the middle for a person
14. from an Arabic word, a small, sparkling disk for decorating clothes
15. from a French word for desk, a chest of drawers or dresser
16. from the French word for Sweden, a velvety-soft leather
17. from a Spanish word meaning "people or community," an Indian village with homes made of adobe and stone
18. from a Spanish word, a blue dye
19. from a Dutch word, a ship used for pleasure or racing
20. sleeping garments, originally from a Persian word

STRATEGIC SPELLING
Using the Memory Tricks Strategy

21.–22. Use memory tricks to help you spell. Create memory tricks for two list words that are hard for you. Underline the matching letters in the list words and helpers.

Did You Know?
Suede became the name of the soft leather because of the French phrase *gants de Suède*, which means "gloves of Sweden."

═	Make a capital.
/	Make a small letter.
∧	Add something.
ℯ	Take out something.
⊙	Add a period.
⏖	New paragraph

PROOFREAD FOR USAGE The verb pairs *bring/take* and *borrow/lend* are often used incorrectly. Don't use one when you mean the other. For example:

Mom has me ~~bring~~ take ∧my little sister to school every day.

Check Verbs If the wrong verb from the pair is used, write the correct one. If the verb in a sentence is correct, write "Correct."

1. She also has me stop at the store so I can bring home milk.
2. In addition, I bring out the garbage every day.
3. In return, she lets me borrow her things.
4. She borrowed me her silk pajamas for a slumber party.
5. She got mad when I forgot to bring them home with me.

PROOFREAD A SELF-PORTRAIT Find the five misspelled words in Kim's self-portrait. Write them correctly. Some may be words you learned before. Fix three errors with verbs too.

> I'm a kaki pants person—no sequins or suade for me! If I need a dress, my sister borrows me one. Mom knows were to find me at home. I'm in my pagamas, sitting in my chair reading. I like to take my friends home so they can meet my family. I like to bring my family when I go places. One time we took a cruise on a yaght.

WRITE A SELF-PORTRAIT Write about yourself in a self-portrait. Try to use three list words and a personal word.

Word List

cafeteria	kimono	gondola	poncho
anchor	catamaran	pueblo	kayak
suede	bungalow	admiral	estate
gingham	yacht	sequin	indigo
mattress	pajamas	bureau	khaki

Personal Words 1.___ 2.___

kayak
admiral
anchor
kimono
pajamas
poncho
indigo
cafeteria
mattress
estate

Review

WORDS IN THE NEWS Write the word from the box that best completes these lines from a newspaper page.

1. Sleep Like a Baby! ___ Sale Today Only!
2. New Ship Dedicated by ___ Sails the Pacific
3. Food in School ___ Found to Be Edible!
4. Sleep in Cuddly Comfort in Our Flannel ___
5. After a Bath, Wrap Yourself in a Japanese Silk ___
6. Ship Loses ___; Floats Out to Sea
7. Paddle a Lake or River in a New ___ from L. L. Lentil
8. Our Dresses, Dyed a Stunning ___, Are Now on Sale!
9. Meteorologist Predicts Rain; Wear Your ___ Outside
10. Railroad Magnate Dies; Sale of His ___ Starts Friday

Word *Study*

ANALOGIES Remember that an **analogy** shows how two pairs of words are related. In the analogy **admiral : ship :: teacher : classroom,** the first word is a worker and the second is a workplace. The analogy is read "admiral is to ship as teacher is to classroom." Some other types of analogies, besides *Worker and Workplace,* are *Synonym*—**humorous : funny :: present : gift**— and *Antonym*—**lost : found :: right : wrong.**

Now that you know some types of analogies, use these words to complete the analogies below: *courageous, cafeteria, laboratory, interesting, inevitable.*

1. university : college :: lunchroom : ___
2. casual : formal :: boring : ___
3. examine : study :: brave : ___
4. sorrow : happiness :: avoidable : ___
5. nurse : hospital :: chemist : ___

Review

Lesson 31: Including All the Letters
Lesson 32: Latin Roots 3
Lesson 33: Prefixes ab-, ad-, co-, com-, con-

Lesson 34: Related Words 3
Lesson 35: Words from Many Cultures 2

REVIEW WORD LIST

1. acquaintance
2. alcohol
3. basically
4. beginning
5. clothes
6. disintegrate
7. extraordinary
8. overrated
9. peculiar
10. respiratory
11. something
12. susceptible
13. veterinarian
14. diversion
15. eventually
16. extrovert
17. facilitate
18. imposing
19. proposal
20. satisfaction
21. abnormal
22. abolish
23. addition
24. adhesive
25. advantage
26. advertisement
27. community
28. complicate
29. controversy
30. cooperate
31. conclude
32. consumption
33. influential
34. persuade
35. prescribe
36. prescription
37. provocative
38. publication
39. publish
40. substantial
41. cafeteria
42. estate
43. kayak
44. khaki
45. kimono
46. mattress
47. pajamas
48. poncho
49. suede
50. yacht

■ PROOFREADING

Find the spelling errors in each passage and write the words correctly. All passages have seven errors except the last one, which has eight.

PROOFREAD A NOTICE

As a result of a proposul by parent organizations, begining next week the cafateria will pubulish the daily lunch menus in the local paper. This will not only fasilitate meal planning for parents but will assure the comunity that students can take advantig of nutritious choices and that tax money is being well-spent.

PROOFREAD A QUESTIONNAIRE

As you may know, the television series *Billy and Pete* has generated some controvoursy. Please take the time to register your opinions about the show.

1. Have you seen an advetisement for the show?
   Yes   No

2. Have you seen the show?   Yes   No

3. Please circle the words that most nearly describe your reaction to the show.
   overated   offensive   pretty good
   provokative   extrordinary

4. If you have not seen the show, do you plan to watch it eventualy?   Yes   No

5. Circle the phrase that most nearly describes your reason for watching television.
   as a divirsion   for education
   for companionship   for current events

PROOFREAD A COMPLAINT

Last week I received a suade vest, a ponsho, and an air matress that I ordered from your catalog. There was substancial damage to the vest when I pulled off an adhesiv sticker that was evidently put there by the manufacturer. Since you guarantee satisifaction on all items, I am hoping to persuaide you to send me a new vest.

PROOFREAD A TELEPHONE MESSAGE

Ben,

    The veternarian called to say that Bubbles has a respitory infection. He is going to perscribe some medicine, and you can pick up the perscription when you pick up Bubbles. He says that basicly Bubbles is fine but very suseptible to infection. He did remark that Bubbles seems to be quite an extravert despite her illness.

            Shana

PROOFREAD A MOVIE REVIEW

Dr. Danger

The flick of the week is *Dr. Danger* starring Vincent Morello as the doctor and Dawn Blythe as his assistant. Dr. Danger lives on an imposeing astate next to a posh yaught club, but they won't let him join because he's too weird. I guess they think a guy who wears a kamono when he paddles his kiyak doesn't fit in. What they don't realize is that Dr. Danger is pretty good at making things disinegrate. His assistant tries to complecate what plot there is with no success. Send this one out to sea.

PROOFREAD A SOCIAL STUDIES REPORT

In 1847 Frederick Douglass started a publucation, *The North Star,* in Rochester, New York. The newspaper was influencal in helping to abolsh slavery and segregation. In adition, Douglass strongly supported women's rights and strongly opposed consumtion of alchol. In his later life, he made the aquaintance of President Lincoln and served as ambassador to Haiti.

PROOFREAD A NARRATIVE PARAGRAPH

The Day the Squirrel Got In

Last week when Dad went to take our family's clean cloths out of the dryer, he heard an abnorml noise. He thought somthing pecuilar was in there, but what? When he opened the dryer, the pagamas seemed to be moving all by themselves! Suddenly, out popped a squirrel trailing a pair of kakhi pants and some underwear. Dad opened the back door, but the squirrel refused to coroperate. Instead, he ran around the laundry room one way while Dad ran around the other. To conclud, we had to call the animal control truck, and two men managed to capture one very scared animal. I mean the squirrel, not Dad.

Vocabulary, Writing, and Reference Resources

Cross-Curricular Lessons

Writer's Handbook

Dictionary Handbook

Spelling Dictionary

Writer's Thesaurus

English/Spanish Word List

Cross-Curricular Lessons

🖐 SOCIAL STUDIES

🍎 HEALTH

💡 SCIENCE

📕 READING

➗ MATHEMATICS

The American Revolution

The American Revolution transformed thirteen British colonies into a new, independent nation. The list words tell about this event, one of the most important in world history. Add two words of your own to the list. Then do the activity. Use your Spelling Dictionary if you need help.

■ GETTING AT MEANING

Time Line Complete the time line with list words.

1770

1767

The British Parliament passes the Townshend Acts, calling for (1) taxes on certain goods coming into the American colonies from Britain.

As a result of mounting tensions, British soldiers panic and fire on a mob of angry colonists, killing several of them, in an event that becomes known as the (2).

1773

To (3) against the hated tea tax, colonists disguised as Indians dump crates of British tea into Boston Harbor.

| 1767 | 1768 | 1769 | 1770 | 1771 | 1772 | 1773 | 1774 |

1775

Colonial citizen-soldiers, known as (4) because of their readiness to fight at a moment's notice, fight British troops, known as (5) because of their bright uniforms, at Lexington and Concord.

1776

The (6) is issued. This defiant document lists the colonists' (7) against Britain's King George III and (8) the united colonies free and independent of British rule.

Choose Sides

Imagine you live in colonial America. Pair up with a partner and choose sides, American and British. If you chose the American side, write some reasons why you should revolt. If you chose the British side, write some reasons why you should remain loyal to Britain. Use your notes as you and your partner discuss the issues, trying to convince each other that your position is the correct one.

1779

American Captain John Paul Jones defeats the British warship *Serapis* in an important (9) battle off the coast of England. Badly damaged, Jones's own ship sinks two days later.

1781

A cornered British army (10) to the Americans at Yorktown, ending the Revolutionary War.

| 1775 | 1776 | 1777 | 1778 | 1779 | 1780 | 1781 |

The Lewis and Clark Expedition

Columbia River
Thomas Jefferson
claim
co-leaders
journals
settlement
Canadian
keelboat
Louisiana
  Purchase
observations

Where did Lewis and Clark explore? What did they find?
The list words tell about their famous expedition. Add two words
of your own. Then do the activity. Use your Spelling Dictionary
if you need help.

■ GETTING AT MEANING

Using a Map Use the map and the pictures to help complete the
sentences with list words.

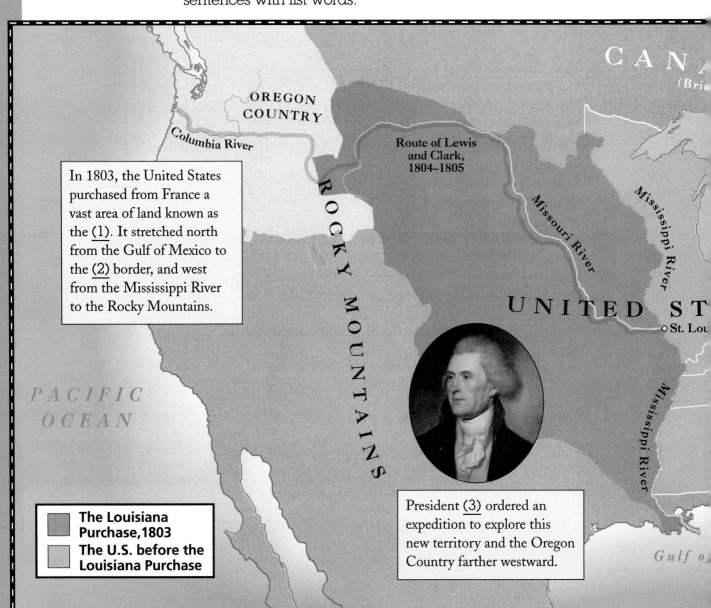

OREGON COUNTRY

Columbia River

Route of Lewis
and Clark,
1804–1805

CANA
(Bri

Missouri River

Mississippi River

UNITED ST
○ St. Lou

Mississippi River

PACIFIC
OCEAN

ROCKY MOUNTAINS

Gulf o

In 1803, the United States
purchased from France a
vast area of land known as
the (1). It stretched north
from the Gulf of Mexico to
the (2) border, and west
from the Mississippi River
to the Rocky Mountains.

President (3) ordered an
expedition to explore this
new territory and the Oregon
Country farther westward.

■ The Louisiana
  Purchase,1803
□ The U.S. before the
  Louisiana Purchase

Meriwether Lewis and William Clark became the expedition's (4).

In May of 1804, the expedition of about forty-five people set out across the Mississippi from St. Louis in two dugout canoes and a flat-bottomed craft called a (5).

In November of 1805, they reached their westward journey's end at the mouth of the (6). Their return trip took six months.

Lewis and Clark made careful (7) of the plants, animals, people, land, and climate along the way, which they recorded in writing in their (8).

This information helped the United States successfully (9) the Oregon Country and played a large part in the eventual (10) of the American West.

homelands
Cherokee
settle
barriers
perish
enforcing
tyrant
invaders
removal
Trail of Tears

The Indian Removal

The list words all deal with President Andrew Jackson's order to remove the Cherokee Indians from their southeastern lands to an area west of the Mississippi River. Although many whites supported the order, others opposed it. Try adding more words to the list, and then do the activity. Use your Spelling Dictionary if you need help.

■ GETTING AT MEANING

For and Against Use the information in the passage to help you complete the speech balloons with list words.

By and large, white pioneers saw American Indians as **barriers** to their goals. The pioneers wanted to **settle** the Indians' lands and, in fact, thought they had the right to do so. The Indians, on the other hand, saw the pioneers as **invaders.** In 1830, President Andrew Jackson sided with the pioneers and ordered the **removal** of the entire **Cherokee** nation from their ancestral **homelands.** Of the fifteen thousand Cherokee forced to move, about one-fourth would **perish** from disease, starvation, and other hardships during the journey west, which came to be called the **"Trail of Tears."** By **enforcing** his decision to move the Indians, Jackson made some people see him as a **tyrant.**

Our (1) belong to us. The white pioneers are (2) in our territory.

DID YOU KNOW?

THE CHOCTAW, CHICKASAW, CREEK, AND SEMINOLE NATIONS ALSO WERE UPROOTED AND RELOCATED DURING JACKSON'S PRESIDENCY.

Slavery

overseer
fugitive
Underground
  Railroad
states' rights
plantations
abolitionist
enslavement
emancipation
secessionist
cotton gin

By 1861, disagreement about slavery had helped bring about the American Civil War between the North and the South. The list words tell about slavery and the controversy it caused. Add two more words about slavery to the list. Then do the activities. Use your Spelling Dictionary if you need it.

■ GETTING AT MEANING

Who Said It? For each statement, write the list word that tells who might have said it in the years before the Civil War. Use the definitions in the box for help.

---

abolitionist

▼

a person who wants to see an institution or custom done away with

fugitive

▼

a person fleeing from danger, an enemy, or justice

overseer

▼

a person who directs workers and their work

secessionist

▼

a person who favors seceding, or withdrawing, from an organization

---

1. "Those slaves don't work nearly hard enough. Why, just yesterday, I had to beat one of them when he took too long getting a drink of water."

2. "Slavery is the great shame of our country. We must continue to speak against it, write against it, oppose it in every way possible."

3. "We left in the darkness—Mama, Papa, and me. For three days now, we've slept by day and run by night. At first, we could hear the master's dogs coming up behind us, but not anymore."

4. "No longer can we pretend that the national government has the interests of the southern states at heart. To preserve our rights, our very way of life, we have no choice but to pull away and form our own nation."

What Is It? Write the list word that each fact describes.

5. Crops such as tobacco, cotton, and sugar cane were planted, tended, and harvested by slaves on these large farms in the South.

6. This mechanical engine, invented by Eli Whitney to separate seeds from fiber, helped make cotton "king" in the South and strengthened the institution of slavery.

7. When this happens, a person's freedom is taken away, and he or she becomes the property of someone else.

8. This secret network of routes and hiding places aided fugitive slaves on their way to freedom in northern states or in Canada.

9. Many southerners used this idea to support their position that individual states, rather than the national government, should have the right to decide whether to allow slavery or not.

10. When this happens, a person is set free from slavery or some other restraint. It comes from the Latin **ex-** (away), **manus** (hand), and **capere** (to take).

THE LIFE OF A SLAVE

What was slavery like from the slaves' point of view? To find out, read *To Be a Slave* by Julius Lester (Dial, 1968), *Now Is Your Time!* by Walter Dean Myers (HarperCollins, 1992), or another book that your librarian recommends. Then write about, or discuss with some classmates, your reactions to the book.

Cowboys

wrangler
longhorn
trail drive
roundup
open range
barbed wire
chuck wagons
lariat
stampede
mustangs

The list words relate to cowboys, people who take care of cattle for ranch owners. The height of the cowboy era lasted from the mid-1860s to the mid-1880s. Add words that you know about cowboys to the list. Then do the activity, using your Spelling Dictionary if you need help.

■ GETTING AT MEANING

A Cowboy Photo Album Use list words to complete the captions for the photographs.

During the height of the cowboy era, most cattle were raised on unfenced grassland known as the (1). Each spring and fall, cowboys held a (2), in which they gathered up the animals, separated the cattle of different ranchers, and branded new calves with their owners' marks.

In a (3), cowboys drove their herds hundreds of miles to railroad stations to ship them to market. At times the cattle would become frightened and rush blindly ahead in a (4), trampling everything in their path.

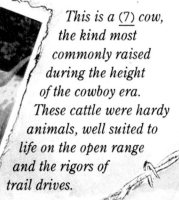

This is a (7) cow, the kind most commonly raised during the height of the cowboy era. These cattle were hardy animals, well suited to life on the open range and the rigors of trail drives.

During roundups and trail drives, (5) carried the cowboys' food, utensils, and bedrolls. The crew on a trail drive included a (6), from the German word wrangein, *who looked after the horses. Later, the term came to mean the same as "cowboy."*

DID YOU KNOW?

It took strong, independent women to journey west during the 1800s. The few who did became the first cowgirls. Since they were doing the same work men were doing, the cowgirls dressed in the same clothing as the men (boots, Stetson hats, and pants) and worked right alongside them—rounding up, branding, and sending cattle to market.

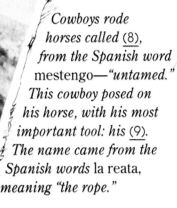

Cowboys rode horses called (8), from the Spanish word mestengo—*"untamed." This cowboy posed on his horse, with his most important tool: his (9). The name came from the Spanish words* la reata, *meaning "the rope."*

This picture shows a ranch of the early 1900s, when the cowboy era was a thing of the past. To protect their crops from cattle, farmers had been fencing their land with (10) since its invention in the mid-1870s.

The Age of Expansion

empire
manifest destiny
foreign policy
cede
annex
imperialism
purchase
yellow
  journalism
treaty
overseas

During the 1800s, the United States expanded west across the continent and beyond. The list words relate to that expansion. Try to add more words to the list, and then do the activities. Use your Spelling Dictionary for help if you need it.

■ GETTING AT MEANING

Map Captions The map shows the westward growth of the United States in the mid- to late 1800s. Use list words to complete the map captions.

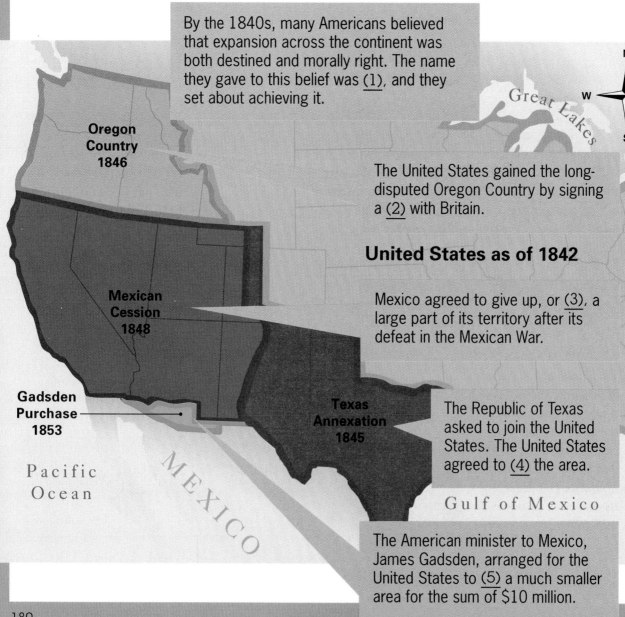

By the 1840s, many Americans believed that expansion across the continent was both destined and morally right. The name they gave to this belief was (1), and they set about achieving it.

Oregon Country 1846

Great Lakes

The United States gained the long-disputed Oregon Country by signing a (2) with Britain.

United States as of 1842

Mexican Cession 1848

Mexico agreed to give up, or (3), a large part of its territory after its defeat in the Mexican War.

Gadsden Purchase 1853

Texas Annexation 1845

The Republic of Texas asked to join the United States. The United States agreed to (4) the area.

Pacific Ocean

MEXICO

Gulf of Mexico

The American minister to Mexico, James Gadsden, arranged for the United States to (5) a much smaller area for the sum of $10 million.

Letters to the Editor In 1898, the people of Cuba (an island southeast of the United States) were in revolt against their Spanish rulers. When the U.S. battleship *Maine* sank near Cuba on February 15, many American newspapers called for war against Spain, and their readers responded. Use list words to complete the letters to the editor.

February 18, 1898

Dear Sir:

My heart leapt at your stirring editorial on the sinking of the Maine by the Spanish. This incident proves that we Americans must look (6), beyond our shores, to expand our territory and defend ourselves against attack. Furthermore, the Cubans despise being part of the Spanish (7) and need our support in their struggle for freedom. War is indeed unpleasant, but war it must be.

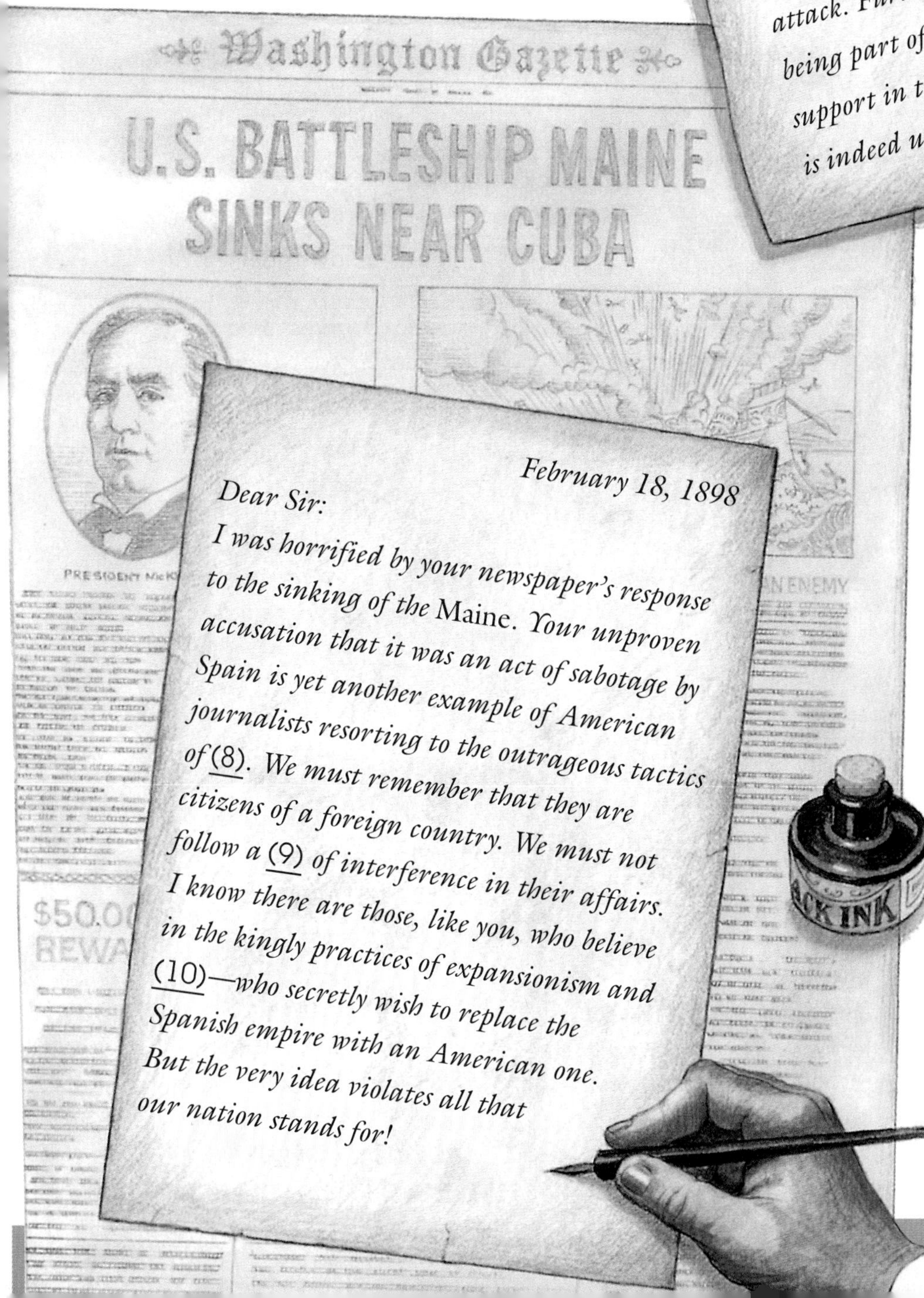

✠ Washington Gazette ✠

U.S. BATTLESHIP MAINE SINKS NEAR CUBA

PRESIDENT McK

$50.00
REWA

February 18, 1898

Dear Sir:

I was horrified by your newspaper's response to the sinking of the Maine. Your unproven accusation that it was an act of sabotage by Spain is yet another example of American journalists resorting to the outrageous tactics of (8). We must remember that they are citizens of a foreign country. We must not follow a (9) of interference in their affairs. I know there are those, like you, who believe in the kingly practices of expansionism and (10)—who secretly wish to replace the Spanish empire with an American one. But the very idea violates all that our nation stands for!

MAPPING THE AMERICAN EMPIRE

BEGINNING IN THE MID-1800S, THE UNITED STATES ACQUIRED VARIOUS POSSESSIONS OVERSEAS. WORK WITH SOME CLASSMATES TO FIND OUT WHEN AND HOW THE UNITED STATES ACQUIRED THOSE POSSESSIONS. THEN MAKE OR OBTAIN A LARGE WORLD MAP AND ATTACH IT TO A BULLETIN BOARD. WRITE A LABEL FOR EACH POSSESSION, BASED ON WHAT YOU HAVE LEARNED.

flappers
Jazz Age
Harlem
speakeasies
Prohibition
skyscrapers
racketeers
Art Deco
Charleston
bootleggers

The Roaring Twenties

After World War I ended in 1918, Americans wanted to relax, have fun, and enjoy their prosperity. The list words relate to the 1920s, an era that came to be called the Roaring Twenties. If you can, add more words about the 1920s to the list. Then do the activity, using your Spelling Dictionary if you need it.

■ GETTING AT MEANING

What's in a Name? The Roaring Twenties got that nickname because they were noisy, energetic, daring years. Use the pictures and captions to help you write the list word that each sentence describes.

During the Roaring Twenties, flappers shocked their elders by rolling down their stockings, raising their hemlines, cutting their hair short, and dancing wild new dances like the Charleston.

1 These outlaws got their name from pickpockets in England who started noisy disturbances to distract their victims.

2 This lively dance of the 1920s, in which the knees twisted in and the heels swung out with every step, takes its name from a city in South Carolina named after an English king.

3 This era of American history, which included the 1920s, takes its name from a word meaning "to forbid."

4 These places were named for the quiet way that customers asked to be let in, so as not to attract attention from neighbors or police officers.

The Twenties was part of the Prohibition era when the manufacture and sale of alcoholic beverages were forbidden by law. To get around this law, bars and clubs known as speakeasies sold illegal liquor supplied by bootleggers. Gangsters and racketeers fought for control of these illegal enterprises.

Jazz originated among black musicians in the South and spread to northern cities. One major center of jazz was Harlem, an African American community in New York City.

5 This center of African American music, literature, and art in New York City was named for the Dutch city of Haarlem.

6 These women were nicknamed for one of their unusual items of clothing: galoshes worn with the buckles unfastened so they flopped back and forth.

7 The name of this distinctive style of design came from the *Exposition Internationale des Arts Décoratifs et Industriels Modernes,* an exposition of decorative and industrial arts held in Paris, France, in 1925.

8 The name for these people, who found all sorts of unusual ways to transport illegal liquor, comes from the early American practice of smuggling bottles inside one's footwear.

9 These buildings, which became increasingly popular in the 1920s, got their name from the topmost sail of clipper ships.

10 This other nickname for the Roaring Twenties grew out of the popularity of a new kind of music that developed from African American spirituals.

In the 1920s the value of urban land skyrocketed. To save land and money, architects designed skyscrapers. Some, such as New York's Chrysler Building, reflected Art Deco, a new style of design that relied on streamlined forms and geometric shapes.

NAME YOUR DECADE

Think about the decade that you live in. What nickname would you give it, and why? Write a paragraph or create a poster that explains and supports the nickname you have chosen.

neutrality
aggression
dictators
Allies
liberation
isolationists
Axis
concentration
  camps
victory
invades

World War II

World War II began on September 1, 1939, when Germany invaded Poland. The war ended when Japan formally surrendered on September 2, 1945. The list words relate to the war and the events that led to it. Add words of your own. Use your Spelling Dictionary if you need help with the activity.

■ GETTING AT MEANING

Newspaper Headlines Use the context clues in the news stories to complete the headlines with list words. (Don't forget to capitalize the words as needed.)

WAR★CHRONICLES

World War II Issue

This is the Enemy

(1) Now Rule Germany, Italy, Soviet Union

August 3, 1934 Adolf Hitler has seized complete control of the German government. With this move, Hitler joins the ranks of rulers with total authority over their nations, including Benito Mussolini of Italy and Joseph Stalin of the Soviet Union.

U.S. Continues Policy of (2)! (3) Are Pleased

August 31, 1935 Congress has voted to ban weapons sales to nations at war in order to avoid involvement in foreign wars. One supporter of the ban stated, "What happens in Europe is the concern of Europeans, not Americans."

GERMANY (4) POLAND!
British, French Response to Act of (5) Expected

September 1, 1939 Yesterday, German forces swarmed into Poland without warning and without provocation. Pledged to defend Poland, Britain and France are expected to respond to the attack by declaring war on Germany.

WAR★CHRONICLES

World War II Issue

U.S. Joins (6) in War Against (7)

December 12, 1941 Following Congress's declaration of war on Japan, Germany and Italy yesterday declared war on the United States. Mussolini once stated that the line between Berlin and Rome would be the axis on which the world would turn. That line now extends to Tokyo. The United States now joins Britain, the Soviet Union, and other nations allied against Japan, Germany, and Italy.

Soldiers Discover Nazis' Victims in (9)

April 30, 1945 With the war in Europe all but over, American and British soldiers moving across Germany have discovered camp after camp with half-dead prisoners waiting for release. It is becoming clear that the Nazis systematically imprisoned, tortured, starved, and murdered millions of civilians, including Jews, Poles, and Russians.

Allies Complete (8) of France

August 27, 1944 One month after breaking through German lines and driving the Germans back across the French countryside, Allied troops rode triumphantly through Paris yesterday. After four years of occupation by Germany, a joyful France and its capital have been freed from Nazi rule.

War Ends in (10) for Allies

September 3, 1945 Yesterday, the war ended as Japan formally surrendered to the Allies, approximately four months after Germany's surrender. The final blows to Japan were struck on August 6 and 9, when American planes dropped atomic bombs on the cities of Hiroshima and Nagasaki.

LIFE ON THE HOME FRONT

Once committed, the American people supported the war effort wholeheartedly. Interview a family member, neighbor, or someone else who was alive during World War II. Ask what the person remembers about such things as "Rosie the Riveter," rationing, war bonds, and scrap drives. Share what you learn with your classmates.

Do the job *HE* left behind

APPLY U.S. EMPLOYMENT SERVICE

Gaining Civil Rights

minority groups
nonviolence
demonstrations
civil disobedience
segregation
affirmative action
boycott
desegregation
franchise
discrimination

Civil rights are the rights that a citizen has, such as the right to fair and equal treatment. In the United States, African Americans and certain other groups have had to struggle to gain their civil rights. The list words relate to that struggle. Try adding other words to the list. Then do the activity. Use your Spelling Dictionary if you need help.

■ GETTING AT MEANING

Using a Time Line Use the time line to help you answer the questions with list words.

1. A nineteenth-century Supreme Court ruling upheld the idea of "separate but equal." What is separation of one racial group from another called?

2. Black people refused to ride the buses in Montgomery, Alabama, to protest segregation. What is this protest method?

3. Martin Luther King, Jr., urged black people to protest unjust civil laws by refusing to obey them. What is this protest method?

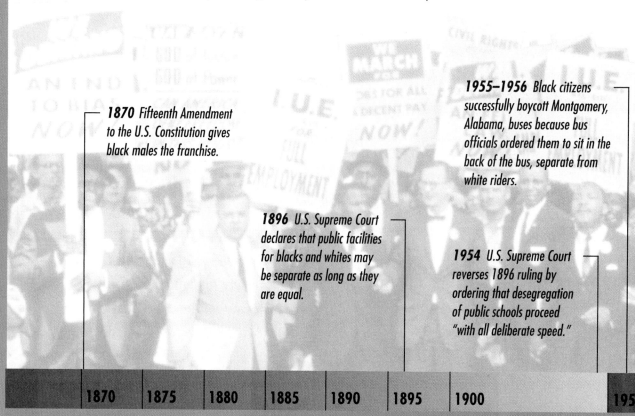

1870 Fifteenth Amendment to the U.S. Constitution gives black males the franchise.

1896 U.S. Supreme Court declares that public facilities for blacks and whites may be separate as long as they are equal.

1955–1956 Black citizens successfully boycott Montgomery, Alabama, buses because bus officials ordered them to sit in the back of the bus, separate from white riders.

1954 U.S. Supreme Court reverses 1896 ruling by ordering that desegregation of public schools proceed "with all deliberate speed."

| 1870 | 1875 | 1880 | 1885 | 1890 | 1895 | 1900 | 1955 |

4. The Fifteenth Amendment gave black males the right to vote. What is another word for "right to vote"?

5. The Civil Rights Act of 1964 stated that businesses must serve all people without regard to race. What is the act of refusing to serve someone because of race?

6. African Americans and other people who differ from the majority of the population in terms of race, religion, or national origin are members of what kinds of groups?

7. When the Supreme Court ordered public schools to stop separating racial groups in 1954, what was it calling for?

8. Martin Luther King, Jr., and his Southern Christian Leadership Conference believed in using only peaceful methods to achieve racial equality. What word describes these methods?

9. Special job training for minority workers is an example of what kind of program?

10. In giving its award to Martin Luther King, Jr., in 1964, the Nobel Peace Prize committee cited the peaceful marches he had led to protest racial injustice. What is another name for protest marches, rallies, and similar gatherings?

1957 SCLC is formed by Martin Luther King, Jr., who urges people to commit acts of civil disobedience to protest racial injustice.

1964 Martin Luther King, Jr., wins Nobel Peace Prize for leading peaceful civil rights demonstrations. Civil Rights Act barring discrimination in public places and by employers becomes law.

1970s To compensate for past discrimination, affirmative action programs set goals for hiring and educating members of minority groups.

| 1960 | 1965 | 1970 |

187

balance
energetic
oxygen
injure
extending
elastic
bounces
strenuous
discipline
muscular
  strength

Physical Fitness

Dance is one road to physical fitness. What other words come to mind when you think of dance as a form of exercise? Add two words to the list. Use your Spelling Dictionary if you need help with the activity.

▉ GETTING AT MEANING

Dance and Fitness Use context clues and your own knowledge to fill in the blanks with list words.

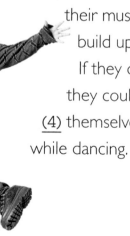

WELCOME TO THE DANCE

These dancers are serious about their work.
They eat right and practice every day.
This kind of life takes a great deal of (1), but they're up to the task. They begin with breathing exercises to help them use (2) efficiently and not run short of breath.

Next, they do exercises to stretch their muscles and build up their (3). If they didn't stretch, they could easily (4) themselves while dancing.

One dancer bends and stretches as she holds on to her partner. Her body is so flexible, you'd think it was made of <u>(5)</u>!

Another dancer <u>(6)</u> all around on springy legs.

Some dancers have so much energy they seem ready to burst. In fact, they're so <u>(7)</u> that it almost makes you tired just watching them!

One dancer practices <u>(8)</u> his arms and lifting his partner overhead.

Another dancer holds steady on one foot for minutes at a time to improve his <u>(9)</u>.

Dancing is hard work! After a <u>(10)</u> day's workout, the classes cool down and then relax for a while.

STUDIO

READY, SET, DANCE

Alone or with a partner, choose a favorite piece of music and create a new dance. As you make up your dance, think about how its different parts or steps benefit you. Do they help your endurance? balance? agility? strength? If you play a sport, how will this exercise help you play it better?

Personal Care

farsighted
iris
calculus
caries
melanin
plaque
mole
sebaceous
  glands
sebum
wart

The words in the list are all about personal health care.
Add more words to the list. Then do the activities. Use your
Spelling Dictionary if you need help.

■ GETTING AT MEANING

Word Origins Use the word origins to help you fill in the blanks
with list words.

Our bodies have ways of protecting themselves. An oil in the
skin, called (1), helps keep our skin from drying out. This oil is
secreted by the (2).

From the Greek word meaning "black" comes (3), the coloring
agent in our skin that helps protect us against the sun's
harmful rays.

Things can go wrong with our bodies too. We can get a (4) on our
skin. But don't be fooled by that old superstition. This is caused by
a virus, not by touching a toad!

When the inside of a tooth decays, (5) can form, leaving
a cavity.

sebum: "grease; oil"

melanos: "black"

wearte: "raised lump"

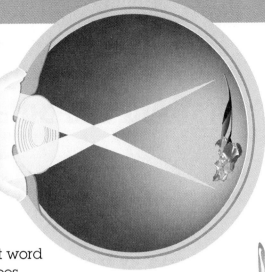

Multiple Meanings Write the list word that each pair of phrases describes.

6
part of the eye that controls the amount of light coming in
flower with sword-shaped leaves

7
hard substance that forms on the teeth
system of calculation $\int x^n dx$

8
dark spot or lump on the skin
small furry animal that lives underground

9
thin film on the surface of the teeth
award for extraordinary achievement

10
eye disorder in which you see distant things more clearly than things that are near
thinking ahead and planning wisely

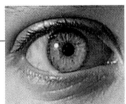

caries: "**decay**"

breathing
prevent
shock
artificial
  respiration
smoke detectors
pedestrians
reflective
emergency
helmet
fire extinguisher

First Aid and Safety

What would you do in an emergency situation? Add two words about first aid or safety to the list. Then complete the activities. Use your Spelling Dictionary if you need help.

■ GETTING AT MEANING

First-Aid Tips Use list words to complete this passage from a first-aid manual.

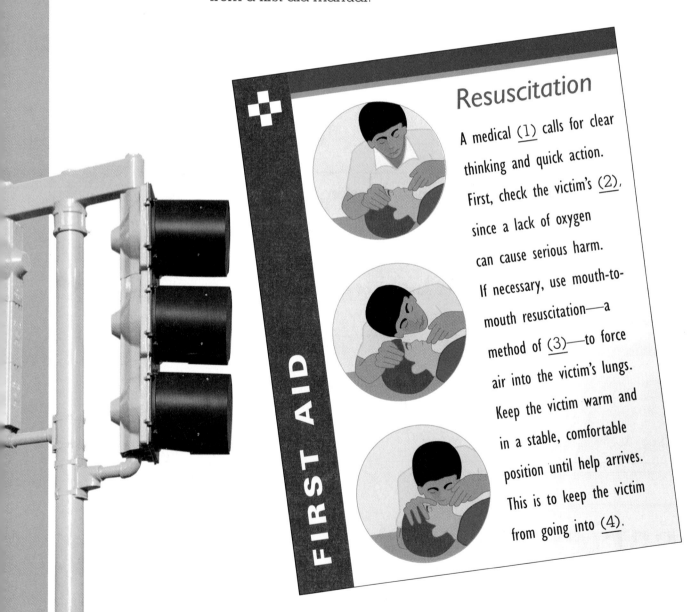

Resuscitation

A medical (1) calls for clear thinking and quick action. First, check the victim's (2), since a lack of oxygen can cause serious harm. If necessary, use mouth-to-mouth resuscitation—a method of (3)—to force air into the victim's lungs. Keep the victim warm and in a stable, comfortable position until help arrives. This is to keep the victim from going into (4).

FIRST AID

Home Safety Tips Complete these safety tips with words from the list.

what kinds of protective clothing and accessories people should wear during certain jobs, sports, or activities. (Your local sporting goods store might be able to help.) Share what you learned in a demonstration speech or in a booklet of safety tips.

SAFETY TIPS

✚

Fire Safety

Be prepared to (5) fires from causing serious damage in your home. Keep a (6) in your kitchen in case of a cooking fire. Since breathing smoke from a fire can cause serious injury or death, install (7) in your home.

Outdoor Safety Tips Complete these safety tips with words from the list.

Be safe outdoors too, whether you're walking or riding. Bike riders and (8) should obey all traffic lights and signals. Protect your head from serious injury by wearing a (9) when you ride. At night, put (10) tape on your clothing and bicycle to let drivers know where you are.

193

Physicians

radiologist
dermatologist
podiatrist
cardiologist
orthopedist
pediatrician
surgeon
neurologist
obstetrician
ophthalmologist

All of the list words name different kinds of physicians. Can you think of two more? Add them to the list and then do the activities. Use your Spelling Dictionary if you need help.

■ GETTING AT MEANING

What Am I? Use a list word to describe each kind of physician.

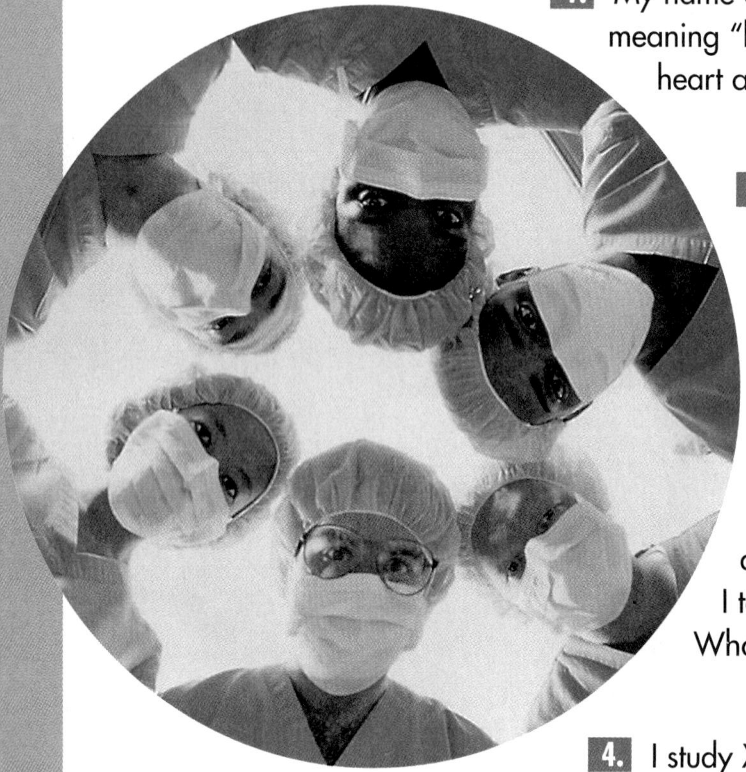

1. My name comes from the Greek word **kardia,** meaning "heart." I specialize in taking care of the heart and blood vessels. What am I?

2. I deal with the structure, functions, and diseases of people's eyes. My name comes from the Greek word **ophthalmos,** meaning "eye." What am I?

3. My name comes from the Greek words **paidos,** meaning "child," and **iatros,** meaning "physician." I take care of babies and children. What am I?

4. I study X rays in order to diagnose and treat medical problems. My name comes from the Latin word **radius,** meaning "ray." What am I?

5. I treat people's skin problems. My name comes from the Greek word **dermatos,** meaning "skin." What am I?

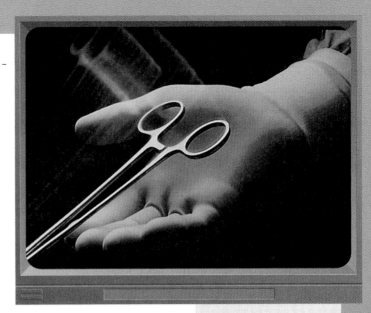

6. My name comes from the Old French word *cirurgien*, meaning "hand work." I perform operations, or surgeries. What am I?

7. My name comes from the Latin word *obstetrica*, meaning "midwife." I treat pregnant women and deliver their babies. What am I?

8. I try to correct the deformities and diseases of bones and joints, especially in children. My name comes from the Greek words *ortho*, meaning "straight"; "correct" and *paidos*, meaning "child." What am I?

9. When people have problems with their feet, they come to. see me. My name comes from the Greek word *podos*, meaning "foot." What am I?

DID YOU KNOW?

Wilhelm Roentgen discovered the X ray in 1895. Within a few months doctors were using this original imaging device to look at broken bones, and they still use Roentgen's X rays today.

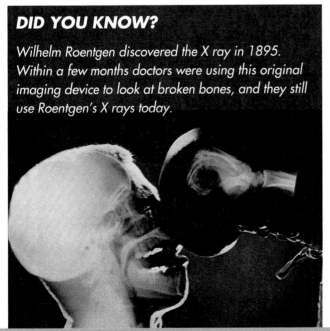

10. I treat diseases of the nervous system. My name comes from the Greek word *neuron*, meaning "nerve." What am I?

A MEDICAL PLOT

Imagine that you're a writer for a TV series that takes place in a hospital. Write a plot outline for a half-hour fictional drama. Tell who, what, where, why, and when. Center your plot on a medical crisis that's resolved by people who work at the hospital—doctors, nurses, etc. You may need to do some medical research for your plot.

DIRECTOR

Force and Motion

Every day, people and things move around you. All motion is caused by force, but not all forces cause motion. Add two force and motion words to the list. Use your Spelling Dictionary if you need help with the activities.

■ GETTING AT MEANING

Which Kind of Friction? Use the drawing to help you decide which kind of friction each item describes.

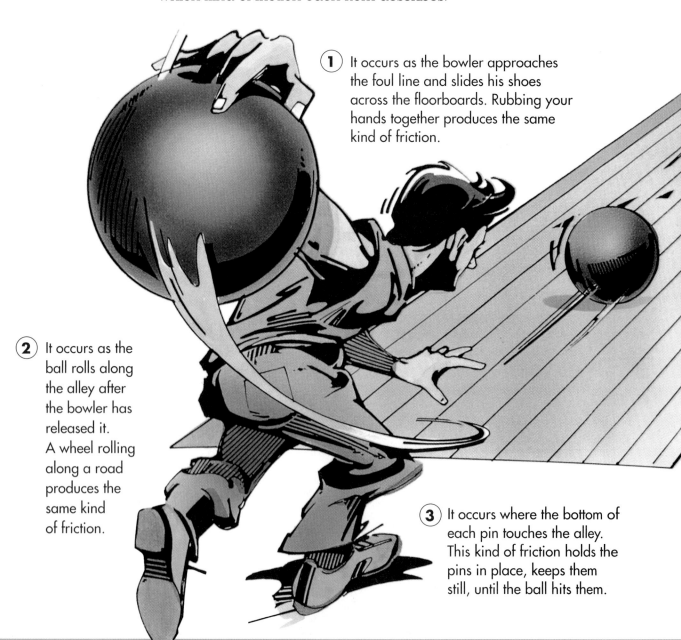

1. It occurs as the bowler approaches the foul line and slides his shoes across the floorboards. Rubbing your hands together produces the same kind of friction.

2. It occurs as the ball rolls along the alley after the bowler has released it. A wheel rolling along a road produces the same kind of friction.

3. It occurs where the bottom of each pin touches the alley. This kind of friction holds the pins in place, keeps them still, until the ball hits them.

Context Clues

Use the drawing and the definitions to help you complete each fact with one of the list words defined at the right.

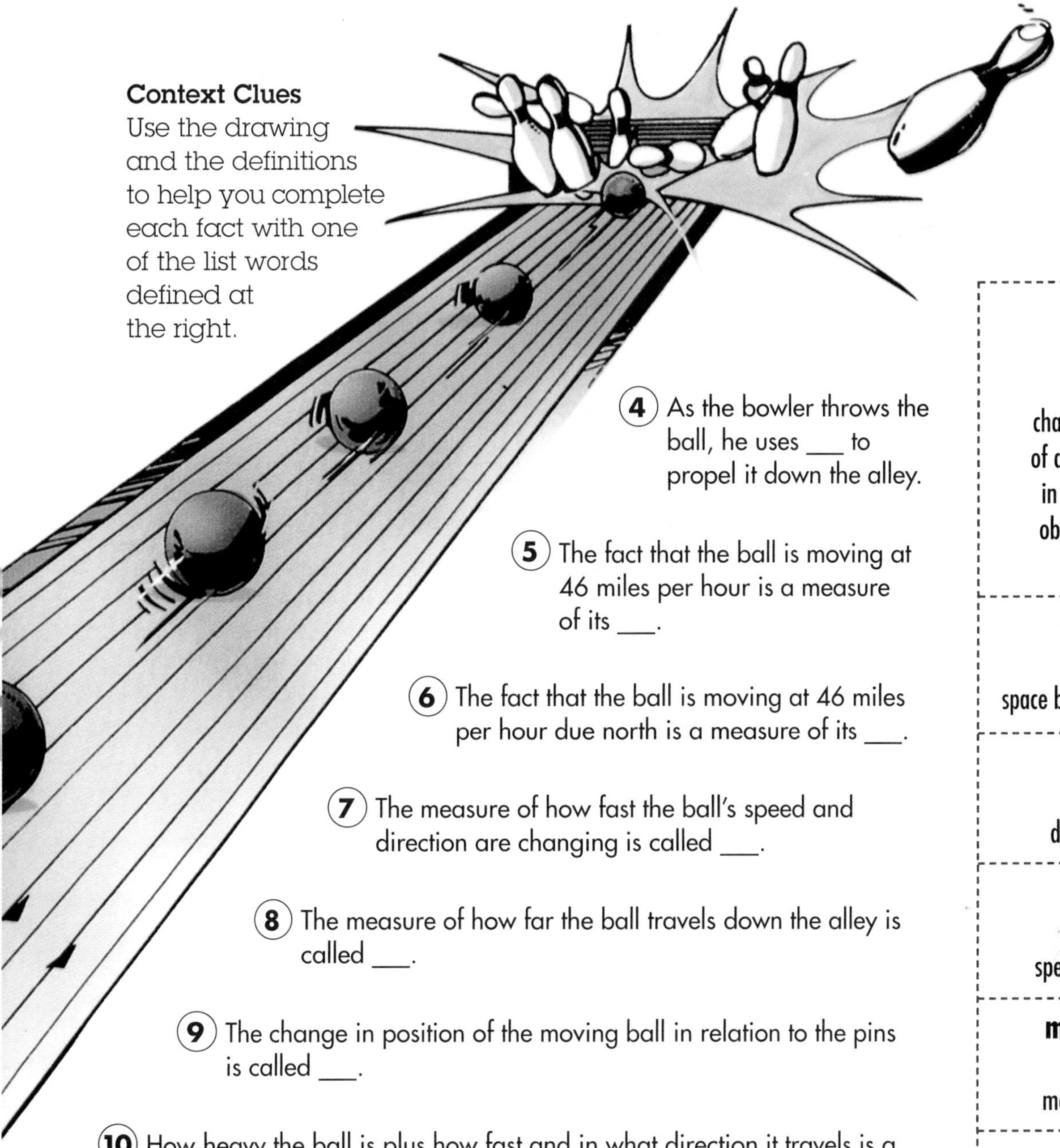

4 As the bowler throws the ball, he uses ___ to propel it down the alley.

5 The fact that the ball is moving at 46 miles per hour is a measure of its ___.

6 The fact that the ball is moving at 46 miles per hour due north is a measure of its ___.

7 The measure of how fast the ball's speed and direction are changing is called ___.

8 The measure of how far the ball travels down the alley is called ___.

9 The change in position of the moving ball in relation to the pins is called ___.

10 How heavy the ball is plus how fast and in what direction it travels is a measure of its ___.

relative motion
↓
change in position of a moving object in relation to an object that is not moving

distance
↓
space between two points

speed
↓
distance/time

velocity
↓
speed + direction

momentum
↓
mass + velocity

acceleration
↓
how fast an object's velocity is changing

force
↓
any action that accelerates an object

TWIST AND SHOUT

SIT IN A CHAIR THAT ROTATES. HOLD A HEAVY OBJECT IN EACH HAND, WITH YOUR ARMS OUTSTRETCHED. HAVE SOMEONE ROTATE YOU SLOWLY AND THEN LET YOU GO AND MOVE AWAY. QUICKLY PULL THE OBJECTS INWARD. WHAT HAPPENS? COMPARE THIS WITH WHAT HAPPENS WHEN A FIGURE SKATER MAKES SIMILAR MOVEMENTS.

atom
electron
proton
neutron
nucleus
atomic number
periodic table
radiation
Geiger counter
nuclear fission

The Atom

The eyes that are reading these words are made up of atoms. So is the brain that is interpreting what the eyes see. In fact, most everything you can think of is made up of atoms. Add two more words about atoms to the list. Then do the activities.

■ GETTING AT MEANING

Interpreting a Diagram Use the paragraph to help you label the diagram with list words.

An **atom** is the smallest bit of an element that has all the characteristics of that element. At the atom's core is the **nucleus.** This nucleus is usually made up of **protons,** which are positively charged, and **neutrons,** which have no charge. Outside of the nucleus are negatively charged particles called **electrons.**

DIAGRAM OF AN **1** ___

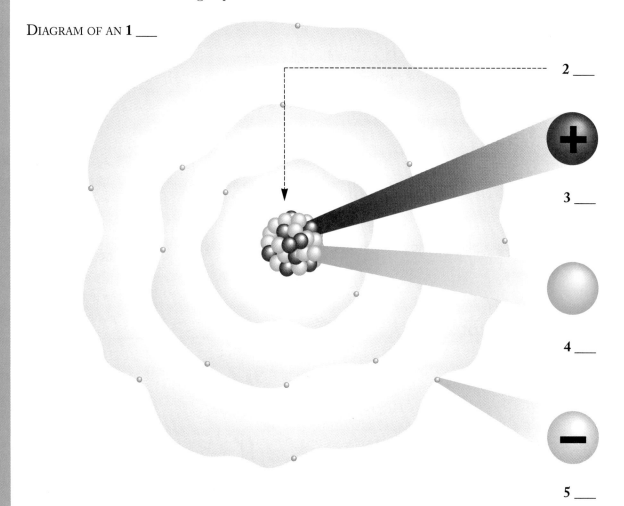

2 ___

3 ___

4 ___

5 ___

Inventors and Their Inventions Read each sentence carefully.
Complete it with the correct word or phrase from the box below.

> atomic number   Geiger counter   nuclear fission
>
> radiation   periodic table

6. In 1895 an X ray, a kind of ___ that could penetrate the human body, was discovered.

7. In 1912, Hans Geiger invented the first instrument to detect radioactivity. It was called the ___.

8. In 1939, scientists discovered that certain heavy nuclei split into lighter nuclei when they absorb certain neutrons. They called this process ___.

9. Russian chemist Dmitri Mendeleev helped develop a systematic arrangement of known chemical elements in the form of a table, which is called the ___ of the elements.

10. In this arrangement, each element is placed according to its ___, from low to high.

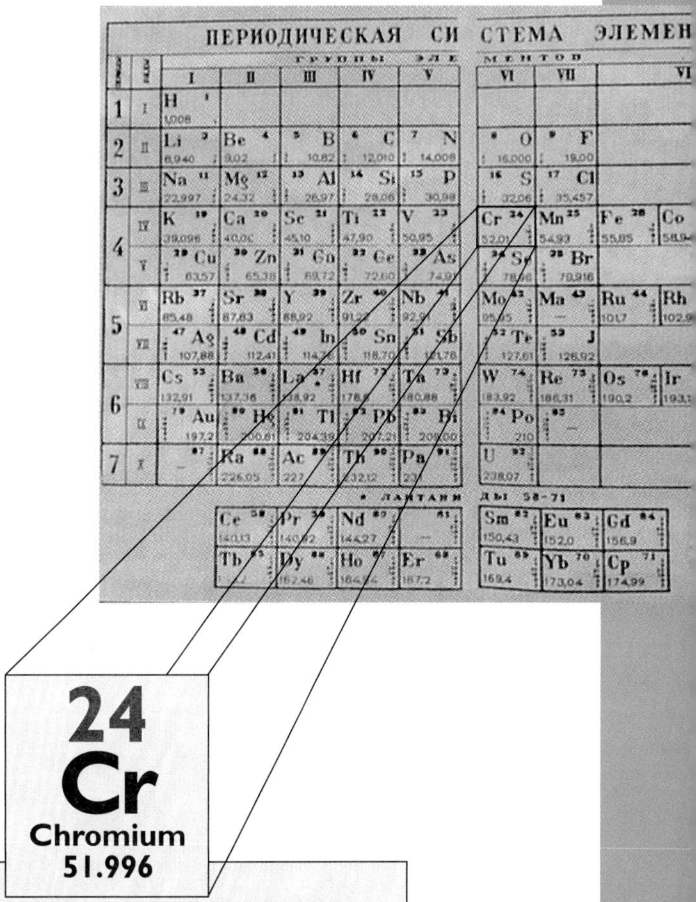

ПЕРИОДИЧЕСКАЯ СИСТЕМА ЭЛЕМЕНТОВ

24
Cr
Chromium
51.996

Name That ELEMENT

These radioactive elements were named for certain people, places, or things. Find out how some of these elements got their names and report your findings on a table or chart.

43 Technetium	86 Radon	90 Thorium	94 Plutonium	98 Californium
61 Promethium	87 Francium	91 Protactinium	95 Americium	99 Einsteinium
84 Polonium	88 Radium	92 Uranium	96 Curium	100 Fermium
85 Astatine	89 Actinium	93 Neptunium	97 Berkelium	101 Mendelevium

Compounds and Mixtures

compound
mixture
chemical
  formula
suspension
emulsifier
solution
solvent
solute
diluted
concentrated

The air you breathe, the food you eat, even your own body—they're all made of compounds and mixtures. Try adding two more words about compounds and mixtures to the list. Then do the activity.

■ GETTING AT MEANING

Cause and Effect Use the definitions above each cause and effect statement to complete it with list words.

chemical formula

mixture two or more substances that are mixed together but not chemically combined

compound substance formed when two or more elements are chemically combined

compound

chemical formula a shorthand way of showing which elements, and how many atoms of each, make up a chemical compound

CAUSE When one atom of sodium and one atom of chlorine chemically combine, **EFFECT** a molecule of the (1) known as salt forms. Salt has the (2) NaCl.

CAUSE When onion, garlic, oregano, and tomato sauce are put together, **EFFECT** a (3) known as spaghetti sauce results.

mixture

suspension

suspension mixture in which the particles of one substance are scattered in another without dissolving

emulsifier a substance that keeps the particles of one liquid mixed into another liquid

emulsifier

solution mixture in which one substance dissolves in another

solution

CAUSE When sugar is dissolved in a mixture of water and lemon juice, **EFFECT** the (4) known as lemonade results.

CAUSE When drops of oil are scattered in vinegar but not dissolved, **EFFECT** a (5) that is used on salads results.

CAUSE When egg yolk is added to vinegar and oil, **EFFECT** the vinegar and oil are kept from separating. The yolk acts as an (6), and mayonnaise is formed.

solvent substance that dissolves other substances

solute the substance being dissolved

diluted weakened or thinned by the addition of liquid

concentrated made stronger by the addition of a solute

concentrated

diluted

CAUSE When extra sugar is added to grape juice, **EFFECT** the grape juice becomes more (7).

CAUSE When extra water is added to grape juice, **EFFECT** the grape juice becomes (8). Since the water dissolves the sugar, the water acts as a (9), while the sugar is a (10).

solvent

solute

TRY THIS EXPERIMENT

Which is a better solvent, cold water or hot? Prepare two clear glasses, one half-full of cold tap water, the other half-full of hot tap water. Stir a teaspoonful of salt into each glass. Does the salt dissolve more quickly in one glass than the other? What can you conclude about hot water versus cold water as a solvent?

Heat and Temperature

contract
temperature
solar collectors
expand
transferred
thermometer
ventilate
insulation
thermostat
heat sources

"It sure is a hot one today!" "Won't it ever cool off?" You hear comments like these every summer, but heat is around you all the time—summer and winter, indoors and out. Add heat words to the list. Use your Spelling Dictionary if you need help with the activity.

■ GETTING AT MEANING

Picture Clues Use the pictures to help you fill in the blanks with list words.

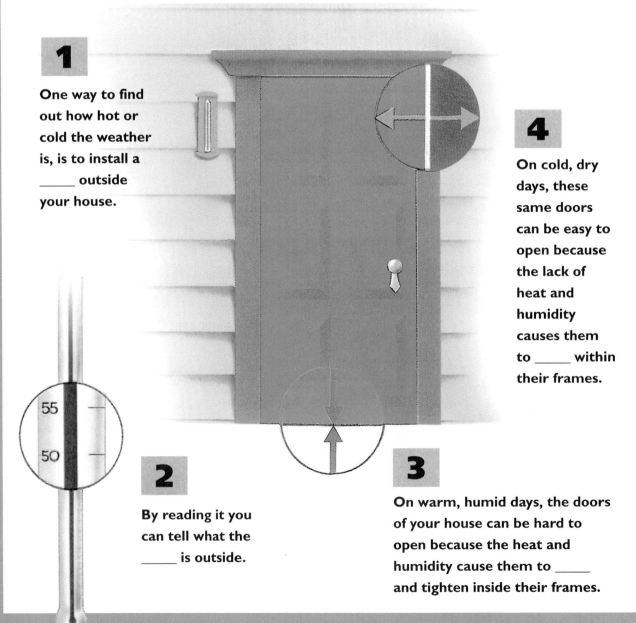

1
One way to find out how hot or cold the weather is, is to install a _____ outside your house.

4
On cold, dry days, these same doors can be easy to open because the lack of heat and humidity causes them to _____ within their frames.

2
By reading it you can tell what the _____ is outside.

3
On warm, humid days, the doors of your house can be hard to open because the heat and humidity cause them to _____ and tighten inside their frames.

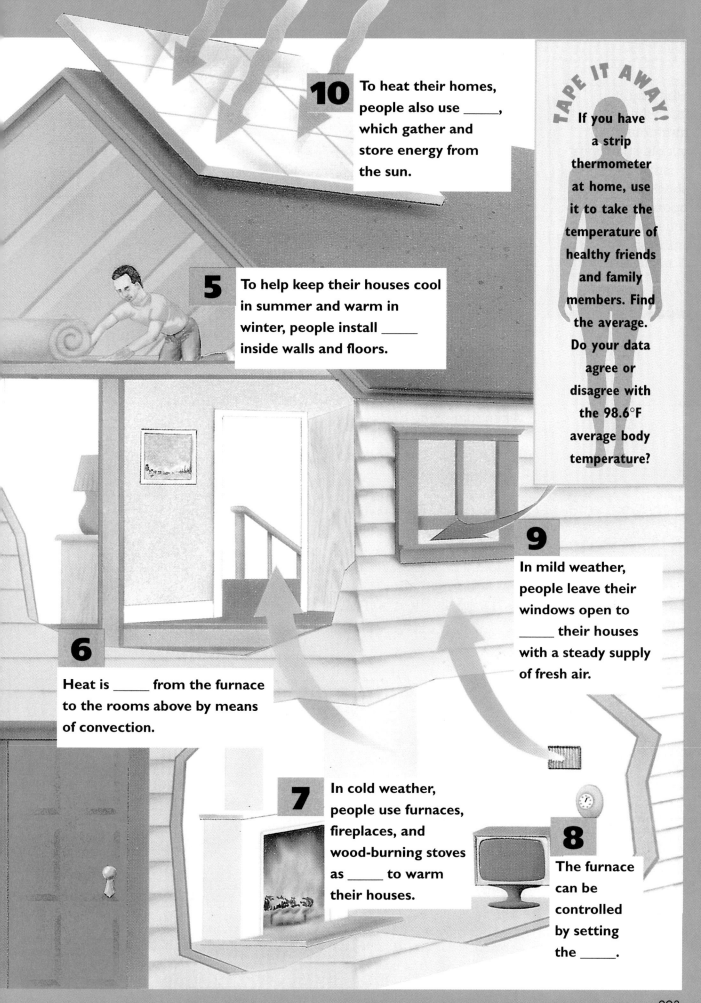

10 To heat their homes, people also use _____, which gather and store energy from the sun.

5 To help keep their houses cool in summer and warm in winter, people install _____ inside walls and floors.

9 In mild weather, people leave their windows open to _____ their houses with a steady supply of fresh air.

6 Heat is _____ from the furnace to the rooms above by means of convection.

7 In cold weather, people use furnaces, fireplaces, and wood-burning stoves as _____ to warm their houses.

8 The furnace can be controlled by setting the _____.

white light
intensity
luminous
visible spectrum
prism
shadow
opaque
reflects
transparent
translucent

Light

The list words are all about light: what it's made of and what it does. Add two more words about light to the list. Then do the activities.

■ GETTING AT MEANING

Light Facts Write the list words from the passage below that facts 1–4 tell about.

Something that gives off its own light is **luminous.**
Intensity is the strength of light falling on an area.
When something turns back light, it **reflects** it.
When something blocks light, a **shadow** forms.

1 The moon does this to sunlight to make moonlight.

2 The farther you move from the source of light, the less of this there is.

3 To tell time from a sundial, you look at this.

4 The sun is. The moon isn't.

Diagram Write the list words from the caption below that numbers 5–7 refer to.

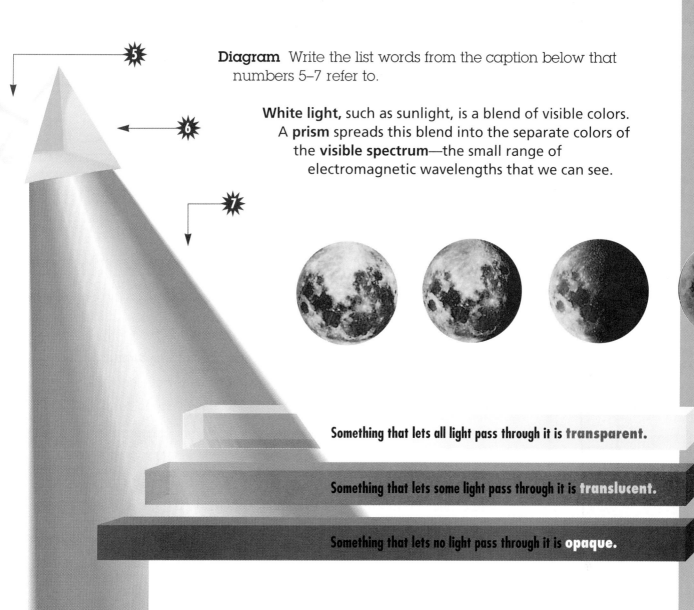

White light, such as sunlight, is a blend of visible colors. A **prism** spreads this blend into the separate colors of the **visible spectrum**—the small range of electromagnetic wavelengths that we can see.

Something that lets all light pass through it is **transparent.**

Something that lets some light pass through it is **translucent.**

Something that lets no light pass through it is **opaque.**

Categorizing Use the definitions of **transparent, translucent,** and **opaque** above to complete the sentences below.

* Sandwich bags, window glass, clean air, and clear nail polish are all _____.

* Aluminum foil, apples, your hand, and an elephant are all _____.

* Waxed paper, fog, lime gelatin, sunglasses, and tissue paper are all _____.

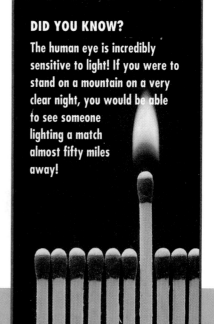

DID YOU KNOW?

The human eye is incredibly sensitive to light! If you were to stand on a mountain on a very clear night, you would be able to see someone lighting a match almost fifty miles away!

Electricity

electric current
batteries
voltage
generator
conductor
insulator
resistance
parallel circuits
series circuits
circuit breaker

Think about all the things that stop working during a power outage. We rely on electricity more than we usually realize. Add two more words to the list. Then do the activities. Use your Spelling Dictionary if you need help.

■ GETTING AT MEANING

The Basics of Electricity Use the drawings and information to help you complete the passages in purple.

Flip on a light switch. An **electric current** starts moving through copper wires in your wall. Metal is a good **conductor** of electricity. A plastic coating around the wires acts as an **insulator** to keep the electricity safely inside the wires.

Turning on the light starts the flow of (1). The wire acts as a (2). The plastic (3) is a safety device.

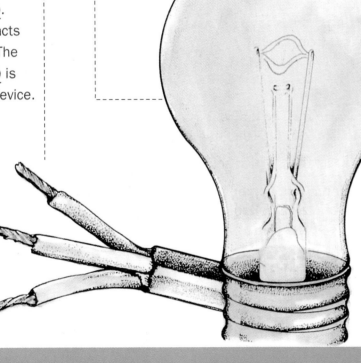

Some appliances use power from electrical outlets. These outlets are connected to wires that eventually connect to a **generator** at a power plant that converts other kinds of energy into electricity. Anything that slows or stops the electric current acts as a **resistance.**

The thin wires in this light bulb glow brightly because of their (4) to electricity. When a lamp is plugged into an outlet, a (5) provides the power to run the light.

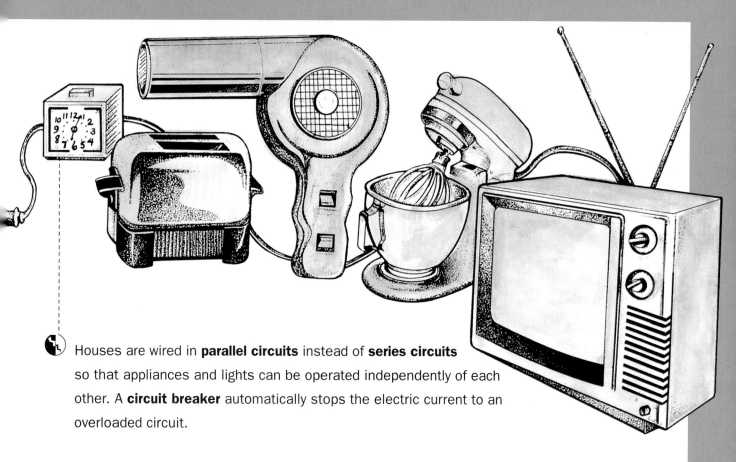

⚡ Houses are wired in **parallel circuits** instead of **series circuits** so that appliances and lights can be operated independently of each other. A **circuit breaker** automatically stops the electric current to an overloaded circuit.

Suppose the toaster burns out but the clock and TV keep running. Then this house is wired in (6). If too many appliances are running at once, a (7) will kick in to prevent a fire. If this house were wired in (8), then all the appliances and lights would have to be on at once or none of them would work.

⚡ **Batteries** turn chemical fuel into electrical energy. The energy a battery gives to the electric current is the **voltage.**

If this radio did not run on (9), you'd have to plug it in to run it. Its low-(10) battery uses very little energy.

MAKE A SIMPLE
ELECTRIC CIRCUIT

You need a low-voltage dry cell battery, two insulated wires with ends stripped, and a light bulb in a socket. Connect the battery to the light with the two wires. When the circuit is complete, the bulb will light up.

Computers

chips
inputting
outputting
CPU
hardware
software
programs
floppy disk
keyboard
personal
  computer

Computers coordinate traffic lights, help people find books in libraries, and read the bar codes at supermarket checkout lines. Add other words about computers to the list. Then do the activities. Use your Spelling Dictionary for help.

■ GETTING AT MEANING

Diagrams Use the diagram and information below to help you fill in the passages on the next page with list words.

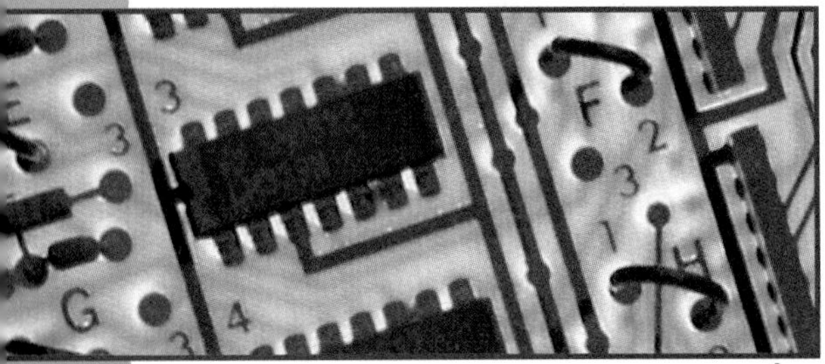

The physical parts of a **personal computer** are called **hardware.** Sets of instructions for a computer are called **programs.** All computer programs taken together are called **software.**

The **CPU** (central processing unit) is the computer's "brain." In it are tiny **chips,** which hold memory.

Inputting is the process of putting information into the computer, usually by typing on the **keyboard.**

Outputting is the process of retrieving information, which usually comes out as a printed page. This information can be stored within the computer as well as on a **floppy disk.**

Stan has twelve computer programs. Nine are games, two are writing programs, and one is a program for composing music. Together, these twelve programs make up Stan's (1) library.

Stan runs these programs on his (2), which consists of a monitor with a screen, a (3) for typing in information, and a Central Processing Unit called a (4), which Stan has nicknamed Brainiac. Stan has taken Brainiac apart to look at the (5) that hold its memory.

Stan works after school at a computer store. He sells both (6), such as monitors and mice, and software. His favorite software (7) are *Babe Ruth's Big League Baseball* and *The Marvelous Mathemagician.*

Stan has bought a new writing program for his computer. It comes on a single (8), which he slides into his computer's disk drive. Seconds later, it's ready to use. Stan begins (9) a story he must write for a composition class. Two hours later he begins (10) his story on his printer; then he settles back to read it.

DID YOU KNOW?

One of the first computer programmers was Rear Admiral Grace Murray Hopper. One day in the 1940s, she found a moth caught in the wires of a computer that had stopped working. Her team pasted the moth in a notebook. It was the first computer "bug." Ever since, the word *bug* has meant a computer problem.

dwarf
double stars
nebula
neutron star
nuclear fusion
black hole
red giant
white dwarfs
supergiants
supernova

SCIENCE

The Stars

Stars are born; they mature, age, and die. Names have been given to their various stages of life. Add other words about stars to the list. Then do the activities. Use your Spelling Dictionary for help.

■ GETTING AT MEANING

A Star Is Born . . . and Dies Read the photo captions on these pages. Then use them and the clues in the sentences to help you fill in the blanks with list words.

New stars are forming through nuclear fusion in this cloud of gas and dust called a nebula.

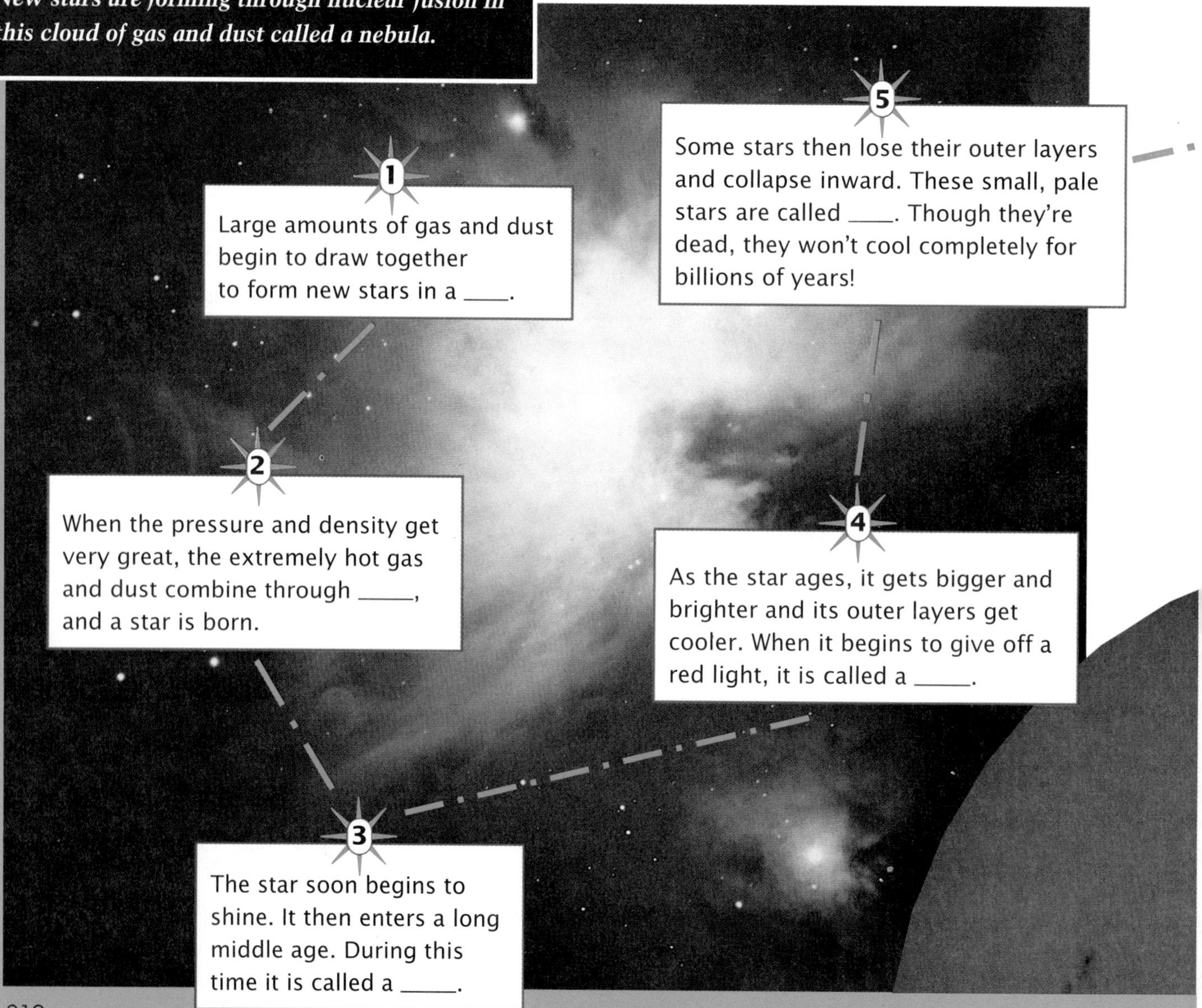

1 Large amounts of gas and dust begin to draw together to form new stars in a ____.

2 When the pressure and density get very great, the extremely hot gas and dust combine through ____, and a star is born.

3 The star soon begins to shine. It then enters a long middle age. During this time it is called a ____.

4 As the star ages, it gets bigger and brighter and its outer layers get cooler. When it begins to give off a red light, it is called a ____.

5 Some stars then lose their outer layers and collapse inward. These small, pale stars are called ____. Though they're dead, they won't cool completely for billions of years!

210

This bright area is the explosion of a supernova.

7 Pairs of stars that are relatively close to each other in space are called ___.

6 Other stars keep growing even larger and brighter as they age. These stars are so huge that they're called ____.

8 A dying star that explodes is called a ____. It can grow bright in days and then take months to fade.

9 Sometimes a supernova leaves behind tightly packed neutrons, which form a ___.

10 After a very large star explodes in a supernova, gravity can pull everything, even light, into the dying star. Because no light escapes, we cannot see this ___.

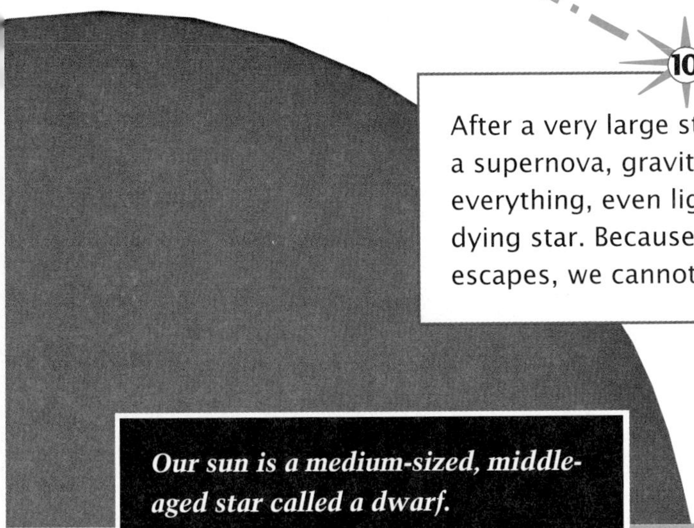

STARRY NIGHT

LOOK IN A LIBRARY FOR A COPY OF VINCENT VAN GOGH'S PAINTING STARRY NIGHT. HOW DO YOU THINK VAN GOGH FELT ABOUT THE STARS? WRITE A SHORT EXPLANATION.

Our sun is a medium-sized, middle-aged star called a dwarf.

211

Looking at Yourself

resolved
positive
sympathetic
timid
strain
objectives
self-image
outgoing
candid
seriously

The list words describe feelings and issues that many adolescents deal with every day. Think of two more words and add them to the list. Then do the activities. Use your Spelling Dictionary for help.

■ GETTING AT MEANING

Dear Friend, . . . Complete each letter with words from the list.

October 15

Dear Jenna,

Moving to a new state can be hard on a person. I've been under some real (1) lately. I'm still the new kid in school, so I haven't made any close friends yet. (You know me—I'm not outspoken and (2) like you are.) I am determined to keep an upbeat, (3) outlook, though, so I've set some definite (4) for myself. What do you think of them?

#1: Don't be so (5)! Put yourself out there and make yourself talk to one new person each day.

#2: Don't take things so (6). Lighten up and laugh more often—especially at yourself.

#3: Like yourself. Maintain a good (7). Accept yourself for who you are, even if other people don't!

So, Jen, write soon and tell me what you honestly think of my objectives.

Take care,
Cassandra

October 22

Dear Cass,

Sorry things are a bit rocky for you there, but they'll get better. You asked what I think of your objectives. Well, since you asked for my (8) opinion . . . I think they're great! I've (9) to use them myself, and I've added one more:

#4: Try to be kind to others and share their feelings—be (10). It may be just as hard for them to make new friends as it is for you!

Write and tell me how things are going.

Keep your chin up,

Jenna

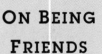

ON BEING FRIENDS

With your classmates, compile a list (or a book) of serious, sarcastic, and humorous quotes on friendship. Here are a few to get you started:

"If you have one true friend you have more than your share."
—Thomas Fuller

"Treat your friends as you do your pictures, and place them in their best light."
—Jennie Jerome Churchill

"Animals are such agreeable friends—they ask no questions, they pass no criticisms."
—George Eliot

"A friend is one who dislikes the same people you dislike."
—Anonymous

overwhelming
perilous
feat
pitfalls
liberate
surviving
suspense
thrive
undaunted
genuine

READING

Meeting Challenges

Many books and articles tell of people meeting challenges. Add two more words about challenges to the list. Use your Spelling Dictionary if you need help with the activity.

■ GETTING AT MEANING

At the Movies Complete the interview with list words. Use the captions to help you.

Guy Nosey: I'm talking with famous film spy Jane Bond on the set of *Taking the Plunge* as she prepares to plunge into this tank, (1) herself from her chains, and swim to safety before the sharks can make a snack of her. Tell us, Jane, why aren't you using a stunt double to accomplish this (2) of daring? It's extremely (3), isn't it?

Jane: Well, Guy, I've practiced this stunt so often that I'm prepared for any of the many (4) that I might encounter. I'm confident my attempt will be an (5) success.

Thrown into shark-infested waters . . .

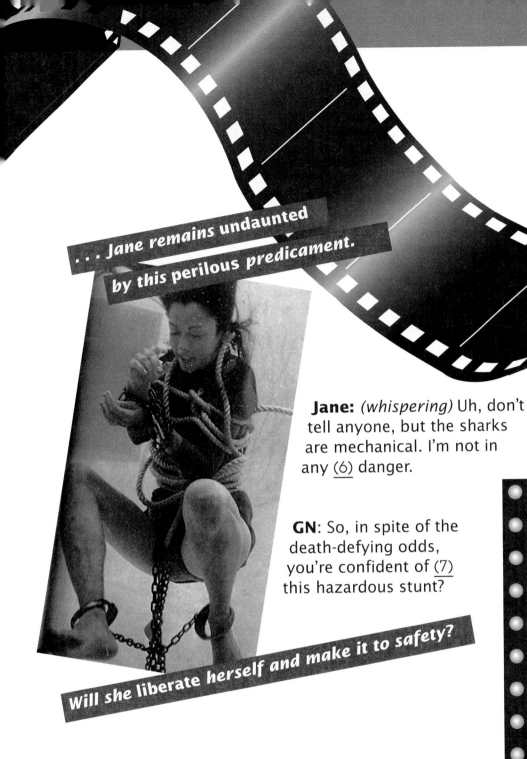

... Jane remains undaunted by this perilous predicament.

Jane: *(whispering)* Uh, don't tell anyone, but the sharks are mechanical. I'm not in any (6) danger.

GN: So, in spite of the death-defying odds, you're confident of (7) this hazardous stunt?

Will she liberate herself and make it to safety?

Jane: As always, I remain (8) in the face of peril. Actually, I (9) on it! *(whispering)* I also could use the publicity. It's good for my career!

GN: Well, ladies and gentleman, there you have it. Now, I don't know about you, but the (10) is killing me. Will Jane be successful, or will she be shark food? I can't wait to see what happens next.

MOVIE POSTER

CREATE AN ADVERTISING POSTER FOR AN ADVENTURE, SCIENCE FICTION, OR HORROR MOVIE. USE LIST WORDS AS WELL AS THEIR SYNONYMS AND ANTONYMS TO DESCRIBE SOME OF THE OTHER CHALLENGES THE MAIN CHARACTERS FACE.

quest
traditional
obstacle
persevered
suitors
expectations
reunion
understanding
melancholy
despair

Searching for Who You Are

Many stories tell of a quest. A man or woman goes in search of something, faces obstacles, and in the end is rewarded. Can you recognize the typical patterns of such a story? Think of two words to add to the list. Use your Spelling Dictionary if you need help with the activity.

■ GETTING AT MEANING

Understanding Traditional Tales
Use the list words to complete this legend.

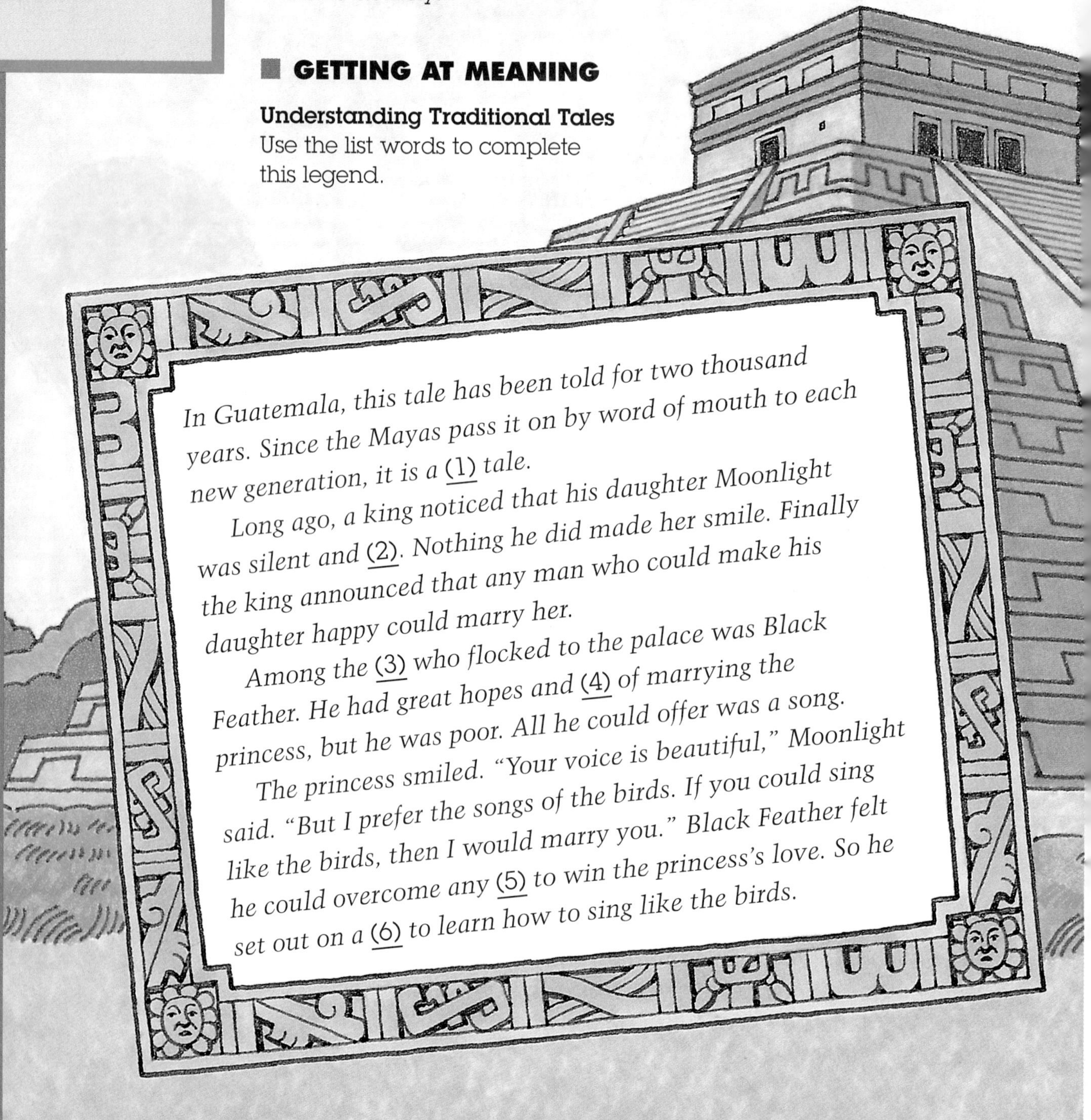

In Guatemala, this tale has been told for two thousand years. Since the Mayas pass it on by word of mouth to each new generation, it is a (1) tale.

Long ago, a king noticed that his daughter Moonlight was silent and (2). Nothing he did made her smile. Finally the king announced that any man who could make his daughter happy could marry her.

Among the (3) who flocked to the palace was Black Feather. He had great hopes and (4) of marrying the princess, but he was poor. All he could offer was a song. The princess smiled. "Your voice is beautiful," Moonlight said. "But I prefer the songs of the birds. If you could sing like the birds, then I would marry you." Black Feather felt he could overcome any (5) to win the princess's love. So he set out on a (6) to learn how to sing like the birds.

216

Black Feather listened to the songs of hundreds of birds, but he could not sing like them. He began to (7) of ever completing his task.

It was then that the Great Spirit of the Woods appeared. "I have watched your struggle," the Great Spirit said. "Because you have (8) and have not given up, I will help you." The Great Spirit hollowed out a tree branch, cut holes in it, and gave it to the young man. "This is a chirimia," the Great Spirit said. "Learn to play it well." Black Feather practiced until he had gained a complete (9) of how to play the flute.

When Black Feather returned to the palace, the princess heard his chirimia. It was filled with the songs of the birds. Black Feather and the princess had a joyful (10) and were soon married. Today in Guatemala, you can still hear the sweet sounds of the chirimia.

MODERN QUESTS

THINK OF A STORY YOU HAVE READ THAT TELLS OF A QUEST.

THE STORY COULD BE MODERN REALISTIC FICTION OR IT COULD BE A TRADITIONAL TALE. MAKE UP A BOOK JACKET THAT HIGHLIGHTS THE QUEST ASPECTS OF THE STORY.

Stories About America

historical fiction
setting
harsh
petition
emigrates
represents
traditions
Civil War
looms
civil rights

Is there a period in American history you're curious about? Historical fiction, fiction based on historical fact, will show you what it was like to live during a time in the past. Think of two more words about historical fiction to add to the word list. Use your Spelling Dictionary if you need help with the activity.

■ GETTING AT MEANING

Plot Summaries Use list words to complete the description of each book. Then think about which book you would most enjoy reading.

[NEBRASKA]

✐ A Czech family struggles to farm despite the rugged, (1) conditions on the Nebraska prairie. Antonia's quiet strength (2) the spirit of all the farmers who first cultivated the soil of the American heartland.

[CALIFORNIA]

[OKLAHOMA]

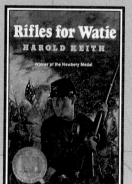

✐ A young Union soldier becomes a spy and briefly joins the Cherokee Indian rebels who fought for the South in the American (5). There is suspense and a realistic view of war in this book of (6).

✐ The San Francisco earthquake of 1906 is only one of the things Moon Shadow copes with when he (3) from China to California to join his father. Moon Shadow is sustained in a hostile new world by the beliefs and values that make up the rich (4) of the Chinese community.

The mill town of Lowell, Massachusetts, seems to offer independence for poor farm girls in the 1840s. But as a factory girl working the huge mechanical (7) that weave cloth for the textile factories, Lyddie faces long hours, low pay, and dangerous work. Should she sign the workers' (8) demanding better conditions, or will that only make things worse?

[MASSACHUSETTS]

North Carolina in 1963 is the (9) of this book. When her Uncle Pete joins the freedom riders, Sheryl realizes that she also wants to help in the (10) movement that is spreading across the country.

[NORTH CAROLINA]

FACTFACTFACTFACTFACT

TURN HISTORY INTO FICTION

FIND AN INFORMATIONAL ARTICLE ON A PERIOD IN U.S. HISTORY YOU'RE INTERESTED IN. HOW COULD YOU TURN THE INFORMATION INTO A FICTIONAL STORY? OUTLINE THE STORY; DESCRIBE THE MAIN CHARACTERS, THE SETTING, AND THE BEGINNING OF THE PLOT.

FICTIONFICTIONFICTION

Consumer Topics

- simple interest
- compound interest
- principal
- unit prices
- commission
- percent of increase
- percent of decrease
- credit
- installments
- budget

For consumers, good money management involves spending and saving in ways that make the most of their earnings. The list words are related to consumer concerns. Add other words that you know, and then do the activity. Use your Spelling Dictionary for help if you need it.

GETTING AT MEANING

Clipping Clues Use the newspaper clippings to complete the paragraphs with list words.

Stan recently graduated from college and started a sales job with a base salary plus a 2 percent (1). Because he wants to make the best use of his money, he prepared a detailed (2) in which he listed his income and expenses. As part of his expenses, he included the monthly payments, or (3), that he makes on the car he purchased on (4) last year.

HELP WANTED SALES

Enthusiastic person wanted for fast-paced sales position. Base salary plus 2 percent **commission** and benefits.

Incredible Deals at Buy-Now Auto Dealership

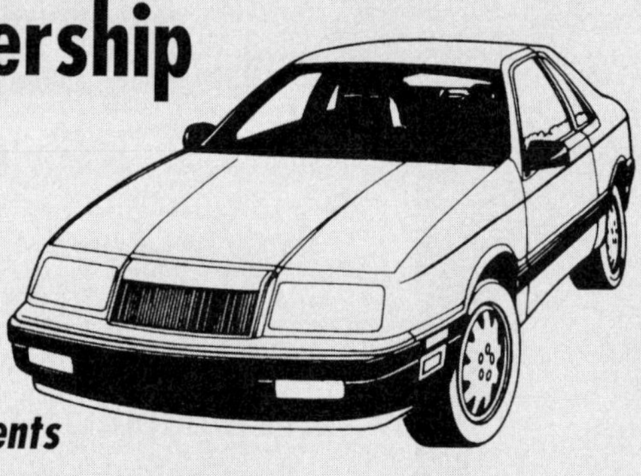

*Special prices on 1,000 new and used cars. Instant **credit** available with **installments** that will fit your **budget**. Don't miss this chance!*

Earn More at Save-Quick Bank

*Don't settle for **simple interest**! Come to Save-Quick Bank and watch your **principal** grow fast with the best **compound interest** plan in town! Earn the maximum interest on interest!*

Smart Shoppers Save $$

By shopping wisely, using coupons, and comparing **unit prices** of competing brands, some shoppers have experienced a **percent of decrease** in their spending even during a time when prices have shown a **percent of increase.**

Stan shops for food carefully, always checking the (5) of all the items he buys. When he noticed prices rising during the last few months, he computed the (6) and found it to be 2 percent. In spite of this, by using coupons and watching ads for sale prices, Stan experienced a $1\frac{1}{2}$ (7) in his own spending during the same period.

With his first paycheck, Stan opened a savings account with a (8) of $100. He chose an account that offered (9) because his savings would increase faster than they would with (10).

DID YOU KNOW?

Buying on credit is nothing new. According to records of the time, some people in ancient Rome paid for their houses using installment plans!

221

The Real Number System

The numbers we deal with in everyday life are in the real number system. The list contains math terminology used to describe real numbers. If you can, add more words to the list. Then do the activities. Use your Spelling Dictionary if you need help.

GETTING AT MEANING

Conversation Clues Study the number line and the five characters' conversation. Then complete the sentences with list words. (Use the number line for items 1–5.)

$$3.45 \times 10^{-2}$$

I AM A NUMBER WRITTEN AS **SCIENTIFIC NOTATION.** MY **STANDARD FORM** IS 0.0345.

"THE THREE OF US ARE RATIONAL NUMBERS."

-0.3

I AM A **REPEATING DECIMAL.** I CAN ALSO BE WRITTEN AS THE FRACTION $-\frac{1}{3}$.

0.5

I AM A **TERMINATING DECIMAL.** I CAN ALSO BE WRITTEN AS THE FRACTION $\frac{1}{2}$.

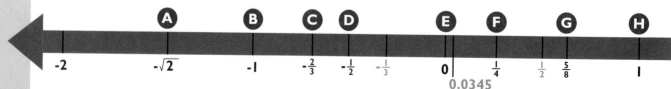

A	B	C	D	E	F	G	H
$-\sqrt{2}$	-1	$-\frac{2}{3}$	$-\frac{1}{2}$ $-\frac{1}{3}$	0	$\frac{1}{4}$	$\frac{1}{2}$ $\frac{5}{8}$	1

-2 ....

0.0345

"WE'RE ALL RE

Find out the distances between the sun and each of the planets in the solar system. On a large sheet of drawing paper or poster board, draw the sun and the planets in their correct positions relative to one another, and label each sun-to-planet distance in both standard form and scientific notation.

1. ALL THE POINTS ON THE NUMBER LINE REPRESENT _____.

2. POINTS A AND J EACH REPRESENT AN _____.

3. IN ITS DECIMAL FORM, POINT C REPRESENTS A _____.

4. EACH OF THE LABELED POINTS EXCEPT A AND J REPRESENTS A _____.

5. IN ITS DECIMAL FORM, POINT G REPRESENTS A _____.

6. SINCE THE SQUARE ROOT OF 64 IS 8, 64 IS A _____.

7. IN 8^3, 8 IS THE _____.

8. SINCE $10^2 = 100$, THE _____ OF 100 IS 10.

Using a Chart Study the chart. Then use it to complete the sentences with list words.

STANDARD FORM	SCIENTIFIC NOTATION
0.0015	1.5×10^{-3}
3,800,000	3.8×10^{6}
9	9.0×10^{0}

9. THE MAXIMUM DISTANCE FROM THE EARTH TO THE SUN IS NINETY-FOUR MILLION FIVE HUNDRED THOUSAND MILES. THAT NUMBER, WRITTEN IN _____, IS 9.45×10^7.

10. IN _____ THAT NUMBER IS WRITTEN 94,500,000.

I AM A **PERFECT SQUARE.** MY **SQUARE ROOT** IS 4 BECAUSE $4^2 = 16$. THE **BASE** IN THE NUMBER 4^2 IS 4.

I AM AN **IRRATIONAL NUMBER.** I CANNOT BE WRITTEN AS A FRACTION. MY DECIMAL FORM DOES NOT REPEAT OR TERMINATE.

$$\sqrt{2}$$

| 1.$\overline{3}$ | $\sqrt{3}$ | 2 | | 3 | | 4 |

AL NUMBERS."

Geometry

Three-dimensional geometric figures can be seen all around us.
The word list contains the names of some of these figures and
various terms used in measuring them. Add more words. Use
your Spelling Dictionary if you need help with the activity.

■ GETTING AT MEANING

Diagrams Study the diagrams on both pages and then complete
the sentences on the next page with list words.

*TO FIND HOW MANY CUBIC UNITS
FIT INSIDE A **THREE-DIMENSIONAL**
FIGURE, COMPUTE ITS **VOLUME.**
TO FIND THE VOLUME OF A
RECTANGULAR PRISM, USE THIS
FORMULA:*

$$V = LWH$$

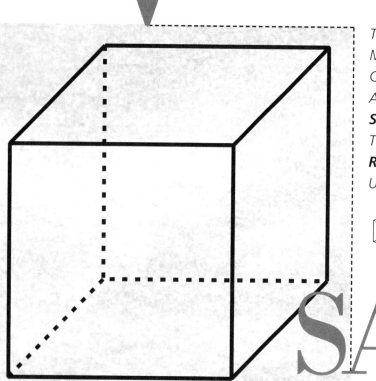

*TO FIND HOW MUCH
MATERIAL IS NEEDED TO
COVER THE OUTSIDE OF
A FIGURE, COMPUTE ITS
SURFACE AREA. TO FIND
THE SURFACE AREA OF A
RECTANGULAR PRISM,
USE THIS FORMULA:*

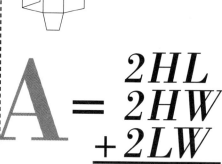

$$SA = \begin{matrix} 2HL \\ 2HW \\ +2LW \end{matrix}$$

OTHER THREE-DIMENSIONAL FIGURES

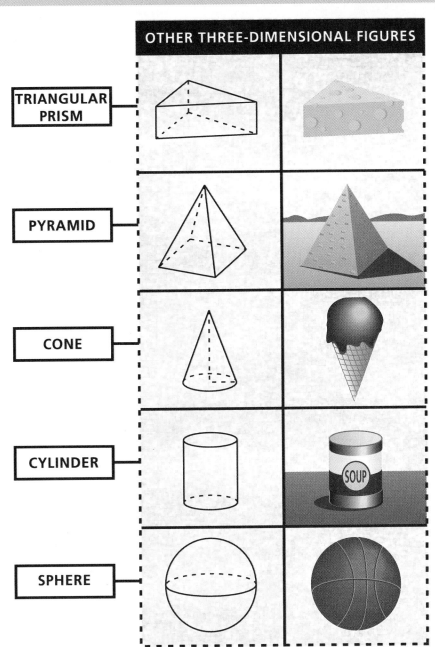

TRIANGULAR PRISM

PYRAMID

CONE

CYLINDER

SPHERE

A SHOE BOX HAS THE SHAPE OF A (1).

THE LEAST AMOUNT OF PAPER NEEDED TO WRAP A GIFT BOX IS THE SAME AS THE (2) OF THE BOX.

THE BASES OF A (3) EACH HAVE THREE SIDES.

A SOUP CAN HAS THE SHAPE OF A (4).

WHEN PACKING A CRATE WITH BOXES, IT WOULD HELP TO KNOW THE (5) OF THE CRATE.

CYLINDERS, PRISMS, AND PYRAMIDS ARE ALL (6) FIGURES.

FOLLOWING A RECIPE IS LIKE USING A (7).

A BASKETBALL HAS THE SHAPE OF A (8).

A (9) AND A (10) EACH HAVE ONLY ONE BASE.

AMAZING ARCHITECTURE

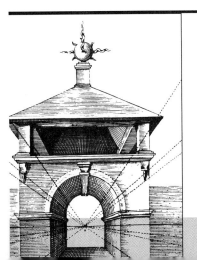

Most buildings are in the shape of a rectangular prism. However, architects sometimes use unusual shapes in their designs. Draw your own design of a building that uses at least three different shapes besides rectangular prisms. Use magazines or books to get ideas. Label each part of the building with its geometric name.

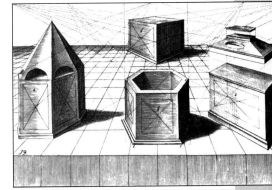

Algebra

evaluate
variable
solve
equation
inequality
solution
mathematical
  expression
parentheses
grouping
  symbols
order of
  operations

Algebra expresses mathematical ideas using numbers, symbols, and variables. The words in the list are important in algebra. Add more words to the list. Use your Spelling Dictionary if you need help with the activities.

■ GETTING AT MEANING

Sentence Completion Read the story carefully. Then choose the correct list word from each pair of list words in brackets on the next page.

Derrick's school is competing in an academic contest. Derrick is on the math team. For the first practice problem, the team must **evaluate** the **mathematical expression** $5x + (x - 4)$ **when** $x = -9$. First a team member substitutes -9 for the **variable** x. Then another member does the subtraction within the **parentheses.** Since there are no other **grouping symbols,** the team members then do the multiplication and addition, using the standard **order of operations.** Another problem requires the team to **solve** the **equation** $x - 17 = 24$. Their answer, $x = 41$, is correct because $41 - 17 = 24$. Another problem involved finding out if -5 is a **solution** for the **inequality** $x + 4 < -24$. The team's answer was "no" because substituting -5 for x does not make the sentence true.

The 1 [equation, mathematical expression] $2x + 3$ does not have any 2 [grouping symbols, variables].

The sentence $3x = -12$ is an 3 [equation, inequality]. If you 4 [evaluate, solve] it correctly, you will find that $x = -4$.

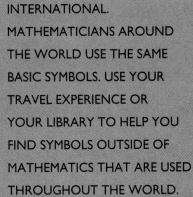

Universal Understanding

THE LANGUAGE OF MATHEMATICS IS INTERNATIONAL. MATHEMATICIANS AROUND THE WORLD USE THE SAME BASIC SYMBOLS. USE YOUR TRAVEL EXPERIENCE OR YOUR LIBRARY TO HELP YOU FIND SYMBOLS OUTSIDE OF MATHEMATICS THAT ARE USED THROUGHOUT THE WORLD. DESCRIBE OR DRAW THESE SYMBOLS.

To 5 [evaluate, solve] $8 - 3(x + 5)$, substitute a number for the 6 [solution, variable], compute within the 7 [parentheses, order of operations], and follow the standard 8 [order of operations, grouping symbols].

The 9 [equation, inequality] $3x + 1 < 9$ has more than one 10 [solution, variable].

DID YOU KNOW?

Algebra is generally considered to have begun in 1591. In that year Francois Vieté, a French mathematician, first used variables to describe patterns. Vieté's work quickly led to a great deal more mathematics being invented.

Consumer Topics 2

Most consumers earn, spend, save, and invest money. The list contains words related to these activities. Add other words, using your Spelling Dictionary if you need help with this activity.

■ GETTING AT MEANING

Family Finances The Matthews family keeps a family income summary, along with some helpful newspaper articles. Study the items from this file and then fill each blank with a list word.

Susan Matthews is learning good financial habits from her parents, Ceretha and Max. When deciding how much she could afford for apartment rent, she knew that she couldn't consider her total salary, or (1), as being available.

She had to subtract (2) first, and then consider the result: her (3).

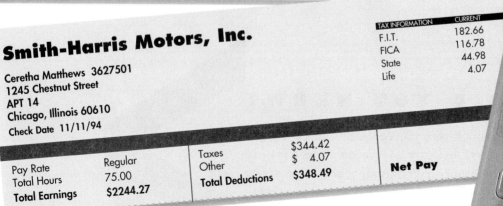

The Home Mart

	MINIMUM DUE	NEW BALANCE	AMOUNT PAID
	20.00	175.98	
	20.00	175.98	

37009-KB

The Home Mart
100 South Mall Plaza
Chicago, IL 60606

ADDRESS
CITY   ST   ZIP
PHONE #
PLEASE INDICATE ANY
ADDRESS OR PHONE #
CHANGES ABOVE

BILLING DATE 11/15/94

ACCOUNT NUMBER 111-333-411

Ceretha Matthews
1245 Chestnut Street
APT 14
Chicago, IL 60610

MAIL THIS PORTION WITH YOUR PAYMENT

1000100040583949944000048396

DATE	REFERENCE	STORE/DEPT	DESCRIPTION	AMOUNT
10/26	01028726	17-48	GOURMET	26.09
11/09	01023455	17-48	APPLIANCES	124.99
11/14	01028911	15-56	HOME ACCENTS	24.90

Smith-Harris Motors, Inc.

Ceretha Matthews 3627501
1245 Chestnut Street
APT 14
Chicago, Illinois 60610
Check Date 11/11/94

TAX INFORMATION	CURRENT	
F.I.T.	182.66	
FICA	116.78	
State	44.98	
Life	4.07	

Pay Rate	Regular	Taxes	$344.42	Net Pay
Total Hours	75.00	Other	$ 4.07	
Total Earnings	**$2244.27**	**Total Deductions**	**$348.49**	

Comparison Shopping Is Worth the Time, Experts Say

Results of a study just release[d] composed of financial expert[s] indicate that in the long run [it] helps consumers save substa[ntial] [on] purchases.

Investment in Local Utility Pays Off!

Municipal Electric Company's increase in **profit** means investors will receive a $0.02 per share increase in dividend. After a somewhat sluggish start, Municipal Electric's market activity appears to have been taking a consistent upward swing. Investors who have been with Municipal Electric from the beginning are really seeing their investments multiply!

Susan also needs to consider other expenses, like (4) bills. Even in applying for charge accounts, Susan makes a careful (5) of the (6) of interest charged by each company. Susan knows that she can avoid a (7) if she pays the new balance each month and never has an (8). Susan recently made an (9) in some stock. If the company she invested in makes a (10), then the value of her stock should increase.

COMPARING CREDIT

Gather data about three different credit cards from department stores, gasoline companies, or banks. Ask about the annual rate, the credit limit, the payment schedule, and the minimum payment required. Also find out if an annual fee is charged and if special discounts are available with the card. Then write a report about your findings.

Writer's Handbook

INTRODUCTION

Spelling is an important part of writing. Since writing is a form of communication, if your spelling is unclear, your communication could be unclear as well. This handbook will tell you some time of the other things you need to know in order to become a better writer.

CONTENTS

Writing Traits

FOCUS/IDEAS

Good writers focus on a **main idea** and develop this idea with strong, supporting details. In addition, they know their purpose for writing. This purpose may be to persuade, to inform, to describe, or to entertain. Your purpose is important because it helps you focus your main idea.

Even a postcard has a main idea and a purpose.

Dear Lee,
    The cookout at camp was great! We sang songs while the hot dogs cooked over the flames and the owls hooted. Wish you were here.
              Best,
              Craig

Main Idea Craig is enjoying camp.
Purpose To inform Lee

Details This postcard gives Lee a glimpse of camp life. Details make the writing lively. Compare these two sentences:
- Camp is busy and fun. (dull, with few details)
- We hike in the green hills, paddle aluminum kayaks, and rehearse for the camp musical. (adds color and information)

STRATEGIES FOR CHOOSING A MAIN IDEA AND PURPOSE
- Choose a topic that you can handle. For example, "The History of the England" is too large a topic for a brief essay.
- Let your purpose fit the topic. For example, a funny story is entertaining; a comparison-contrast of two movies is informative.

ORGANIZATION

Every piece of writing needs some kind of **organization**. Writing's structure is like the frame of a house. It holds everything together and gives a shape to ideas and details.

Here are some ways to organize your writing:
- A narrative with a beginning, middle, and end
- A step-by-step set of instructions
- A comparison-contrast of two people, places, or things
- A description of something from left to right
- An explanation of causes and effects
- A persuasive piece with the best reason last

Before you write, consider how best to shape your ideas. For example, if you were explaining how to build a birdhouse, a set of instructions would work. If you are sharing a personal experience, a narrative is the form to use.

Deciding on the form of your writing is just the first step. Consider how all of your ideas connect to the topic. What organization would best present your ideas?

STRATEGIES FOR ORGANIZING YOUR IDEAS
- Create a graphic organizer such as a web, outline, chart, or sketch.
- Order the steps from first to last.
- Introduce characters, set the scene, and show action.
- Save the most important idea until last, and build up to it.
- Use sequence words such as *first, later,* and *now.*
- Use signal words such as *both* and *neither* to show comparisons.

VOICE

Every writer has a **voice**—a personality that comes through in the tone and style of a piece of writing. Voice shows that a writer knows and cares about a topic. It also reveals a certain style and tone.

A writer with a strong, clear voice speaks directly to readers and keeps their attention.

- I stood on the bridge and looked at the water. (weak voice)
- I leaned over the railing of the bridge, scowling down at the muddy, brown waters of the river. (strong voice)

Your voice should take into account what the reader needs to know. Your topic, audience, and purpose will determine your voice.

STRATEGIES FOR DEVELOPING YOUR VOICE

- Be sure of your purpose and audience. A review of a school play that flopped might have a humorous, light voice. An argument for more lifeguards at the town beach demands a serious, thoughtful voice.
- Select words that match your voice. When you write dialogue for characters in a story, you can use contractions *(I've, it's)* along with slang. Figurative language can make your voice interesting and colorful. Formal writing, such as research reports and business letters, requires exact, objective vocabulary.
- Remember that your voice shapes and controls your ideas. Whatever you write about, express yourself in an engaging, appropriate voice.

WORD CHOICE

Good writers always search for the perfect **words** to express an idea. Precise nouns, strong verbs, and vivid adjectives make their writing unforgettable.

The examples below show how careful word choice brings writing to life.

- London is an example of a foggy city and is covered with thick clouds much of the time. (dull and wordy)
- London's fog is a fine mist that blankets its streets and chills its citizens. (vivid and precise)

STRATEGIES FOR IMPROVING YOUR WORD CHOICE

- Appeal to the senses. (*The elephant's hide was cracked like dry earth* instead of *The elephant's skin looked dry; The moon hangs like a pearl earring* instead of *The moon is white and round*)
- Use precise nouns. (*heron* instead of *bird; skyscraper* instead of *building*)
- Harness the power of strong verbs. (*whisper* instead of *say; galloped* instead of *ran*)
- Eliminate wordiness. (*I believe* instead of *It is my opinion that*)
- Banish empty words such as *good, cute, stuff,* and *nice.* Choose words with meaning. (*The cellar held battered trunks, rusted lawnmowers, and countless cardboard boxes* instead of *The cellar was full of stuff*)
- Try rewriting sentences that depend on linking verbs such as *is, am,* and *were.* (*The bell jangled in my ears* instead of *The bell was loud*)
- Find words that make magic on the page: *shadowy, harsh, glimmer, devastated.* Jot these words down in a writer's notebook for future reference.

SENTENCES

> Good writing has a natural flow. **Sentences** that vary in structure and length create a readable style. When writing follows the rhythms of speech, it is a pleasure to read aloud.

Here are some ways to improve your sentences.
- Vary sentence types. Use interrogative, exclamatory, and imperative sentences along with declarative sentences.
- Write sentences of varying lengths.
- Begin sentences with words other than *the, I,* or *it.*
- Use connectors. Show relationships between ideas with words such as *although, but, next, while,* and *however.* Don't rely too heavily on *and, so,* and *because.*

STRATEGY FOR IMPROVING YOUR SENTENCES

Reread a piece of your writing and number each sentence. Then make a chart like the one below and examine each sentence.

Sentence number	Number of words	First word	Type of sentence (Interrogative, Declarative Imperative, Exclamatory)	Connector words

As you fill out your chart, look for areas to improve. You may learn that you overuse *but* or *and* to connect ideas. Maybe your sentences could be longer and more varied. When you revise your writing, improve these areas.

CONVENTIONS

Conventions are rules for written language. They are the signals that writers use to make their meaning clear to readers. For example, sentences begin with a capital letter and end with punctuation. Paragraphs are indented to show where a new idea begins. Grammar and spelling follow patterns.

Writing with strong conventions is easier to read.

- sam and he frens walkd to the stor they buyed ice creem (weak conventions)
- Sam and his friends walked to the store. They bought ice cream. (strong conventions)

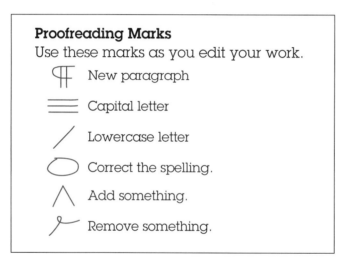

Proofreading Marks
Use these marks as you edit your work.

New paragraph

Capital letter

Lowercase letter

Correct the spelling.

Add something.

Remove something.

STRATEGIES FOR FOLLOWING WRITING CONVENTIONS

- Make sure sentences are complete, with correct capitalization and punctuation.
- Use a dictionary or spell-checker to check spelling.
- Choose the correct forms of pronouns, especially pronouns that are compound subjects or objects.
- Do not change verb tenses without a reason.
- Check the use of apostrophes in possessive nouns and contractions.

Taking Writing Tests

These tips should make the task of taking writing tests easier.

GENERAL GUIDELINES FOR WRITING TESTS

- **Follow instructions carefully.** Listen closely for how much time you have, what you should use to write (pen, pencil, or computer), when you should begin and end, and any special instructions.
- **Read the assignment and identify the key words.** Before you begin writing, make sure you clearly understand what the directions are asking you to do. Here are some key words that often appear in test directions:

    Categorize or *Classify:* Sort ideas or facts into groups.

    Compare and Contrast: Point out similarities (compare) and differences (contrast).

    Defend: Give evidence to show why a view is right.

    Define: Tell what something is or means.

    Describe: Create a word picture with details and examples.

    Discuss: State your ideas about what something means.

    Evaluate: Give your opinion, with support, on whether an idea is good or bad, right or wrong.

    Explain: Make something clear by giving reasons, examples, or steps.

    Summarize: State main points, or retell important parts of a story.

- **Plan how you'll use your time.** Allot some time at the start to plan out what you will write. Save time at the end to reread and catch any errors.
- **Write a strong opening** to catch your readers' attention. Be sure it specifically addresses the topic of the assignment.
- **Use specific facts and details** to develop your ideas. Be sure to put them in the proper order or form.
- **Take time to wrap things up.** Don't stop writing just because your time is up. Use the last few minutes to write a strong conclusion that pulls things together.

Models

NARRATIVE WRITING

Narrative writing tells a story, which always has a beginning, middle, and end. Sometimes it entertains, instructs, or helps the reader understand an issue or event.

> Last summer, while hiking on Mount Neeweeshaw, I walked into a waking nightmare. My dad and I stopped to rest. It was scorching, so I wandered over to sit in the shade of a boulder.
>
> Then I heard a strange buzzing. A warning bell went off in my head. Danger is near! My heart thumped like a wild rabbit, but I didn't move a muscle. Moving just my eyes, I could see a shape like a coil of rope. It was a big snake! I knew by the diamond pattern on its back and the rattles at the end of its tail that I was in trouble. The rattler was warning, "I will strike!"
>
> Sweat ran down my arms and legs. I wanted like crazy to run away, but somehow I made myself sit still. Finally, the snake slithered off. The danger had passed, but I was still shaking.

What makes it sound writing? Here's how the writer uses the six traits of good writing to make the piece enjoyable to read.

Focus/Ideas Details focused on writer's terrified reaction
Organization Strong beginning, middle, and end; connectors clarify sequence, cause and effect (*so, then, finally*)
Voice Writer's personal involvement clear (*warning bell went off in my head, heart thumped like a wild rabbit*)
Word Choice Exact nouns (*boulder, rattler*); strong verbs (*thumped, slithered*); vivid adjectives (*scorching, diamond*)
Sentences Good sentence variety; mimics natural speech
Conventions No errors

EXPOSITORY WRITING

Expository writing is meant to inform the reader. It often describes a process or offers a report on an event of some kind.

Everybody loves pizza, and this French bread pizza is quick and easy to make. First, get out the things you need: a sharp knife, a cookie sheet, a loaf of French bread, pizza sauce, shredded mozzarella cheese, and any other toppings you want.

Next, turn the oven on to 400°F. While it is heating up, carefully slice the bread in half the long way. Now spread pizza sauce to cover the top of the bread. Then cover the sauce with cheese. How much you use depends on how much you like cheese. Do not put on too much cheese, or some will fall off the bread and onto the cookie sheet.

Finally, add your favorite toppings, such as peppers, olives, sausage, or pepperoni. Place your pizza on the cookie sheet and bake it for 15 minutes. Let it cool for a few minutes and bite in!

What makes it sound writing? Here's how the writer uses the six traits of good writing to make the piece informative and enjoyable to read.

Focus/Ideas Clear main idea; all details explain the steps clearly

Organization Clear introduction; steps in order; helpful connectors (*First, Next, While, Now, Then, Finally*)

Voice Warm and helpful, but serious about process

Word Choice Precise nouns (*knife, cookie sheet, loaf, pizza sauce*) and specific verbs (*slice, spread, cover, bake*)

Sentences Imperative sentences consistent with how-to format

Conventions No errors

DESCRIPTIVE WRITING

Descriptive writing portrays people, places, and things in lively, vivid writing.

Some people think a fish makes a poor pet, but they never met my goldfish Mutt. He may not fetch or purr, but Mutt is beautiful, smart, and entertaining.

While most goldfish are solid orange-gold, Mutt looks as though an artist painted parts of him a velvety black. When he swims, his long fins and tail wave and shimmer. He is a silk kite with streamers.

I think Mutt is intelligent because he knows when it is time to eat. As soon as I get the food flakes, he glides close to me and points his mouth at the surface. He likes attention and comes close when I press my face to the glass. Then, at bedtime, he retires to his plastic "house."

Watching Mutt swim gracefully and slowly or dart like lightning around his aquarium keeps me entertained for hours. If I am tired or upset, Mutt gives me a calm, restful feeling.

What makes it sound writing? Here's how the writer uses the six traits of good writing to make the piece lively and enjoyable to read.

Focus/Ideas Strong, specific details that bring subject into focus

Organization Organized by traits, one per paragraph; strong beginning and ending

Voice Clear communication of bond with pet; strong writer presence (*I press my face to the glass*)

Word Choice Vivid verbs and modifiers that appeal to sight (*fetch, velvety, shimmer, gracefully, dart*), hearing (*purr*), and feeling (*calm, restful*); metaphor (*a silk kite with streamers*)

Sentences Interest through varied kinds and lengths of sentences; combined ideas

Conventions No errors

PERSUASIVE WRITING

Persuasive writing attempts to convince readers to accept a writer's position on a particular issue.

Go, Bulldogs, go! We should adopt the bulldog as our school mascot because there is so much to admire in a bulldog.

First, we say that the dog is a person's best friend. A best friend is always there for you and supports you. Loyalty is part of a winning attitude for people, too.

Second, like all dogs, bulldogs love people. A bulldog takes care of its family. For example, it would defend you from harm. Students at Benton Elementary are like a family, and a bulldog mascot would stand for the way we take care of each other.

Most important, a bulldog is strong and a great fighter. Once it grabs on, it doesn't let go. Don't we want to have that kind of staying power? If we play a game or meet a goal, we will give it our best and won't quit.

Now, don't you think Benton Bulldogs has a nice ring to it?

What makes it sound writing? Here's how the writer uses the six traits of good writing to make the piece convincing and enjoyable to read.

Focus/Ideas Opinion clearly stated; developed with good supporting reasons and details

Organization Strong introduction; topic sentences give reasons in logical order; most important reason given last

Voice Writer's enthusiasm and personality evident

Word Choice Persuasive words with emotional appeal (*best friend, winning attitude, love, takes care of, family, staying power*)

Sentences Varied structures and kinds; connectors aid flow (*first, second, for example, most important, now*)

Conventions No errors

The Writing Process

Producing a polished piece of writing takes several steps: Prewrite, Draft, Revise, Edit, and Publish.

1. PREWRITE: THINK BEFORE YOU WRITE

Just as it's easier to see in the dark if you have a flashlight, it's easier to write something if you have a plan to guide you. Before you begin writing, take some time and plan ahead.

- **Select a topic.** You can decide what you want to write about by going through your writing journal and rereading your thoughts, feelings, and observations. You might also look through books, magazines, or newspapers for ideas.
- **Determine your purpose and audience.** What is your purpose for writing? Do you want to express certain feelings or opinions? Do you want to explain something? Inform, persuade, or entertain? Who is your audience? Will you address ascertain group, or are you writing only for yourself?
- **Narrow your topic.** Make sure your ideas really do focus on a specific topic. To do this, you might create a web, develop a written outline, logically group words or phrases that pertain to the topic you've chosen.
- **Gather information about your topic.** Depending on what you're writing about, you might take notes from different sources; conduct interviews; list points you want to make; arrange events on a time line; or note how things look, sound, smell, taste, and feel.
- **Organize your information.** Depending on your type of writing and your purpose for writing, you will need to organize by time order, special order, or order of importance.

Prewriting Strategy
Create a Word Web

Word webs can help you narrow your topic. Place your topic in a center oval, then list each word and idea in separate ovals, radiating out from the topic oval. This helps you generate new ideas related to your subject matter, while getting down to specific—thus manageable—issues concerning your topic.

2. DRAFT: PUT YOUR IDEAS ON PAPER

Gather your writing materials, including your prewriting notes and any other resources you may need, and find a quiet, comfortable place to write. Plan on writing for at least twenty minutes. If you have trouble starting, these strategies might help:

- **Set a goal.** Tell yourself you'll write a certain amount, then stick to it.
- **Review your resources.** Examine your notes or journal to come up with an idea for a good opening line or paragraph.
- **Get started!** Set aside all concerns for perfect spelling, punctuation, or capitalization during this drafting stage. You'll have time to revise later. For now, just begin with a sentence that states your main idea in a direct and interesting way. Then let your ideas flow freely.

Drafting Strategy
Write a Strong Opening Paragraph
Attract attention to your writing with an effective opening paragraph. One of the following may help you create a "strong lead":
- An interesting quotation
- A surprising statement
- A detailed, creative description

3. REVISE: MAKE CHANGES TO YOUR DRAFT

When you revise, you reread what you have written, looking for ways to improve it. To begin revising, read your draft to yourself to catch such errors as unclear or unnecessary sentences or ideas that are out of order. Then discuss your writing with other classmates or your teacher. Read your draft aloud and ask for reactions. Did your listeners understand what you were trying to say? Can they suggest ways to improve it?

The following changes may help clarify your writing:
- **Add and subtract** words or ideas.
- **Move** words, sentences, or paragraphs.
- **Substitute** words or ideas to improve your draft.

Revising Strategy
Ask Questions

The questions you ask will depend on your purpose, audience, and type of writing. Here are some questions to help you revise your work:

- Does my writing have a clear beginning, middle, and end?
- Does each paragraph have a topic sentence that sets up or states the main idea?
- Do all my details, events, or reasons support this main idea?
- Are all events, steps, or reasons in the right order?
- Are there any extra or inexact words I should delete or replace? (for example, *because* instead of *the reason was because, devour* instead of *eat*)
- Should I delete any information that doesn't relate to the topic?
- Do I need to add or rearrange information?
- Does any voice shine through? (for example, *he collapsed onto the sofa* instead of *he sat down*)
- Are all my facts and figures correct?
- Have I used language appropriate for my audience and type of writing?
- Are there words or phrases I have overused? Can I replace any of them with synonyms?

4. EDIT: POLISH YOUR WRITING

After revising your first draft, check to see that your work follows conventions. Look for errors in grammar, punctuation, capitalization, and spelling. Proofread once after revising your draft to be sure you have included all corrections. Then proofread again after finishing your final draft.

Use the following questions as a proofreading checklist:
- Did I capitalize all proper nouns and proper adjectives?
- Is each sentence correctly punctuated?
- Have I avoided fragments and run-on sentences?
- Did I keep the correct verb tense throughout?
- Do all subjects and verbs agree?
- Did I check the spelling of any unfamiliar words?
- Did I indent every paragraph?
- If there is a special format for this type of writing, did I follow it?

Editing Strategy
Use Proofreading Marks

The proofreading marks on page 236 can provide you with a quick and efficient way to edit your draft. Give your draft a final read, and use a red pen or pencil to mark errors in grammar, spelling, and punctuation either in the margin or within the text.

5. PUBLISH: LET YOUR WORK SHINE

You do most of your classroom writing with paper and pen. However, the following are some other ways you might present your work:

- Read it aloud
- Share with a few classmates in a writer's circle
- Post it on a class Web site
- Publish it in a school newspaper
- Include it in an illustrated class book
- Submit it to a magazine for publication

Publishing Strategy
Look Your Best

Your teacher may have his or her own rules for how an assignment should look. Be sure you know what those rules are. In general, though, you should make sure that your work is as neat and as easy to read as possible. For instance, indent the first line of each paragraph. Use one-inch margins along the edges of the paper. If you write by hand, write neatly. If you use a computer, choose a clean, easy-to-read font and size. The two examples below have the same text, but the first is much easier to read.

To this day, I have no idea how all those marbles got in there.

To this day, I have no idea how all those marbles got in there.

Dictionary Handbook

Understanding and Using the Dictionary

Have you ever stopped while you were writing to wonder how to spell a word, or while you were reading to wonder what a certain word meant or how to pronounce it? You can find the answers to questions like these when you know how to use a dictionary. This handbook will help you to do this.

1. How do I look up a word quickly?

The **entry words** in a dictionary are arranged in alphabetical order. To find a word quickly, use the pairs of words at the top outside corner of each page—**guide words.** They tell you the first and last entry words on that page. If your word falls in-between the guide words, then you know it's somewhere on that page.

For example, if the guide words are **fly l fog,** you'll find *focus* on that page, but to find *fish* you'll have to turn back a few pages.

Exercise 1   Write two entry words that would appear on the same dictionary page as each set of guide words.

1. remodel l saffron
2. thicken l thistle
3. fellowship l formula
4. captain l center
5. able l arch
6. reindeer l represent
7. fit l foot
8. sick l snowball

2. How do I look up a word I don't know how to spell?

The key is finding out how the word begins. For example, suppose you need to correct this misspelling: "He wanted to become a *sitizen*." How else might the word begin? Think about what letters could make the sound /s/ at the beginning of this word. You know that the letters **s** and **c** are common spellings of this sound, so you try them out.

First, you try *sitizen*. You look through the **guide words** until you find the page headed **sir | size**, but *sitizen* isn't there. So you try *citizen*, and there it is on the page headed **cistern | civilize.**

Exercise 2   Use your Spelling Dictionary to find out which word in each pair is spelled correctly. Write the correct spelling and the guide words from the dictionary page where each is found.

1. dilute—delute
2. engagement—ingagement
3. fenomenon—phenomenon
4. cronicle—chronicle
5. sculpture—skulpture
6. sentennial—centennial

3. What do I do if I still can't find the word?

Most dictionaries have a spelling chart that shows all the possible spellings for each English sound. The part of the chart for the sound /k/ is shown.

k   **c**oat, **k**ind, ba**ck**, e**ch**o, a**ch**e, **q**uit, a**cc**ount, anti**que**, ex**c**ite, a**cq**uire

Notice that there are ten possible spellings for this sound in English. Use the spelling chart if you still can't find a word after you've looked up every spelling you can think of.

Exercise 3   Use the spelling chart called "Spellings of English Sounds" at the beginning of your Spelling Dictionary to answer these questions.

1. How many ways can the sound /f/ be spelled?
2. Which word in the chart has the sound /yü/ spelled the same as in *hue?*
3. Which word in the chart has the sound /zh/ spelled the same as in *treasure?*
4. How many ways can the sound /ə/ be spelled?
5. What are the five ways that the sound /n/ can be spelled?
6. What are the four ways that the sound /r/ can be spelled?

4. How do I know which definition fits my word?

Many words have more than one meaning. In fact, a word like cut has dozens of meanings. You can use the **context** of the word, the **parts of speech** labels, and the **illustrative phrases** and **sentences** provided to help you choose the proper **definition** of your word. What is the definition of the word *fine* in this sentence? "The artist used a single-bristle brush to paint his subject's fine, black eyelashes."

> **fine** (fīn), *adj.* **1** of very high quality; very good; excellent: *a fine view, a fine scholar.* **2** very thin or slender: *fine wire.* **3** sharp: *a tool with a fine edge.* **4** polished; elegant; refined: *fine manners.* **5** subtle: *The law makes fine distinctions.* **6** good-looking; handsome: *a fine young man.* **7** clear; bright: *fine weather.* —**fine′ly**, *adv.* —**fine′ness**, *n.*

From the context of the sentence, you know that the definition you are looking for means "very thin." Reading the definitions, you can see that the one you want is definition 2: very thin or slender.

Exercise 4   Write the part of speech and the number of the definition that fits the italicized word in each sentence. Use your Spelling Dictionary.

1. Our church held a *bazaar* to raise money for the fire victims.
2. Dotted *lines* separated the four lanes of the highway.
3. To everyone's relief, Alice's tumor turned out to be *benign*.
4. We knew just the right *accessories* to go with Jay's suit.
5. We sat on the shore and watched the *outgoing* tide.

5. How can I find out how to pronounce a word?

The entry word is broken into **syllables.** Right after it comes the pronunciation, enclosed in parentheses: **mix▪ture** (miks′chər). The **accent mark** tells you which syllable to emphasize.

The **pronunciation key,** which appears on every page in most dictionaries, shows how to sound out the pronunciations.

Some words can be said in more than one way. For example, two pronunciations are given in your Spelling Dictionary for *advertisement* (ad′vər tīz′mənt or ad vėr′tis mənt). The pronunciation (ad′vər tīz′mənt) is given first, not because it is more correct than (ad vėr′tis mənt), but because it is used by more people. If you say (ad vėr′tis mənt), you are just as correct as those people who say (ad′vər tīz′mənt).

Exercise 5 Write the word that each pronunciation represents. Use the pronunciation key below to help you.

1. (slüth)
2. (ang′kər)
3. (pol′ə se)
4. (ek′sər sīz)
5. (reb′əl or ri bel′)

6. (nō wun)
7. (byùr′ō)
8. (mag′nit)
9. (kwest)
10. (lug′ij)

a	hat	ī	ice	ù	put	ə stands for	
ā	age	o	not	ü	rule	a	in about
ä	far, calm	ō	open	ch	child	e	in taken
âr	care	ȯ	saw	ng	long	i	in pencil
e	let	ô	order	sh	she	o	in lemon
ē	equal	oi	oil	th	thin	u	in circus
ėr	term	ou	out	ŦH	then		
i	it	u	cup	zh	measure		

6. How do I find the correct spelling for a word that is not an entry word?

Sometimes when you add endings such as **-ed, -ing, -s,** and **-es** to words, the spelling changes. These are not listed as entry words. To find the correct spellings of these forms, look up the base word and find the **related forms** in the entry.

Exercise 6 In your Spelling Dictionary, look up the base word of each misspelled related form. Write the related form correctly.

1. manicureist
2. volcanos
3. purchaseable

4. rationaly
5. commutted
6. crisises

7. What if my dictionary lists two ways to spell a word?

Some words may be spelled in more than one way. Sometimes this is shown in a single entry, with the more common spelling first: **R.S.V.P.** or **r.s.v.p.** Other times, different spellings are listed as separate entries, and the definition is given under the more common spelling:

> **ar∎chae∎ol∎o∎gy** (är′kē ol′ə jē), *n.* the scientific study of the people, customs, and life of ancient times. Also, **archeology.**
> **ar∎che∎ol∎o∎gy** (är′kē ol′ə jē), *n.* archaeology.

Exercise 7   Look up these words in your Spelling Dictionary. Write the more common spelling for each word.

1. cuing, cueing
2. teddy bear, Teddy bear
3. extravert, extrovert
4. mah-jongg, mah-jong

8. How do I find out where a word in our language came from originally?

A dictionary also gives you information about how words came into our language. An explanation of a word's origin is called an **etymology**. A word's etymology is usually found at the end of the entry, enclosed in brackets. Read this entry for *calligraphy*.

> **cal ▪ lig ▪ ra ▪ phy** (kə lig′rə fē), *n.* beautiful handwriting. [< Greek *kalligraphia* < *kallos* beauty + *graphein* write]

From the etymology you learn that *calligraphy* came to our language from Greek and means "beautiful writing."

Exercise 8   Use your Spelling Dictionary to find the etymologies of the following words. Write the language, languages, or other source each word came from.

1. liaison
2. mosquito
3. catamaran
4. tycoon
5. okra
6. weird
7. therapy
8. boycott

9. What else can I find in a dictionary entry?

Sometimes an entry is followed by a **synonym study**. These explain subtle differences between words that are closely related in meaning. Look at this entry for the word *revenge:*

> **re ▪ venge** (ri venj′), *n.* harm done in return for a wrong; satisfaction obtained by repayment of an injury, etc.; vengeance: *take revenge, get revenge.* —*v.t.* do harm in return for. See synonym study below
> **Syn.** *v.t.* **Revenge, avenge** mean to punish someone in return for a wrong. **Revenge** applies when it is indulged in to get even: *Gangsters revenge the murder of one of their gang.* **Avenge** applies when the punishment seems just: *They fought to avenge the enemy's invasion of their country.*

Exercise 9   Use **revenge** and **avenge** each in a sentence to illustrate their differences in meaning.

10. Why are there two different entries for some words?

These words are homographs. A **homograph** is a word that is spelled the same as another word but has a different origin and meaning. Look at the two entries for *low*.

> **low**[1] (lō), *adj.* **1** not high or tall; short: *low walls, a low hedge.* **2** in a low place: *a low shelf.* **3** small in amount, degree, force, value, etc.; moderate: *a low price.* —*adv.* **1** in, at, or to a low portion, point, degree, etc.: *Supplies are running low.* **2** near the ground, floor, or base: *fly low.* **3** softly; quietly; not loudly. [< Scandinavian (Old Icelandic) *lāgr*].

> **low**[2] (lō), *v.i., v.t.* make the sound of a cow; moo. —*n.* the sound a cow makes; mooing. [Old English *hlōwan*]

If you look at the etymologies of the two words, you will see that *low*[1] is originally from the Scandinavian word *lāgr* and *low*[2] is originally from the Old English word *hlōwan*.

Exercise 10 Use a dictionary to look up these homographs. Explain the differences in their origins and meanings. (Note: You won't find these in your Spelling Dictionary.)

1. row[1], row[2]
2. net[1], net[2]
3. league[1], league[2]
4. pro[1], pro[2]
5. hip[1], hip[2], hip[3]
6. rail[1], rail[2], rail[3]

Spelling Dictionary

Parts of a Dictionary Entry

1 ↓ **2** ↓ **3** ↓ **4** ↓

heavy (hev′ē), *adj.,* **heav·i·er,**
heav·i·est, *adv.* —*adj.* **1** hard to lift or
carry; of great weight: *a heavy*
load. See synonym study below. ⟧ **5**
2 of great amount, force, or
intensity: *A heavy rain drenched* ←**6**
us. —*adv.* **hang heavy,** pass slowly **7**
and uninterestingly: *The time hung*
heavy on my hands. (Old English ←**8**
hefig < hebban heave) —**heav′i ness,** ←**9**
10 ⟦ *n.* **Syn.** *adj.* **1 Heavy** and **weighty**
mean of great weight. **Heavy,**
when used figuratively, suggests
something pressing down on the
mind or feelings: *The President has*
heavy responsibilities. **Weighty** is
used chiefly figuratively, applying
to something of great importance:
She made a weighty
announcement.

1 Entry word
2 Pronunciation
3 Part-of-speech label
4 Inflected forms
5 Definition
6 Illustrative sentence
   or phrase
7 Idiom
8 Etymology
9 Run-on entry
10 Synonym study

Full Pronunciation Key

a	hat, cap	**i**	it, pin	**p**	paper, cup	**v**	very, save
ā	age, face	**ī**	ice, five	**r**	run, try	**w**	will, woman
ä	father, far			**s**	say, yes	**y**	young, yet
â	care, hair	**j**	jam, enjoy	**sh**	she, rush	**z**	zero, breeze
		k	kind, seek	**t**	tell, it	**zh**	measure,
b	bad, rob	**l**	land, coal	**th**	thin, both		seizure
ch	child, much	**m**	me, am	**�245H**	then, smooth		
d	did, red	**n**	no, in			**ə**	represents:
		ng	long, bring				a in about
e	let, best			**u**	cup, butter		e in taken
ē	equal, be	**o**	hot, rock	**u̇**	full, put		i in pencil
ėr	term, learn	**ō**	open, go	**ü**	rule, move		o in lemon
		ȯ	all, saw				u in circus
f	fat, if	**ô**	order, store				
g	go, bag	**oi**	oil, voice				
h	he, how	**ou**	house, out				

The contents of the dictionary entries in this book have been adapted from
the *Scott, Foresman Advanced Dictionary,* Copyright © 1993, 1988, 1983,
1979 by Scott, Foresman and Company.

Spellings of English Sounds*

Symbol	Spellings	Symbol	Spellings
a	at, plaid, half, laugh	ng	long, ink, handkerchief, tongue
ā	able, aid, say, age, eight, they, break, vein, gauge, crepe, beret	o	odd, honest
ä	father, ah, calm, heart, bazaar, yacht, sergeant	ō	open, oak, toe, own, home, oh, folk, though, bureau, sew, brooch, soul
âr	dare, aerial, fair, prayer, where, pear, their, they're	ȯ	all, author, awful, broad, bought, walk, taught, cough, Utah, Arkansas
b	bad, rabbit	ô	order, board, floor, tore
ch	child, watch, future, question	oi	oil, boy
d	did, add, filled	ou	out, owl, bough, hour
e	end, said, any, bread, says, heifer, leopard, friend, bury	p	pay, happy
		r	run, carry, wrong, rhythm
ē	equal, eat, eel, happy, cities, vehicle, ceiling, receive, key, these, believe, machine, liter, people	s	say, miss, cent, scent, dance, tense, sword, pizza, listen
		sh	she, machine, sure, ocean, special, tension, mission, nation
ėr	stern, earth, urge, first, word, journey	t	tell, button, two, Thomas, stopped, doubt, receipt, pizza
f	fat, effort, laugh, phrase		
g	go, egg, guest, ghost, league	th	thin
		ŦH	then, breathe
gz	example, exhaust	u	up, oven, trouble, does, flood
h	he, who, jai alai, Gila monster	u̇	full, good, wolf, should
hw	wheat	ü	food, junior, rule, blue, who, move, threw, soup, through, shoe, two, fruit, lieutenant
i	it, England, ear, hymn, been, sieve, women, busy, build, weird		
		v	very, have, of, Stephen
ī	I, ice, lie, sky, type, rye, eye, island, high, eider, aisle, height, buy, coyote	w	will, quick
		y	yes, opinion
		yü	use, few, cue, view, vacuum
j	jam, gem, exaggerate, schedule, badger, bridge, soldier, large, allegiance	z	zero, has, buzz, scissors, xylophone
k	coat, kind, back, echo, ache, quit, account, antique, excite, acquire	zh	measure, garage, division
		ə	alone, complete, moment, authority, bargain, April, cautious, circus, pageant, physician, oxygen, dungeon, tortoise
l	land, tell		
m	me, common, climb, solemn, palm		
n	no, manner, knife, gnaw, pneumonia		

*Not all English spellings of these sounds are included in this list.

A

ab·bre·vi·ate (ə brē′vē āt), *v.t.*, **-at·ed, -at·ing.** shorten (a word or phrase) so that a part stands for the whole: *"Hour" is abbreviated to "hr."* [< Late Latin *abbreviatum* shortened < Latin *ad-* to + *brevis* short.]

ab·bre·vi·a·tion (ə brē′vē ā′shən), *n.* part of a word or phrase standing for the whole; shortened form: *"Dr." is an abbreviation of "Doctor."*

ab·duct (ab dukt′), *v.t.* carry off (a person) by force or by trickery; kidnap. [< Latin *abductum* led away < *ab-* away + *ducere* to lead] —**ab·duc′tion,** *n.*

ab·nor·mal (ab nôr′məl), *adj.* away from the normal; deviating from the ordinary conditions, the standard, or a type. See **irregular** for synonym study.

a·bol·ish (ə bol′ish), *v.t.* do away with completely; put an end to: *Slavery was abolished in the United States in 1865.* [< Middle French *aboliss-,* a form of *abolir* < Latin *abolere* destroy] —**a·bol′ish·a·ble,** *adj.*

ab·o·li·tion·ist (ab′ə lish′ə nist), *n.* **1** person who advocates abolition of any institution or custom. **2 Abolitionist,** person in the 1830s to 1860s who favored the compulsory abolition of slavery.

a·bra·sive (ə brā′siv), *n.* substance that erodes, grinds, or polishes a surface by friction. Sandpaper, pumice, and emery are abrasives. —**a·bra′sive·ness,** *n.*

ab·sorb (ab sôrb′), *v.t.* **1** take in or suck up (a liquid or gas): *The sponge absorbed the spilled milk.* **2** take in and make a part of itself; assimilate: *The U.S. has absorbed millions of immigrants.* [< Latin *absorbere* < *ab-* from + *sorbere* suck in] —**ab·sorb′a·ble,** *adj.*

ab·stain (ab stān′), *v.i.* **1** hold oneself back voluntarily, especially because of one's principles; refrain. **2** refrain from voting. [< Old French *abstenir* < Latin *abstinere* < *abs-* off + *tenere* to hold]

ab·sten·tion (ab sten′shən), *n.* **1** an abstaining; abstinence. **2** fact of not voting: *There were 5 votes in favor, 4 against, and 3 abstentions.*

ac·cel·e·ra·tion (ak sel′ə rā′shən), *n.* rate of change of velocity, expressed in meters/second/second.

acceleration
acceleration of
race cars

ac·ces·sor·y (ak ses′ər ē), *n., pl.* **-sor·ies,** *adj.* —*n.* **1** subordinate part or detail; adjunct. **2** Often, **accessories,** *pl.* nonessential but usually desirable additional clothing, equipment, etc. —*adj.* added; extra; additional.

ac·com·pa·ny (ə kum′pə nē), *v.t.,* **-nied, -ny·ing.** go in company with. [< Middle French *accompagner* take as a companion < *a-* to + *compain* companion]

ac·cor·di·on (ə kôr′dē ən), *n.* a portable musical wind instrument played by pressing the keys and the bellows to force air through the reeds. —*adj.* having folds like an accordion: *a skirt with accordion pleats.* [< German *Akkordion*]

ac·cu·mu·late (ə kyü′myə lāt), *v.,* **-lat·ed, -lat·ing.** —*v.t.* collect little by little. —*v.i.* grow into a heap by degrees; pile up; gather: *Dust had accumulated in the house.* [< Latin *accumulatum* heaped up < *ad-* in addition + *cumulus* a heap]

ac·cur·a·cy (ak′yər ə sē), *n.* condition of being without errors or mistakes; precise correctness; exactness.

a·chieve·ment (ə chēv′mənt), *n.* something achieved or won by exertion; accomplishment; feat: *Martin Luther King, Jr., won the Nobel Prize for his achievements.*

ac·knowl·edg·ment (ak nol′ij mənt), *n.* **1** something given or done to show that one has received a service, favor, gift, message, etc. **2** act of admitting the existence or truth of anything; admission.

ac·quit·tance (ə kwit′ns), *n.* a written release from a debt or obligation.

a·cre·age (ā′kər ij), *n.* **1** number of acres. **2** land sold by the acre.

a·crop·o·lis (ə krop′ə lis), *n.* **1** the high, fortified part or citadel of an ancient Greek city. **2 the Acropolis,** the citadel of Athens on which the Parthenon was built. [< Greek *akropolis* < *akros* highest part + *polis* city]

ad·di·tion (ə dish′ən), *n.* **1** operation, indicated by the sign +, of collecting separate numbers or quantities into one number or quantity known as the sum. **2** part added to a building.

ad·here (ad hir′), *v.i.,* **-hered, -her·ing.** stick fast; remain firmly attached; cling (*to*). [< Latin *adhaerere* < *ad-* to + *haerere* to stick]

ad·her·ent (ad hir′ənt), *n.* a faithful supporter or follower: *an adherent of the conservative party.* —*adj.* sticking fast; attached.

ad·he·sion (ad hē′zhən), *n.* act or condition of adhering; sticking fast. [< Latin *adhaesionem* < *adhaerere.* See ADHERE.]

ad·he·sive (ad hē′siv), *n.* **1** gummed tape used to hold bandages in place; adhesive tape. **2** glue, paste, or other substance for sticking things together. —*adj.* holding fast; adhering easily; sticky. —**ad·he′sive·ly,** *adv.*

ad·ja·cent (ə jā′snt), *adj.* lying near or close; adjoining; next: *The house adjacent to ours has been sold.* [< Latin *adjacentem* < *ad-* near + *jacere* to lie] —**ad·ja′cent·ly,** *adv.*

ad·journ (ə jėrn′), *v.t.* put off until a later time; postpone: *The members of the club voted to adjourn.* —*v.i.* stop business or proceedings for a time; recess: *The court adjourned from Friday until Monday.* [< Old French *ajorner* < *a* to + *jorn* day]

ad·mir·al (ad′mər əl), *n.* **1** the commander of a navy or fleet. **2** officer in the United States Navy ranking next below a fleet admiral and next above a vice-admiral. [earlier *amiral* < Old French < Arabic *amīr al* chief of the]

ad·van·tage (ad van′tij), *n., v.,* **-taged, -tag·ing.** —*n.* a favorable circumstance or condition; any gain resulting from a better or superior position; benefit: *the advantages of good health and a sound education.* See synonym study below. —*v.t.* give an advantage to; help; benefit. [< Old French *advantage* < *avant* before < Latin *abante*]

Syn. *n.* **1 Advantage, benefit, profit** mean gains of different kinds. **Advantage** applies to a gain resulting from a position of superiority over others: *In most sports, a well-coordinated person has an advantage over those with* less coordination. **Benefit** applies to gain in personal or social improvement: *The general relaxation of the body is one of the chief benefits of swimming.* While **profit** applies especially to material gain it is also applied to gain in anything valuable: *There is profit even in mistakes.*

ad·van·ta·geous (ad′vən tā′jəs), *adj.* giving an advantage or advantages; favorable; beneficial.

ad·vent (ad′vent), *n.* a coming; arrival: *the advent of the new year, the advent of industrialism.* [< Latin *adventum* < *ad-* to + *venire* come]

ad·ven·tur·ous (ad ven′chər əs), *adj.* enterprising; daring.

ad·ver·si·ty (ad vėr′sə tē), *n., pl.* **-ties.** condition of being in unfavorable circumstances, as financial circumstances.

ad·ver·tise·ment (ad′vər tīz′mənt, ad vėr′tis mənt), *n.* a public notice or announcement, now always paid for, recommending some product or service.

ad·vo·cate (*v.* ad′və kāt; *n.* ad′və kit, ad′və kāt), *v.,* **-cat·ed, -cat·ing,** *n.* —*v.t.* speak or write in favor of. —*n.* person who defends, maintains, or publicly recommends a proposal, belief, etc.; supporter. [< Latin *advocatum* summoned < *ad-* to + *vocare* to call]

aer·i·al (âr′ē əl), *n.* the antenna of a radio, television set, etc. —*adj.* carried out from or done by aircraft: *an aerial photograph.*

aer·o·bics (âr′ō′biks), *n.* a system of physical exercises that increases the body's consumption of oxygen and improves the functioning of the circulatory system. [< *aerob(ic)* + *-ics*]

aes·thet·ic (es thet′ik), *adj.* based on or determined by beauty rather than by practically useful, scientific, or moral considerations. [< Greek *aisthētikos* sensitive, perceptive < *aisthanesthai* perceive] —**aes·thet′i·cal·ly,** *adv.*

af·fec·tive (af′ek tiv), *adj.* having to do with the emotions; emotional.

adversity
adversity caused by a flash flood in Australia

a	hat	**ī**	ice	**u̇**	put	**ə** stands for
ā	age	**o**	not	**ü**	rule	**a** in about
ä	far, calm	**ō**	open	**ch**	child	**e** in taken
âr	care	**ȯ**	saw	**ng**	long	**i** in pencil
e	let	**ô**	order	**sh**	she	**o** in lemon
ē	equal	**oi**	oil	**th**	thin	**u** in circus
ėr	term	**ou**	out	**ŦH**	then	
i	it	**u**	cup	**zh**	measure	

af·firm·a·tive ac·tion (ə fér′mə tiv ak′shən), a program that encourages the employment of women and minorities in order to compensate for past discrimination.

af·ter·wards (af′tər wərdz), *adv.* later.

ag·gra·vate (ag′rə vāt), *v.t.,* **-vat·ed, -vat·ing. 1** make more burdensome; make worse: *The danger was aggravated by rebellion at home.* **2** INFORMAL. annoy; irritate; exasperate. [< Latin *aggravatum* made heavy < *ad-* on, to + *gravis* heavy]

ag·gres·sion (ə gresh′ən), *n.* practice of making assaults or attacks on the rights or territory of others as a method or policy. [< Latin *aggressionem* < *ad-* up to + *gradi* to step]

ag·gres·sive (ə gres′iv), *adj.* very active; energetic.

aisle (īl), *n.* passage between rows of seats in a hall, theater, school, etc. [< Middle French *ele* < Latin *ala* wing]

à la carte (ä′ lə kärt′), with a stated price for each dish (instead of one price for the whole meal). [< French, according to the bill of fare]

al·co·hol (al′kə hòl), *n.* the colorless, flammable, volatile liquid in wine, beer, whiskey, gin, and other fermented and distilled liquids that makes them intoxicating. [< Medieval Latin, originally, "fine powder," then "essence" < Arabic *al-kuhl* the powdered antimony]

algae

growing **algae**

al·gae (al′jē), *n.pl.* group of related organisms, mostly aquatic and often independently mobile, containing chlorophyll but lacking true stems, roots, or leaves. [< Latin, plural of *alga* seaweed]

all-A·mer·i·can (òl′ə mer′ə kən), *adj.* made up entirely of Americans or American elements. —*n.* (in sports) a player who is all-American.

al·ler·gic (ə lér′jik), *adj.* having an allergy: *allergic to eggs.*

Al·lies (al′īz), *n.pl.* the countries that fought against Germany, Italy, and Japan in World War II.

al·lot (ə lot′), *v.t.,* **-lot·ted, -lot·ting.** divide and distribute in parts or shares. [< Middle French *allotir* < *a-* to + *lot* lot]

al·low (ə lou′), *v.,* **al·lowed, al·low·ing.** let (someone) do something; permit: *The class was not allowed to leave.* [< Old French *alouer* < Latin *allaudare* approve < *ad-* to + *laudare* to praise]

amphibian

a long-tailed

amphibian

all read·y (òl′ red′ē), completely ready: *She was all ready to begin exercising.* See **already.**

all to·geth·er (òl′ tə geᴛʜ′ər), everyone in a group: *We were all together for the picnic.* See **altogether.**

al·lude (ə lüd′), *v.i.,* **-lud·ed, -lud·ing.** refer indirectly (to); *I didn't tell him of your decision; I didn't even allude to it.* [< Latin *alludere* < *ad-* + *ludere* to play]

a lot (ə lot′), very much: *She misses her cat a lot.*

a·loud (ə loud′), *adv.* loud enough to be heard; not in a whisper; loudly.

al·read·y (òl red′ē), *adv.* **1** before this time: *We arrived at noon but you had already left.* **2** by this time; even now: *Are you finished already?* [for *all ready*]

al·to·geth·er (òl′tə geᴛʜ′ər), *adv.* **1** to the whole extent; completely; entirely: *The house was altogether destroyed by fire.* **2** on the whole; considering everything: *Altogether, I'm sorry it happened.* **3** in all: *Altogether there were 14 books.*

am·a·teur (am′ə chər, am′ə tər), *n.* **1** person who does something for pleasure, not for money or as a profession. **2** person who does something rather poorly. —*adj.* made or done by amateurs. [< French < Latin *amator* lover < *amare* to love]

am·bi·dex·trous (am′bə dek′strəs), *adj.* able to use both hands equally well.

am·bu·lance (am′byə ləns), *n.* an automobile, boat, or aircraft equipped to carry sick or injured.

am·phib·i·an (am fib′ē ən), *n.* any of a class of cold-blooded vertebrates with moist, scaleless skin that, typically, lay eggs in water where the young hatch and go through a larval or tadpole stage, breathing by means of gills. Frogs, toads, newts, and salamanders belong to this class.

a·nal·y·sis (ə nal′ə sis), *n.,* pl. **-ses** (-sēz′). **1** a breaking up of anything complex into its various simple elements. **2** this process as a method of studying the nature of a thing. [< Greek < *analyein* loosen up < *ana-* up + *lyein* loosen]

an·chor (ang′kər), *n.* a heavy, shaped piece of iron or steel lowered into the water to hold a ship or boat fixed in a particular place. —*v.t.* hold in place with an anchor. [Old English *ancor* < Latin *ancora* < Greek *ankyra*]

an·cient (ān'shənt), *adj.* **1** of or belonging to times long past: *ancient records.* **2** of great age; very old: *the ancient hills.* —*n.* a very old person. [< Old French *ancien* < Late Latin *anteanus* former < Latin *ante* before]

an·nex (*v.* ə neks'; *n.* an'eks), *v.t.* join or add to a larger or more important thing: *The United States annexed Texas in 1845.* —*n.* an addition to an existing building. [< Latin *annexum* bound to < *ad-* to + *nectere* to bind]

an·ni·hi·late (ə nī'ə lāt), *v.t.,* **-lat·ed, -lat·ing.** destroy completely; wipe out of existence: *The flood annihilated over thirty towns and villages.* [< Late Latin *annihilatum* brought to nothing < Latin *ad-* to + *nihil* nothing] —**an·ni'hi·la'tive,** *adj.* —**an·ni'hi·la'tor,** *n.*

an·nu·al (an'yü əl), *adj.* **1** coming once a year: *A birthday is an annual event.* **2** in a year; for a year: *an annual salary of $12,000.* [< Late Latin *annualis* < Latin *annus* year] —**an'nu·al·ly,** *adv.*

an·nu·al rate (an'yü əl rāt'), amount of interest charged or earned in a year.

an·nu·i·ty (ə nü'ə tē, ə nyü'ə tē), *n.,* *pl.* **-ties.** sum of money paid every year or at certain regular times. [< Medieval Latin *annuitatem* < Latin *annuus* yearly < *annus* year]

a·no·rak (an'ə räk'), *n.* a heavy jacket with a fur hood, worn in arctic regions. [< Eskimo (Greenland) *ánorâq* clothing]

an·te·bel·lum (an'ti bel'əm), *adj.* **1** before the war. **2** before the American Civil War. [< Latin *ante bellum* before the war]

an·ti·air·craft (an'tē âr'kraft'), *adj.* used in defense against enemy aircraft.

an·ti·bi·ot·ic (an'ti bī ot'ik), *n.* substance produced by a living organism, especially a bacterium or a fungus, that destroys or weakens harmful microorganisms.

an·ti·bod·y (an'ti bod'ē), *n., pl.* **-bod·ies.** a protein substance produced in the blood or tissues that destroys or weakens bacteria or neutralizes poisons.

an·ti·dote (an'ti dōt), *n.* medicine or remedy that counteracts the effects of a poison: *Milk is an antidote for some poisons.* [< Greek *antidoton* < *anti-* against + *didonai* give]

an·ti·freeze (an'ti frēz'), *n.* liquid with a low freezing point added to the cooling medium in the radiator of an internal-combustion engine to prevent the system from freezing.

an·ti·his·ta·mine (an'ti his'tə mēn'), *n.* any of various drugs that inhibit or relieve the effects of histamine in the body, used in the treatment of colds and allergies.

an·ti·mis·sile (an'ti mis'əl), *adj.* designed or used to intercept and destroy enemy missiles.

an·ti·sep·tic (an'tə sep'tik), *n.* substance that prevents the growth of germs that cause infection.

an·ti·so·cial (an'ti sō'shəl), *adj.* **1** against the general welfare: *antisocial behavior.* **2** opposed to friendly relationship and normal companionship with others.

an·ti·trust (an'ti trust'), *adj.* opposed to trusts or other business monopolies: *antitrust legislation.*

an·y·more (en'ē môr', en'ē mōr'), *adv.* at present; now; currently.

an·y more (en'ē môr'), more than one has already had: *I am too tired to play any more games with you.*

an·y·way (en'ē wā), *adv.* **1** in any case; at least: *I am coming anyway, no matter what.* **2** in any way whatever. **3** carelessly.

an·y way (en'ē wā'), no matter which way: *Any way I go, my dog Ginger finds me.*

a·part (ə pärt'), *adv.* **1** to pieces; in pieces; in separate parts: *Take the watch apart.* **2** away from each other. —*adj.* separate.

a part (ə pärt), thing that helps to make up a whole: *A chapter is a part of a book.*

ancient (def. 1)
ancient ruins in Turkey

a	hat	**ī**	ice	**u̇**	put	**ə** stands for	
ā	age	**o**	not	**ü**	rule	**a**	in about
ä	far, calm	**ō**	open	**ch**	child	**e**	in taken
âr	care	**ȯ**	saw	**ng**	long	**i**	in pencil
e	let	**ô**	order	**sh**	she	**o**	in lemon
ē	equal	**oi**	oil	**th**	thin	**u**	in circus
ėr	term	**ou**	out	**ŦH**	then		
i	it	**u**	cup	**zh**	measure		

a·part·heid (ə pärt′hāt, ə pärt′hīt), *n.* racial segregation, especially as was practiced by law in the Republic of South Africa. [< Afrikaans, separateness]

a·pol·o·gy (ə pol′ə jē), *n., pl.* **-gies.** words of regret for an offense or accident; expressing regret and asking pardon. [< Late Latin *apologia* a speech in defense < Greek < *apo-* + *legein* speak]

ap·pre·hend (ap′ri hend′), *v.t.* formally arrest or seize (a person): *The suspect was apprehended.* [< Latin *apprehendere* < *ad-* upon + *prehendere* seize]

ap·pre·hen·sive (ap′ri hen′siv), *adj.* afraid that some misfortune is about to occur; fearful.

ap·pro·pri·ate (*adj.* ə prō′prē it; *v.* ə prō′prē āt), *adj., v.,* **-at·ed, -at·ing.** *adj.* especially right or proper for the occasion; suitable; fitting: *Plain, simple clothes are appropriate for school wear.* —*v.t.* set apart for a special purpose: *The legislature appropriated a billion dollars for foreign aid.* [< Late Latin *appropriatum* made one's own < Latin *ad-* to + *proprius* one's own] —**ap·pro′pri·ate·ly,** *adv.*

ap·ro·pos (ap′rə pō′), *adv.* fittingly; opportunely. —*adj.* to the point; fitting; suitable. [< French *à propos* to the purpose]

a·rach·no·pho·bi·a (ə rak′nə fō′bē ə), *n.* an abnormal fear of spiders.

ar·chae·ol·o·gy (är′kē ol′ə jē), *n.* the scientific study of the people, customs, and life of ancient times.

archaeology
Archaeology helps reconstruct a picture of life in the past.

ar·chi·pel·a·go (är′kə pel′ə gō, är′chə pel′ə gō), *n., pl.* **-gos** or **-goes.** group of many islands. [< Italian *arcipelago* < *arci-* chief + *pelago* sea]

ar·chi·tec·ture (är′kə tek′chər), *n.* science or art of planning and designing buildings.

arc·tic (ärk′tik, är′tik), *adj.* at or near the North Pole: *the arctic fox.* [< Greek *arktikos* of the Bear (constellation) < *arktos* bear]

ar·gu·ment (är′gyə mənt), *n.* discussion by persons who disagree.

ar·ma·dil·lo (är′mə dil′ō), *n., pl.* **-los.** any of several small, burrowing, chiefly nocturnal mammals ranging from Texas to tropical America. Armadillos are covered with an armorlike shell of small, bony plates. [< Spanish, diminutive of *armado* armed (one) < Latin *armatum* armed]

ar·range·ment (ə rānj′mənt), *n.* **1** a putting or a being put in proper order. **2** something arranged in a particular way.

Art De·co (ärt dā′kō), a decorative style of the 1920s and 1930s which used vivid colors, bold outline, and geometrical forms. [< French *Art Déco*, short for *Arts Décoratifs* Decorative Arts]

ar·ti·cle (är′tə kəl), *n.,* a written composition on a special subject forming part of the contents of a magazine, newspaper, or book. [< Old French < Latin *articulus,* diminutive of *artus* joint]

ar·ti·fact (är′tə fakt), *n.* anything made by human skill or work, especially a tool or weapon. [< Latin *artem* art + *factum* made]

ar·ti·fi·cial in·tel·li·gence (är′tə fish′əl in tel′ə jəns), ability of a computer to closely mimic human thinking.

ar·ti·fi·cial res·pi·ra·tion (är′tə fish′əl res′pə rā′shən), the first-aid procedure used to restore normal breathing to a person who has stopped breathing by forcing air alternately into and out of the lungs.

as·cent (ə sent′), *n.* **1** act of going up; rising: *early balloon ascents.* **2** act of climbing a ladder, mountain, etc.

as·sem·bly (ə sem′blē), *n., pl.* **-blies.** group of people gathered together for some purpose: *The principal addressed the school assembly.*

as·sent (ə sent′), *v.i.* express agreement; agree; consent: *Everyone assented to the plans for the dance.* [< Latin *assentire* < *ad-* along with + *sentire* feel, think]

as·sist·ance (ə sis′təns), *n.* an assisting; help; aid.

as·sist·ant (ə sis′tənt), *n.* person who assists another, especially as a subordinate in some office or work. —*adj.* helping; assisting.

a·sym·met·ri·cal (ā′sə met′rə kəl), *adj.* not symmetrical.

at·om (at′əm), *n.* the smallest particle of an element that has all the characteristics of that element. [< Latin *atomus* < Greek *atomos* indivisible < *a-* not + *tomos* a cutting]

a·tom·ic num·ber (ə tom′ik num′bər), the number of protons in an atom's nucleus.

a·tro·cious (ə trō′shəs), *adj.* monstrously wicked or cruel: *an atrocious crime.* —**a·tro′cious·ly,** *adv.*

a·troc·i·ty (ə tros′ə tē), *n., pl.* **-ties.** monstrous wickedness or cruelty. [< Latin *atrocitatem* < *atrox* fierce]

at·tend·ance (ə ten′dəns), *n.* **1** act of attending. **2** number of people present; persons attending. **3 take attendance,** call the roll.

aus·pi·cious (ȯ spish′əs), *adj.* with signs of success; favorable.

au·to·mat·ic (ȯ′tə mat′ik), *adj.* (of machinery, etc.) moving or acting by itself; regulating itself: *an automatic elevator.* [< Greek *automatos* self-acting] —**au′to·mat′i·cal·ly,** *adv.*

a·vail·a·ble (ə vā′lə bəl), *adj.* **1** that can be used or secured: *She is not available for the job; she has other work.* **2** that can be had: *All available tickets were sold.*

a·venge (ə venj′), *v.,* **a·venged, a·veng·ing.** —*v.t.* take revenge for or on behalf of: *Hamlet avenged his father's murder.* See **revenge** for synonym study. —*v.i.* get revenge. [< Old French *avengier* < *a-* to + *vengier* avenge < Latin *vindicare*] —**a·veng′er,** *n.*

awk·ward (ȯk′wərd), *adj.* not graceful or skillful in movement; clumsy: *The seal is awkward on land.* [< obsolete *awk* perversely, in the wrong way < Scandinavian (Old Icelandic) *öfugr* + *-ward*] —**awk′ward·ly,** *adv.*

ax·is (ak′sis), *n.* **the Axis,** Germany, Italy, Japan, and their allies, during World War II. [< Latin]

B

ba·con (bā′kən), *n.* **1** salted and smoked meat from the back and sides of a hog. **2 bring home the bacon, a** succeed; win. **b** earn a living. [< Middle French < Germanic]

bag·gage (bag′ij), *n.* the trunks, bags, suitcases, etc., that a person takes along when traveling; luggage. [< Old French *baggage* < *bague* bundle]

bal·ance (bal′əns), *n., v.,* **-anced, -anc·ing.** —*n.* steady condition or position; steadiness. —*v.t.* keep a steady condition or position. [< Old French < Late Latin *bilancem* two-scaled < Latin *bi-* two + *lanx*]

bam·boo (bam bü′), *n., pl.* **-boos.** any of various species of woody or treelike tropical or semitropical grasses. [< Dutch *bamboe* < Malay *bambu*]

ban·jo (ban′jō), *n., pl.* **-jos.** a musical instrument having four or five strings, played by plucking the strings with the fingers. [probably of Bantu origin]

barbed wire (bärbd′ wīr′), wire with sharp points on it every few inches, used for fences.

ba·rom·e·ter (bə rom′ə tər), *n.* **1** instrument for measuring the pressure of air, used in determining height above sea level and in predicting probable changes in the weather. **2** something that indicates changes: *His newspaper column is a barometer of public opinion.* [< Greek *baros* weight + English *-meter*]

bar·ri·er (bar′ē ər), *n. pl.* **bar·ri·ers,** something that stands in the way; obstacle. [< Anglo-French *barrere* < *barre* bar]

base (bās), *n.* **1** (of an exponent) a number raised to a power. In 4^3, 4 is the base. **2** (geometry) a name used for a side of a polygon or surface of a space figure.

bash·ful (bash′fəl), *adj.* uneasy in unaccustomed situations or in the presence of others; embarrassed.

ba·sic (bā′sik), *adj.* of, at, or forming a base; fundamental: *Addition and subtraction are some of the basic processes of arithmetic.* —*n.* an essential part. —**ba′si·cal·ly,** *adv.*

ba·tik (bə tēk′), *n.* method of executing designs on textiles by covering the material with wax in a pattern, dyeing the parts left exposed, and then removing the wax. [< Javanese *batik*]

bamboo
Bamboo is a treelike grass that grows in groves.

banjo
A **banjo** has a head and neck like a guitar and a body like a tambourine.

a	hat	ī	ice	u̇	put	ə stands for	
ā	age	o	not	ü	rule	a	in about
ä	far, calm	ō	open	ch	child	e	in taken
âr	care	ȯ	saw	ng	long	i	in pencil
e	let	ô	order	sh	she	o	in lemon
ē	equal	oi	oil	th	thin	u	in circus
ėr	term	ou	out	ᴛʜ	then		
i	it	u	cup	zh	measure		

bazaar (def. 1)
a **bazaar** for shopping and browsing

bat·ter·y (bat′ər ē), *n., pl.* **-ter·ies.**
1 a single electric cell: *a flashlight battery.* **2** set of two or more electric cells connected together for the production of electric current: *a car battery.*

ba·zaar (bə zär′), *n.* **1** (in various countries of Asia) a marketplace consisting of a street or streets full of small shops and booths. **2** sale of articles held for some charity or purpose. [< Persian *bāzār*]

be·cause (bi kôz′), *conj.* for the reason that; since: *Children play ball because it's fun.* —*adv.* **because of,** by reason of; on account of. [Middle English *bi cause* by (the) cause]

be·fore (bi fôr′), *prep.* **1** earlier than: *Come before five o'clock.* **2** in front of; in advance of; ahead of: *Walk before me.* **3** rather than; sooner than: *I will die before giving in.* **4** in the presence of or sight of: *perform before an audience.* —*adv.* **1** earlier; sooner. **2** in front; in advance; ahead: *I went before to see if the road was safe.* **3** until now; in the past: *I didn't know that before.* —*conj.* **1** previously to the time when: *I would like to talk to her before she goes.* **2** rather than; sooner than: *I will die before I give in.* [Old English *beforan*]

be·gin·ning (bi gin′ing), *n.* **1** a start: *make a good beginning.* **2** first part. —*adj.* that begins.

be·lieve (bi lēv′), *v.,* **-lieved, -liev·ing.** —*v.t.* accept as true or real: *We all believe that the earth is round.* —*v.i.* have faith (in a person or thing); trust: *We believe in our friends.* [Old English *belēfan*]

bel·li·cose (bel′ə kōs), *adj.* fond of fighting and quarreling; warlike. [< Latin *bellicosus* < *bellum* war]

bel·lig·er·ent (bə lij′ər ənt), *adj.* fond of fighting; tending or inclined to war. —*n.* person engaged in fighting with another person. [< Latin *belligerantem* < *bellum* war + *gerere* to wage]

ben·e·fac·tor (ben′ə fak′tər), *n.* person who has helped others, either by gifts or kind acts. [< Late Latin < Latin *benefactum* befitted < *bene* well + *facere* do]

ben·e·fi·cial (ben′ə fish′əl), *adj.* producing good; favorable; helpful: *Sunshine is beneficial.*

ben·e·fi·ci·ar·y (ben′ə fish′ē er′ē), *n., pl.* **-ar·ies.** person who receives or is to receive money or property from an insurance policy, a will.

ben·e·fit (ben′ə fit), *n.* anything which is for the good of a person or thing; advantage; help. See **advantage** for synonym study. —*v.t.* give benefit to; be good for: *Rest will benefit a sick person.* [< Anglo-French *benfet* < Latin *benefactum* good deed < *bene* well + *facere* do]

be·nev·o·lent (bə nev′ə lənt), *adj.* wishing or intended to promote the happiness of others; charitable.

be·nign (bi nīn′), *adj.* **1** kindly in feeling; benevolent; gracious: *a benign old woman.* **2** not dangerous to health; not malignant: *a benign tumor.* [< Latin *benignus* < *bene* well + *-gnus* born]

bi·o·chem·ist (bī′ō kem′ist), *n.* an expert in the science that deals with the chemical processes of living matter; biological chemistry.

bi·og·ra·pher (bī og′rə fər), *n.* person who writes a biography.

bi·og·ra·phy (bī og′rə fē), *n., pl.* **-phies.** an account of a person's life.

bi·ol·o·gy (bī ol′ə jē), *n.* the scientific study of living organisms, including their origins, structures, activities, and distribution. Botany and zoology are branches of biology.

bi·on·ic (bī on′ik), *adj.* having both biological and electronic parts.

bi·on·ics (bī on′iks), *n.* study of the anatomy and physiology of animals as a basis for new or improved electronic devices. [< *bio(logy)* + *(electro)nics*]

bi·op·sy (bī′op sē), *n., pl.* **-sies.** examination of cells or tissues taken from a living body, for diagnosis. [< *bio-* + Greek *opsis* a viewing]

bi·zarre (bə zär′), *adj.* strikingly odd in appearance or style. [< French < Spanish *bizarro* brave < Italian *bizzarro* angry < *bizza* anger]

black hole (blak′ hōl′), region of space in which so much mass is concentrated that nothing, not even light, can escape; the result of the death of massive stars.

BLT, abbreviation for a kind of sandwich: bacon, lettuce, and tomato.

boc·cie (boch′ē), *n.* an Italian form of the game of bowls, played outdoors on a narrow, enclosed court. [< Italian *bocce,* plural of *boccia* ball]

book·keep·er (bůk′kē′pər), *n.* person who keeps a record of accounts.

black hole
a mysterious **black hole** in space

boom (büm), *n.* a long pole or beam, used to extend the bottom of a sail.

boot·leg·ger (büt/leg/ər), *n., pl.* **boot·leg·gers.** person who sells, transports, or makes goods (especially alcoholic liquor) unlawfully. [from practice of smuggling liquor in boot legs]

borsch (bôrsh), *n.* a Russian soup consisting of meat stock, cabbage, and onions, colored red with beet juice and served with sour cream. [< Russian *borshch*]

Bos·ton Mas·sa·cre (bò/stən mas/ə kər), violent encounter between American colonists and British soldiers in Boston, March 5, 1770.

bouil·lon (bùl/yon), *n.* a clear, thin soup. [< French < *bouillir* to boil]

bounce (bouns), *v.*, **bounces, bounced, bounc·ing,** *v.i.* spring into the air like a rubber ball. —*n.* a springing back; bound; rebound. [Middle English *bunsen*]

boy·cott (boi/kot), *v.t.* combine against (a person, business, nation, etc.) in agreement not to buy from, sell to, or associate with and try to keep others from doing so. [< Captain Charles C. *Boycott,* 1832-1897, English land agent in Ireland whose tenants and neighbors boycotted him when he refused to lower rents]

breath·ing (brē/ᴛʜing), *n.* respiration. —*adj.* living.

breath·tak·ing (breth/tā/king), *adj.* thrilling; exciting.

brev·i·ty (brev/ə tē), *n.* shortness in speech or writing. [< Latin *brevitatem* < *brevis* short]

brief (brēf), *adj.* using few words; concise. —*n.* a short statement; summary. [< Old French *bref* < Latin *brevem* short] —**brief/ly,** *adv.*

budg·et (buj/it), *n.* estimate of the amount of money that will probably be received and spent for various purposes in a given time. —*v.i.* draw up or prepare a budget. [< Middle French *bougette,* diminutive of *bouge* bag < Latin *bulga*]

bul·lion (bùl/yən), *n.* gold or silver in the form of ingots or bars. [< Anglo-French < Old French *bouillir* to boil; influenced by Old French *billon* debased metal]

bun·ga·low (bung/gə lō), *n.* a small house, usually of one story or a story and a half, with low, sweeping lines.

bur·eau (byùr/ō), *n., pl.* **bur·eaus** (byùr/ōz). chest of drawers for clothes, often having a mirror; dresser. [< French, desk (originally cloth-covered) < Old French *burel,* diminutive of *bure* coarse woolen cloth < Late Latin *burra*]

bur·eau·crat (byùr/ə krat), *n.* official in a bureaucracy.

C

caf·e·ter·i·a (kaf/ə tir/ē ə), *n.* restaurant where people wait on themselves. [< Mexican Spanish *cafetería* coffee shop < *café* coffee]

cake (kāk), *n.* **1** a baked mixture of flour, sugar, eggs, flavoring, and other things. **2 take the cake,** SLANG. **a** win first prize. **b** excel. [probably < Scandinavian (Old Icelandic) *kaka*]

cal·cu·lus (kal/kyə ləs), *n., pl.* **-li** (-lī), **-lus·es.** plaque that has hardened on the teeth; called tartar.

cal·lig·ra·phy (kə lig/rə fē), *n.* beautiful handwriting. [< Greek *kalligraphia* < *kallos* beauty + *graphein* write]

cal·lous (kal/əs), *adj.* hard or hardened, as parts of the skin that are exposed to constant pressure.

cal·lus (kal/əs), *n.* a hard, thickened place on the skin. [< Latin]

cam·ou·flage (kam/ə fläzh), *n., v.,* **-flaged, -flag·ing.** —*n.* a disguise or false appearance serving to conceal. The white fur of a polar bear is a natural camouflage. —*v.t.* give a false appearance to in order to conceal; disguise. [< French < *camoufler* to disguise]

calligraphy

an inscription in

calligraphy

a	hat	**ī**	ice	**ù**	put	**ə** *stands for*	
ā	age	**o**	not	**ü**	rule	**a**	in about
ä	far, calm	**ō**	open	**ch**	child	**e**	in taken
âr	care	**ò**	saw	**ng**	long	**i**	in pencil
e	let	**ô**	order	**sh**	she	**o**	in lemon
ē	equal	**oi**	oil	**th**	thin	**u**	in circus
ėr	term	**ou**	out	**ᴛʜ**	then		
i	it	**u**	cup	**zh**	measure		

Ca·na·di·an (kə nā′dē ən), *adj.* of Canada or its people. —*n.* native or inhabitant of Canada.

ca·nas·ta (kə nas′tə), *n.* a card game similar to rummy, played with two decks of cards plus four jokers. [< Spanish, literally, basket, ultimately < Latin *canistrum*]

can·cel·la·tion (kan′sə lā′shən), *n.* 1 a canceling. 2 a being canceled.

can·did (kan′did), *adj.* saying openly what one really thinks; frank and sincere; outspoken: *a candid reply.* [< Latin *candidus* white < *candere* to shine] —**can′did·ness,** *n.*

can·ta·loupe (kan′tl ōp), *n.* kind of muskmelon with a hard, rough rind and sweet, juicy, orange flesh. [< French *cantaloup* < Italian *Cantalupo* papal estate near Rome where first cultivated]

cantaloupe

a **cantaloupe** cut

into halves

can·vas (kan′vəs), *n.* piece of canvas on which an oil painting is painted. —*adj.* made of canvas. [< Old French *canevas* < Latin *cannabis* hemp]

can·vass (kan′vəs), *v.t.* go through (a city, district, etc.) asking for votes, orders, donations. —*n.* act or process of canvassing. [< obsolete verb *canvass* toss (someone) in a sheet, (later) shake out, discuss < *canvas*] —**can′vass·er,** *n.*

cap·i·tal·ism (kap′ə tə liz′əm), *n.* an economic system based on the ownership of land, factories, and other productions by private individuals or groups of individuals who compete with one another.

cap·ture (kap′chər), *v.,* **-tured, -tur·ing,** *n.* —*v.t.* make a prisoner of; take by force, skill, or trickery; seize. —*n.* capturing. [< Latin *captura* a taking < *capere* take]

car·a·way (kar′ə wā), *n.* plant of the same family as parsley that yields fragrant, spicy seeds which are used to flavor bread, rolls, cakes, etc. [< Arabic *karawyā*]

car·di·ol·o·gist (kär′dē ol′ə jist), *n.* an expert in cardiology, a branch of medicine dealing with the heart and the diagnosis and treatment of its diseases.

car·i·ca·ture (kar′ə kə chùr), *n., v.,* **-tured, -tur·ing.** —*n.* picture, cartoon, or description that exaggerates the peculiarities of a person or the defects of a thing. —*v.t.* make a caricature of. [< French < Italian *caricatura* < *caricare* overload, exaggerate < Late Latin *carricare* to load < Latin *carrus* wagon]

catastrophe

the **catastrophe** of

Hurricane Camille in

Louisiana, 1969

car·ies (kâr′ēz, kâr′ē ēz), *n., pl.* **car·ies.** 1 decay of teeth or bones. 2 cavity formed in a tooth by such decay. [< Latin]

car·tog·ra·pher (kär tog′rə fər), *n.* maker of maps or charts.

cas·ta·net (kas′tə net′), *n.* one of a pair of instruments held in the hand and clicked together to beat time for dancing or music. [< Spanish *castañeta* < Latin *castanea*]

cat·a·ma·ran (kat′ə mə ran′), *n.* boat with two hulls side by side joined by crosspieces. [< Tamil *kattamaram* tied tree]

ca·tas·tro·phe (kə tas′trə fē), *n.* a sudden, widespread, or extraordinary disaster; great calamity or misfortune. [< Greek *katastrophē* an overturning < *kata-* down + *strephein* to turn]

cau·cus (kȯ kəs), *n.* a meeting of members or leaders of a political party to choose candidates, etc. —*v.i.* hold a caucus. [probably of Algonquian origin]

cede (sēd), *v.t.,* **ced·ed, ced·ing.** give up; surrender; hand over to another: *Spain ceded the Philippines to the United States.* [< Latin *cedere* yield, go]

cen·ten·ni·al (sen ten′ē əl), *adj.* 1 of or having to do with 100 years or the 100th anniversary. 2 100 years old. —*n.* 1 a 100th anniversary. 2 celebration of the 100th anniversary. [< Latin *centum* hundred + English *(bi)ennial*]

cen·ter·board (sen′tər bôrd′), *n.* a movable keel of a sailboat. It is lowered through a slot in the bottom of a boat to prevent drifting to leeward.

cen·ti·me·ter (sen′tə mē′tər), *n.* unit of length equal to ¹⁄₁₀₀ of a meter.

cen·ti·pede (sen′tə pēd′), *n.* any of a class of flat, wormlike arthropods with many pairs of legs, the front pair of which are clawlike and contain poison glands. [< Latin *centipeda* < *centum* hundred + *pedem* foot]

chal·lenge (chal′ənj), *v.,* **-lenged, -leng·ing,** *n.* —*v.t.* call to a game or contest. —*n.* a call to a game or contest. [< Old French *chalenger* < Latin *calumniari* to slander < *calumnia* false accusation] —**chal′leng·er,** *n.*

char·i·ta·ble (châr′ə tə bəl), *adj.* 1 generous in giving to poor, sick, or helpless people. 2 of or for charity.

Charles·ton (chärlz/tən), *n.* a lively ballroom dance, especially popular in the 1920s.

chem·i·cal for·mu·la (kem/ə kəl fôr/myə lə), expression showing by chemical symbols the composition of a compound, such as H_2O.

Cher·o·kee (cher/ə kē), *n., pl.* **-kee** or **-kees.** member of a tribe of Iroquois Indians of the southern Appalachians, now living mostly in Oklahoma.

chip (chip), *n., pl.* **chips.** in electronics: **a** a small piece of semiconductor material, usually silicon, which holds an integrated circuit. **b** an integrated circuit.

chop su·ey (chop/ sü/ē), fried or stewed meat and vegetables cut up and cooked in a sauce. It is served with rice. [< Chinese (Canton) *tsap sui* odds and ends]

cho·re·o·graph (kôr/ē ə graf), *v.t.* arrange or design dancing for.

chor·tle (chôr/tl), *v.,* **-tled, -tling,** *n.* —*v.i., v.t.* chuckle or snort with glee. —*n.* a gleeful chuckle or snort. [blend of *chuckle* and *snort;* coined by Lewis Carroll] —**chor/tler,** *n.*

chron·ic (kron/ik), *adj.* **1** lasting a long time: *Rheumatism is often a chronic disease.* **2** suffering long from an illness: *a chronic invalid.* **3** never stopping; constant; habitual: *a chronic liar.* [< Greek *chronikos* of time < *chronos* time] —**chron/i·cal·ly,** *adv.*

chron·i·cle (kron/ə kəl), *n., v.,* **-cled, -cling.** —*n.* record of events in the order in which they took place; history; story. —*v.t.* write the history of; tell the story of.

chron·o·graph (kron/ə graf), *n.* instrument for measuring very short intervals of time accurately, such as a stopwatch. [< Greek *chronos* time + English *-graph*]

chron·o·log·i·cal (kron/ə loj/ə kəl), *adj.* of or in accordance with chronology; arranged in the order in which the events happened. —**chron/o·log/i·cal·ly,** *adv.*

chry·san·the·mum (krə san/thə məm), *n.* any of a genus of plants of the composite family that have many-petaled round flowers of various colors and that bloom in the fall. [< Latin < Greek *chrysanthemon* < *chrysos* gold + *anthemon* flower]

chuck wag·ons (chuk/ wag/ənz), (in the western United States) wagons or trucks, that carry food and cooking equipment for workers.

cin·na·mon (sin/ə mən), *n.* spice made from the dried, reddish-brown inner bark of a laurel tree of the East Indies. [< Latin < Greek *kinnamon;* of Semitic origin]

cir·cuit break·er (sėr/kit brā/kər), safety device that switches off when too much current flows in a circuit.

cir·cum·lo·cu·tion (sėr/kəm lō kyü/shən), *n.* use of several or many words instead of one or a few.

cir·cum·scribe (sėr/kəm skrīb/), *v.t.,* **-scribed, -scrib·ing.** draw a line around; mark the boundaries of; bound. [< Latin *circumscribere* < *circum* around + *scribere* write]

cir·cum·stance (sėr/kəm stans), *n.* condition that accompanies an act or event. [< Latin *circumstantia* < *circumstare* surround < *circum* around + *stare* stand]

cir·cum·stan·tial (sėr/kəm stan/shəl), *adj.* depending on or based on circumstances: *Stolen jewels found in a person's possession are circumstantial evidence.*

cir·cum·vent (sėr/kəm vent/), *v.t.* **1** get the better of or defeat by trickery; outwit: *circumvent the law.* **2** go around. [< Latin *circumventum* circumvented < *circum* around + *venire* come] —**cir/cum·ven/tion,** *n.*

civ/il dis·o·be·di·ence (siv/əl dis/ə bē/dē əns), deliberate, public refusal to obey a law that one considers unjust. Civil disobedience is often used as a form of protest.

cinnamon
different forms of the spice **cinnamon**

a	hat	ī	ice	u̇	put	ə stands for	
ā	age	o	not	ü	rule	a	in about
ä	far, calm	ō	open	ch	child	e	in taken
âr	care	ȯ	saw	ng	long	i	in pencil
e	let	ô	order	sh	she	o	in lemon
ē	equal	oi	oil	th	thin	u	in circus
ėr	term	ou	out	ŦH	then		
i	it	u	cup	zh	measure		

Civil War

Christian Fleetwood, an
honored soldier from the
Civil War

civ·il rights (siv′əl rīts′), the rights of a citizen, guaranteed to all citizens of the United States, regardless of race, color, religion, or sex.

Civ·il War (siv′əl wôr′), war between the northern and southern states of the United States from 1861 to 1865; War Between the States.

claim (klām), *v.t.* say one has (a right, title, possession, etc.) and demand that others recognize it; assert one's right to: *claim a tract of land.* —*n.* something that is claimed. [< Old French *claimer, clamer* < Latin *clamare* call, proclaim] —**claim′a·ble,** *adj.*

clean·li·ness (klen′lē nis), *n.* cleanness; habitual cleanness.

clothes (klōz, klōᴛʜz), *n.pl.* coverings for a person's body; clothing.

co·ed·u·ca·tion·al (kō′ej ə kā′shə nəl), *adj.* educating boys and girls or men and women together in the same school or classes.

co·ex·ist (kō′ig zist′), *v.i.* exist together or at the same time.

co·he·sive (kō hē′siv), *adj.* tending to hold together; sticking together. —**co·he′sive·ly,** *adv.* —**co·he′sive·ness,** *n.*

co-lead·ers (kō′lē′dərz), two or more people who together assume the responsibilities of leadership.

col·lage (kə läzh′), *n.* picture made by pasting on a background such things as parts of photographs and newspapers, fabric, and string. [< French, pasting, gluing < Greek *kolla* glue]

col·lapse (kə laps′), *v.,* **-lapsed, -laps·ing,** *n.* —*v.i.* break down; fail suddenly. —*n.* a falling or caving in; sudden shrinking together. [< Latin *collapsum* fallen completely < *com-* completely + *labi* to fall]

col·lect·i·ble (kə lek′tə bəl), *adj.* able to be collected. —*n.* anything that is collected, especially unusual or dated objects having little worth.

col·lege (kol′ij), *n.* institution of higher learning that gives degrees.

col·lo·qui·al (kə lō′kwē əl), *adj.* used in everyday, informal talk, but not in formal speech or writing.

colo·nel (ker′nl), *n.* a commissioned officer in the army, air force, or Marine Corps ranking next above a lieutenant colonel and next below a brigadier general. [< Middle French *coronel, colonel* < Italian *colonello* commander of a regiment < *colonna* military column < Latin *columna* column]

co·los·sal (kə los′əl), *adj.* of huge size.

Co·lum·bi·a Riv·er (kə lum′bē ə riv′ər), river flowing from British Columbia through E Washington and between Washington and Oregon into the Pacific. 1214 mi.

com·mand (kə mand′), *v.t.* **1** give an order to; direct. **2** have authority or power over; be in control of; govern: *to command a ship.* **3** have a position of control over; rise high above; overlook: *A hilltop commands the plain around it.* —*n.* **1** an order; direction: *The admiral obeyed the queen's command.* **2** authority; power; control: *The rebels are now in command of the government.* [< Old French *comander* < Popular Latin *commandare,* alteration of Latin *commendare* commend]

com·mand·er (kə man′dər), *n.* **1** person who commands. **2** officer in charge of an army or a part of an army. **3** a navy officer ranking next below a captain and next above a lieutenant commander.

com·man·do (kə man′dō), *n., pl.* **com·man·dos. 1** soldier trained to make brief surprise raids in enemy territory. **2** group of such soldiers. [< Afrikaans *kommando*]

com·mem·o·rate (kə mem′ə rāt′), *v.,* **-rat·ed, -rat·ing.** preserve or honor the memory of. [< Latin *commemoratum* remembered < *com-* + *memorare* bring to mind]

com·men·da·tion (kom′ən dā′shən), *n.* praise; approval.

com·mis·e·rate (kə miz′ə rāt′), *v.t., v.i.* **-rat·ed, -rat·ing.** feel or express sorrow for another's suffering or trouble; sympathize with. [< Latin *commiseratum* pitied < *com-* + *miser* wretched] —**com·mis′e·ra′tion,** *n.*

com·mis·sion (kə mish′ən), *n.* percentage of the amount of business done, paid to the agent who does it. [< Latin *commissionem* < *committere* commit]

com·mit (kə mit′), *v.t.,* **-mit·ted, -mit·ting. 1** do or perform (usually something wrong): *commit a crime.* **2** hand over for safekeeping; deliver. **3** send to prison or an asylum. **4** give over; carry over; transfer: *commit a poem to memory.* **5** reveal (one's opinion). **6** involve; pledge. [< Latin *committere* < *com-* with + *mittere* send, put] —**com·mit′ta·ble,** *adj.*

com·mu·ni·ty (kə myü′nə tē), *n., pl.* **-ties.** all the people living in the same place and subject to the same laws; people of any town.

com·mute (kə myüt′), *v.,* **-mut·ed, -mut·ing,** *n.* —*v.i.* travel regularly to and from work especially between suburb and downtown. —*n.* the distance ordinarily traveled by a commuter. [< Latin *commutare* < *com-* + *mutare* to change]

com·par·a·ble (kom′pər ə bəl), *adj.* able to be compared.

com·par·i·son (kəm par′ə sən), *n.* act or process of comparing; finding the likenesses and differences.

com·pas·sion·ate (kəm pash′ə nit), *adj.* desiring to relieve another's suffering; sympathetic. —**com·pas′sion·ate·ly,** *adv.*

com·pat·i·ble (kəm pat′ə bəl), *adj.* able to exist well together. [< Medieval Latin *compatibilem* < Latin *compati* suffer with] —**com·pat′i·bil′i·ty,** *n.*

com·pete (kəm pēt′), *v.i.,* **-pet·ed, -pet·ing. 1** try hard to obtain something wanted by others; be rivals. **2** take part (in a contest). [< Latin *competere* < *com-* together + *petere* seek]

com·pe·tence (kom′pə təns), *n.* ability; fitness.

com·pli·cate (kom′plə kāt), *v.t.,* **-cat·ed, -cat·ing.** make hard to understand, settle, cure, etc.; mix up; make complex. [< Latin *complicatum* folded together < *com-* together + *plicare* to fold]

com·po·sure (kəm pō′zhər), *n.* calmness; quietness; self-control.

com·pound (*adj.* kom′pound; *n.* kom′pound), *adj.* formed by the joining of two or more words. "Steamship," "high school," and "hit-and-run" are compound words. —*n.* substance formed by chemical combination of two or more elements in definite proportions by weight. [< Old French *compondre* put together < Latin *componere* < *com-* together + *ponere* put]

com·pound in·ter·est (kom′pound in′tər ist), interest paid on both the original sum of money borrowed or invested and interest added to it.

com·pre·hend (kom′pri hend′), *v.t.* understand the meaning of: *He comprehends the theory.* [< Latin *comprehendere* < *com-* + *prehendere* seize]

com·pre·hen·sion (kom′pri hen′shən), *n.* act or power of understanding; ability to get the meaning.

con·cen·trat·ed (kon′sən trā′tid), *adj.* (of liquids and solutions) made strong or stronger: *concentrated orange juice.*

con·cen·tra·tion camps (kon′sən trā′shən kamps′), camps where political enemies, prisoners of war, or members of minority groups are held by government order.

con·cert (kon′sərt), *n.* a musical performance in which several musicians or singers take part. [< French < Italian *concerto* < Latin *concertare* strive with < *com-* with + *certare* strive]

con·clude (kən klüd′), *v.t.,* **-clud·ed, -clud·ing.** bring to an end; finish. [< Latin *concludere* < *com-* up + *claudere* to close]

con·clu·sion (kən klü′zhən), *n.* final part; end. [< Latin *conclusionem* < *concludere* conclude]

con·clu·sive (kən klü′siv), *adj.* decisive; convincing; final. —**con·clu′sive·ly,** *adv.* —**con·clu′sive·ness,** *n.*

con·dem·na·tion (kon′dem nā′shən), *n.* **1** a condemning: *the condemnation of an unsafe bridge.* **2** a being condemned: *His condemnation made him an outcast.*

con·duc·tor (kən duk′tər), *n.* thing that transmits heat, electricity, light, sound, etc. Copper is a good conductor of heat and electricity.

cone (kōn), *n.* a solid figure formed by connecting a circle to a point not in the plane of the circle. [< Latin *conus* < Greek *konos* pine cone, cone]

concert
young clarinetists
playing a **concert**

a	hat	ī	ice	u̇	put	ə stands for	
ā	age	o	not	ü	rule	a	in about
ä	far, calm	ō	open	ch	child	e	in taken
âr	care	ȯ	saw	ng	long	i	in pencil
e	let	ô	order	sh	she	o	in lemon
ē	equal	oi	oil	th	thin	u	in circus
ėr	term	ou	out	ᴛʜ	then		
i	it	u	cup	zh	measure		

constellation

Sagittarius is a southern **constellation** between Scorpio and Capricorn.

con·fer·ence (kon′fər əns), *n.*
1 meeting of interested persons to discuss a particular subject.
2 association of schools, churches, etc., joined together for some special purpose.

con·fes·sion (kən fesh′ən), *n.* **1** an owning up; acknowledgment; admission. **2** admission of guilt.

con·ges·tion (kən jes′chən), *n.* an overcrowded condition.

con·grat·u·late (kən grach′ə lāt), *v.t.*, **-lat·ed, -lat·ing.** express one's pleasure at the happiness or good fortune of. [< Latin *congratulatum* congratulated < *com-* + *gratus* pleasing]

con·grat·u·la·tion (kən grach′ə lā′shən), *n.* **1** a congratulating. **2 congratulations,** *pl.* expression of pleasure at another's happiness.

con·nois·seur (kon′ə sėr′), *n.* a critical judge of art or of matters of taste; expert. [< Old French < *connoistre* know < Latin *cognoscere*]

con·science (kon′shəns), *n.* sense of right and wrong; ideas and feelings within a person that warn of what is wrong. [< Latin *conscientia* < *conscire* be conscious]

con·sci·en·tious (kon′shē en′shəs), *adj.* careful to do what one knows is right; controlled by conscience.

con·sen·sus (kən sen′səs), *n.* general agreement; opinion of all or most of the people consulted. [< Latin < *consentire* consent]

con·sent (kən sent′), *v.i.* give approval or permission; agree. —*n.* approval; permission; assent. [< Latin *consentire* < *com-* with + *sentire* feel, think] —**con·sent′er,** *n.*

con·se·quence (kon′sə kwens), *n. pl.,* **con·se·quenc·es.** result or effect; outcome.

con·ser·va·tion (kon′sər vā′shən), *n.* a preserving from harm or decay; protecting from loss or from being used up: *the conservation of forests.*

con·spir·a·tor (kən spir′ə tər), *n.* person who conspires; plotter.

con·spire (kən spīr′), *v.,* **-spired, -spir·ing.** —*v.i.* **1** plan secretly with others to do something unlawful or wrong; plot. **2** act together: *All things conspired to make her birthday a happy one.* —*v.t.* plot (something evil or unlawful). [< Latin *conspirare*, originally, breathe together < *com-* + *spirare* breathe] —**con·spir′er,** *n.*

con·stel·la·tion (kon′stə lā′shən), *n.* group of stars usually having a recognized shape. The Big Dipper is the easiest constellation to locate. [< Late Latin *constellationem* < Latin *com-* together + *stella* star]

con·struc·tion (kən struk′shən), *n.* **1** act of constructing; building. **2** thing constructed; building.

con·sume (kən süm′), *v.t.,* **-sumed, -sum·ing. 1** use up; spend. **2** eat or drink up. [< Latin *consumere* < *com-* + *sumere* take up]

con·sump·tion (kən sump′shən), *n.* **1** a consuming; using up; use: *We took along some food for consumption on our trip.* **2** amount used up: *The consumption of fuel oil is much greater in winter.* [< Latin *consumptionem* < *consumere* consume]

con·tem·po·rar·y (kən tem′pə rer′ē), *adj., n., pl.* **-rar·ies.** —*adj.* **1** belonging to or living in the same period of time: *Walt Whitman and Emily Dickinson were contemporary poets.* **2** of or having to do with the present time; modern: *contemporary literature.* —*n.* person living in the same period of time as another or others. [< *con-* together + Latin *temporarius* belonging to time < *tempus* time]

con·tract (kən trakt′), *v.t.* draw together; make shorter, narrower, or smaller: *contract a muscle. The earthworm contracted its body.* [< Latin *contractum* drawn together < *com-* + *trahere* to draw]

con·tro·ver·sy (kon′trə vėr′sē), *n., pl.* **-sies. 1** an arguing a question about which differences of opinion exist. **2** quarrel; wrangle. [< Latin *controversia* < *contra-* against + *versum* turned]

con·ven·ience (kən vē′nyəns), *n.* **1** fact or quality of being convenient: *The convenience of packaged goods increases their sale.* **2** comfort; advantage; accommodation.

con·ven·tion·al (kən ven′shə nəl), *adj.* **1** depending on conventions; customary: *"Good morning" is a conventional greeting.* **2** acting or behaving according to commonly accepted and approved ways. **3** of the usual type or design; commonly used or seen: *conventional furniture.* —**con·ven′·tion·al·ly,** *adv.*

con·vert (kən vėrt′), *v.t.* turn to another use; change into an object or material of a different form, character, or function: *These machines convert cotton into cloth.* [< Latin *convertere* < *com-* around + *vertere* to turn]

con·vict (*v.* kən vikt′; *n.* kon′vikt), *v.t.* prove guilty. —*n.* person serving a prison sentence for some crime. [< Latin *convictum* overcome, defeated < *com-* + *vincere* conquer]

con·vince (kən vins′), *v.t.,* **-vinced, -vinc·ing.** make a (person) feel sure; cause to believe; persuade by argument or proof: *The mistakes you made convinced me you had not studied your lesson.* [< Latin *convincere* < *com-* + *vincere* conquer] —**con·vin′ci·ble,** *adj.*

co·op·e·rate (kō op′ə rāt′), *v.i.,* **-rat·ed, -rat·ing.** work together; unite in producing a result. [< Late Latin *cooperatum* worked together < *co-* + *operari* to work]

co·or·di·na·tion (kō ôrd′n ā′shən), *n.* harmonious adjustment or working together.

cor·por·al (kôr′pər əl), *n.* the lowest-ranking noncommissioned officer in the army, ranking next below a sergeant and next above a private first class, usually in charge of a squad.

cor·po·ra·tion (kôr′pə rā′shən), *n.* group of persons with authority to act as a single person.

corps (kôr), *n., pl.* **corps** (kôrz). **1** branch of specialized military service: *the Army Medical Corps.* **2** group of people with special training, organized for working together: *a corps of nurses.* [< French < Latin *corpus* body. Doublet of CORPSE, CORPUS.]

corpse (kôrps), *n.* a dead human body. [< Old French *corps, cors* < Latin *corpus* body]

cor·pus·cle (kôr′pus′əl), *n.* any of the cells that form a large part of the blood, lymph, etc. [< Latin *corpusculum,* diminutive of *corpus* body]

cor·rupt (kə rupt′), *adj.* **1** influenced by bribes; dishonest: *a corrupt judge.* **2** morally bad; evil; wicked. —*v.t.* **1** bribe. **2** make evil or wicked. [< Latin *corruptum* corrupted, broken < *com-* + *rumpere* to break] —**cor·rupt′ly,** *adv.* —**cor·rupt′ness,** *n.*

cor·rupt·i·ble (kə rup′tə bəl), *adj.* that can be corrupted.

cos·mo·pol·i·tan (koz′mə pol′ə tən), *adj.* **1** free from national or local prejudices; feeling at home in all parts of the world. **2** belonging to all parts of the world; not limited to any one country or its inhabitants. —*n.* a person who feels at home all over.

cot·ton gin (kot′n jin′), machine for separating the fibers of cotton from the seeds; gin.

coun·ter·feit (koun′tər fit), *v.t.* copy (money, handwriting, pictures, etc.) in order to deceive or defraud; forge. —*n.* copy made to deceive or defraud and passed as genuine; forgery. —**count′ter·feit′er,** *n.*

cou·ra·geous (kə rā′jəs), *adj.* full of courage; brave; fearless. —**cou·ra′geous·ly,** *adv.*

cous·cous (küs′küs′), *n.* a North African dish consisting of coarsely ground hard wheat that has been soaked in water and steamed in broth. [< French, ultimately < Arabic *kaskasa* to grind, pound]

CPU, central processing unit (part of a computer which interprets and carries out instructions, and in which data are processed).

cred·it (kred′it), *n.* **1** delayed payment; time allowed for delayed payment. **2** on credit, on a promise to pay later. [< Middle French *crédit* < Italian *credito* < Latin *creditum* a loan < *credere* trust, entrust, believe]

cri·sis (krī′sis), *n., pl.* **cri·ses.** (-sēz′). a deciding event. [< Latin < Greek *krisis* < *krinein* decide]

cri·ter·i·on (krī tir′ē ən), *n., pl.* **cri·ter·i·a.** rule or standard for making a judgment; test. [< Greek *kritērion* < *krinein* decide, judge]

coordination
The gymnast exhibits **coordination** on the balance beam.

cotton gin
Eli Whitney's **cotton gin**

a	hat	ī	ice	u̇	put	ə stands for	
ā	age	o	not	ü	rule	a	in about
ä	far, calm	ō	open	ch	child	e	in taken
âr	care	ȯ	saw	ng	long	i	in pencil
e	let	ô	order	sh	she	o	in lemon
ē	equal	oi	oil	th	thin	u	in circus
ėr	term	ou	out	ᵺ	then		
i	it	u	cup	zh	measure		

crit·i·cal (krit/ə kəl), adj. 1 inclined to find fault or disapprove: a critical disposition. 2 full of danger or difficulty: The patient was critical. —crit/i·cal·ly, adv.

crit·i·cism (krit/ə siz/əm), n. unfavorable remarks or judgments; disapproval; faultfinding: I am the object of your criticism.

cri·tique (kri tēk/), n., v., -tiqued, -tiqu·ing. —n. a critical essay or review. —v.t. write a review of: criticize. [< French]

cro·quet (krō kā/), n. an outdoor game played by driving wooden balls through wickets with mallets. [< French, dialectal variant of crochet]

cue (kyü), n., v., cued, cue·ing or cu·ing. —n. action, speech, or word which gives the signal for an actor, singer, musician, etc., to enter or to begin. —v.t. provide (a person) with a cue or hint.

cul·tur·al (kul/chər əl), adj. of or having to do with culture: Music and art are cultural studies. —cul/tur·al·ly, adv.

cus·tom·ar·y (kus/tə mer/ē), adj. 1 according to custom; as a habit; usual; habitual: customary greetings. 2 holding or held by custom; established by custom. —cus/tom·ar/i·ly, adv.

cyl·in·der (sil/ən dər), n. a solid figure with two circular bases that are parallel and congruent. [< Latin cylindrus < Greek kylindros < kylindein to roll]

cym·bal (sim/bəl), n. one of a pair of brass or bronze plates, used as a musical instrument. Cymbals make a loud, ringing sound. [Old English cimbal < Latin cymbalum < Greek kymbalon < kymbē hollow of a vessel] —cym/bal·ist, n.

Declaration of Independence The **Declaration of Independence** helped establish our country's freedom from Great Britain.

D

day·dream (dā/drēm/), n. 1 dreamy thinking about pleasant things. 2 something imagined but not likely to come true. —v.i. think dreamily about pleasant things. —day/dream/er, n.

day·light-sav·ing time (dā/līt/sā/ving tīm/), time that is one hour ahead of standard time. Clocks are set ahead one hour in the spring and back one hour in the fall.

day·time (dā/tīm/), n. time when it is day and not night.

de·ceit·ful (di sēt/fəl), adj. 1 ready or willing to deceive. 2 meant to deceive; deceiving; misleading. —de·ceit/ful·ness, n.

Dec·la·ra·tion of In·de·pend·ence (dek/lə rā/shən əv in/di pen/dəns), the public statement adopted by the Second Continental Congress on July 4, 1776, in which the American colonies declared themselves free and independent of Great Britain.

de·com·pose (dē/kəm pōz/), v., -posed, -pos·ing. —v.t. rot; decay. —v.i. become rotten; decay. —de/com·pos/a·ble, adj.

de·duct·i·ble (di duk/tə bəl), adj. that can be deducted.

de·duc·tion (di duk/shən), n., pl. de·duc·tions. 1 act of deducting; subtraction. 2 amount deducted.

de·fen·si·ble (di fen/sə bəl), adj. 1 that can be defended. 2 justifiable. —de·fen/si·bil/i·ty, n. —de·fen/si·bly, adv.

de·fine (di fīn/), v.t., -fined, -fin·ing. make clear the meaning of; explain: A dictionary defines words. [< Latin definire to limit < de- down + finis end] —de·fin/a·ble, adj.

def·i·ni·tion (def/ə nish/ən), n. statement that makes clear the meaning of a word.

de·hy·drate (dē hī/drāt), v., de·hy·drat·ed, de·hy·drat·ing. —v.t. take water or moisture from; dry: dehydrate vegetables. —v.i. lose water or moisture. [< de- remove + Greek hydōr water] —de/hy·dra/·tion, n.

del·i·cate (del/ə kit), adj. of fine weave, quality, or make; easily torn; thin. [< Latin delicatus pampered] —del/i·cate·ly, adv. —del/i·cate·ness, n.

del·i·ca·tes·sen (del/ə kə tes/n), n. 1 sing. in use. store that sells prepared foods, such as cooked meats, smoked fish, cheese, salads, pickles, sandwiches, etc. 2 pl. in use. the foods sold at such a store. [< German Delikatessen, plural of Delikatesse delicacy]

de·mand (di mand/), v.t. 1 ask for as a right: The accused demanded a trial by jury. 2 ask for with authority: The teacher demanded quiet during the exam. 3 ask to know or to be told: demand an answer. 4 call for; require; need: Training a puppy demands patience. [< Latin demandare < de- + mandare to order]

de·moc·ra·cy (di mok′rə sē), *n., pl.*
-cies. 1 government that is run
by the people who live under it.
2 country, state, or community
having such a government.
[< Greek *dēmokratia* < *dēmos*
people + *kratos* rule]

de·mo·graph·ic (dē′mə graf′ik,
dem′ə graf′ik), *adj.* of or having
to do with demography.

de·mog·ra·phy (di mog′rə fē), *n.*
science dealing with statistics of
human populations, including size,
diseases, number of births, deaths,
etc. [< Greek *dēmos* people]

dem·on·stra·tion (dem′ən strā′shən),
n., pl. **dem·on·stra·tions.** parade
or meeting to protest or to make
demands: *The tenants held a
demonstration against the rent.*

de·pend·ent (di pen′dənt), *adj.*
relying on another for help,
support, etc.: *A child is dependent
on its parents.* —*n.* person who is
supported by another.
—**de·pend′ent·ly,** *adv.*

der·ma·tol·o·gist (der′mə tol′ə jist), *n.*
a doctor who specializes in
dermatology, a branch of
medicine that deals with the skin,
its structure, and its diseases.

de·scribe (di skrīb′), *v.t.,* **-scribed,
-scrib·ing.** tell or write about;
give a picture or an account of in
words. [< Latin *describere* < *de-*
+ *scribere* write] —**de·scrib′a·ble,**
adj.

de·seg·re·gate (dē seg′rə gāt), *v.,*
-gat·ed, -gat·ing. —*v.t.* abolish
racial segregation in: *desegregate
a public school.* —*v.i.* become
desegregated.
—**de·seg′re·ga′tion,** *n.*

de·spair (di spâr′), *n.* loss of hope;
a being without hope; a feeling
that nothing good can happen
to one; helplessness. —*v.i.* lose
hope; be without hope. [< Old
French *desperer* lose hope < Latin
desperare < *de-* out of, without +
sperare to hope]

de·struc·tive (di struk′tiv), *adj.*
destroying; causing destruction.
—**de·struc′tive·ness,** *n.*

de·tain (di tān′), *v.t.* **1** keep from
going; hold back. **2** keep from
going away; hold as a prisoner.
3 withhold. [< Old French *detenir*
< Latin *detinere* < *de-* + *tenere* to
hold] —**de·tain′ment,** *n.*

de·ten·tion (di ten′shən), *n.* **1** act of
detaining; holding back. **2** a
keeping in custody; confinement.
[< Late Latin *detentionem* < Latin
detinere detain]

di·ag·no·sis (dī′əg nō′sis), *n., pl.*
di·ag·no·ses (-sēz′). **1** act or
process of identifying a disease
by careful investigation of its
symptoms. **2** conclusion reached
after a careful study of symptoms
or facts. [< Greek < *dia-* apart +
gignoskein know]

di·a·logue (dī′ə lòg), *n.*
1 conversation between two or
more persons. **2** conversation in
a play, novel, story, etc. [< Greek
dialogos < *dia-* between + *logos*
speech]

di·am·e·ter (dī am′ə tər), *n.*
1 a line segment passing from one
side through the center of a circle,
sphere, etc., to the other side. **2** the
length of such a line segment;
measurement from one side to the
other through the center. [< Greek
diametros < *dia-* + *metron*
measure]

dic·ta·tor (dik′tā tər), *n., pl.*
dic·ta·tors. person exercising
absolute authority, without having
any claim, seizes control of a
government.

dif·fer·ent (dif′ər ənt), *adj.* **1** not alike;
not like; unlike: *A boat is different
from an automobile.* **2** not the
same; separate; distinct.
—**dif′fer·ent·ly,** *adv.*

dif·fe·ren·ti·ate (dif′ə ren′shē āt), *v.t.,*
-at·ed, -at·ing. make different;
cause to have differences.

di·lem·ma (də lem′ə), *n.* situation
requiring a choice between two
alternatives, which are or appear
equally unfavorable; difficult
choice. [< Greek *dilēmma* < *di-*
two + *lēmma* premise]

despair
a look of **despair**
on a young man's face

dialogue
performers involved in
a **dialogue**

a	hat	**ī**	ice	**u̇**	put	**ə** stands for	
ā	age	**o**	not	**ü**	rule	**a**	in about
ä	far, calm	**ō**	open	**ch**	child	**e**	in taken
âr	care	**ȯ**	saw	**ng**	long	**i**	in pencil
e	let	**ô**	order	**sh**	she	**o**	in lemon
ē	equal	**oi**	oil	**th**	thin	**u**	in circus
ėr	term	**ou**	out	**ʹH**	then		
i	it	**u**	cup	**zh**	measure		

discipline

Training a horse requires patience and **discipline.**

di·lute (də lüt′, dī lüt′), v., **di·lut·ed, di·lut·ing,** adj. —v.t. make weaker or thinner by adding water or some other liquid. —adj. weakened or thinned by the addition of water or some other liquid. [< Latin *dilutum* washed away < *dis-* + *luere* to wash]

dis·as·trous (də zas′trəs), adj. bringing disaster; causing much suffering or loss. —**dis·as′trous·ness,** n.

dis·ci·pline (dis′ə plin), n., v., **-plined, -plin·ing.** —n. training, especially training of the mind or character. —v.t. bring to a condition of order and obedience; bring under control; train. [< Latin *disciplina* < *discipulus* pupil] —**dis′ci·plin·er,** n.

dis·crim·i·na·tion (dis krim′ə nā′shən), n. a difference in attitude or treatment shown to a particular person, class, etc.: *racial discrimination.*

dis·in·te·grate (dis in′tə grāt), v., **-grat·ed, -grat·ing.** —v.t. break up; separate into small parts or bits. —v.i. become disintegrated; break up. —**dis·in′te·gra′tor,** n.

dis·miss (dis mis′), v.t., **dis·missed, dis·miss·ing,** 1 send away; allow to go: *At noon the teacher dismissed the class.* 2 put out of mind; stop thinking about: *Dismiss your troubles.* [< Latin *dismissum* sent away < *dis-* + *mittere* to send]

dis·pos·a·ble (dis pō′zə bəl), adj. 1 that can be disposed of after use. 2 at one's disposal; available.

dis·tance (dis′təns), n. length of a path over which an object travels, usually expressed in meters or kilometers.

dis·trac·tion (dis trak′shən), n. act of turning aside or drawing away the mind, attention, etc.

dis·trib·ute (dis trib′yüt), v.t., **-ut·ed, -ut·ing.** give some of to each; divide and give out in shares; deal out: *distribute candy.* [< Latin *distributum* divided < *dis-* apart, individually + *tribuere* assign]

di·ver·sion (də vėr′zhən), n. distraction from work, care, etc.; amusement; entertainment; pastime: *Baseball is my favorite diversion.*

di·vis·i·ble (də viz′ə bəl), adj. 1 capable of being divided. 2 capable of being divided without leaving a remainder. —**di·vis′i·bly,** adv.

does·n't (duz′nt), does not.

distance

a mountain in the far **distance**

dou·ble stars (dub′əl stärz′), two stars so close together that they look like one to the naked eye.

drown (droun), v.i. die under water or other liquid because of lack of air to breathe. [Old English *druncnian*]

dwarf (dwôrf), n., pl. **dwarfs** n. any of a class of stars of small size and luminosity, including the sun.

E

e·co·nom·ic (ē′kə nom′ik, ek′ə nom′ik), adj. of or having to do with economics. Economic problems have to do with the production, distribution, and consumption of goods and services.

ed·i·ble (ed′ə bəl), adj. fit to eat; eatable. —n. **edibles,** pl. things fit to eat; food. [< Late Latin *edibilis* < Latin *edere* eat]

ef·fec·tive (ə fek′tiv), adj. 1 able to produce an effect: *an effective order.* 2 producing the desired effect; getting results: *an effective medicine.* —**ef·fec′tive·ly,** adv. —**ef·fec′tive·ness,** n.

ef·fer·ves·cence (ef′ər ves′ns), n. 1 act or process of bubbling. 2 liveliness and gaiety.

ef·fi·cient (ə fish′ənt), adj. able to produce the effect wanted without waste of time, energy. [< Latin *efficientem* < *ex-* + *facere* do, make] —**ef·fi′cient·ly,** adv.

egg (eg), n. 1 the round or oval body, covered with a shell or membrane, laid by the female of birds, reptiles, amphibians, fishes, insects, etc., that do not bring forth living young. 2 **walk on eggs,** proceed or act cautiously. [< Scandinavian (Old Icelandic)] —**egg′like′,** adj.

e·las·tic (i las′tik), adj. 1 having the quality of returning to its original size, shape, or position after being stretched, squeezed, bent. 2 springing back; springy: *an elastic step.* —n. tape, cloth, cord, etc., woven partly of rubber. [< New Latin *elasticus* < Greek *elastos* ductile, driven < *elaunein* to drive] —**e·las′ti·cal·ly,** adv.

e·lec·tric cur·rent (i lek′trik kėr′ənt), the flow of electric charge, expressed in amperes.

e·lec·tron (i lek′tron), n. a negatively charged particle, often found in an atom, that usually moves around a nucleus. [< *electr(ic)* + *-on*]

el·e·gance (el′ə gəns), *n.* **1** good taste; refined grace and richness; luxurious beauty. **2** elegant.

el·o·quence (el′ə kwəns), *n.* flow of speech that has grace and force.

el·o·quent (el′ə kwənt), *adj.* **1** having eloquence. **2** very expressive: *eloquent eyes.* [< Latin *eloquentem* speaking out < *ex-* out + *loqui* speak] —**el′o·quent·ly,** *adv.*

e·lude (i lüd′), *v.t.,* **e·lud·ed, e·lud·ing.** avoid or escape by cleverness, quickness, etc.; slip away from; evade. [< Latin *eludere* < *ex-* out + *ludere* to play]

e·man·ci·pate (i man′sə pāt), *v.t.,* **-pat·ed, -pat·ing.** release from slavery or restraint; set free. [< Latin *emancipatum* set free < *ex-* away + *manus* hand + *capere* to take] —**e·man′ci·pa′tor,** *n.*

e·man·ci·pa·tion (i man′sə pā′shən), *n.* a release from slavery or restraint.

em·bar·go (em bär′gō), *n., pl.* **em·bar·goes. 1** an order of a government forbidding merchant ships to enter or leave its ports. **2** any restriction put on commerce by law. [< Spanish < *embargar* restrain, ultimately < Latin *in-* + Popular Latin *barra* bar]

em·bar·rass·ment (em bar′əs mənt), *n.* **1** act of embarrassing. **2** condition of being embarrassed.

e·mer·gen·cy (i mėr′jən sē), *n., pl.* **-cies,** *adj.* —*n.* a sudden need for immediate action. —*adj.* for a time of sudden need: *an emergency brake.*

em·i·grant (em′ə grənt), *n. pl.,* **em·i·grants,** *adj.* —*n.* person who leaves his or her own country or region to settle in another. —*adj.* leaving one's country to settle in another.

em·i·grate (em′ə grāt), *v.i.,* **em·i·grates, em·i·grat·ed, em·i·grat·ing.** leave one's own country or region to settle in another. [< Latin *emigratum* moved out < *ex-* out + *migrare* to move]

em·i·nent (em′ə nənt), *adj.* **1** above all or most others; outstanding; distinguished. **2** conspicuous; noteworthy. **3** standing out above other things; prominent. [< Latin *eminentem* standing out, prominent < *ex-* out + *minere* jut] —**em′i·nent·ly,** *adv.*

e·mo·tion·al (i mō′shə nəl), *adj.* **1** showing emotion: *an emotional reaction.* **2** appealing to the emotions. —**e·mo′tion·al·ly,** *adv.*

em·pire (em′pīr), *n.* group of countries or states under one ruler or government: *The Roman Empire consisted of many separate territories.* [< Old French < Latin *imperium* < *imperare*]

e·mul·si·fi·er (i mul′ sə fī ər), *n.* substance that keeps the particles of one liquid mixed in another liquid.

en·close (en klōz′), *v.t.,* **-closed, -clos·ing. 1** shut in on all sides; surround. **2** put a wall or fence around. **3** place in an envelope or package along with something else: *She enclosed a check.*

en·clo·sure (en klō′zhər), *n.* **1** a space that is enclosed. **2** thing that encloses. A wall or fence is an enclosure.

en·core (äng′kôr, än′kôr), *interj., n.,* —*interj.* once more; again. —*n.* a demand by the audience for the repetition of a song, etc., or for another appearance of the performer or performers. [< French]

en·cour·age·ment (en kėr′ij mənt), *n.* **1** condition of being or feeling encouraged. **2** something that encourages. **3** act of encouraging.

en·dan·ger (en dān′jər), *v.t.* cause danger to; expose to loss or injury.

en·dur·ance (en dùr′əns, en dyùr′əns), *n.* **1** power to last and to withstand hard wear: *A runner must have great endurance.* **2** power to put up with.

en·er·get·ic (en′ər jet′ik), *adj.* full of energy; eager to work.

emergency
an ambulance rushing
to an **emergency**

a	hat	**ī**	ice	**ù**	put		**ə** stands for	
ā	age	**o**	not	**ü**	rule		**a**	in about
ä	far, calm	**ō**	open	**ch**	child		**e**	in taken
âr	care	**ò**	saw	**ng**	long		**i**	in pencil
e	let	**ô**	order	**sh**	she		**o**	in lemon
ē	equal	**oi**	oil	**th**	thin		**u**	in circus
ėr	term	**ou**	out	**ᴛʜ**	then			
i	it	**u**	cup	**zh**	measure			

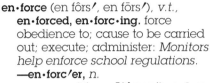

enforce | evidence

en·force (en fôrs′, en fōrs′), *v.t.*, **en·forced, en·forc·ing.** force obedience to; cause to be carried out; execute; administer: *Monitors help enforce school regulations.* —**en·forc′er,** *n.*

en·gage·ment (en gāj′mənt), *n.* **1** a promise or pledge to marry; betrothal. **2** appointment made to meet someone at a certain time.

en·slave (en slāv′), *v.t.*, **-slaved, -slav·ing.** make a slave or slaves of; take away freedom from. —**en·slave′ment,** *n.*

en·ter·tain·ment (en′tər tān′mənt), *n.* thing that interests, pleases, or amuses. A show or a circus is an entertainment.

en·tre·pre·neur (än′ trə prə nėr′), *n.* person who organizes and manages a business or industrial enterprise, attempting to make a profit but taking the risk of a loss. [< French < *entreprendre* undertake]

en·vel·op (en vel′əp), *v.t.* **1** wrap or cover; enfold. **2** hide; conceal: *Fog enveloped the village.* [< Old French *enveloper* < *en-* in + *voloper* to wrap] —**en·vel′op·er,** *n.*

en·ve·lope (en′və lōp, än′və lōp), *n.* a paper cover in which a letter or anything flat can be mailed, filed, etc. It can usually be folded over and sealed by wetting a gummed edge.

en·vi·a·ble (en′vē ə bəl), *adj.* to be envied; worth having; desirable.

en·vi·ron·ment (en vī′rən mənt), *n.* **1** all the surrounding things, conditions, and influences affecting the development of living things. **2** condition of the air, water, soil, etc.; natural surroundings. —**en·vi′ron·men′tal,** *adj.*

en·vi·sion (en vizh′ən), *v.t.* picture in one's mind.

en·vy (en′vē), *n.*, *pl.* **-vies,** *v.*, **-vied, -vy·ing.** —*n.* feeling of discontent, dislike, or desire because another has what one wants. —*v.t.* envy toward. [< Old French *envie* < Latin *invidia,* ultimately < *invidere* look with enmity at < *in-* against + *videre* see]

ep·i·dem·ic (ep′ə dem′ik), *n.* the rapid spread of a disease so that many people have it at the same time. [< Greek *epidēmia* a stay, visit, prevalence (of a disease) < *epi-* among + *dēmos* people]

ep·i·logue (ep′ə lòg), *n.* **1** a concluding section added to a novel, poem, etc., that rounds out or interprets the work. **2** speech or poem, addressed to the audience by one of the actors at the end of a play. [< Greek *epilogos,* ultimately < *epi-* above + *legein* speak]

e·qua·tion (i kwā′zhən), *n.* a mathematical sentence that states the equality of expressions.

es·pe·cial·ly (e spesh′ə lē), *adv.* more than others; specially; chiefly.

es·tate (e stāt′), *n.* **1** a large piece of land belonging to a person; landed property: *a beautiful estate with a country house.* **2** that which a person owns; property; possessions: *When she died, her estate was divided up.*

eu·lo·gy (yü′lə jē), *n.*, *pl.* **-gies.** speech or writing in praise of a person or thing, especially a deceased person. [< Greek *eulogia* < *eu-* well + *legein* speak]

e·val·u·ate (i val′yü āt), *v.t.*, **-at·ed, -at·ing.** find out the value or the amount of; estimate the worth or importance of; appraise.

e·ven (ē′vən), *adj.* **1** having the same height everywhere; level; flat; smooth: *Even country has no hills.* **2** at the same level; in the same plane or line. —*v.t.* make level or equal; make even: *She evened the edges by trimming them.* —*adv.* in an even manner. —**e′ven·ly,** *adv.* —**e′ven·ness,** *n.*

e·ven·tu·al·ly (i ven′chü ə lē), *adv.* in the end; finally.

eve·ry day (ev′rē dā′), all the days: *Every day is better than the last.*

eve·ry·day (ev′rē dā′), *adj.* **1** of every day; daily: *Accidents are everyday occurrences.* **2** for every ordinary day; not for Sundays or holidays: *She wears everyday clothes to work.* **3** not exciting.

eve·ry·thing (ev′rē thing), *pron.* every thing; all things. —*n.* something extremely important.

ev·i·dence (ev′ə dəns), *n.* **1** anything that shows what is true and what is not; facts; proof: *The evidence showed that he had not been near the place.* See synonym study below. **2** indication; sign: *A smile gives evidence of pleasure.* **Syn.** *n.* **1 Evidence, testimony, proof** mean that which tends to demonstrate the truth or falsity of something. **Evidence** applies to facts that indicate, without fully proving, that something is so:

entertainment

entertainment by the Morris Dancers in Covent Garden, England

Running away was evidence of his guilt. **Testimony** applies to any speech or action which serves as evidence of something: *Her testimony contradicted that of the preceding witness.* **Proof** means evidence so full and convincing as to leave no doubt or little doubt: *The signed receipt is proof that the letter was delivered.*

ex·ag·ge·rate (eg zaj′ə rāt′), *v.,* **-rat·ed, -rat·ing.** —*v.t.* make (something) greater than it is. [< Latin *exaggeratum* heaped up < *ex-* up + *agger* to heap]

ex·cel·lent (ek′sə lənt), *adj.* of unusually good quality; better than others. —**ex′cel·lent·ly,** *adv.*

ex·cep·tion·al (ek sep′shə nəl), *adj.* out of the ordinary; unusual. —**ex·cep′tion·al·ly,** *adv.*

ex·cite·ment (ek sīt′mənt), *n.* **1** an excited condition. **2** thing that excites. **3** an exciting; arousing.

ex·claim (ek sklām′), *v.i., v.t.* say or speak suddenly in surprise or strong feeling; cry out. [< Latin *exclamare* < *ex-* out + *clamare* cry out] —**ex·claim′er,** *n.*

ex·cla·ma·tion (ek′sklə mā′shən), *n.* something exclaimed; interjection. *Ah!* and *oh!* are exclamations.

ex·er·cise (ek′sər sīz), *n., v.,* **-cised, -cis·ing.** —*n.* **1** active use of the body or mind for their improvement or as a means of training for any kind of activity. **2** something that gives practice and training or causes improvement. —*v.i.* take exercise; go through exercises. [< Old French *exercice* < Latin *exercitium* < *exercere* keep busy < *ex-* out + *arcere* prevent]

ex·ist·ence (eg zis′təns), *n.* **1** being. **2** occurrence; presence.

ex·pand (ek spand′), *v.t.* **1** make larger; increase in size; enlarge. **2** spread out; open out; unfold. —*v.i.* grow or become larger. [< Latin *expandere* < *ex-* out + *pandere* to spread] —**ex·pand′a·ble,** *adj.*

ex·pec·ta·tion (ek′spek tā′shən), *n., pl.* **ex·pec·ta·tions.** an expecting; anticipation.

ex·pire (ek spīr′), *v.,* **-pired, -pir·ing.** —*v.i.* **1** come to an end: *You must obtain a new license when your old one expires.* **2** die. —*v.t.* breathe out (air). [< Latin *exspirare* < *ex-* out + *spirare* breathe]

ex·pres·sion (ek spresh′ən), *n.* **1** a putting into words; expressing: *the expression of an idea.* **2** word or group of words used as a unit: *"Shake a leg" is a slang expression.* **3** indication of feeling, spirit, character; look that shows feeling. —**ex·pres′sion·less,** *adj.*

ex·tend (ek stend′), *v.t.,* **ex·tend·ed, ex·tend·ing. 1** stretch out: *extend your hand.* **2** continue or prolong in time, space, or direction. [< Latin *extendere* < *ex-* out + *tendere* to stretch]

ex·tra·cur·ric·u·lar (ek′strə kə rik′yə lər), *adj.* outside the regular course of study: *Football and debating are extracurricular activities.*

ex·traor·di·nar·y (ek strôr′də ner′ē), *adj.* beyond what is ordinary; very unusual or remarkable; exceptional. —**ex·traor′di·nar′i·ly,** *adv.*

ex·tra·sen·sor·y (ek′strə sen′sər ē), *adj.* beyond the normal range of the senses.

ex·tra·ter·res·tri·al (ek′strə tə res′trē əl), *adj.* outside the earth or its atmosphere.

ex·trav·a·gant (ek strav′ə gənt), *adj.* **1** spending carelessly and lavishly; wasteful. **2** beyond the bounds of reason; excessive: *an extravagant price.* [< Medieval Latin *extravagantem* < Latin *extra-* outside + *vagari* to wander] —**ex·trav′a·gant·ly,** *adv.*

ex·tro·vert (ek′strə vėrt′), *n.* person tending to act rather than think. Extroverts are more interested in what is going on around them than in their own thoughts. Also, **extravert.** [< *extro-* outside (variant of *extra-*) + Latin *vertere* to turn]

exercise (def. 1)
participating in a road race for **exercise**

expression (def. 3)
a cheerful **expression**

a	hat	**ī**	ice	**u̇**	put		**ə** stands for	
ā	age	**o**	not	**ü**	rule		**a**	in about
ä	far, calm	**ō**	open	**ch**	child		**e**	in taken
âr	care	**ȯ**	saw	**ng**	long		**i**	in pencil
e	let	**ô**	order	**sh**	she		**o**	in lemon
ē	equal	**oi**	oil	**th**	thin		**u**	in circus
ėr	term	**ou**	out	**ŦH**	then			
i	it	**u**	cup	**zh**	measure			

F

floe (def. 2)

an ice **floe**

fa·cil·i·tate (fə sil′ə tāt), *v.t.*, **-tat·ed, -tat·ing.** make easy; lessen the labor of: *A computer facilitates many tasks.* —**fa·cil·i·ta′tor,** *n.*

fac·sim·i·le (fak sim′ə lē), *n.* an exact copy or likeness; perfect reproduction. [< Latin *fac* make + *simile* similar, like]

fac·tion (fak′shən), *n.* group of persons in a political party, church, club, etc., acting together or having a common purpose. [< Latin *factionem* party, class, originally, a doing < *facere* do]

fail·ure (fā′lyər), *n.* a being unable to do or become what is wanted, expected; not succeeding.

fa·mil·iar (fə mil′yər), *adj.* **1** known from constant association; well-known: *a familiar face.* **2** of everyday use; common; ordinary. **3** well-acquainted; versed: *He is familiar with French.* [< Latin *familiaris < familia*]

far·sight·ed (fär′sī′tid), *adj.* seeing distant things more clearly than near ones because the parallel light rays entering the eye come to a focus behind, rather than on, the retina. —**far′sight′ed·ness,** *n.*

fat (fat), *n.* **1** a white or yellow oily substance formed in animal tissue, made up chiefly of carbon, hydrogen, and oxygen. **2** **chew the fat,** SLANG. talk, especially in an idle fashion; chat. [Old English]

fa·vor·ite (fā′vər it), *adj.* liked better than others. —*n.* person or thing preferred above others.

feat (fēt), *n.* a great or unusual deed; act showing great skill, strength, or daring; achievement. [< Old French *fait* < Latin *factum* (thing) done]

fe·ro·cious (fə rō′shəs), *adj.* savagely cruel or destructive; fierce. [< Latin *ferocem* fierce] —**fe·ro′cious·ly,** *adv.* —**fe·ro′cious·ness,** *n.*

fe·roc·i·ty (fə ros′ə tē), *n., pl.* **-ties.** savage cruelty; fierceness.

Fer·ris wheel (fer′is hwēl′), a large, upright wheel rotating about a fixed axis, with swinging seats hanging from its rim. [< George W. G. *Ferris,* 1859–1896, American engineer, the inventor]

fer·ti·lize (fėr′tl īz), *v.t.,* **-lized, -liz·ing.** put fertilizer on.

fi·nal·ly (fī′nl ē), *adv.* **1** at the end; at last. **2** in such a way as to decide or settle the question.

floriculture

beautiful **floriculture**

at the Kew Gardens

in London

fi·nance charge (fī′nans chärj′), amount of interest charged to borrow money, usually in percent.

fin·ger (fing′gər), *n.* **1** one of the five slender divisions that end the hand, especially the four excluding the thumb. **2 have a finger in the pie, a** take part or share in a project; help to do something. **b** interfere or meddle. [Old English] —**fin′ger·like′,** *adj.*

fire ex·tin·guish·er (fīr′ ek sting′gwish ər), a portable container filled with chemicals which can be sprayed on a fire to put it out.

flam·boy·ant (flam boi′ənt), *adj.* **1** gorgeously brilliant; flaming; showily striking: *flamboyant colors.* **2** very ornate; much decorated; florid: *flamboyant architecture.* **3** given to display; ostentatious; showy. **4** having wavy lines or flamelike curves: *flamboyant designs.* [< French] —**flam·boy′ant·ly,** *adv.*

flam·ma·ble (flam′ə bəl), *adj.* easily set on fire; inflammable.

flap·per (flap′ər), *n., pl.* **flap·pers.** a young woman of the 1920s who dressed unconventionally and behaved with some freedom.

floe (flō), *n.* **1** field or sheet of floating ice. **2** a floating piece broken off from such a field or sheet. [< Scandinavian (Norwegian) *flo*]

flop·py disk (flop′ē disk′), a flexible plastic disk with a magnetic surface, used for computer data storage.

flo·ri·cul·ture (flôr′ə kul′chər), *n.* cultivation of flowers or flowering plants, especially ornamental plants. —**flo′ri·cul′tur·ist,** *n.*

for·bid·den (fər bid′n), *adj.* not allowed; against the law or rules; prohibited. —*v.* a pp. of **forbid.**

force (fôrs), *n.* any action that accelerates an object, expressed in newtons. [< Old French, ultimately < Latin *fortis* strong] —**force′less,** *adj.* —**forc′er,** *n.*

fo·reign pol·i·cy (fôr′ən pol′ə sē), plan of action adopted as tactically or strategically best by a government for managing affairs with other nations.

fore·see (fôr sē′), *v.,* **-saw, -seen, -see·ing.** —*v.t.* see or know beforehand; anticipate. —*v.i.* use foresight. —**fore·se′er,** *n.*

fore·word (fôr′wėrd′), *n.* a brief introduction or preface to a book, speech, etc.

for·feit (fôr′fit), *v.t.* lose or have to give up by one's own act, neglect, or fault. —*n.* loss or giving up of something as a penalty. [< Old French *forfait* a forfeit < *forfaire* transgress, do wrong] —**for′feit·er**, *n.*

for·mu·la (fôr′myə lə), *n., pl.* **-las** or **-lae.** an equation that states a general fact or rule by using variables. [< Latin, diminutive of *forma* form]

for·syth·i·a (fôr sith′ē ə), *n.* any of a genus of shrubs of the olive family, having many bell-shaped, yellow flowers. [< New Latin < William *Forsyth*, 1737–1804, British horticulturist]

found·ry (foun′drē), *n., pl.* **-ries.** place where metal is melted and molded; place where things are made of molten metal.

fran·chise (fran′chīz), *n.* right to vote: *The United States gave women the franchise in 1920.* [< Old French < *franc* free]

fu·gi·tive (fyü′jə tiv), *n.* person who is fleeing or who has fled from danger, an enemy, justice, etc. [< Latin *fugitivus* < *fugere* flee]

fun·nel (fun′l), *n.* **1** a tapering utensil with a wide, cone-shaped mouth ending in a tube, used to prevent spilling in pouring liquids, powder, grain, etc., into containers with small openings. **2** anything shaped like a funnel. [< Old French *fonel*, ultimately < Late Latin *fundibulum* < Latin *infundibulum* < *in-* in + *fundere* pour]

fuse (fyüz), *n., v.,* **fused, fus·ing.** —*n.* wire or strip of easily fusible metal inserted in an electric circuit that melts and breaks the connection when the current becomes dangerously strong. —*v.t.* join together by melting; melt. —*v.i.* become melted; melt together: *Copper and zinc fuse to make brass.* [< Latin *fusum* poured, melted < *fundere* pour, melt] —**fuse′less**, *adj.*

G

ga·lumph (gə lumf′), *v.i.* gallop in a clumsy way: *cows galumphing home.* [perhaps blend of *gallop* and *triumph*; coined by Lewis Carroll]

gas·o·hol (gas′ə hȯl), *n.* a fuel for internal-combustion engines, composed of ninety percent unleaded gasoline and ten percent ethyl alcohol. [blend of *gasoline* and *alcohol*]

Gei·ger count·er (gī′gər koun′tər), an instrument used to detect radiation from radioactive material. [< Hans *Geiger*, 1882–1947, German physicist]

gen·e·ra·tor (jen′ə rā′tər), *n.* a device that uses electromagnetic induction to change mechanical energy into electricity.

gen·tle (jen′tl), *adj.,* **-tler, -tlest. 1** not severe, rough; mild. **2** soft; low. [< Old French *gentil* < Latin *gentilis* of the (same) family, national < *gentem* family, nation]

gen·u·ine (jen′yü ən), *adj.* **1** actually being what it seems or is claimed to be; real; true. **2** without pretense; sincere; frank. [< Latin *genuinus* native, natural, ultimately < *gignere* beget]

ge·og·ra·phy (jē og′rə fē), *n., pl.* **-phies. 1** study of the earth's surface, climate, continents, etc. **2** the surface features of a place or region: *the geography of Ohio.* [< Greek *geōgraphia* < *gē* earth + *graphein* describe]

ge·om·e·try (jē om′ə trē), *n.* branch of mathematics which studies the relationship of points, lines, angles, and surfaces of figures in space; the mathematics of space. [< Greek *geōmetria* < *gē* earth + *-metria* measuring]

ghet·to (get′ō), *n., pl.* **ghet·tos. 1** part of a city where any racial group or nationality lives. **2** (formerly) a part of a city in Europe where Jews were required to live. [< Italian]

funnel (def. 2) the **funnel** of a tornado approaching Enid, Oklahoma

a	hat	ī	ice	u̇	put	ə stands for	
ā	age	o	not	ü	rule	a	in about
ä	far, calm	ō	open	ch	child	e	in taken
âr	care	ȯ	saw	ng	long	i	in pencil
e	let	ô	order	sh	she	o	in lemon
ē	equal	oi	oil	th	thin	u	in circus
ėr	term	ou	out	ᴛʜ	then		
i	it	u	cup	zh	measure		

ging·ham (ging′əm), *n.* a cotton cloth made from colored threads. Its patterns are usually in stripes, plaids, or checks. [< French *guingan* < Malay *ginggang* striped]

gi·raffe (jə raf′), *n.* a large African mammal that chews its cud and has a very long neck, long legs, and a spotted skin. [< Italian *giraffa* < Arabic *zarāfah*]

glimpse (glimps), *n., v.,* **glimpsed, glimps·ing.** —*n.* **1** a short, quick view or look. **2** a short, faint appearance. —*v.t.* catch a short, quick view of. [Middle English *glimsen*]

gnu (nü, nyü), *n., pl.* **gnus** or **gnu.** a large African antelope with an oxlike head, curved horns, high shoulders, and a long tail; wildebeest. [< Kaffir *nqu*]

go·ing to (gō′ing tù), intending to; planning to: *I am going to read this novel.*

gon·do·la (gon′dl ə), *n.* a long, narrow boat with a high peak at each end, rowed or poled by a single oar. It is used on the canals of Venice. [< Italian]

gou·lash (gü′läsh), *n.* stew made of beef or veal and vegetables. [< Hungarian *gulyás (hús)* herdsman's (meat)]

gov·ern·ment (guv′ərn mənt, guv′ər mənt), *n.* rule or authority over a country, state, district, etc.; authoritative direction of the affairs of state.

grad·u·ate (*v.* graj′ü āt; *n., adj.* graj′ü it), *v.,* **-at·ed, -at·ing,** *n., adj.* —*v.i.* finish a course of study at a school, college, or university and receive a diploma or other document saying so. —*n.* person who had graduated and has a diploma. —*adj.* that has graduated. [< Medieval Latin *graduatum* graduated < Latin *gradus* step, degree]

grad·u·a·tion (graj′ü ā′shən), *n.* **1** a graduating from a school, college, or university. **2** ceremony of graduating; graduating exercises.

gra·ham crack·ers (grā′əm krak′ərz), *n.* crackers made from whole-wheat flour, including all the bran. [< Sylvester *Graham,* 1794–1851, American minister and dietary reformer, who advocated the use of this flour]

gram·mat·i·cal·ly (grə mat′ik lē), *adv.* according to the rules and principles of grammar.

grand·daugh·ter (grand′dô′tər), *n.* daughter of one's son or daughter.

graph·ic (graf′ik), *adj.* **1** producing by words the effect of a picture; lifelike; vivid: *a graphic description of a battle.* **2** of or about graphs and their use. —*n.* an etching, drawing, lithograph, etc.; any work of the graphic arts. [< Latin *graphicus* < Greek *graphikos* < *graphein* write] —**graph′ic·al·ly,** *adv.*

great-aunt (grāt′ant′), *n.* grandaunt.

great-grand·moth·er (grāt′grand′muŦH′ər), *n.* grandmother of one's father or mother.

griev·ance (grē′vəns), *n., pl.* **griev·an·ces.** a real or imagined wrong; reason for being angry or annoyed; cause for complaint.

griev·ous (grē′vəs), *adj.* **1** hard to bear; causing great pain or suffering; severe: *grievous cruelty.* **2** very evil or offensive; outrageous. —**griev′ous·ly,** *adv.*

gross in·come (grōs′ in′kum′), the total amount of money earned.

group·ing sym·bols (grü′ping sim′belz), symbols, such as parentheses, brackets, and fraction bars that group numbers and/or variables together.

guar·an·tee (gar′ən tē′), *n., v.,* **-teed, -tee·ing.** —*n.* a promise or pledge to replace or repair a purchased product, return the money paid, etc., if the product is not as represented. —*v.t.* stand back of; give a guarantee for.

guard·ed (gär′did), *adj.* kept safe; carefully watched over; defended; protected. —**guard′ed·ly,** *adv.* —**guard′ed·ness,** *n.*

Gua·te·ma·la (gwä′tə mä′lə), *n.* country in NW Central America. 6,817,000 pop.; 42,000 sq. mi. (108,800 sq. km.) *Capital:* Guatemala City. —**Gua′te·ma′lan,** *adj., n.*

gul·li·ble (gul′ə bəl), *adj.* easily deceived or cheated.

gum·bo (gum′bō), *n., pl.* **-bos. 1** the okra plant. **2** its sticky pods. **3** soup usually made of chicken and rice and thickened with these pods. [of Bantu origin]

gun (gun), *n.* weapon with a metal tube for shooting bullets or shells. **jump the gun, a** start too soon; start before the signal to do so. **b** get a head start on one's opposition. [< Scandinavian (Old Icelandic) *Gunnhildr,* woman's name]

granddaughter granddaughters and grandmother sharing some affection

H

half·way (haf′wā′), *adv.* half the way; half the required distance: *The rope reached only halfway around the tree.* —*adj.* midway.

ham·mock (ham′ək), *n.* a hanging bed or couch made of canvas, netted cord, etc., suspended by cords or ropes at both ends. [< Spanish *hamaca* < Taino]

hand·cuff (hand′kuf′), *n.* one of a pair of metal rings joined by a short chain and locked around the wrists of a prisoner. —*v.t.* put handcuffs on.

hard·ware (härd′wâr′), *n.* the mechanical parts of a computer, teaching machine, nuclear reactor, etc.

har·dy (här′dē), *adj.*, **-di·er, -di·est.** able to bear hard treatment, fatigue, etc.; strong; robust: *hardy frontier settlers.* —**har′di·ly,** *adv.* —**har′di·ness,** *n.*

Har·lem (här′ləm), *n.* northern section of Manhattan, bordering the Harlem and East rivers.

harsh (härsh), *adj.* rugged; bleak: *a harsh coast.* [Middle English *harsk* < Scandinavian (Danish) *harsk* rancid] —**harsh′ly,** *adv.* —**harsh′ness,** *n.*

have to (haf′ tü), be required to, must: *You have to be on time.*

haz·ard·ous (haz′ər dəs), *adj.* full of risk; dangerous; perilous.

heart·y (här′tē), *adj.*, **heart·i·er, heart·i·est,** *n.*, *pl.* **heart·ies.** —*adj.* **1** warm and friendly; genuine; sincere. **2** strong and well; vigorous. —*n.* a brave and good comrade.

heat sourc·es (hēt′ sôr′səz), anything that can give off heat because its temperature is higher than that of its surroundings.

hel·i·cop·ter (hel′ə kop′tər), *n.* type of aircraft without wings, lifted from the ground and supported in the air by one or more horizontal propellers or rotors. [< French *hélicoptère* < Greek *helix, helikos* spiral + *pteron* wing]

hel·met (hel′mit), *n.* a covering made of steel, leather, plastic, or some other sturdy material, worn to protect the head. [< Old French; of Germanic origin]

he·ro·ic (hi rō′ik), *adj.* **1** of, like, or suitable for a hero, his deeds, or his qualities; brave, great, or noble. **2** of or about heroes and their deeds; epic. **3** unusually daring or bold. —**he·ro′i·cal·ly,** *adv.*

her·o·ism (her′ō iz′əm), *n.* **1** actions and qualities of a hero or heroine; great bravery; daring courage. **2** a doing something noble at great cost to oneself; a very brave act.

hes·i·tate (hez′ə tāt), *v.i.*, **-tat·ed, -tat·ing. 1** feel that perhaps one should not; be unwilling; not want: *I hesitated to interrupt you.* **2** stop for an instant; pause. [< Latin *haesitatum* stuck fast < *haerere* stick fast] —**hes′i·tat′er,** *n.*

hick·o·ry (hik′ər ē), *n.*, *pl.* **-or·ies.** any of a genus of North American trees of the same family as the walnut, bearing a hard nut with an edible, sweet kernel. [alteration of earlier *pohickery*; of Algonquian origin]

hid·e·ous (hid′ē əs), *adj.* very ugly; frightful; horrible. [< Old French *hideus* < *hide* fear, horror] —**hid′e·ous·ness,** *n.*

hin·drance (hin′drəns), *n.* **1** person or thing that hinders. **2** act of hindering. See **obstacle** for synonym study.

his·to·ri·cal fic·tion (hi stôr′ə kəl fik′shən), novels, plays, and other prose writings about imaginary people and happenings that take place in the past.

ho·gan (hō′gän′), *n.* dwelling used by the Navajos. Hogans are built with logs and mounded over with earth. [< Navajo *hoghan* house]

home·land (hōm′land′), *n.*, *pl.* **home·lands.** country that is one's home; one's native land.

hom·i·ny (hom′ə nē), *n.* whole or coarsely ground hulled corn, usually eaten boiled.

hazardous

hazardous barrels of toxic waste

helicopter

a	hat	ī	ice	u̇	put	ə stands for	
ā	age	o	not	ü	rule	a	in about
ä	far, calm	ō	open	ch	child	e	in taken
âr	care	ȯ	saw	ng	long	i	in pencil
e	let	ô	order	sh	she	o	in lemon
ē	equal	oi	oil	th	thin	u	in circus
ėr	term	ou	out	ᴛʜ	then		
i	it	u	cup	zh	measure		

hors d'oeu·vre (ôr′ dèrv′), *pl.* **hors d'oeu·vres** (ôr′ dèrvz′), **hors d'oeu·vre.** relish, light food, or dainty sandwich served as an appetizer before the regular courses of a meal. [< French, literally, apart from (the main) work]

hy·drant (hī′drənt), *n.* a large, upright cylinder with a valve for drawing water directly from a water main; fireplug.

hy·drau·lic (hī drò′lik), *adj.* 1 having to do with water or other liquids at rest or in motion. 2 operated by the pressure of water or other liquids in motion, especially when forced through an opening or openings. [< Latin *hydraulicus*, ultimately < Greek *hydōr* water + *aulos* pipe]

hy·dro·e·lec·tric (hī′drō i lek′trik), *adj.* of or having to do with the generation of electricity by water power.

hy·dro·gen (hī′drə jən), *n.* a colorless, odorless, gaseous element that burns easily and weighs less than any other element. It combines with oxygen to form water. [< French *hydrogène* < *hydro-* + *-gène* -gen]

hy·dro·pho·bi·a (hī′drə fō′bē ə), *n.* an abnormal fear of water.

hy·per·crit·i·cal (hī′pər krit′ə kəl), *adj.* too critical.

hyp·o·crite (hip′ə krit), *n.* 1 person who pretends to be very good or religious. 2 person who is not sincere; pretender. [< Greek *hypokritēs* actor < *hypo-* under + *kritēs* a judge]

igloo

Inuit youngsters in an

igloo

I

i·den·ti·fy (ī den′tə fī), *v.t.*, **-fied, -fy·ing.** recognize as being, or show to be, a particular person or thing; prove to be the same. —**i·den′ti·fi′a·ble,** *adj.* —**i·den′ti·fi′a·bly,** *adv.*

ig·loo (ig′lü), *n., pl.* **-loos.** a dome-shaped hut used by Eskimos, often built of blocks of hard snow. [< Eskimo *igdlu* house]

im·me·di·ate·ly (i mē′dē it lē), *adv.* at once; without delay.

im·mi·grant (im′ə grənt), *n., pl.* **im·mi·grants.** person who comes into a foreign country or region to live there: *Canada has many immigrants from Europe.*

immigrant

immigrants on Ellis Island in the 1900s

im·mi·grate (im′ə grāt), *v.i.,* **-grat·ed, -grat·ing.** come into a foreign country or region to live there.

im·mi·gra·tion (im′ə grā′shən), *n.* 1 a coming into a foreign country or region to live there. 2 the persons who immigrate; immigrants.

im·mi·nent (im′ə nənt), *adj.* likely to happen soon; about to occur: *Black clouds show rain is imminent.* [< Latin *imminentem* overhanging, threatening] —**im′mi·nent·ly,** *adv.*

im·mune (i myün′), *adj.* protected from disease, poison, etc.; having immunity: *Vaccination makes a person practically immune to polio.* [< Latin *immunis*, originally, free from obligation < *in-* not + *munia* duties, services]

im·mu·nize (im′yə nīz), *v.t.,* **-nized, -niz·ing.** give immunity to; make immune: *Vaccination immunizes people against smallpox.* —**im′mu·ni·za′tion,** *n.*

im·pa·la (im pä′lə, im pal′ə), *n.* a medium-sized reddish-brown antelope, found in eastern and southern Africa and noted for long leaps. The male has long curved horns. [< Zulu]

im·pede (im pēd′), *v.t.,* **-ped·ed, -ped·ing.** stand in the way of; hinder; obstruct. [< Latin *impedire* < *in-* on + *pedem* foot]

im·ped·i·ment (im ped′ə mənt), *n.* 1 hindrance; obstruction. 2 some physical defect, a speech defect.

im·per·cep·ti·ble (im′pər sep′tə bəl), *adj.* that cannot be perceived or felt; very slight. —**im′per·cep′ti·bly,** *adv.*

im·per·i·al·ism (im pir′ē ə liz′əm), *n.* policy of extending the rule or authority of one country over other countries and colonies.

im·port (*v.* im pôrt′; *n.* im′pôrt), *v.t.* bring in from a foreign country for sale or use: *The United States imports coffee from Brazil.* —*n.* article imported: *Rubber is a useful import.* [< Latin *importare* < *in-* in + *portare* carry]

im·pos·ing (im pō′zing), *adj.* impressive because of size, appearance, dignity, etc.

im·ply (im plī′), *v.t.,* **-plied, -ply·ing.** mean without saying so; express indirectly; suggest: *Her smile implied that she had forgiven us.* [< Old French *emplier* involve, put (in) < Latin *implicare* < *in-* in + *plicare* to fold]

im·pres·sion (im presh′ən), *n.* **1** effect produced on the senses or mind. **2** effect produced by any operation or activity.

im·prove·ment (im prüv′mənt), *n.* a making better; becoming better.

in·born (in′bôrn′), *adj.* born in a person; instinctive; natural.

in·con·ceiv·a·ble (in′kən sē′və bəl), *adj.* **1** impossible to imagine. **2** hard to believe; incredible. —**in′con·ceiv′a·bly**, *adv.*

in·con·tro·vert·i·ble (in′kon trə vėr′tə bəl), *adj.* that cannot be disputed or denied.

in·cor·po·rate (*v.* in kôr′pə rāt′; *adj.* in kôr′pər it), *v.,* **-rat·ed, -rat·ing,** *adj.* —*v.t.* make (something) a part of something else; join or combine (something) with something else. —*adj.* united; combined; incorporated. [< Latin *incorporatum* formed into a body < *in-* into + *corpus* body]

in·de·struct·i·ble (in′di struk′tə bəl), *adj.* that cannot be destroyed. —**in′de·struct′i·bly**, *adv.*

in·di·go (in′də gō), *n., pl.* **-gos,** *adj.* —*n.* a blue dye formerly obtained from various plants, but now usually made artificially. —*adj.* deep violet-blue. [< Spanish *índigo* < Latin *indicum* < Greek *indikon,* originally adjective, Indian]

in·e·qual·i·ty (in′i kwol′ə tē), *n., pl.* **-ties.** a mathematical sentence with one of the following symbols: <, >, ≤ , ≥.

in·ev·i·ta·ble (in ev′ə tə bəl), *adj.* not to be avoided; sure to happen. [< Latin *inevitabilis* < *in-* not + *evitare* avoid < *ex-* out + *vitare* shun] —**in·ev′i·ta·bly**, *adv.*

in·fer (in fėr′), *v.,* **-ferred, -fer·ring.** —*v.t.* find out by a process of reasoning from something known or assumed; conclude: *People inferred that so able a governor would make a good President.* —*v.i.* draw inferences. [< Latin *inferre* introduce, bring in < *in-* in + *ferre* bring] —**in·fer′a·ble**, *adj.*

in·fer·ence (in′fər əns), *n.* **1** process of inferring. **2** that which is inferred; conclusion.

in·flame (in flām′), *v.t.,* **-flamed, -flam·ing. 1** make more violent; excite: *The stirring speech inflamed the crowd.* **2** make unnaturally hot, red, sore, or swollen. [< Latin *inflammare* < *in-* in + *flamma* flame]

in·flu·ence (in′flü əns), *n., v.,* **-enced, -enc·ing.** —*n.* **1** power of persons or things to act on others, seen only in its effects: *the influence of the moon on the tides.* **2** power to produce an effect without using force or authority. —*v.t.* have an influence on: *The moon influences the tides.* [< Medieval Latin *influentia* emanation from the stars believed to affect human destiny, originally, a flowing in < Latin *in-* in + *fluere* to flow]

in·flu·en·tial (in′flü en′shəl), *adj.* **1** having much influence: *Influential friends helped her to get a job.* **2** using influence; producing results. —**in′flu·en′tial·ly**, *adv.*

i·ni·ti·a·tion (i nish′ē ā′shən), *n.* ceremonies by which one is admitted to a group or society.

in·jure (in′jər), *v.t.,* **-jured, -jur·ing. 1** do damage to; harm; hurt: *I injured my arm while skiing.* **2** be unfair to; do injustice or wrong to.

in·no·cent (in′ə sənt), *adj.* **1** doing no wrong or evil; free from sin or wrong; not guilty. **2** without knowledge of evil: *A baby is innocent.* —*n.* an innocent person. [< Latin *innocentem* < *in-* not + *nocere* to harm] —**in′no·cent·ly**, *adv.*

in·put (in′pùt′), *v.,* **in·put, in·put·ting,** *n.* —*v.t.* put in; introduce. —*n.* information or instructions put into a computer.

in·scrip·tion (in skrip′shən), *n.* something inscribed; words, names, letters, etc., written or engraved on stone, metal, paper. [< Latin *inscriptionem* < *inscribere*]

impression (def. 2) The flood left an **impression** in the mud.

inscription an **inscription** on Thomas Jefferson's gravestone

a	hat	ī	ice	ù	put	ə stands for
ā	age	o	not	ü	rule	a in about
ä	far, calm	ō	open	ch	child	e in taken
âr	care	ȯ	saw	ng	long	i in pencil
e	let	ô	order	sh	she	o in lemon
ē	equal	oi	oil	th	thin	u in circus
ėr	term	ou	out	ŦH	then	
i	it	u	cup	zh	measure	

in·sen·si·tive (in sen′sə tiv), *adj.*
1 not sensitive; not able to feel or
notice. **2** slow to feel or notice.
—**in·sen′si·tive·ly,** *adv.*
—**in·sen′si·tive·ness,** *n.*

in·spect (in spekt′), *v.t.* **1** look over
carefully; examine: *A dentist
inspects my teeth twice a year.*
2 examine formally; look over
officially: *All mines are inspected
by government officials.* [< Latin
inspectum looked over < *in-* +
specere to look]
—**in·spect′a·ble,** *adj.*

in·spec·tion (in spek′shən), *n.*
an inspecting; examination.

in·stall·ment (in stȯl′mənt), *n., pl.*
in·stall·ments. part of a sum of
money or of a debt to be paid at
certain stated times: *The table cost
$100; we paid for it in installments.*

in·stinc·tive (in stingk′tiv), *adj.* of or
having to do with instinct; caused
or done by instinct; born in an
animal or person, not learned: *The
spinning of webs is instinctive in
spiders.* —**in·stinc′tive·ly,** *adv.*

in·struc·tion·al (in struk′shə nəl), *adj.*
of or for instruction; educational.

in·struc·tor (in struk′tər), *n.* person
who instructs; teacher.

in·suf·fi·cient (in′sə fish′ənt), *adj.*
not sufficient; lacking in what is
needed; inadequate.
—**in′suf·fi′cient·ly,** *adv.*

in·su·late (in′sə lāt), *v.t.,* **-lat·ed,
-lat·ing. 1** keep from losing or transferring electricity, heat, sound, etc.,
especially by covering, packing, or
surrounding with a nonconducting
material. **2** set apart; separate from
others; isolate. [< Latin *insula* island]

in·su·la·tion (in′sə lā′shən), *n.* **1** an
insulating. **2** a being insulated.
3 material used in insulating.

in·su·la·tor (in′sə lā′tər), *n.* that
which insulates; something that
prevents the passage of electricity,
heat, or sound; nonconductor.

in·tel·li·gence (in tel′ə jəns), *n.* ability
to learn and know; quickness of
understanding; mind.

in·ten·si·ty (in ten′sə tē), *n., pl.* **-ties.**
amount or degree of strength of
electricity, heat, light, sound, etc.,
per unit of area, volume, etc.

in·ter·cept (in′tər sept′), *v.t.* take or
seize on the way from one place
to another: *intercept a letter,
intercept a messenger.* [< Latin
interceptum caught between,
interrupted < *inter-* between
+ *capere* to take, catch]
—**in′ter·cep′tion,** *n.*

intensity
The **intensity** of the
lava from a volcano
changes the environment.

in·ter·change·a·ble (in′tər chān′jə
bəl), *adj.* **1** capable of being used
or put in place of each other.
2 able to change places.
—**in′ter·change′a·bly,** *adv.*

in·ter·con·nect (in′tər kə nekt′), *v.t.*
connect with each other.
—**in′ter·con·nec′tion,** *n.*

in·ter·dis·ci·pli·nar·y (in′tər dis′ə plə
ner′ē), *adj.* between different fields
of study.

in·ter·fere (in′tər fir′), *v.i.,* **-fered,
-fer·ing. 1** get in the way of each
other; come into opposition; clash.
2 mix in the affairs of others;
meddle. [< Old French *entreferir*
strike each other < *entre-* between
+ *ferir* to strike] —**in′ter·fer′er,** *n.*

in·ter·me·di·ate[1] (in′tər mē′dē it),
adj. being or occurring between;
middle: *Gray is intermediate
between black and white.* —*n.*
person who acts between others
to bring about an agreement;
mediator. [< Latin *intermedius
< inter-* between + *medius* in the
middle]

in·ter·me·di·ate[2] (in′tər mē′dē āt),
v.i., **-at·ed, -at·ing.** come in to help
settle a dispute; mediate. [< *inter-*
+ *mediate,* verb]

in·ter·min·gle (in′tər ming′gəl), *v.t.,
v.i.,* **-gled, -gling.** mix together.

in·ter·mis·sion (in′tər mish′ən), *n.*
a time between periods of activity;
pause: *The band played only with
a short intermission at ten.*

in·ter·na·tion·al (in′tər nash′ə nəl),
adj. **1** between or among nations:
*A treaty is an international
agreement.* **2** having to do with
the relations between nations.
—**in′ter·na′tion·al·ly,** *adv.*

in·ter·per·son·al (in′tər pėr′sə nəl),
adj. between persons.

in·ter·pre·ta·tion (in tėr′prə tā′shən),
n. an interpreting; explanation.

in·ter·sec·tion (in′tər sek′shən), *n.*
point, line, or place where one
thing crosses another.
—**in′ter·sec′tion·al,** *adj.*

in·ter·vene (in′tər vēn′), *v.i.,* **-vened,
-ven·ing.** come between persons or
groups to help settle a dispute; act
as an intermediary: *The President
was asked to intervene in the coal
strike.* [< Latin *intervenire < inter-*
between + *venire* come]
—**in′ter·ve′nor, in′ter·ven′er** *n.*

in·ter·ven·tion (in′tər ven′shən), *n.*
1 an intervening. **2** interference,
especially by one nation in the
affairs of another.

in·tra·mur·al (in′trə myur′əl), *adj.*
1 within the walls; inside. **2** carried on by members of the same school.

in·tra·mus·cu·lar (in′trə mus′kyə lər), *adj.* within or into a muscle: *intramuscular injection.*

in·tra·state (in′trə stāt′), *adj.* within a state, especially within a state of the United States: *intrastate commerce.*

in·tra·ve·nous (in′trə vē′nəs), *adj.*
1 within a vein or the veins.
2 into a vein or veins.
—in′tra·ve′nous·ly, *adv.*

in·tro·vert (in′trə vért′), *n.* person exhibiting introversion. —*v.t.*
1 direct (one's thoughts, etc.) inward or upon oneself. **2** turn or bend inward: *introverted toes.*
[< *intro-* within + Latin *vertere* to turn]

in·trude (in trüd′), *v.*, **-trud·ed, -trud·ing.** —*v.i.* force oneself in; come unasked and unwanted: *If you are busy, I will not intrude.* —*v.t.* give unasked and unwanted; force in: *intrude one's opinions upon others.* [< Latin *intrudere* < *in-* in + *trudere* to thrust]
—in·trud′er, *n.*

in·tru·sion (in trü′zhən), *n.* act of intruding; coming unasked and unwanted.

in·tu·i·tion (in′tü ish′ən, in′tyü ish′ən), *n.* immediate perception or understanding of truths, facts, etc., without reasoning. [< Late Latin *intuitionem* a gazing at < Latin *intueri* consider, look upon < *in-* + *tueri* to look]

in·tu·i·tive (in tü′ə tiv, in tyü′ə tiv), *adj.* perceiving or understanding by intuition: *an intuitive mind.*
—in·tu′i·tive·ly, *adv.*
—in·tu′i·tive·ness, *n.*

in·vade (in vād′), *v.*, **in·vades, in·vad·ed, in·vad·ing.** —*v.t.*
1 enter with force or as an enemy for conquest or spoils: *Soldiers invaded the country.* **2** enter as if to take possession: *Tourists invaded the city.* **3** interfere with; encroach upon; violate: *The law punishes*

people who invade the rights of others. —*v.i.* make an invasion. [< Latin *invadere* < *in-* in + *vadere* go, walk]

in·vad·er (in vād′ər) *n., pl.* **in·vad·ers.** person, animal, or thing that enters as if to take possession.

in·va·sion (in vā′zhən), *n.* an invading; entering by force or as an enemy. [< Late Latin *invasionem* < *invadere*]

in·ves·ti·gate (in ves′tə gāt), *v.t.*, **-gat·ed, -gat·ing.** look into thoroughly; examine closely: *investigate a complaint.* [< Latin *investigatum* traced, searched out < *in-* in + *vestigare* to track, trace < *vestigium* footstep, vestige]
—in·ves′ti·ga′tor, *n.*

in·vest·ment (in vest′mənt), *n.* something that is expected to yield money as income or profit or both.

in·vin·ci·ble (in vin′sə bəl), *adj.* unable to be conquered; impossible to overcome: *invincible courage, an invincible fighter.* [< Latin *invincibilis* < *in-* not + *vincere* conquer] **—in·vin′ci·bly,** *adv.*

in·voke (in vōk′), *v.t.*, **-voked, -vok·ing. 1** call on in prayer; appeal to for help or protection. **2** ask earnestly for; beg for: *The condemned criminal invoked the judge's mercy.* [< Latin *invocare* < *in-* on + *vocare* to call]
—in·vok′er, *n.*

IQ, intelligence quotient.

i·ris (ī′ris), *n.* **1** any of a genus of plants with sword-shaped leaves and large, showy flowers most of which have three upright parts and three drooping parts; fleur-de-lis. **2** the flower of any of these plants. **3** the colored part around the pupil of the eye. The iris controls the amount of light entering the eye. [< Latin, rainbow < Greek]

ir·ra·tion·al num·ber (i rash′ə nəl num′bər), a number that cannot be written as a fraction; a nonrepeating decimal.

							ə stands for	
a	hat	ī	ice	u̇	put		ə stands for	
ā	age	o	not	ü	rule		a	in about
ä	far, calm	ō	open	ch	child		e	in taken
âr	care	ȯ	saw	ng	long		i	in pencil
e	let	ô	order	sh	she		o	in lemon
ē	equal	oi	oil	th	thin		u	in circus
ėr	term	ou	out	ŦH	then			
i	it	u	cup	zh	measure			

ir·reg·u·lar (i reg′yə lər), *adj.* 1 not regular; not according to rule; out of the usual order or natural way. 2 not according to law or morals: *irregular behavior.* See synonym study below. —ir·reg′u·lar·ly, *adv.* **Syn.** *adj.* 1,2 **Irregular, abnormal** mean out of the usual or natural order or pattern. **Irregular** means not according to the accepted standard: *She has irregular habits.* **Abnormal** means a deviation from what is regarded as normal, average, or typical for the class: *Seven feet is an abnormal height for a person.*

ir·rel·e·vant (i rel′ə vənt), *adj.* not to the point; off the subject: *an irrelevant question.* —ir·rel′e·vant·ly, *adv.*

ir·rev·o·ca·ble (i rev′ə kə bəl), *adj.* 1 not able to be revoked; final: *an irrevocable decision.* 2 impossible to call or bring back. —ir·rev′o·ca·bly, *adv.*

ir·ri·tate (ir′ə tāt), *v.t.*, -tat·ed, -tat·ing. make impatient or angry; annoy; provoke; vex: *Their constant interruptions irritated me.* [< Latin *irritatum* enraged, provoked]

isle (īl), *n.* 1 a small island. 2 island. [< Old French < Latin *insula*]

i·so·la·tion·ist (ī′sə lā′shə nist, is′ə lā′shə nist), *n.*, *pl.* i·so·la·tion·ists. person who believes in or favors isolationism. —*adj.* of or having to do with isolationists or isolationism.

journal

a **journal** for personal thoughts

J

jai a·lai (hī′ ä lī′), game similar to handball, played on a walled court with a hard ball, popular in Spain and Latin America; pelota. [< Spanish < Basque < *jai* festival + *alai* merry]

jazz (jaz), *n.* class of music in which melody is subordinate to syncopated rhythms, characterized by improvisation, the use of dissonances, sliding from tone to tone, and the imitation of vocal effects by the instruments. Jazz is native to the United States, and developed from early Afro-American spirituals and folk music. [probably an African American word, of west African origin]

Jazz Age (jaz′ āj′), term used to describe the 1920s in the United States, when jazz music first became an important part of American culture.

Jef·fer·son (jef′ər sən), *n.* **Thomas,** (tom′əs), *n.* 1743–1826, American statesman, third president of the United States, from 1801 to 1809. He drafted the Declaration of Independence.

jeop·ar·dize (jep′ər dīz), *v.t.*, -dized, -diz·ing. put in danger; risk.

jin·rik·i·sha (jin rik′shə, jin rik′shȯ), *n.* a small, two-wheeled carriage with a folding top, pulled by a runner, formerly used in the Orient. [< Japanese *jinrikisha* < *jin* man + *riki* strength + *sha* cart]

jour·nal (jėr′nl), *n.*, *pl.* jour·nals. a daily record of events or occurrences.

jour·nal·ism (jėr′nl iz′əm), *n.* work of writing for, editing, managing, or publishing a newspaper or magazine.

judg·ment (juj′mənt), *n.* 1 result of judging; opinion or estimate. 2 ability to form sound opinions; power to judge well; good sense.

ju·di·cial (jü dish′əl), *adj.* 1 of or by judges; having to do with courts or the administration of justice. 2 of or suitable for a judge; impartial; fair. [< Latin *judicialis* < *judicium* judgment < *judicem* judge]

ju·di·cious (jü dish′əs), *adj.* having, using, or showing good judgment; wise; sensible. —ju·di′cious·ly, *adv.*

juke·box (jük′boks′), *n.* an automatic phonograph operated by inserting a coin in a slot. The records to be played are selected by pushing a button. [< Gullah *juke* disorderly, of west African origin + English *box*]

jur·is·dic·tion (jur′is dik′shən), *n.* 1 right, power, or authority to administer justice or exercise judicial functions. 2 authority; power; control. [< Latin *jurisdictionem* < *jus, juris* law + *dicere* say]

jur·y (jur′ē), *n.*, *pl.* jur·ies. group of persons selected to hear evidence in a court of law and sworn to give a decision in accordance with the evidence presented to them. [< Anglo-French *jurie* < Old French *jurer* swear < Latin *jurare* < *jus, juris* law]

jus·ti·fi·ca·tion (jus′tə fə kā′shən), *n.* 1 a justifying. 2 a being justified.

jus·ti·fy (jus′tə fī), *v.t.*, -fied, -fy·ing. show to be just or right; give a good reason for; defend. [< Old French *justifier* < Late Latin *justificare* < Latin *justus* just + *facere* make] —jus′ti·fi′er, *n.*

K

ka·lei·do·scope (kə lī′də skōp), *n.* tube containing bits of colored glass and two mirrors. As it is turned, it reflects continually changing patterns. [< Greek *kalos* pretty + *eidos* shape + English -*scope*]

ka·ra·te (kä rä′tē), *n.* a Japanese method of fighting without weapons by striking with the hands, elbows, knees, and feet at certain vulnerable parts of the opponent's body. [< Japanese]

kay·ak (kī′ak), *n.* an Eskimo canoe made of skins stretched over a light frame of wood or bone with an opening in the middle for a person. —*v.i.* go in a kayak. [< Eskimo]

keel (kēl), *n.* the main timber or steel piece that extends the whole length of the bottom of a ship or boat. The whole ship is built up on the keel.

keel·boat (kēl′bōt′), *n.* a large, shallow barge, with a keel and covered deck, formerly used on the Missouri and other rivers.

ker·nel (kėr′nl), *n.* **1** the softer part inside the hard shell of a nut or inside the stone of a fruit. **2** grain or seed of wheat, corn, or other cereal plant.

key·board (kē′bôrd′), *n.* the set of keys in a piano, organ, computer.

khak·i (kak′ē, kä′kē), *n.* **1** a dull yellowish brown. **2** a heavy twilled wool or cotton cloth of this color, much used for soldiers' uniforms. **3** khakis, *pl.* uniform made of this cloth. [< Hindi *khākī*, originally, dusty < Persian *khāk* dust]

ki·mo·no (kə mō′nə), *n., pl.* -nos. **1** a loose outer garment held in place by a wide sash, worn by Japanese men and women. **2** a woman's loose dressing gown. [< Japanese]

kind of (kīnd′ əv), sort of, in a way.

knowl·edge·a·ble (nol′i jə bəl), *adj.* well-informed, especially about a particular subject.

kum·quat (kum′kwot), *n.* any of several yellow or orange fruits somewhat like a small orange, having a sour pulp and a sweet rind. Kumquats are used in preserves and candy. [< Chinese (Canton) *kam* golden + *kwat* orange]

L

lar·i·at (lar′ē ət), *n.* **1** rope for fastening horses, mules, to a stake. **2** lasso. [< Spanish *la reata* the rope]

la·ser (lā′zər), *n.* device which generates and amplifies light waves in a narrow and extremely intense beam of light of only one wavelength going in only one direction. Laser beams are used to cut materials and remove diseased body tissues. [< l(ight) a(mplification by) s(timulated) e(mission of) r(adiation)]

launch (lònch), *n.* **1** an open motorboat used for pleasure trips, ferrying passengers, etc. **2** the largest boat carried by a warship. [< Spanish and Portuguese *lancha* kind of long boat < Malay *lancharān* < *lanchār* fast]

lee·ward (lē′wərd, lü′ərd), *adj., adv.* **1** on the side away from the wind. **2** in the direction toward which the wind is blowing.

left field (left fēld), **1** (in baseball) the section of the outfield beyond third base. **2 out in left field,** SLANG. out of contact with reality; unreasonable or improbable. —**left fielder.**

leg·is·la·ture (lej′ə slā′chər), *n.* group of persons that has the duty and power of making laws.

lem·ming (lem′ing), *n.* any of several genera of small, mouselike, arctic rodents, having a short tail and furry feet. [< Norwegian]

lem·on·ade (lem′ə nād′), *n.* drink made of lemon juice, sugar, and water.

kayak
Inuks maneuvering a
kayak

left field (def. 1)
a view of **left field** during a baseball game

a	hat	**ī**	ice	**u̇**	put	**ə** stands for	
ā	age	**o**	not	**ü**	rule	**a**	in about
ä	far, calm	**ō**	open	**ch**	child	**e**	in taken
âr	care	**ȯ**	saw	**ng**	long	**i**	in pencil
e	let	**ô**	order	**sh**	she	**o**	in lemon
ē	equal	**oi**	oil	**th**	thin	**u**	in circus
ėr	term	**ou**	out	**ᴛ͟ʜ**	then		
i	it	**u**	cup	**zh**	measure		

loom

Peruvian women

working on a

loom

le·o·tard (lē′ə tärd), *n.* Usually, **leotards**, *pl.* a tight-fitting one-piece garment, with or without sleeves, worn by dancers, acrobats. [< French *léotard* < *Jules Léotard*, French aerialist of the 1800's]

li·a·ble (lī′ə bəl), *adj.* **1** subject to the possibility; likely or possible, especially unpleasantly likely: *That glass is liable to break.* **2** exposed to or in danger of something likely.

li·ai·son (lē′ā zon′, lē ā′zon), *n.* **1** connection between military units, branches of a service, etc., to secure proper cooperation. **2** similar connection or communication between civilian bodies, such as companies, etc. [< French < Latin *ligationem* a binding < *ligare* to bind]

li·bel (lī′bəl), *n., v.,* **-beled, -bel·ing** or **-belled, -bel·ling.** —*n.* a written or published statement, picture, etc., tending to damage a person's reputation or subject someone to public ridicule and disgrace. —*v.t.* make false or damaging statements about. [< Old French, a formal written statement < Latin *libellus*, diminutive of *liber* book]

lib·er·al (lib′ər əl), *adj.* **1** giving or given freely; generous. **2** plentiful; abundant; ample: *a liberal supply of food.* **3** not narrow in one's views and ideas; broad-minded. —*n.* person who holds liberal principles. [< Latin *liberalis* befitting free people, honorable, generous < *liber* free] —**lib′er·al·ly,** *adv.* —**lib′er·al·ness,** *n.*

lib·e·rate (lib′ə rāt′), *v.t.,* **-rat·ed, -rat·ing.** set free; free or release from slavery, prison, confinement, etc. [< Latin *liberatum* freed < *liber* free] —**lib′e·ra′tor,** *n.*

lib·e·ra·tion (lib′ə rā′shən), *n.* **1** a setting free. **2** a being set free.

life ex·pect·an·cy (līf′ ek spek′tən sē), the average number of remaining years that a person at a given age can expect to live.

life·guard (līf′gärd′), *n.* person trained in lifesaving who is employed on a beach or at a swimming pool to help in case of accident or danger to swimmers.

life in·sur·ance (līf′ in shùr′əns), **1** insurance by which a specified sum of money is paid to the insured person's survivors at the person's death. **2** sum paid by the insurance company at death.

life jack·et (līf′ jak′it), a sleeveless jacket filled with a light material, such as kapok, or with compressed air, worn as a life preserver.

life-size (līf′sīz′), *adj.* as big as the living person, animal, etc.; equal in size to the original.

life·time (līf′tīm′), *n.* time of being alive; period during which a life lasts. —*adj.* for life.

lim·ou·sine (lim′ə zēn′, lim′ə zēn′), *n.* a large automobile or small bus used to transport passengers to or from an airport, a bus station, etc. [< French < *Limousin*, former French province]

line (līn), *n., v.,* **lined, lin·ing.** —*n.* **1** a long narrow mark. **2** row of persons or things: *a line of trees.* **3 out of line, a** in disagreement. **b** uncalled-for; not suitable or proper. —*v.t.* arrange a line along; form a line along. [fusion of Old English *līne,* line, rope, and Old French *ligne* line, both ultimately < Latin *linea* line, linen thread < *linum* flax]

lip·stick (lip′stik′), *n.* a small stick of a waxlike cosmetic, used for coloring the lips.

long·horn (lòng′hôrn′), *n.* one of a breed of cattle with very long horns, formerly common in the southwestern United States and Mexico.

loom (lüm), *n., pl.* **looms.** frame or machine for weaving yarn or thread into cloth.

lo·qua·cious (lō kwā′shəs), *adj.* talking much; fond of talking. —**lo·qua′cious·ly,** *adv.* —**lo·qua′cious·ness,** *n.*

Lou·i·si·an·a Pur·chase (lü ē′zē an′ə pėr′chəs), large region that the United States bought from France in 1803. It extended from the Mississippi River to the Rocky Mountains and from Canada to the Gulf of Mexico.

luck·i·ly (luk′ə lē), *adv.* by good luck; fortunately.

luff (luf), *v.i.* turn the bow of a ship toward the wind; sail into the wind. —*n.* **1** act of turning the bow of a ship toward the wind. **2** the forward edge of a fore-and-aft sail.

lug·gage (lug′ij), *n.* baggage, especially of a traveler or passenger; suitcases and the like.

lu·mi·nous (lü′mə nəs), *adj.* shining by its own light: *The sun and stars are luminous bodies.* —**lu′mi·nous·ly,** *adv.* —**lu′mi·nous·ness,** *n.*

M

ma·chet·e (mə shet′ē, mə chet′ē), *n.* a large, heavy knife, used as a tool for cutting brush, sugar cane, etc., and as a weapon. [< Spanish]

mac·ra·mé (mak′rə mä), *n.* a coarse lace or fringe made by knotting thread or cord in patterns. [< French *macramé* < Italian *macramè* < Turkish *makrama* napkin]

mag·nate (mag′nāt), *n.* an important, powerful, person. [< Late Latin *magnatem* < Latin *magnus* great]

mag·net (mag′nit), *n.* **1** stone or piece of metal that has the property of attracting iron or steel. **2** anything that attracts.

mag·nif·i·cent (mag nif′ə sənt), *adj.* **1** richly colored or decorated; splendid; grand; stately. **2** noble; exalted. —**mag·nif′i·cent·ly**, *adv.*

mah-jongg or **mah·jong** (mä′jong′), *n.* game of Chinese origin played by four people with 144 oblong tiles. Each player tries to form winning combinations by drawing or discarding. [< dialectal Chinese *ma chiang*, literally, sparrows (from a design on the pieces)]

man·a·cle (man′ə kəl), *n., v.,* **-cled, -cling.** —*n.* **1** Usually, **manacles,** *pl.* fetter for the hands; handcuff. **2** anything that fetters; restraint. —*v.t.* put manacles on. [< Old French *manicle* < Latin *manicula,* diminutive of *manus* hand]

man·age (man′ij), *v.,* **-aged, -ag·ing,** —*v.t.* **1** guide or handle with skill or authority; control; direct. **2** succeed in accomplishing; contrive; arrange. **3** make use of: *manage tools well.* —*v.i.* **1** conduct affairs. **2** get along: *manage on one's income.* [earlier *manege* < Italian *managgiare* handle or train (horses) < *mano* hand < Latin *manus*] —**man′age·a·ble,** *adj.*

man·age·ment (man′ij mənt), *n.* **1** a managing or handling; control; direction. **2** persons that manage a business.

man·date (man′dāt), *n.,* **1** an order or command: *a royal mandate.* **2** order from a higher court or official to a lower one. [< Latin *mandatum* < *mandare* to order]

man·i·cure (man′ə kyùr), *v.,* **-cured, -cur·ing,** *n.* —*v.t., v.i.* care for (the fingernails and hands); trim, clean, and polish (the fingernails). —*n.* the care of the hands. [< French < Latin *manus* hand + *cura* care] —**man′i·cur′ist,** *n.*

man·i·fest des·ti·ny (man′ə fest des′tə nē), the belief in the 1840s in the inevitable territorial expansion of the United States.

ma·nip·u·late (mə nip′yə lāt), *v.t.,* **-lat·ed, -lat·ing.** handle or treat, especially skillfully: *manipulate clay into a pot.* [< Latin *manipulus* handful < *manus* hand + root of *plere* to fill] —**ma·nip′u·la′tion,** *n.* —**ma·nip′u·la′tor,** *n.*

ma·nip·u·la·tive (mə nip′yə lə tiv), *adj.* of or having to do with manipulation.

man·ne·quin (man′ə kən), *n.* figure of a person used by tailors, artists, stores, etc.

man·ner·ism (man′ə riz′əm), *n.* an odd trick or habit; way of acting.

man·u·fac·ture (man′yə fak′chər), *v.,* **-tured, -tur·ing,** *n.* —*v.t.* make by hand or by machine; produce by human labor, especially in large quantities with the help of machines. —*n.* act or process of manufacturing. [< Middle French < Medieval Latin *manufactura* < Latin *manu facere* make by hand]

man·u·script (man′yə skript), *n.* book or paper written by hand or with a typewriter. Before printing was invented, all books and papers were handwritten manuscripts. —*adj.* written by hand. [< Latin *manu scriptus* written by hand]

ma·ra·ca (mə rä′kə), *n.* a percussion instrument consisting of seeds, pebbles, etc., enclosed in a dry gourd and shaken like a rattle. [< Portuguese < Tupi]

mah-jongg

a winning hand in

mah-jongg

a	hat	**ī**	ice	**ù**	put	**ə** stands for	
ā	age	**o**	not	**ü**	rule	**a**	in about
ä	far, calm	**ō**	open	**ch**	child	**e**	in taken
âr	care	**ȯ**	saw	**ng**	long	**i**	in pencil
e	let	**ô**	order	**sh**	she	**o**	in lemon
ē	equal	**oi**	oil	**th**	thin	**u**	in circus
ėr	term	**ou**	out	**ŦH**	then		
i	it	**u**	cup	**zh**	measure		

mar·a·thon (mar′ə thon), *n.*
1 a footrace of 26 miles, 385 yards (42.2 kilometers). 2 any race over a long distance.

ma·rim·ba (mə rim′bə), *n.* a musical instrument somewhat like a xylophone. [of Bantu origin]

marsh·mal·low (märsh′mal′ō, märsh′mel′ō), *n.* a soft, white, spongy candy, covered with powdered sugar, made from corn syrup, sugar, starch, and gelatin.

marsupial

A kangaroo is a

marsupial.

mar·su·pi·al (mär sü′pē əl), *n.* any of an order of mammals having a pouch covering the mammary glands on the abdomen, in which the female nurses and carries her incompletely developed young. Kangaroos belong to this order.

mast (mast), *n.* a long pole of wood or metal rising from the keel of a vessel set upright on a ship to support the yards, sails, rigging, etc. [Old English *mæst*]

ma·ter·i·al·ism (mə tir′ē ə liz′əm), *n.* tendency to care too much for the things of this world and to neglect spiritual needs.

math·e·mat·i·cal ex·pres·sion (math′ə mat′ə kəl ek spresh′ən), a mathematical phrase that uses numbers, variables, and operation symbols to represent a value.

mat·i·nee (mat′n ā′), *n.* a dramatic or musical performance held in the afternoon. [< French *matinée* < Old French *matin* morning]

mat·tress (mat′ris), *n.* 1 a covering of strong cloth stuffed with cotton, foam rubber, etc., and sometimes containing springs, used on a bed. 2 air mattress. [< Old French *materas* < Italian *materasso* < Arabic *al-matrah* the cushion]

Ma·ya (mī′ə, mä′yə), *n., pl.* **Ma·yas** or **Ma·ya** for 1. 1 member of an ancient American Indian people of Central America and Mexico. The Mayas had a highly developed civilization from about A.D. 350 to about A.D. 800. 2 their language. —**Ma′yan,** *adj., n.*

may·be (mā′bē), *adv.* it may be; possibly; perhaps. → **maybe, may be.** *Maybe* is an adverb; *may be* is a verb form: *Maybe you'll have better luck next time. He may be the next mayor.*

may be (mā′ bē′), could be, might be: *This may be his last chance.*

mean·time (mēn′tīm′), *n.* time between. —*adv.* 1 in the intervening time; in the time between. 2 at the same time.

me·di·o·cre (mē′dē ō′kər), *adj.* neither good nor bad; of average quality. [< Latin *mediocris,* originally, halfway up < *medius* middle + *ocris* jagged mountain]

meg·a·lop·o·lis (meg′ə lop′ə lis), *n.* a large metropolitan area, often including several cities. [< Greek *megas, megalou* great + *polis* city]

mel·an·chol·y (mel′ən kol′ē), *n., adj.* —*n.* condition of sadness and low spirits; gloominess. —*adj.* depressed in spirits; sad. [< Greek *melancholia* < *melanos* black + *cholē* bile]

mel·a·nin (mel′ə nən), *n.* any of a class of dark-brown or black pigments that help protect the skin against sun damage. [< Greek *melanos* black]

me·men·to (mə men′tō), *n., pl.* **me·men·tos** or **me·men·toes.** something serving as a reminder of what is past or gone; souvenir. [< Latin, remember]

mem·o·ra·ble (mem′ər ə bəl), *adj.* worth remembering; not to be forgotten; notable: *a memorable trip.* —**mem′or·a·bly,** *adv.*

mem·o·ran·dum (mem′ə ran′dəm), *n., pl.* **mem·o·ran·da** (mem′ə ran′də). a short written statement for future use; note to aid one's memory. [< Latin, (thing) to be remembered]

me·tab·o·lism (mə tab′ə liz′əm), *n.* the sum of the physiological processes by which an organism maintains life. [< Greek *metabolē* change < *meta-* after + *bolē* a throwing]

met·ro·nome (met′rə nōm), *n.* device that can be adjusted to make loud ticking sounds at different speeds. Metronomes are used especially to mark time for persons practicing on musical instruments. [< Greek *metron* measure + *-nomos* regulating < *nemein* regulate]

me·trop·o·lis (mə trop′ə lis), *n.* a large city; important center, especially the center of some activity: *a financial metropolis.* [< Greek *mētropolis* < *mētēr* mother + *polis* city]

mile·age (mī′lij), *n.* 1 miles covered or traveled: *Our car's mileage last year was 10,000 miles.* 2 miles traveled per gallon of gasoline.

milk (milk), *n.* 1 the whitish liquid secreted by the mammary glands of female mammals for the nourishment of their young.

2 cry over spilt milk, to waste sorrow or regret on what has happened and cannot be remedied.

mi·nor·i·ty group (mə nôr′ə tē grüp′), *n., pl.* **mi·nor·i·ty groups.** a group of people who differ from the majority of the population in terms of race, religion, or national origin.

min·ute·man (min′it man′), *n., pl.* **min·ute·men.** member of the American militia just before and during the Revolutionary War. They kept themselves ready for military service at a minute's notice.

mi·nu·ti·a (mi nü′shē ə, mi nyü′ shē ə), *n. sing.* of **minutiae.**

mi·nu·ti·ae (mi nü′shē ē, mi nyü′shē ē), *n. pl.* very small matters; trifling details. [< Latin, trifles, plural of *minutia* smallness < *minutum*]

mir·a·cle (mir′ə kəl), *n.* **1** a wonderful happening that is contrary to or independent of the known laws of nature, and is therefore ascribed to God or some supernatural being or power. **2** something marvelous; a wonder. [< Latin *miraculum,* ultimately < *mirus* wonderful]

mis·cel·la·ne·ous (mis′ə lā′nē əs), *adj.* not all of one kind or nature; of mixed composition or character: [< Latin *miscellaneus* < *miscellus* mixed < *miscere* to mix]

mis·chie·vous (mis′chə vəs), *adj.* **1** causing mischief; naughty. **2** full of pranks and teasing fun. —**mis′chie·vous·ly,** *adv.* —**mis′chie·vous·ness,** *n.*

mix·ture (miks′chər), *n.* **1** what has been mixed; product of mixing. **2** two or more substances mixed together but not chemically combined. [< Latin *mixtura* < *miscere* to mix]

moc·ca·sin (mok′ə sən), *n.* a soft leather shoe originally worn by North American Indians, typically without heels; the sole and the sides stitched to the upper part with rawhide. [of Algonquian origin]

mois·ture (mois′chər), *n.* slight wetness. Dew is moisture that collects at night on cool surfaces.

mole (mōl), *n.* a spot or lump on the skin that is usually brown or black.

mo·men·tum (mō men′təm), *n., pl.* **-tums, -ta** (-tə). measure of the strength of an object's motion, depending on both an object's mass and its velocity.

mon·strous (mon′strəs), *adj.* **1** of extremely large size; huge; enormous. **2** shocking; horrible; dreadful. —**mon′strous·ly,** *adv.*

mo·ped (mō′ped), *n.* motorbike which can be pedaled as a vehicle or operated with a motor at up to 30 miles (48 kilometers) an hour. [blend of *motor* and *pedal*]

mort·gage (môr′gij), *n., v.,* **-gaged, -gag·ing.** —*n.* a legal right or claim to a piece of property, given as security in case the loaned money is not repaid when due. —*v.t.* give a lender a claim to (one's property) in case a debt is not paid when due. [< Old French < *mort* dead + *gage* pledge]

mo·sa·ic (mō zā′ik), *n.* decoration made of small pieces of stone, glass, wood, etc., of different colors inlaid to form a picture or design. [< Medieval Latin *mosaicus, musaicus* of the Muses, artistic]

mo·squi·to (mə skē′tō), *n., pl.* **mo·squi·toes.** any of a family of small, slender insects with two wings. The females can pierce the skin of humans and animals and draw blood, causing itching. [< Spanish, diminutive of *mosca* fly < Latin *musca*]

mo·to·cross (mō′tō krȯs′), *n.* a motorcycle race run over cross-country trails rather than on a paved track. [< French *moto-cross* <*moto* motorcycle + *cross* (-country) a cross-country race < English *cross-country,* adjective]

mo·tor·cade (mō′tər kād), *n.* procession or long line of auto-mobiles. [< *motor* + (*caval*)*cade*]

mot·to (mot′ō), *n., pl.* **-toes** or **-tos.** a brief sentence adopted as a rule of conduct: *"Think before you speak"* is a good motto.

minuteman

minutemen

getting ready to march

a	hat	**ī**	ice	**u̇**	put	**ə** stands for	
ā	age	**o**	not	**ü**	rule	**a**	in about
ä	far, calm	**ō**	open	**ch**	child	**e**	in taken
âr	care	**ȯ**	saw	**ng**	long	**i**	in pencil
e	let	**ô**	order	**sh**	she	**o**	in lemon
ē	equal	**oi**	oil	**th**	thin	**u**	in circus
ėr	term	**ou**	out	**ᴛH**	then		
i	it	**u**	cup	**zh**	measure		

natural

a **natural** arch

mug·wump (mug′wump′), *n.* person who is independent in politics. [< Massachuset *mukquomp* chief]

muk·luk (muk′luk), *n.* a high, waterproof boot, often made of sealskin, worn by Eskimos and others in arctic regions. [< Eskimo *muklok* large seal]

mur·mur (mėr′mər), *n.* 1 a soft, low, indistinct sound that rises and falls a little and goes on without breaks. 2 complaint made under the breath, not aloud. —*v.t.* utter in a murmur. [< Latin]

mus·cu·lar strength (mus′kyə lər strengkth′), *n.* the ability of muscles to put forth force.

musk·rat (musk′rat′), *n., pl.* **-rats** or **-rat.** a water rodent of North America, like a rat, but larger, having webbed hind feet, a glossy coat, and a musky smell.

mus·tang (mus′tang), *n., pl.* **mus·tangs.** a small, wiry, wild or half-wild horse of the North American plains, descended from domesticated Spanish stock. [< Spanish *mestengo* untamed]

N

na·ive (nä ēv′), *adj.* simple in nature; like a child; not sophisticated. [< French *naïve,* feminine of *naïf* < Latin *nativus*] —**na·ive′ly,** *adv.*

na·po·le·on (nə pō′lē ən), *n.* kind of pastry with a custard, cream, or jam filling. [< *Napoleon I*]

nar·rate (nar′āt, na rāt′), *v.t.,* **-rat·ed, -rat·ing.** give an account of; tell (a story, etc.): *narrate an incident.* [< Latin *narratum* made known, told] —**nar′ra·tor,** *n.*

nar·ra·tive (nar′ə tiv), *n.* story or account; tale. —*adj.* that narrates. —**nar′ra·tive·ly,** *adv.*

NASA (nas′ə), *n.* National Aeronautics and Space Administration (an agency of the United States government established to direct and aid civilian research and development in aeronautics and aerospace technology).

NATO (nā′tō), *n.* North Atlantic Treaty Organization (an alliance of sixteen Western nations providing military cooperation, originally formed in 1949).

nat·ur·al (nach′ər əl), *adj.* produced by nature; based on some state of things in nature. —*n.* that which is natural. —**nat′ur·al·ness,** *n.*

naval

a **naval** ship at sea

nat·ur·al·ist (nach′ər ə list), *n.* 1 person who makes a study of living organisms, especially in their native habitats. 2 writer or artist who practices naturalism.

na·ture (nā′chər), *n.* 1 all things except those made by human beings; the world: *the wonders of nature.* 2 the sum total of the forces at work throughout the universe: *the laws of nature.*

na·val (nā′vəl), *adj.* 1 of or for warships or the navy: *a naval officer.* 2 having a navy.

neb·u·la (neb′yə lə), *n., pl.* **-lae** (-lē′), **-las.** mass of dust particles and gases in outer space (**galactic nebula**), which may either be dark or appear as a haze illuminated by stars. [< Latin, mist, cloud]

neck (nek), *n.* 1 the part of the body that connects the head with the shoulders. 2 the part of a garment that fits the neck. 3 **neck and neck, a** abreast. **b** running equal or even in a race or contest. [Old English *hnecca*] —**neck′less,** *adj.*

ne·go·ti·ate (ni gō′shē āt), *v.,* **-at·ed, -at·ing.** —*v.i.* talk over and arrange terms; confer; consult. —*v.t.* arrange for: *They finally negotiated a peace treaty.* [< Latin *negotiatum* engaged in business < *negotium* business < *neg-* not + *otium* ease, leisure] —**ne·go′ti·a′tion,** *n.* —**ne·go′ti·a′tor,** *n.*

net in·come (net′ in′kum′), the amount of money remaining after deductions.

neu·rol′o·gist (nu̇ rol′ə jist, nyu̇ rol′ə jist), *n.* an expert who studies the nervous system and its diseases.

neu·tral (nü′trəl, nyü′trəl), *adj.* 1 on neither side in a quarrel or war. 2 of or belonging to a neutral country or neutral zone: *a neutral port.* —*n.* a person or country not taking part in a quarrel or war. [< Latin *neutralis* of neuter gender < *neuter*] —**neu′tral·ly,** *adv.*

neu·tral·i·ty (nü tral′ə tē, nyü tral′ə tē), *n.* the attitude or policy of a nation that does not take part directly or indirectly in a war.

neu·tron (nü′tron, nyü′tron), *n.* a particle having no electric charge and found either by itself or in a nucleus. [< *neutr(al)* + *-on*]

neu·tron star (nü′tron stär′, nyü′tron stär′), star in which the inward force of gravity is balanced by the outward pressure of packed neutrons.

nom de plume (nom′ də plüm′), *n.*,
pl. **noms de plume** (nomz′ də
plüm′). pen name. [formed in
English from French *nom* name,
de of, *plume* pen]

non·vi·o·lence (non vī′ə ləns), *n.*
belief in the use of peaceful
methods to achieve any goal.

no one (nō′ wun′), no person; nobody.

nor·mal (nôr′məl), *adj.* of the usual
standard; regular; usual: *The
normal temperature of the human
body is 98.6 degrees.* **—nor′mal·ly,**
adv.

no·tice·a·ble (nō′ti sə bəl), *adj.*
1 easily seen or noticed; observable.
2 worth noticing; deserving notice.
—no′tice·a·bly, *adv.*

nu·cle·ar fis·sion (nü′klē ər fish′ən,
nyü′klē ər fish′ən), the splitting of
an atomic nucleus into two parts,
especially when bombarded by a
neutron. Fission is used to induce
the chain reaction in an atomic
bomb.

nu·cle·ar fu·sion (nü′klē ər fyü′zhən,
nyü′klē ər fyü′zhən), the
combining of two atomic nuclei to
produce a nucleus of greater mass.
Fusion releases vast amounts of
energy and is used to produce the
reaction in a hydrogen bomb.

nu·cle·us (nü′klē əs, nyü′klē əs), *n.*,
pl. **-cle·i** (klē ī), **-cle·us·es.** the
central part of an atom, consisting
of a proton or protons, neutrons,
and other particles. [< Latin, kernel
< *nux, nucis* nut]

nui·sance (nü′sns, nyü′sns), *n.* thing
or person that annoys, troubles,
offends, or is disagreeable;
annoyance. [< Old French
< *nuire* to harm < Latin *nocere*]

---

o

ob·jec·tive (əb jek′tiv), *n.*, *pl.* **ob·jec·
tives.** something aimed at; object;
goal: *My objective is to play tennis
better.* **—ob·jec′tive·ly,** *adv.*
—ob·jec′tive·ness, *n.*

ob·ser·va·tion (ob′zər vā′shən), *n.*
1 act, habit, or power of seeing
and noting. **2** Often, **observations,**
pl. something seen and noted;
information secured by observing.

ob·sta·cle (ob′stə kəl), *n.* something
that stands in the way or stops
progress. [< Latin *obstaculum* < *ob-*
in the way of + *stare* to stand]
**Syn. Obstacle, obstruction,
hindrance** mean something that
gets in the way of action or
progress. **Obstacle** applies to
something that stands in the way
and must be moved or overcome
before one can continue toward a
goal: *A fallen tree across the road
was an obstacle to our car.*
Obstruction applies especially to
something that blocks a passage:
*The enemy built obstructions in
the road.* **Hindrance** applies to
something that holds back or
makes progress difficult: *Noise
is a hindrance to studying.*

ob·ste·tri·cian (ob′stə trish′ən), *n.*
doctor who specializes in obstetrics,
a branch of medicine concerned
with caring for and treating
women before, in, and after
childbirth. [< Latin *obstetrica*
< *obstetrix* midwife < *ob-* by
+ *stare* to stand]

ob·struc·tion (əb struk′shən), *n.* thing
that obstructs; something in the
way: *The whirlpool was an
obstruction to navigating the river.*
See **obstacle** for synonym study.

oc·ca·sion·al (ə kā′zhə nəl), *adj.*
happening or coming now and
then, or once in a while.
—oc·ca′sion·al·ly, *adv.*

oc·cur·rence (ə kėr′əns), *n.* **1** an
occurring: *The occurrence of
storms delayed our trip.* **2** event;
happening; incident.

o·kra (ō′krə), *n.* **1** a tall plant of the
mallow family, cultivated for its
sticky pods, which are used in
soups and as a vegetable. **2** the
pods. [< a west African word]

o·mis·sion (ō mish′ən), *n.* **1** an
omitting. **2** a being omitted.

observation (def. 1)
a science **observation**
in a laboratory

a	hat	**ī**	ice	**u̇**	put	**ə** stands for	
ā	age	**o**	not	**ü**	rule	**a**	in about
ä	far, calm	**ō**	open	**ch**	child	**e**	in taken
âr	care	**o̅**	saw	**ng**	long	**i**	in pencil
e	let	**ô**	order	**sh**	she	**o**	in lemon
ē	equal	**oi**	oil	**th**	thin	**u**	in circus
ėr	term	**ou**	out	**ᴛʜ**	then		
i	it	**u**	cup	**zh**	measure		

o·mit (ō mit′), *v.t.,* **o·mit·ted, o·mit·ting. 1** leave out. **2** fail to do; neglect: *They omitted making their beds.* [< Latin *omittere* < *ob-* by + *mittere* let go]

o·paque (ō pāk′), *adj.* any object which light does not pass through. [< Latin *opacus* dark, shady]

o·pen (ō′pən), *adj.* **1** letting (anyone or anything) in or out; not shut; not closed. **2** not having its door, gate, lid, etc., closed; not closed up: *an open box.* —*v.t.* move or turn away from a shut or closed position to allow passage; give access to. —**o′pen·ly,** *adv.* —**o′pen·ness,** *n.*

open range

o·pen range (ō′pən rānj′), large, unfenced area of grassland and water for raising cattle or sheep.

oph·thal·mol·o·gist (of′thal mol′ə jist, op′thal mol′ə jist), *n.* doctor who specializes in ophthalmology, a branch of medicine that deals with the structure, functions, and diseases of the eye.

op·ti·mism (op′tə miz′əm), *n.* **1** tendency to look on the bright side of things. **2** belief that everything will turn out for the best. [< French *optimisme* < Latin *optimus* best]

o·rang·u·tan (ô rang′ù tan′), *n.* a large ape of the forests of Borneo and Sumatra, that has very long arms and long, reddish-brown hair. [< Malay < *orang* man + *utan* of the woods]

or·der of op·e·ra·tions (ôr′dər əv op′ə rā′shənz), in mathematics, the order in which the operations are done within an expression.

or·di·nar·y (ôrd′n er′ē), *adj.* **1** according to habit or custom; usual; regular; normal. **2** not special; common; everyday; average. [< Latin *ordinarius* < *ordinem* order] —**or′di·nar′i·ness,** *n.*

o·ri·ga·mi (ôr′ə gä′mē), *n.* the Japanese art of folding paper to make decorative objects, such as figures of birds and flowers. [< Japanese]

or·tho·pe·dist (ôr′thə pē′dist), *n.* doctor who specializes in orthopedics, a branch of surgery that deals with the deformities and diseases of bones and joints, especially in children. [< *ortho-* + Greek *paidos* child]

out·go·ing (out′gō′ing), *n.* a going out. —*adj.* **1** outward bound; going out; departing. **2** friendly and helpful to others; sociable.

out·put (out′pùt′), *n., v.,* **out·put, out·put·ting.** —*n.* information put out by or delivered by a computer. —*v.t.* deliver information.

out·ra·geous (out rā′jəs), *adj.* very offensive or insulting; shocking. —**out·ra′geous·ly,** *adv.* —**out·ra′geous·ness,** *n.*

out·side (out′sīd′), *n.* **1** side or surface that is out; outer part: *the outside of a house.* **2** space or position that is beyond or not inside. —*adv.* on or to the outside.

out·spo·ken (out′spō′kən), *adj.* not reserved; frank: *an outspoken person.* —**out′spo′ken·ness,** *n.*

out·stand·ing bal·ance (out stan′ding bal′əns), the difference between the amount one owes or has withdrawn from an account and the amount one is owed or deposits in an account.

o·ver·do (ō′vər dü′), *v.t.,* **-did** (-did′), **-done** (-dun′), **-do·ing. 1** do or attempt to do too much: *She overdoes exercise.* **2** cook too much: *The meat is overdone.*

o·ver·due (ō′vər dü′, ō′vər dyü′), *adj.* more than due; due some time ago but not yet arrived, paid, etc.: *The train is overdue.*

o·ver·rate (ō′vər rāt′), *v.t.,* **o·ver·rat·ed, o·ver·rat·ing.** rate or estimate too highly.

o·ver·seas (ō′vər sēz′), *adv.* across the sea; abroad.

o·ver·se·er (ō′vər sē′ər), *n.* one who oversees others or their work.

o·ver·whelm·ing (ō′vər hwel′ming), *adj.* too many, too great, or too much to be resisted; overpowering. —**o′ver·whelm′ing·ly,** *adv.*

ox·y·gen (ok′sə jən), *n.* a colorless, odorless, tasteless gaseous element that forms about one fifth of the atmosphere by volume. Animals and plants cannot live, and fire will not burn, without oxygen. [< French *oxygène* < Greek *oxys* sharp + *-genēs* born]

P

pag·eant (paj′ənt), *n.* an elaborate spectacle; procession in costume; pomp; display; show: *The coronation of a new ruler is always a splendid pageant.*

pains·tak·ing (pānz′tā′king), *adj.* **1** very careful; particular; scrupulous. **2** marked or characterized by attentive care. —**pains′tak′ing·ly,** *adv.*

paint·er¹ (pān'tər), *n*. **1** person who paints pictures; artist. **2** person who paints houses, etc. [< Old French *peinteur*, ultimately < Latin *pictorem* < *pingere* to paint]

paint·er² (pān'tər), *n*. a rope, usually fastened to the bow of a boat, for tying it to a ship, etc. [probably < Middle French *pentoir* hanging cordage < Latin *pendere* to hang]

pa·ja·mas (pə jä'məz, pə jam'əz), *n.pl.* sleeping or lounging garments consisting of a jacket or blouse and loose trousers. [< Hindustani *pājāmā* < Persian *pāe* leg + *jāmah* garment]

pal·an·quin (pal'ən kēn'), *n*. a covered platform enclosed at the sides, often with a couch, that is carried by poles resting on the shoulders of four or six men, formerly used in the Orient. [< Portuguese *palanquim* < Malay *palangki* couch]

par·a·graph (par'ə graf), *n*. group of sentences relating to the same idea or topic and forming a distinct part of a chapter, letter, or other piece of writing. Usually begin a paragraph on a new line and indent. [< Greek *paragraphos* line (in the margin) marking a break in sense < *para-¹* + *graphein* write]

par·al·lel cir·cuits (par'ə lel sér'kits), the paths of electric current connecting several electrical devices in which the removal of one device does not break the electrical flow to the other devices.

par·a·pher·nal·ia (par'ə fər nā'lyə), *n., pl. or sing*. **1** personal belongings. **2** equipment; outfit. [< Medieval Latin < Greek *parapherna* a woman's personal property besides her dowry < *para-¹* + *phernē* dowry]

pa·ren·the·sis (pə ren'thə sis), *n., pl.* **pa·ren·the·ses** (-sēz'). **1** word, phrase, sentence, etc., inserted within a sentence to explain or qualify something. **2** either or both of two curved lines ( ) used to set off such an expression.

par·ka (pär'kə), *n*. a fur jacket with a hood, worn in Alaska and in northeastern Asia.

par·lia·ment (pär'lə mənt), *n*. council or congress that is the highest lawmaking body in some countries. [< Old French *parlement* < *parler* speak.]

par·mi·gia·na (pär'mə jä'nə, pär'mə zhä'nə), *adj*. cooked or sprinkled with Parmesan cheese. [< Italian, feminine of *parmigiano* of Parma]

par·take (pär tāk'), *v.i.,* **-took, -tak·en, -tak·ing. 1** eat or drink some; take some. **2** take or have a share.

part·ner·ship (pärt'nər ship), *n*. **1** a being a partner; joint interest; association: *a business partnership.* **2** company or firm with two or more members who share in the risks and profits of the business.

pas·sage (pas'ij), *n*. **1** hall or way through or between parts of a building; passageway; corridor. **2** means of passing; way through.

pas·time (pas'tīm'), *n*. a pleasant way of passing time; amusement; recreation; diversion; games.

pea soup (pē' süp'), thick soup made with mashed (split) peas, other vegetables, and sometimes ham.

pe·can (pi kän', pi kan', pē'kan), *n*. an olive-shaped, edible nut with a smooth, thin shell, that grows on a hickory tree common in the southern and central United States. [< Cree *pakan* hard-shelled nut]

pe·cu·liar (pi kyü'lyər), *adj*. out of the ordinary; strange; odd; unusual. [< Latin *peculiaris* of one's own < *peculium* private property < *pecu* money, cattle] —**pe·cu'liar·ly,** *adv*.

ped·es·tal (ped'i stəl), *n*. **1** base on which a column or a statue stands. **2** any base; support; foundation.

pe·des·tri·an (pə des'trē ən), *n., pl.* **pe·des·tri·ans.** person who goes on foot; walker. —*adj.* going on foot; walking. [< Latin *pedester* on foot < *pedem* foot]

passage (def. 1)
a **passage** outside the building

a	hat	ī	ice	u̇	put	ə stands for	
ā	age	o	not	ü	rule	a	in about
ä	far, calm	ō	open	ch	child	e	in taken
âr	care	ȯ	saw	ng	long	i	in pencil
e	let	ô	order	sh	she	o	in lemon
ē	equal	oi	oil	th	thin	u	in circus
èr	term	ou	out	ᵺ	then		
i	it	u	cup	zh	measure		

pe·di·a·tri·cian (pē′dē ə trish′ən), *n.* doctor who specializes in pediatrics, a branch of medicine dealing with children's diseases and the care of babies and children.

ped·i·gree (ped′ə grē′), *n.* **1** list of ancestors of a person or animal. **2** line of descent; ancestry; lineage. [< Middle French *pie de grue* foot of crane (because a symbol resembling the toes of a bird was used in showing descent)]

pe·dom·e·ter (pi dom′ə tər), *n.* instrument for recording the number of steps taken by the person who carries it and thus measuring the distance traveled in walking. [< French *pédomètre* < Latin *pedem* foot + Greek *metron* measure]

personal computer

pem·mi·can (pem′ə kən), *n.* dried, lean meat pounded into a paste with melted fat and pressed into cakes. It was an important food among certain tribes of North American Indians. [< Cree *pimikan*]

per·ceive (pər sēv′), *v.t.,* **-ceived, -ceiv·ing. 1** be aware of through the senses; see, hear, taste, smell, or feel. **2** take in with the mind; observe; understand. [< Old French *perceivre* < Latin *percipere* < *per*- thoroughly + *capere* to grasp] **—per·ceiv′a·ble,** *adj.* **—per·ceiv′er,** *n.*

per·cent of de·crease (pər sent′ əv dē′krēs), amount of decrease expressed as a percent.

per·cent of in·crease (pər sent′ əv in′krēs), amount of increase expressed as a percent.

per·cep·tion (pər sep′shən), *n.* **1** act of perceiving: *His perception of the change came in a flash.* **2** understanding that is the result of perceiving: *I now have a clear perception of what went wrong.* [< Latin *perceptionem* < *percipere* perceive. < *per*- thoroughly + *capere* grasp]

pe·ren·ni·al (pə ren′ē əl), *adj.* **1** lasting through the whole year: *a perennial stream.* **2** lasting for a very long time; enduring. **3** (of a plant) lasting more than two years. **—n.** a perennial plant. [< Latin *perennis* < *per*- through + *annus* year] **—pe·ren′ni·al·ly,** *adv.*

per·fect square (pėr′fikt skwâr′), a number whose square root is a positive or negative whole number, or zero.

per·haps (pər haps′), *adv.* it may be; maybe; possibly. [Middle English *per happes* by chances]

per·il·ous (per′ə ləs), *adj.* full of peril; dangerous. **—per′il·ous·ly,** *adv.* **—per′il·ous·ness,** *n.*

per·i·od·ic ta·ble (pir′ē od′ik tā′bəl), table in which the chemical elements, arranged in the order of their atomic numbers, are shown in related groups.

per·ish (per′ish), *v.i.* be destroyed; die: *Soldiers perish in battle.* [< Old French *periss-*, a form of *perir* < Latin *perire* < *per*- to destruction + *ire* go]

per·jur·y (pėr′jər ē), *n., pl.* **-jur·ies.** act or crime of willfully giving false testimony or withholding evidence while under oath.

per·mis·sive (pər mis′iv), *adj.* **1** not forbidding; tending to permit; allowing. **2** permitted; allowed. **—per·mis′sive·ly,** *adv.* **—per·mis′sive·ness,** *n.*

per·pe·trate (pėr′pə trāt), *v.t.,* **-trat·ed, -trat·ing.** do or commit (a crime, fraud, trick, or anything bad or foolish). [< Latin *perpetratum* perpetrated < *per*- thoroughly + *patrare* perform] **—per′pe·tra′tion,** *n.* **—per′pe·tra′tor,** *n.*

per·pet·u·ate (pər pech′ü āt), *v.t.,* **-at·ed, -at·ing.** make perpetual; keep from being forgotten. **—per·pet′u·a′tion,** *n.* **—per·pet′u·a′tor,** *n.*

per·se·cute (pėr′sə kyüt), *v.t.,* **-cut·ed, -cut·ing. 1** cause to suffer repeatedly; do harm to persistently; oppress. **2** annoy; harass. **—per·se·cu′tor,** *n.*

per·se·ver·ance (pėr′sə vir′əns), *n.* a sticking to a purpose or an aim; a persevering; tenacity.

per·se·vere (pėr′sə vir′), *v.i.,* **per·se·vered, per·se·ver·ing.** continue steadily in doing something hard; persist. [< Latin *perseverare* < *per*- thoroughly + *severus* strict]

per·sist·ent (pər sis′tənt), *adj.* **1** not giving up, especially in the face of dislike, disapproval, or difficulties; persisting; persevering. **2** going on; continuing; lasting: *a persistent headache that lasted for three days.* **—per·sist′ent·ly,** *adv.*

per·son·al com·put·er (pėr′sə nəl kəm pyü′tər), a small computer for use at home or work which consists of a monitor with a screen, a keyboard, and a CPU.

per·spec·tive (pər spek′tiv), *n.* **1** art of picturing objects on a flat surface so as to give the appearance of distance or depth. **2** view of things or facts in which they are in the right relations: *a lack of perspective.* **3** a mental view, outlook, or prospect. [< Medieval Latin *perspectiva (ars)* (science) of optics < Latin *perspicere* look through < *per-* through + *specere* to look] —**per·spec′tive·ly,** *adv.*

per·spi·ra·tion (pėr′spə rā′shən), *n.* the salty fluid secreted by sweat glands through pores of the skin.

per·suade (pər swād′), *v.t.,* **-suad·ed, -suad·ing.** win over to do or believe; make willing or sure by urging; convince. [< Latin *persuadere* < *per-* thoroughly + *suadere* to urge] —**per·suad′er,** *n.*

per·sua·sion (pər swā′zhən), *n.* a persuading: *All our persuasion was of no use; she would not come here.*

per·sua·sive (pər swā′siv), *adj.* able, intended, or fitted to persuade.
—**per·sua′sive·ly,** *adv.*
—**per·sua′sive·ness,** *n.*

per·tain (pər tān′), *v.i.* **1** belong or be connected as a part, possession. **2** have to do with; be related; refer. [< Old French *partenir* < Latin *pertinere* reach through, connect < *per-* through + *tenere* to hold]

per·ti·nent (pėrt′n ənt), *adj.* having to do with what is being considered; relating to the matter in hand; to the point. [< Latin *pertinentem* pertaining] —**per′ti·nent·ly,** *adv.*

pe·ti·tion (pə tish′ən), *n.* a formal request to a superior or to one in authority for some privilege, right, benefit, etc.: *Many people signed a petition asking the city council for a new library.* [< Latin *petitionem* < *petere* seek]

phe·nom·e·non (fə nom′ə non), *n., pl.* **-na** (or **-nons** for 2). **1** fact, event, or circumstance that can be observed. **2** an extraordinary or remarkable person or thing. [< Greek *phainomenon* < *phainesthai* appear]

pho·tog·ra·phy (fə tog′rə fē), *n.* process, art, or business of taking photographs.

pic·tur·esque (pik′chə resk′), *adj.* quaint or interesting enough to be used as the subject of a picture.

pip·sis·se·wa (pip sis′ə wə), *n.* any of a genus of low, creeping evergreen plants whose leaves are used in medicine as a tonic, etc. [< Cree *pipisisikweu*]

pis·ta·chi·o (pi stä′shē ō, pi stash′ē ō), *n., pl.* **-chi·os,** *adj.* —*n.* **1** a greenish nut having a flavor that suggests almond. **2** a small tree that it grows on, belonging to the same family as the sumac. —*adj.* light-green. [< Italian *pistacchio,* ultimately < Persian *pistah*]

pit·fall (pit′fól′), *n., pl.* **pit·falls.** **1** a hidden pit to catch animals or human beings. **2** any trap or hidden danger.

plan·ta·tion (plan tā′shən), *n., pl.* **plan·ta·tions.** a large farm or estate, especially in a tropical or semitropical region, on which cotton, tobacco, sugar cane, rubber trees, etc., are grown. The work on a plantation is done by laborers who live there.

plaque (plak), *n.* **1** a thin, flat, ornamental plate or tablet of metal, porcelain, etc., usually intended to be hung up as a wall decoration. **2** a thin film of saliva and food particles which forms on the surface of the teeth.

pleas·ure (plezh′ər), *n.* a feeling of being pleased; enjoyment; delight.

po·di·a·trist (pə dī′ə trist), *n.* person who treats ailments of the human foot; chiropodist.

pol·i·cy (pol′ə sē), *n., pl.* **-cies.** plan of action adopted as tactically or strategically best by a government, person, etc.; way of managing affairs so as to achieve some purpose.

po·lit·i·cal (pə lit′ə kəl), *adj.* of or concerned with politics: *political parties.* —**po·lit′i·cal·ly,** *adv.*

a	hat	**ī**	ice	** u̇**	put	**ə**	*stands for*
ā	age	**o**	not	**ü**	rule	**a**	in about
ä	far, calm	**ō**	open	**ch**	child	**e**	in taken
âr	care	**ȯ**	saw	**ng**	long	**i**	in pencil
e	let	**ô**	order	**sh**	she	**o**	in lemon
ē	equal	**oi**	oil	**th**	thin	**u**	in circus
ėr	term	**ou**	out	**ᵮH**	then		
i	it	**u**	cup	**zh**	measure		

pol·i·tics (pol'ə tiks), *n. sing.* or *pl.*
1 management of political affairs;
the science and art of government.
2 political principles or opinions.

pon·cho (pon'chō), *n., pl.* **-chos.**
a large piece of cloth, often
waterproof, with a slit in the middle
for the head to go through.
Ponchos are worn in South
America as cloaks. [< Spanish
< Araucanian *pontho*]

poncho
wearing **ponchos**
in Bolivia

por·ce·lain (pôr'sə lin), *n.* **1** a very
fine earthenware, usually having
a translucent white body and a
transparent glaze; china. **2** dish or
other object made of this material.

port (pôrt), *n.* the side of a ship or
aircraft to the left of a person
facing the bow or front. —*adj.* on
the left side of a ship or aircraft.
—*v.t., v.i.* turn or shift to the left
side. [origin uncertain]

port·fo·li·o (pôrt fō'lē ō), *n., pl.* **-li·os.**
1 a portable case for loose papers,
drawings, etc.; briefcase. **2** position
and duties of a cabinet member,
diplomat, or minister of state.
3 holdings in the form of stocks,
bonds, etc. [< Italian *portafoglio*,
ultimately < Latin *portare* carry
+ *folium* sheet, leaf]

pos·i·tive (poz'ə tiv), *adj.* **1** admitting
of no question; without doubt:
positive proof. **2** showing
agreement or approval.
—**pos'i·tive·ly,** *adv.*

pos·ses·sive (pə zes'iv), *adj.*
1 desirous of ownership: *a
possessive nature.* **2** asserting or
claiming ownership: *a possessive
manner.* —**pos·ses'sive·ly,** *adv.*
—**pos·ses'sive·ness,** *n.*

pos·si·ble (pos'ə bəl), *adj.* **1** that can
be; that can be done; that can
happen: *Come if possible.* **2** that
can be true or a fact: *It is possible
that she went.* **3** that can be done,
chosen, etc., properly. —*n.*
something that is possible;
possibility.

post·age (pō'stij), *n.* amount paid
on anything sent by mail.

post·script (pōst'skript), *n.* addition
to a letter, written after the writer's
name has been signed.

pos·ture (pos'chər), *n., v.,* **-tured,
-tur·ing.** —*n.* **1** position of the body;
way of holding the body: *Good
posture is important for health.*
2 condition; situation; state: *In the
present posture of public affairs it
is difficult to predict what will
happen.* **3** mental or spiritual
attitude. —*v.i.* **1** take a certain
posture: *The dancer postured
before the mirror, bending and
twisting her body.* **2** pose for effect.
—*v.t.* put in a certain posture.
[< French < Italian *postura* < Latin
positura < *ponere* to place]

prec·e·dent (pres'ə dənt), *n.* **1** action
that may serve as an example or
reason for a later action. **2** (in law)
a judicial decision, case, etc., that
serves as a pattern in future
situations that are similar.

pre·dic·a·ment (pri dik'ə mənt), *n.* an
unpleasant, difficult, or dangerous
situation. [< Late Latin
praedicamentum quality, category
< Latin *praedicare* to predicate]

pre·dis·po·si·tion (prē'dis'pə zish'ən),
n. previous inclination.

pre·fer (pri fér'), *v.,* **-ferred, -fer·ring.**
—*v.t.* like better; choose rather: *She
prefers reading to sewing.* —*v.i.*
have or express a preference: *I will
come later, if you prefer.* [< Latin
praeferre put before < *prae-* pre-
+ *ferre* carry]

pref·er·a·ble (pref'ər ə bəl), *adj.* to
be preferred; more desirable.
—**pref'er·a·bil'i·ty,** *n.*
—**pref'er·a·ble·ness,** *n.*
—**pref'er·a·bly,** *adv.*

pref·e·ren·tial (pref'ə ren'shəl), *adj.*
of, giving, or receiving preference.

prej·u·di·cial (prej'ə dish'əl), *adj.*
causing prejudice or disadvantage;
hurtful; detrimental.
—**prej'u·di'cial·ly,** *adv.*

pre·lim·i·nar·y (pri lim'ə ner'ē), *adj.,
n., pl.* **-nar·ies.** —*adj.* coming
before the main business; leading
to something more important. —*n.*
a preliminary step; something
preparatory.

pre·oc·cu·pa·tion (prē ok'yə
pā'shən), *n.* **1** act of preoccupying.
2 condition of being preoccupied.

pre·pos·ter·ous (pri pos'tər əs), *adj.*
contrary to nature, reason, or
common sense; absurd; senseless.
[< Latin *praeposterus* with the
posterior in front < *prae-* pre- +
posterus coming after, behind]
—**pre·pos'ter·ous·ly,** *adv.*

pre·scribe (pri skrīb'), *v.,* **-scribed,
-scrib·ing.** —*v.t.* **1** lay down as a
rule to be followed; order; direct.
2 order as a remedy or treatment:
The doctor prescribed quinine.
—*v.i.* give medical advice; issue a
prescription. [< Latin *praescribere*
write before < *prae-* pre- + *scribere*
write]

pre·scrip·tion (pri skrip′shən), *n.*
1 act of prescribing. 2 something prescribed; order; direction.
3 a written direction or order for preparing and using a medicine.

pres·i·den·cy (prez′ə dən sē), *n., pl.* **-cies.** 1 office of president. 2 time in which a president is in office.

pres·sure (presh′ər), *n., v.,* **-sured, -sur·ing.** —*n.* 1 the continued action of a weight or force.
2 force per unit of area: *There is a pressure of 27 pounds to the square inch in this tire.* —*v.t.* force or urge by exerting pressure: *The salesman tried to pressure my father into buying the car.*
—**pres′sure·less,** *adj.*

pres·tige (pre stēzh′), *n.* reputation, influence, or distinction based on what is known of one's abilities, achievements, and opportunities. [< Middle French, illusion, magic spell < Latin *praestigiae* tricks]

pre·sume (pri züm′), *v.t.,* **-sumed, -sum·ing.** take for granted without proving; suppose. [< Latin *praesumere* take for granted < *prae-* pre- + *sumere* take]

pre·sump·tion (pri zump′shən), *n.* unpleasant boldness.

pre·vent (pri vent′), *v.t.* 1 stop or keep (from): *I will come if nothing prevents me from doing so.* 2 keep from happening: *Rain prevented the game.* [< Latin *praeventum* forestalled < *prae-* pre- + *venire* come] —**pre·vent′er,** *n.*

pre·ven·tion (pri ven′shən), *n.* a preventing: *the prevention of fire.*

pre·vi·ous (prē′vē əs), *adj.* coming or going before; that came before; earlier. [< Latin *praevius* leading the way < *prae-* pre- + *via* road] —**pre′vi·ous·ly,** *adv.*

prin·ci·pal (prin′sə pəl), *adj.* 1 sum of money on which interest is paid.
2 money or property from which income or interest is received.

prism (priz′əm), *n.* a wedge-shaped transparent object that separates light into its different wavelengths (colors). [< Greek *prisma* something sawed off, prism < *priein* to saw]

prob·a·ble (prob′ə bəl), *adj.*
1 likely to happen: *Cooler weather is probable after this shower.*
2 likely to be true: *Indigestion is the probable cause of your pain.* [< Latin *probabilis* < *probare* to prove] —**prob′a·bly,** *adv.*

pro·claim (prə klām′), *v.t.,* **pro·claims, pro·claimed, pro·claim·ing.** make known publicly and officially; declare publicly. [< Latin *proclamare* < *pro-* forth + *clamare* to shout]

proc·la·ma·tion (prok′lə mā′shən), *n.* an official announcement; public declaration.

prof·it (prof′it), *n.* Often, **profits,** *pl.* the gain from a business; what is left when the cost of goods and of carrying on the business is subtracted from the amount of money taken in. See **advantage** for synonym study. —*v.i.* make a gain from a business; make a profit. [< Old French < Latin *profectus* advance < *proficere* make progress < *pro-* forward + *facere* to make] —**prof′it·er,** *n.*

pro·found (prə found′), *adj.* 1 very deep: *a profound sigh, a profound sleep.* 2 deeply felt; very great: *profound despair, profound sympathy.* [< Latin *profundus* < *pro-* before + *fundus* bottom] —**pro·found′ly,** *adv.*

pro·gram (prō′gram), *n., pl.* **pro·grams.** *v.,* **pro·grams, pro·grammed, pro·gram·ming** or **pro·grams, pro·gramed, pro·gram·ing.** —*n.* set of instructions for an electronic computer or other automatic machine outlining the steps to be performed by the machine in a specific operation. —*v.t.* prepare a set of instructions for (a computer or other automatic machine). [< Greek *programma* proclamation, ultimately < *pro-* forth + *graphein* write]

presidency (def. 1)
the seal from the office of
the **presidency**

							stands for
a	hat	**ī**	ice	**u̇**	put	**ə**	
ā	age	**o**	not	**ü**	rule	**a**	in about
ä	far, calm	**ō**	open	**ch**	child	**e**	in taken
âr	care	**ȯ**	saw	**ng**	long	**i**	in pencil
e	let	**ô**	order	**sh**	she	**o**	in lemon
ē	equal	**oi**	oil	**th**	thin	**u**	in circus
ėr	term	**ou**	out	**ᴛʜ**	then		
i	it	**u**	cup	**zh**	measure		

publish (def. 1)
published magazines for
distribution

pueblo
a **pueblo** in the
southwest

prog·ress (*n.* prog′res; *v.* prə gres′),
n. **1** an advance or growth;
development; improvement: *the
progress of science.* **2** a moving
forward; going ahead: *make rapid
progress on a journey.* —*v.i.* get
better; advance; develop.

pro·hi·bi·tion (prō′ə bish′ən), *n.*
1 law or laws against making or
selling alcoholic liquors. **2** Often,
Prohibition. period between 1920
and 1933 when national prohibition
was in force in the United States.

pro·logue (prō′lóg), *n.* **1** introduction
to a novel, poem, or other literary
work. **2** speech or poem addressed
to the audience by one of the
actors at the beginning of a play.
[< Greek *prologos* < *pro-* before +
logos speech]

pro·mote (prə mōt′), *v.t.,* **-mot·ed,
-mot·ing. 1** raise in rank, condition,
or importance; elevate: *Pupils who
pass the test will be promoted.*
2 help to develop or establish;
cause to advance; further.
—**pro·mot′a·ble,** *adj.*

proof (prüf), *n.* **1** way or means of
showing beyond doubt the truth of
something: *Is what you say a guess
or have you proof?* See **evidence** for
synonym study. **2** establishment of
the truth of anything. [< Old French
prouve < Late Latin *proba* < Latin
probare prove]

pro·pos·al (prə pō′zəl), *n.* **1** what
is proposed; plan, scheme, or
suggestion. **2** offer of marriage.

pros·e·cute (pros′ə kyüt), *v.t.,* **-cut·ed,
-cut·ing.** bring before a court of
law: *Reckless drivers will be
prosecuted.* [< Latin *prosecutum*
followed after < *pro-* forth + *sequi*
follow]

pro·tect (prə tekt′), *v.t.* shield from
harm or danger; shelter; defend;
guard. [< Latin *protectum* covered
up, protected < *pro-* in front +
tegere to cover]

pro·tec·tion (prə tek′shən), *n.* act of
protecting; condition of being kept
from harm; defense.

pro·test (*n., adj.* prō′test; *v.* prə test′),
n. statement that denies or objects
strongly: *They yielded only after
protest.* —*adj.* characterized by
protest; expressing protest or
objection against some condition:
a protest movement. —*v.t.* object
to: *protest a decision.* [< Middle
French < *protester* to protest < Latin
protestari < *pro-* before + *testis*
witness] —**pro·test′a·ble,** *adj.*
—**pro·test′er,** *n.*

pro·ton (prō′ton), *n.* a positively
charged particle found free or in
a nucleus. [< Greek *prōton* first]

pro·voc·a·tive (prə vok′ə tiv), *adj.*
1 irritating; vexing. **2** tending or
serving to call forth action, thought,
laughter, anger, etc.: *a provocative
remark.* —**pro·voc′a·tive·ly,** *adv.*
—**pro·voc′a·tive·ness,** *n.*

pro·voke (prə vōk′), *v.t.,* **-voked,
-vok·ing. 1** make angry; vex. **2** stir
up; excite: *The insult provoked him
to anger.* **3** call forth; bring about;
start into action; cause. [< Latin
provocare < *pro-* forth + *vocare*
to call]

PS, postscript.

pub·li·ca·tion (pub′lə kā′shən), *n.*
book, newspaper, or magazine;
anything that is published.

pub·lish (pub′lish), *v.t.* **1** prepare and
offer (a book, paper, map, piece of
music, etc.) for sale or distribution.
2 bring out the book or books of:
publish an author. [< Old French
publiss-, a form of *publier* to
publish < Latin *publicare*
< *publicus* public]
—**pub′lish·a·ble,** *adj.*

pueb·lo (pweb′lō), *n., pl.* **-los.** an
Indian village consisting of houses
built of adobe and stone, usually
with flat roofs and often several
stories high. [< Spanish, people,
community < Latin *populus*]

punc·tu·al (pungk′chü əl), *adj.* on
time; prompt: *be punctual to the
minute.* [< Latin *punctum* point]
—**punc′tu·al·ly,** *adv.*
—**punc′tu·al·ness,** *n.*

pur·chase (pėr′chəs), *v.t.,* **-chased,
-chas·ing.** get by paying a price;
buy: *purchase a new car.*
[< Anglo-French *purchacer* pursue
< Old French *pur-* forth + *chacier*
to chase] —**pur′chas·a·ble,** *adj.*
—**pur′chas·er,** *n.*

pyr·a·mid (pir′ə mid), *n.* the solid
figure formed by connecting points
of a polygon to a point not in the
plane of the polygon. [< Greek
pyramidos] —**pyr′a·mid′ic,** *adj.*

py·ro·pho·bi·a (pī′rə fō′bē ə), *n.* an
abnormal fear of fire.

Q

quest (kwest), *n.* **1** a search or hunt.
2 expedition of knights. —*v.t.*
search or seek for; hunt. [< Old
French *queste* < Popular Latin
quaesita < Latin *quaerere* seek]
—**quest′er,** *n.*

ques·tion·a·ble (kwes′chə nə bəl), *adj.* open to question or dispute; doubtful; uncertain: *a questionable statement.* —**ques′tion·a·bly,** *adv.*

queue (kyü), *n., v.,* **queued, queu·ing** or **queue·ing.** —*n.* **1** braid of hair hanging down from the back of the head. **2** a line of people, automobiles, etc. —*v.i.* form or stand in a long line. [< French < Latin *coda, cauda* tail] —**queu′er,** *n.*

R

rack·et·eer (rak′ə tir′), *n., pl.* **rack·et· eers.** person who extorts money through bribery, by threatening violence, or by some other illegal means. —*v.i.* extort money in this way.

ra·dar (rā′där), *n.* instrument for determining the distance, direction, speed, etc., of unseen objects by the reflection of microwave radio waves. [< *ra(dio) d(etecting) a(nd) r(anging)*]

ra·di·a·tion (rā′dē ā′shən), *n.* **1** a transfer of energy through space in waves. **2** either radiant energy or sub-atomic particles given off during radioactivity or fission.

ra·di·ol·o·gist (rā′dē ol′ə jist), *n.* an expert in radiology, the science dealing with X rays or the rays from radioactive substances, especially for medical diagnosis or treatment.

ra·di·us (rā′dē əs), *n., pl.* **-di·i** (-dē ī), **-di·us·es.** any line segment going straight from the center to the outside of a circle or a sphere. Any spoke in a wheel is a radius. [< Latin, ray, spoke of a wheel]

ram·bunc·tious (ram bungk′shəs), *adj.* wild and noisy; boisterous. —**ram·bunc′tious·ness,** *n.*

ra·tion·al (rash′ə nəl), *adj.* **1** reasoned out; sensible; reasonable. **2** able to think and reason clearly. —**ra′tion·al·ly,** *adv.*

ra·tion·ale (rash′ə nal′), *n.* the fundamental reason. [< Latin, neuter of *rationalis* rational < *rationem* reckoning]

ra·tion·al num·ber (rash′ə nəl num′bər), any number that can be written as a fraction; a terminating or repeating decimal.

real estate (rē′əl e stāt′), land together with the buildings, fences, trees, water, minerals, etc., that belong with it.

re·al·ism (rē′ə liz′əm), *n.* **1** thought and action based on realities. **2** (in art and literature) the picturing of life as it actually is.

re·al·ize (rē′ə līz), *v.t.,* **-ized, -iz·ing. 1** understand clearly; be fully aware of: *She realizes how hard you worked.* **2** make real; bring into actual existence: *Her uncle's present made it possible for her to realize her dream.*

re·al·ly (rē′ə lē), *adv.* **1** actually; truly; in fact: *things as they really are.* **2** indeed: *Oh, really?*

re·al num·ber (rē′əl num′bər), *n., pl.* **re·al num·bers.** any rational or irrational number.

re·as·sure (rē′ə shùr′), *v.t.,* **-sured, -sur·ing. 1** restore to confidence. **2** assure again or anew. —**re′as·sur′ing·ly,** *adv.*

reb·el (*n., adj.* reb′əl; *v.* ri bel′), *n., adj., v.,* **re·belled, re·bel·ling.** —*n.* person who resists or fights against authority instead of obeying. —*adj.* defying law or authority: *a rebel army.* —*v.i.* resist or fight against law or authority. [< Old French *rebelle* < Latin *rebellem* disorderly < *rebellare* be disorderly, rebel, ultimately < *re-* again + *bellum* war]

re·cede (ri sēd′), *v.i.,* **-ced·ed, -ced·ing.** go or move backward. [< Latin *recedere* < *re-* back + *cedere* go]

re·ces·sion (ri sesh′ən), *n.* period of temporary business reduction, shorter and less extreme than a depression.

real estate

a	hat	**ī**	ice	**u̇**	put	**ə** stands for	
ā	age	**o**	not	**ü**	rule	**a**	in about
ä	far, calm	**ō**	open	**ch**	child	**e**	in taken
âr	care	**ȯ**	saw	**ng**	long	**i**	in pencil
e	let	**ô**	order	**sh**	she	**o**	in lemon
ē	equal	**oi**	oil	**th**	thin	**u**	in circus
ėr	term	**ou**	out	**ŦH**	then		
i	it	**u**	cup	**zh**	measure		

redcoat

the English **redcoats**

re·con·nais·sance (ri kon′ə sens), *n.* examination or survey, especially for military purposes. [< French]

re·con·struct (rē′kən strukt′), *v.t.* construct again; rebuild; make over.

re·cord (*v.* ri kôrd′; *n., adj.* rek′ərd), *v.t.* set down in writing so as to keep for future use. —*n.* **1** anything written and kept. **2 off the record,** not to be recorded or quoted. —*adj.* making or affording a record: *a record wheat crop.* [< Old French *recorder* < Latin *recordari* remember, call to mind < *re-* back + *cordis* heart, mind] —re·cord′a·ble, *adj.*

rec·tan·gu·lar prism (rek tang′gyə lər priz′əm), a polyhedron whose congruent and parallel bases are rectangles.

red·coat (red′kōt′), *n., pl.* red·coats. (in former times) a British soldier.

red gi·ant (red′ jī′ənt), first stage of a star as it begins to die; a rather large star that glows slightly reddish, since it is relatively cool.

ref·er·ence (ref′ər əns), *n.* **1** statement, book, etc., referred to. **2** something used for information or help: *A dictionary is a reference.*

re·fer·ral (ri fér′əl), *n.* **1** act of referring. **2** person who is referred.

re·flect (ri flekt′), *v.t.,* re·flects, re·flect·ed, re·flect·ing. turn back or throw back (light, heat, sound, etc.). [< Latin *reflectere* < *re-* back + *flectere* to bend]

re·flec·tive (ri flek′tiv), *adj.* that reflects; reflecting: *the reflective surface of polished metal.* —re·flec′tive·ly, *adv.*

re·fresh·ment (ri fresh′mənt), *n.* **1** a refreshing. **2** a being refreshed. **3** thing that refreshes. **4 refreshments,** *pl.* food or drink: *serve refreshments at a party.*

re·frig·e·ra·tor (ri frij′ə rā′tər), *n.* box, room, etc., that keeps foods and other items cool, usually by mechanical means.

re·fund (*v.* ri fund′; *n.* rē′fund), *v.t.* make return or restitution of (money received or taken); pay back. —*n.* **1** a return of money paid. **2** the money paid back. [< Latin *refundere* < *re-* back + *fundere* pour] —re·fund′a·ble, *adj.*

re·fuse (ri fyüz′), *v.t.,* -fused, -fus·ing. say no to; decline to accept; reject: *refuse an offer.* [< Old French *refuser* < Latin *refusum* poured back < *re-* + *fundere* pour] —re·fus′a·ble, *adj.* —re·fus′er, *n.*

refreshment (def. 3)

Lemonade is a cool

refreshment.

re·gal (rē′gəl), *adj.* **1** belonging to a king or queen; royal. **2** fit for a king or queen; stately; splendid; magnificent. [< Latin *regalis* < *regem* king] —re′gal·ly, *adv.*

re·ga·li·a (ri gā′lē ə), *n.pl.* the emblems of royalty. Crowns and scepters are regalia. [< Latin, royal things]

re·gard·less (ri gärd′lis), *adj.* with no heed; careless: *regardless of expense.* —*adv.* in spite of what happens. —re·gard′less·ly, *adv.*

re·gime (ri zhēm′), *n.* **1** system, method, or form of government or rule. **2** any prevailing political or social system. [< French *régime* < Latin *regimen*]

reg·i·ment (*n.* rej′ə mənt; *v.* rej′ə ment), *n.* a military unit consisting of several battalions or squadrons, usually commanded by a colonel. —*v.t.* treat in a strict or uniform manner. [< Late Latin *regimentum* rule < Latin *regere* to rule]

re·gion·al (rē′jə nəl), *adj.* of or in a particular region: *a regional storm.*

reg·u·lar (reg′yə lər), *adj.* **1** fixed by custom or rule; usual; ordinary; normal: *Six o'clock was her regular hour of rising.* **2** coming, acting, or done again and again at the same time. —*n.* member of a regularly paid group of any kind: *The fire department was made up of regulars and volunteers.* [< Latin *regularis* < *regula* rule]

reg·u·lar·ly (reg′yə lər lē), *adv.* **1** in a regular manner. **2** at regular times.

reg·u·late (reg′yə lāt), *v.t.,* -lat·ed, -lat·ing. **1** control by rule, principle, or system: *regulate the behavior of students.* **2** keep at some standard: *regulate the air.*

rein·deer (rān′dir′), *n., pl.* -deer. a large deer with branching antlers, native to Greenland and northern regions of the Old World, used to pull sleighs and for meat, milk, and hides. [< Scandinavian (Old Icelandic) *hreindȳi* < *hreinn* reindeer + *dȳr* animalȳ]

rel·a·tive mo·tion (rel′ə tiv mō′shən), changing position with respect to the position of another object.

re·li·a·ble (ri lī′ə bəl), *adj.* worthy of trust; that can be depended on. —re·li′a·bil′i·ty, *n.*

re·mem·brance (ri mem′brəns), *n.* **1** power to remember; act of remembering; memory. **2** any thing or action that makes one remember a person; keepsake.

re·mote con·trol (ri mōt′ kən trōl′),
control from a distance of a
machine, operation, etc., usually
by electrical impulses or signals.

re·mov·al (ri mü′vəl), *n.*
1 a removing; taking away.
2 a change of place or location.

ren·dez·vous (rän′də vü), *n., pl.* **-vous**
(-vüz), *v.,* **-voused** (-vüd), **-vous·ing**
(-vü′ing). —*n.* an appointment or
engagement to meet at a fixed
place or time; meeting by
agreement. —*v.t.* bring together
(troops, ships, space capsules, etc.)
at a fixed place. [< Middle French
< *rendez-vous* present yourself!]

re·peat·ed (ri pē′tid), *adj.* said, done,
or made more than once.
—**re·peat′ed·ly,** *adv.*

re·peat·ing dec·i·mal (ri pē′ting
des′ə məl), decimal in which the
same figure or series of figures is
repeated indefinitely. EXAMPLES:
.3333+, .2323+.

re·per·cus·sion (rē′pər kush′ən), *n.*
1 an indirect influence or reaction
from an event: *repercussions of a
scandal.* **2** sound flung back; echo.

re·port card (ri pôrt′ kärd′), a report
sent regularly by a school to
parents or guardians, indicating
the quality of a student's work.

rep·re·hend (rep′ri hend′), *v.t.*
reprove, rebuke, or blame. [< Latin
reprehendere, originally, pull back
< *re-* back + *prehendere* to grasp]

rep·re·hen·si·ble (rep′ri hen′sə bəl),
adj. deserving reproof, rebuke, or
blame. —**rep′re·hen′si·bil′i·ty,** *n.*

rep·re·sent (rep′ri zent′), *v.t.,*
**rep·re·sents, rep·re·sent·ed,
rep·re·sent·ing. 1** stand for; be a
sign or symbol of: *The 50 stars in
our flag represent the 50 states.*
2 act in place of; speak and act
for.

re·sem·blance (ri zem′bləns), *n.*
1 similar appearance; likeness:
*Twins often show great
resemblance.* **2** a copy; image.

re·sent·ment (ri zent′mənt), *n.* the
feeling that one has at being
injured or insulted; indignation.

re·served (ri zėrvd′), *adj.* **1** kept in
reserve; kept by special arrange-
ment: *a reserved seat.* **2** set apart:
a reserved section at the stadium.
3 self-restrained in action or
speech. —**re·serv′ed·ly,** *adv.*

res·i·den·tial (rez′ə den′shəl), *adj.*
1 of, having to do with, or suitable
for homes or residences: *a
residential district.* **2** of or having
to do with residence. **3** serving or
used as a residence: *a residential
building.* —**res′i·den′tial·ly,** *adv.*

re·sist (ri zist′), *v.t.* **1** act against;
strive against; oppose: *The window
resisted all efforts to open it.*
2 strive successfully against; keep
from. [< Latin *resistere* < *re-* back
+ *sistere* make a stand]
—**re·sist′er,** *n.*

re·sist·i·ble (ri zis′tə bəl), *adj.* that
can be resisted.

re·sist·ance (ri zis′təns), *n.* the
measure of how much the flow
of electric current is opposed,
expressed in ohms.

re·solve (ri zolv′), *v.,* **re·solved,
re·solv·ing,** *n.* —*v.t.* make up one's
mind; determine; decide: *resolve
to do better work in the future.*
—*n.* thing determined on.
determination. [< Latin *resolvere*
< *re-* back + *solvere* to loosen]
—**re·solv′a·ble,** *adj.* —**re·solv′er,** *n.*

res·pi·ra·tion (res′pə rā′shən), *n.* act
of inhaling and exhaling; breathing.

res·pir·a·to·ry (res′pər ə tôr′ē), *adj.*
having to do with or used for
respiration. The lungs are
respiratory organs.

re·trieve (ri trēv′), *v.t.,* **-trieved,
-triev·ing.** get again; recover:
retrieve a lost pocketbook. —*n.*
act of retrieving; recovery. [< Old
French *retruev-,* a form of *retrouver*
find again < *re-* again + *trouver* to
find]

re·un·ion (rē yü′nyən), *n.* **1** a coming
together again. **2** a being reunited.

rev·eil·le (rev′ə lē), *n.* a signal on a
bugle or drum to waken soldiers or
sailors in the morning. [< French
réveillez(-vous) awaken!]

residential (def. 1)
a **residential**
neighborhood

a	hat	ī	ice	ů	put	ə stands for	
ā	age	o	not	ü	rule	a	in about
ä	far, calm	ō	open	ch	child	e	in taken
âr	care	ȯ	saw	ng	long	i	in pencil
e	let	ô	order	sh	she	o	in lemon
ē	equal	oi	oil	th	thin	u	in circus
ėr	term	ou	out	ᴛʜ	then		
i	it	u	cup	zh	measure		

re·venge (ri venj′), n., v., -venged, -veng·ing. —n. harm done in return for a wrong; satisfaction obtained by repayment of an injury, etc.; vengeance: *take revenge, get revenge.* —v.t. do harm in return for. See synonym study below. [< Middle French < *revenger* avenge < Latin *re-* back + *vindicare* avenge]
Syn. *v.t.* **Revenge, avenge** mean to punish someone in return for a wrong. **Revenge** applies when it is indulged in to get even: *Gangsters revenge the murder of one of their gang.* **Avenge** applies when the punishment seems just: *They fought to avenge the enemy's invasion of their country.*
re·vi·tal·ize (rē vī′tə līz), v.t., -ized, -iz·ing. restore to vitality; put new life into. —**re·vi·tal·i·za′tion,** n.
re·voke (ri vōk′), v., -voked, -vok·ing, n. —v.t. take back; repeal; cancel; withdraw: *revoke a driver's license.* —n. (in cards) a failure to follow suit when one can and should; renege. [< Latin *revocare* < *re-* back + *vocare* to call]
ric·o·chet (rik′ə shā′), n., v., -cheted (-shād′), -chet·ing (-shā′ing). —n. the skipping or jumping motion of an object after glancing off a flat surface. —v.i. move with a skipping or jumping motion. [< French]
ri·dic·u·lous (ri dik′yə ləs), adj. deserving ridicule; laughable; absurd. —**ri·dic′u·lous·ly,** adv. —**ri·dic′u·lous·ness,** n.
ro·de·o (rō′dē ō, rō dā′ō), n., pl. -de·os. contest or exhibition of skill in roping cattle, riding horses, etc. [< Spanish < *rodear* go around, ultimately < Latin *rota* wheel]
role mod·el (rōl′ mod′l), person whose patterns of behavior influence another's attitudes and actions.
roll·ing fric·tion (rōl′ing frik′shən), weak, backwards force that arises as a round object rolls over a surface.
roof (rüf, rů̇f), n. 1 the top covering of a building. 2 something like it: *the roof of a car.* 3 **go through the roof** or **hit the roof,** INFORMAL. become very excited. [Old English *hrōf*] —**roof′like′,** adj.
round·up (round′up′), n. 1 act of driving or bringing cattle together from long distances. 2 the people and horses that do this.

roof (def. 1)
tiled **roofs** in Holland

R.S.V.P. or **r.s.v.p.,** please answer [for French *répondez s'il vous plaît*].
rud·der (rud′ər), n. 1 a flat piece of wood or metal hinged vertically to the rear end of a boat or ship and used to steer it. 2 a similar piece on an aircraft. [Old English *rōthor*]
RV, recreational vehicle.

S

sac·char·in (sak′ər ən), n. a very sweet crystalline substance obtained from coal tar, used as a substitute for sugar.
sa·fa·ri (sə fär′ē), n. 1 journey or hunting expedition in eastern Africa. 2 any long trip or expedition. [< Swahili < Arabic *safar* a journey]
saf·fron (saf′rən), n. 1 an autumn crocus with purple flowers having orange-yellow stigmas. 2 an orange-yellow coloring matter obtained from the dried stigmas of this crocus. Saffron is used to color and flavor candy, rice, etc. —adj. orange-yellow. [< Old French *safran*, ultimately < Arabic *za'farān*]
sam·pan (sam′pan), n. any of various small boats used in the rivers and coastal waters of China, Japan, and southeast Asia. [< Chinese *san pan*, literally, three boards]
sat·is·fac·tion (sat′i sfak′shən), n. 1 act of satisfying; fulfillment of conditions or desires. 2 condition of being satisfied, or pleased and contented.
scen·ic (sē′nik, sen′ik), adj. 1 of or having to do with natural scenery. 2 having much fine scenery; picturesque: *a scenic highway.* 3 of or having to do with stage scenery or stage effects. —**scen′i·cal·ly,** adv.
sci·en·tif·ic no·ta·tion (sī′ən tif′ik nō tā′shən), a way to write a number as the product of a power of 10 and a number greater than or equal to 1 and less than 10.
sci·en·tist (sī′ən tist), n. person who has expert knowledge of some branch of science, especially a physical or natural science.
scrib·ble (skrib′əl), v., -bled, -bling, n. —v.t. write or draw carelessly or hastily. —v.i. make marks that do not mean anything. —n. something scribbled. [< Medieval Latin *scribillare*, ultimately < Latin *scribere* write]

scu·ba (skü′bə), *n.* portable breathing equipment, including one or more tanks of compressed air, used by underwater swimmers and divers. —*v.i.* swim underwater using this equipment. [< *s(elf) c(ontained) u(nderwater) b(reathing) a(pparatus)*]

sculp·ture (skulp′chər), *n.*, *v.*, **-tured, -tur·ing.** —*n.* **1** art of making figures by carving, modeling, casting, etc. **2** piece of such work. —*v.t.* make (figures) by carving, modeling, casting, etc. [< Latin *sculptura*, variant of *scalptura* < *scalpere* carve]

se·ba·ceous gland (si bā′shəs gland′), *n.*, *pl.* **se·ba·ceous glands.** gland in an inner layer of the skin that supplies oil to the skin and hair.

se·bum (sē′bəm), *n.* the fatty secretion of the sebaceous glands. [< Latin, tallow, grease]

se·ces·sion·ist (si sesh′ə nist), *n.* **1** person who favors secession. **2** person who secedes.

seg·re·ga·tion (seg′rə gā′shən), *n.* separation of one racial group from another or from the rest of society, as in schools, housing.

self-es·teem (self′e stēm′), *n.* thinking well of oneself; self-respect; conceit.

self-im·age (self′im′ij), *n.* the conception one has of oneself, of one's abilities and ambitions, etc.

se·mes·ter (sə mes′tər), *n.* a division, often one half, of a school year, usually lasting from 15 to 18 weeks.

sen·sa·tion·al (sen sā′shə nəl), *adj.* **1** very good, exciting, etc.; outstanding; spectacular: *the outfielder's sensational catch.* **2** arousing or trying to arouse strong or excited feeling. —**sen·sa′tion·al·ly,** *adv.*

sense (sens), *n.* **1** power of an organism to know what happens outside itself. Sight, hearing, touch, taste, and smell are the five principal senses. **2** feeling: *a sense of warmth.* [< Latin *sensus* < *sentire* perceive, know, feel]

sen·si·ble (sen′sə bəl), *adj.* having or showing good sense or judgment: wise. —**sen′si·ble·ness,** *n.* —**sen′si·bly,** *adv.*

sen·si·bil·i·ty (sen′sə bil′ə tē), *n.*, *pl.* **-ties. 1** ability to feel or perceive. **2** sensitiveness.

sen·si·tiv·i·ty (sen′sə tiv′ə tē), *n.* quality of being sensitive.

sen·si·tize (sen′sə tīz), *v.t.*, **-tized, -tiz·ing.** make sensitive. Camera films have been sensitized to light. —**sen′si·tiz′er,** *n.*

sen·ti·men·tal (sen′tə men′tl), *adj.* **1** having or showing much tender feeling: *sentimental poetry.* **2** likely to act from feelings rather than from logical thinking. —**sen′ti·men′tal·ly,** *adv.*

sep·a·rate (*v.* sep′ə rāt′; *adj.* sep′ər it), *v.*, **-rat·ed, -rat·ing,** *adj.* —*v.t.* **1** be between; keep apart; divide. **2** take apart; part; disjoin: *separate church and state.* —*v.i.* **1** draw, come, or go apart; become disconnected or disunited. **2** part company. —*adj.* **1** apart from others: *in a separate room.* **2** divided; not joined. **3** individual; single. [< Latin *separatum* put apart, divided < *se-* apart + *parare* prepare] —**sep′ar·ate·ly,** *adv.* —**sep′ar·ate·ness,** *n.*

se·quin (sē′kwən), *n.* a small spangle used to ornament dresses, scarfs.

ser·geant (sär′jənt), *n.* a noncommissioned military officer ranking above a corporal.

ser·ies cir·cuits (sir′ēz sėr′kits), the paths of electric current connecting several electrical devices one after the other so that the removal of one device breaks the electrical flow to the other devices.

ser·i·ous (sir′ē əs), *adj.* **1** showing deep thought or purpose; thoughtful; grave: *a serious manner.* **2** in earnest; not joking; sincere. —**ser′i·ous·ly,** *adv.* —**ser′i·ous·ness,** *n.*

scuba

a diver using **scuba** gear

a	hat	ī	ice	u̇	put		ə stands for
ā	age	o	not	ü	rule	a	in about
ä	far, calm	ō	open	ch	child	e	in taken
âr	care	ȯ	saw	ng	long	i	in pencil
e	let	ô	order	sh	she	o	in lemon
ē	equal	oi	oil	th	thin	u	in circus
ėr	term	ou	out	ŦH	then		
i	it	u	cup	zh	measure		

set·ting (set′ing), *n.* **1** scenery of a play. **2** place, time, etc., of a play or story.

set·tle (set′l), *v.t.,* **-tled, -tling. 1** cause to take up residence in a place. **2** establish colonies in; colonize. [Old English *setlan* < *setl* a sitting place, seat]

set·tle·ment (set′l mənt), *n.* **1** act of settling. **2** settling of persons in a new country or area; colonization.

sev·en·ty-two (sev′ən tē tü′), seventy plus two.

shad·ow (shad′ō), *n.* an area that is not lit or is only partially lit because an object is blocking light from reaching it. **—shad′ow·er,** *n.* **—shad′ow·less,** *adj.* **—shad′ow·like′,** *adj.*

sheet (shēt), *n.* rope or chain that controls the angle at which a sail is set. [Old English *scēata* lower part of a sail]

shock (shok), *n.* condition of physical collapse or depression, accompanied by a sudden drop in blood pressure, often resulting in unconsciousness. Shock may set in after a severe injury, great loss of blood, or a sudden emotional disturbance. [probably < French *choc,* noun, *choquer,* verb] **—shock′a·ble,** *adj.*

shop·ping cen·ter (shop′ing sen′tər), group of stores built as a unit on or near a main road, especially in a suburban or new community.

sil·hou·ette (sil′ü et′), *n., v.,* **-et·ted, -et·ting. —***n.* an outline portrait, especially in profile, cut out of a black paper or drawn and filled in with some single color. —*v.t.* show in outline. [< Étienne de *Silhouette,* 1709–1767, French finance minister]

sim·ple in·ter·est (sim′pəl in′tər ist), interest paid on the sum of money saved.

si·mul·cast (sī′məl kast′), *v.,* **-cast** or **-cast·ed, -cast·ing,** *n.* —*v.t., v.i.* transmit a program over radio and television simultaneously. —*n.* broadcast transmitted over radio and television simultaneously.

Sioux (sü), *n., pl.* **Sioux** (sü, süz) for 1. **1** member of an American Indian tribe living on the plains of northern United States and southern Canada; Dakota. **2** the Siouan language of this tribe.

sis·ter-in-law (sis′tər in lò′), *n., pl.* **sis·ters-in-law. 1** sister of one's husband or wife. **2** wife of one's brother. **3** wife of the brother of one's husband or wife.

skyscraper

a modern **skyscraper** in Hong Kong

sit·com (sit′kom′), *n.* INFORMAL. situation comedy.

sky·scrap·er (skī′skrā′pər), *n., pl.* **sky·scrap·ers.** a very tall building.

sla·lom (slä′ləm, slal′əm), *n.* (in skiing) a zigzag race downhill. [< Norwegian < *slad* bent, sloping + *lom* path, trail]

sleep·i·ness (slē′pē nis), *n.* a feeling of drowsiness, almost sleeping.

sleuth (slüth), *n.* **1** bloodhound. **2** INFORMAL. detective. —*v.i.* INFORMAL. be or act like a detective.

slid·ing fric·tion (slīd′ing frik′shən), backwards force that exists between the surfaces of objects that are sliding over each other.

slosh (slosh), *v.i.* splash in or through slush, mud, or water. —*v.t.* pour or dash (liquid) upon. —*n.* **1** slush. **2** INFORMAL. a watery or weak drink. [perhaps blend of *slop* and *slush*]

smoke de·tec·tor (smōk′ di tek′tər), *n., pl.* **smoke de·tec·tors.** a device that sounds an alarm when it detects the presence of smoke inside.

sna·fu (sna fü′), SLANG. —*n.* a snarled or confused state of things. —*adj.* snarled; confused. —*v.t.* **1** put in disorder or in a chaotic state. **2** botch. [< the initial letters of "situation normal—all fouled up"]

snor·kel (snôr′kəl), *n.* a curved tube which enables swimmers to breathe underwater while swimming near the surface. —*v.i.* swim underwater using a snorkel.

soft·ware (sòft′wâr′), *n.* program for a computer system.

so·lar col·lec·tor (sō′lər kə lek′tər), *n., pl.* **so·lar col·lec·tors.** an object that traps the sun's energy and heats up a fluid.

so·lil·o·quy (sə lil′ə kwē), *n., pl.* **-quies. 1** a talking to oneself. **2** speech made by an actor to himself or herself when alone.

sol·ute (sol′yüt, sō′lüt), *n.* solid, gas, or liquid dissolved in a liquid to make a solution. [< Latin *solutum* dissolved]

so·lu·tion (sə lü′shən), *n.* **1** process of dissolving; the mixing of a solid, liquid, or gas with another solid, liquid, or gas so that the molecules of each are evenly distributed. **2** (in mathematics) a value of a variable that makes an equation true. [< Latin *solutionem* a loosing < *solvere* loosen]

solve (solv), *v.t.,* **solved, solv·ing.** find the answer to; clear up: explain. [< Latin *solvere* loosen]

sol·vent (sol′vənt), *adj.* able to dissolve: *Gasoline is a solvent liquid that removes grease spots.* —*n.* substance, usually a liquid, that can dissolve other substances. [< Latin *solventem* loosening, paying]

some·thing (sum′thing), *n.* some thing; a particular thing not named or known. —*adv.* somewhat; to some extent or degree.

soph·o·more (sof′ə môr), *n.* student in the second year of high school or college.

spa·cious (spā′shəs), *adj.* **1** having much space or room; large: *the spacious rooms of the old castle.* **2** of great extent or area. —**spa′cious·ly,** *adv.* —**spa′cious·ness,** *n.*

speak·eas·y (spēk′ē′zē), *n., pl.* **speak·eas·ies.** SLANG. place where alcoholic liquors are sold contrary to law.

spe·cies (spē′shēz), *n., pl.* **-cies.** group of related organisms that have certain permanent characteristics in common and are able to interbreed. A species ranks next below a genus and may be divided into several varieties, races, or breeds. Wheat is a species of grass.

speed (spēd), *n.* rate of motion; found by dividing the distance an object moves by the time the object takes to go that distance and usually expressed in meters/seconds.

speed·om·e·ter (spē dom′ə tər), *n.* instrument to indicate the speed of an automobile or other vehicle, and often the distance traveled.

sphere (sfir), *n.* a round solid figure whose surface is at all points equally distant from the center.

spir·i·tu·al (spir′ə chü əl), *adj.* **1** of or having to do with the spirit or soul. **2** of or having to do with the church; sacred; religious. —*n.* a sacred song or hymn as originally created or interpreted by the Negroes of the southern United States. —**spir′i·tu·al·ly,** *adv.* —**spir′i·tu·al·ness,** *n.*

splat·ter (splat′ər), *v.t., v.i.* splash or spatter. —*n.* a splash or spatter.

sports·cast (spôrts′kast′), *n.* broadcast of a sporting event.

sports·man·ship (spôrts′mən ship), *n.* qualities or conduct of a sportsman; fair play.

square root (skwâr′ rüt′), number that produces a given number when multiplied by itself: *The square root of 16 is 4.*

squig·gle (skwig′əl), *n., v.,* **-gled, -gling.** —*n.* a wriggly twist or curve. —*v.t.* make twisting or curving lines. —*v.i.* twist and turn about. [blend of *squirm* and *wriggle*]

sta·bil·i·ty (stə bil′ə tē), *n.* a being fixed in position.

sta·ble (stā′bəl), *adj.* **1** not likely to fall or be overturned: *a stable government.* **2** not likely to give way; steady; firm: *a stable support.* **3** not likely to change in nature or purpose; steadfast.

stage fright (stāj′ frīt′), nervous fear of appearing before an audience.

stam·pede (stam pēd′), *n.* a sudden scattering or headlong flight of a frightened herd of cattle, horses.

stan·dard form (stan′dərd fôrm′), the notation for writing numbers using the digits 0–9 and each place representing a power of ten.

star·board (stär′bərd), *n.* the right side of a ship, boat, or aircraft, when facing forward. [Old English *stēorbord* the side from which a vessel was steered < *stēor* steering paddle + *bord* side (of a ship)]

states' rights (stāts′ rīts′), powers belonging to the individual states of the United States, under the Constitution. The doctrine of states' rights holds that all powers which the Constitution does not specifically delegate to the federal government and does not specifically deny to the individual states belong to the states.

stat·ic fric·tion (stat′ik frik′shən), force in the direction that opposes any motion between the surfaces of objects that are touching but not moving past each other.

a	hat	ī	ice	u̇	put	**ə stands for**	
ā	age	o	not	ü	rule	a	in about
ä	far, calm	ō	open	ch	child	e	in taken
âr	care	ȯ	saw	ng	long	i	in pencil
e	let	ô	order	sh	she	o	in lemon
ē	equal	oi	oil	th	thin	u	in circus
ėr	term	ou	out	ᵺ	then		
i	it	u	cup	zh	measure		

stim·u·lus (stim′yə ləs), *n., pl.* **-li** (-lī). something that stirs to action or effort; incentive: *Ambition is a great stimulus.*

stor·age (stôr′ij), *n.* **1** act or tact of storing goods. **2** condition of being stored. Cold storage is used to keep eggs and meat from spoiling.

straight-faced (strāt′fāst′), *adj.* showing no emotion, humor, etc.

straight·for·ward (strāt′fôr′wərd), *adj.* **1** honest; frank. **2** going straight ahead; direct. —*adv.* directly. —**straight′for′ward·ness,** *n.*

strain (strān), *v.i.* be injured or damaged by too much effort. —*n.* **1** any severe, trying, or wearing pressure: *the strain of worry.* **2** effect of such pressure on the body or mind. —**strain′less,** *adj.*

stra·te·gic (strə tē′jik), *adj.* **1** of strategy; based on strategy; useful in strategy: *a strategic retreat.* **2** important in strategy: *a strategic link in national defense.* —**stra·te′gi·cal·ly,** *adv.*

stra·te·gi·cal (strə tē′jə kəl), *adj.* strategic.

strat·e·gy (strat′ə jē), *n., pl.* **-gies.** **1** science or art of war; the planning and directing of military movements and operations. **2** the skillful planning and management of anything. [< Greek *stratēgia* < *stratēgos* general < *stratos* army + *agein* to lead]

stren·u·ous (stren′yü əs), *adj.* **1** very active. **2** full of energy. **3** requiring much energy: *strenuous exercise.* —**stren′u·ous·ly,** *adv.* —**stren′u·ous·ness,** *n.*

struc·tur·al (struk′chər əl), *adj.* **1** used in building. **2** of or having to do with structure or structures: *The geologist showed the structural difference in rocks of different ages.* —**struc′tur·al·ly,** *adv.*

stub·born (stub′ərn), *adj.* **1** fixed in purpose or opinion; not giving in to argument or requests. **2** characterized by obstinacy: *a stubborn refusal.* **3** hard to deal with or manage: *a stubborn cough.* —**stub′born·ly,** *adv.* —**stub′born·ness,** *n.*

sub·com·mit·tee (sub′kə mit′ē), *n.* a small committee chosen from and acting under a larger general committee for some special duty.

sub·di·vi·sion (sub′də vizh′ən), *n.* **1** division into smaller parts. **2** part of a part. **3** tract of land divided into building lots.

sub·head (sub′hed′), *n.* a subordinate heading or title.

sub·head·ing (sub′hed′ing), *n.* subhead.

sub·ma·rine (*n., v.* sub′mə rēn′; *adj.* sub′mə rēn′), *n., v.,* **-rined, -rin·ing,** *adj.* —*n.* boat that can operate under water, used in warfare for attacking enemy ships with torpedoes and for launching missiles. —*v.t.* attack or sink by a submarine. —*adj.* under the surface of the sea; underwater.

sub·merge (səb mėrj′), *v.,* **-merged, -merg·ing.** —*v.t.* **1** put under water; cover with water. **2** cover; bury. —*v.i.* sink under water; go below the surface. [< Latin *submergere* < *sub-* under + *mergere* to plunge]

sub·or·di·nate (*adj., n.* sə bôrd′n it; *v.* sə bôrd′n āt), *adj., n., v.,* **-nat·ed, -nat·ing.** —*adj.* **1** lower in rank: *In the army, lieutenants are subordinate to captains.* **2** lower in importance; secondary. —*n.* a subordinate person or thing. —*v.t.* make subordinate: *He subordinated his wishes to those of his guests.* [< Medieval Latin *subordinatum* lowered in rank < Latin *sub-* under + *ordinem* order] —**sub·or′di·nate·ly,** *adv.* —**sub·or′di·nate·ness,** *n.*

sub·scribe (səb skrīb′), *v.i.,* **-scribed, -scrib·ing. 1** promise to give or pay money: *subscribe to several charities.* **2** promise to accept and pay for a number of copies of a newspaper, magazine, etc.: *We subscribe to a few magazines.* [< Latin *subscribere* < *sub-* under + *scribere* write] —**sub·scrib′er,** *n.*

sub·script (sub′skript), *adj.* written underneath or low on the line. —*n.* number, letter, or other symbol written underneath and to one side of a symbol. In H_2SO_4 the 2 and 4 are subscripts.

sub·sec·tion (sub′sek′shən), *n.* part of a section.

sub·stance (sub′stəns), *n.* **1** what a thing consists of; matter; material. **2** the real, main, or important part of anything: *The substance of an education is its effect on your life.* **3** the real meaning: *Give the substance of the speech in your own words.* **4** solid quality; body. **5** wealth; property: *a person of substance.* [< Old French < Latin *substantia* < *substare* stand firm < *sub-* up to + *stare* to stand]

sub·stan·tial (səb stan/shəl), *adj.*
1 having substance; material; real;
actual: *People and things are
substantial; dreams and ghosts
are not.* 2 strong; firm; solid: *The
house is substantial enough to
last a hundred years.* 3 large;
important; ample: *make a
substantial improvement in
health.* —**sub·stan/tial·ly,** *adv.*

sub·ter·ra·ne·an (sub/tə rā/nē ən),
adj. underground: *A subterranean
passage led from the castle to a
cave.* [< Latin *subterraneus* < *sub-*
under + *terra* earth]

sub·trac·tion (səb trak/shən), *n.*
operation of subtracting one
number or quantity from another.

sub·ur·ban (sə bėr/bən), *adj.* 1 of,
having to do with, or in a suburb:
*We have excellent suburban train
service.* 2 characteristic of a
suburb or its inhabitants.

sub·ur·ban·ite (sə bėr/bə nīt), *n.*
person who lives in a suburb.

suede (swād), *n.* a soft leather that
has a velvety nap on one or both
sides. —*adj.* made of suede: *a
suede jacket.* [< French (*gants de*)
Suède (gloves from) Sweden]

suf·fi·cient (sə fish/ənt), *adj.* as much
as is needed; enough: *sufficient
proof.* —**suf·fi/cient·ly,** *adv.*

suite (swēt; *also* süt for 2), *n.* 1 set of
connected rooms to be used by
one person or family. 2 set of
furniture that matches; suit. 3 any
set or series of like things. [< French
< Old French *siute* < Popular Latin
sequita]

suit·or (sü/tər), *n., pl.* **suit·ors.** 1 man
who is courting a woman. 2 person
bringing suit in a court of law.

su·ki·ya·ki (sü/kē yä/kē, skē yä/kē),
n. a Japanese dish consisting
mainly of cooked, thinly sliced
meat, onions, bamboo shoots,
and various other vegetables.
[< Japanese]

sun·di·al (sun/dī/əl), *n.* instrument
for telling the time of day by the
position of a shadow cast by the
sun; dial.

su·per·car·go (sü/pər kär/gō), *n., pl.*
su·per·car·goes. officer on a
merchant ship who represents the
owner and has charge of the cargo
and the business affairs of the
voyage.

su·per·fi·cial (sü/pər fish/əl), *adj.* 1
on the surface; at the surface: *His
burns were superficial and soon
healed.* 2 concerned with or
understanding only what is on the
surface; not thorough; shallow:
*superficial education, superficial
knowledge.* —**su·per·fi/cial·ly,** *adv.*

su·per·gi·ant (sü/pər jī/ənt), *n., pl.*
su·per·gi·ants. star more massive
than the sun in a late stage in its
life in which it becomes even
larger and brighter than a red
giant.

su·per·im·pose (sü/pər im pōz/), *v.t.,*
-posed, -pos·ing. put on top of
something else.

su·per·mar·ket (sü/pər mär/kit), *n.*
a large grocery store in which
customers select their purchases
from open shelves.

su·per·nat·ur·al (sü/pər nach/ər əl),
adj. above or beyond what is
natural: *supernatural voices.*
—**su/per·nat/ur·al·ly,** *adv.*
—**su/per·nat/ur·al·ness,** *n.*

su·per no·va (sü/pər nō/və), *n., pl.*
-vas. explosive death of a massive,
supergiant star.

su·per·script (sü/pər skript), *adj.*
written above. —*n.* number, letter,
etc., written above and to one side
of a symbol. In $a^3 \times b^n$ the 3 and
the *n* are superscripts.

su·per·sede (sü/pər sēd/), *v.t.,*
-sed·ed, -sed·ing. take the place
of; cause to be set aside; displace:
*Electric lights have superseded
gaslights.* [< Latin *supersedere* be
superior to, refrain from < *super-*
above + *sedere* sit]
—**su/per·sed/er,** *n.*

su·per·son·ic (sü/pər son/ik), *adj.*
1 greater than the speed of sound
in air or in some other medium.
2 capable of moving faster than
sound: *supersonic aircraft.*

supersonic (def. 2)
the **supersonic**
Concorde

a	hat	**ī**	ice	**u̇**	put	**ə** stands for	
ā	age	**o**	not	**ü**	rule	**a**	in about
ä	far, calm	**ō**	open	**ch**	child	**e**	in taken
âr	care	**ȯ**	saw	**ng**	long	**i**	in pencil
e	let	**ô**	order	**sh**	she	**o**	in lemon
ē	equal	**oi**	oil	**th**	thin	**u**	in circus
ėr	term	**ou**	out	**ᴛʜ**	then		
i	it	**u**	cup	**zh**	measure		

suspend (def. 1)

This bridge is

suspended on cables

between towers.

su·per·sti·tion (sü′pər stish′ən), *n.*
1 an unreasoning fear of what is unknown or mysterious; unreasoning expectation. **2** belief or practice founded on ignorant fear or mistaken reverence: *A common superstition considers 13 an unlucky number.* [< Latin *superstitionem*, originally, a standing over, as in wonder or awe < *super-* above + *stare* to stand]

sup·posed to (sə pōzd′ tü), permitted to, expected to.

sur·face ar·e·a (sér′fis âr′ē ə), the sum of the areas of all the surfaces of a solid figure.

sur·geon (sér′jən), *n.* doctor who performs operations; medical practitioner who specializes in surgery.

sur·ren·der (sə ren′dər), *v.* **sur·ren·ders, sur·ren·dered, sur·ren·der·ing.** —*v.t.* give up (something) to the possession or power of another; yield (*to*): *The general surrendered the fort to the enemy.* —*n.* act of surrendering. [< Old French *surrendre* < *sur-* over + *rendre* render]

sur·veil·lance (sər vā′ləns), *n.* **1** watch kept over a person. **2** supervision. [< French < *sur-* over + *veiller* to watch]

sur·vive (sər vīv′), *v.*, **sur·vived, sur·viv·ing.** —*v.t.* live longer than; remain alive after: *He survived his wife by three years.* —*v.i.* continue to live; remain alive; live on. [< Old French *sourvivre* < *sur-* over + *vivre* to live]

sus·cep·ti·ble (sə sep′tə bəl), *adj.* **1** easily influenced by feelings or emotions; very sensitive: *Poetry appealed to his susceptible nature.* **2 susceptible to,** easily affected by; liable to; open to: *Vain people are susceptible to flattery.* [< Late Latin *susceptibilis*, ultimately < Latin *sub-* up + *capere* to take] —**sus·cep′ti·bly,** *adv.*

sus·pend (sə spend′), *v.t.* **1** hang down by attaching to something above: *The lamp was suspended from the ceiling.* **2** hold in place as if by hanging. **3** stop for a while: *suspend work.*

sus·pense (sə spens′), *n.* **1** condition of being uncertain. **2** anxious uncertainty; anxiety: *Parents may feel suspense when their children are very sick.* [< Old French (*en*) *suspens* (in) abeyance, ultimately < Latin *suspendere*]

sus·pen·sion (sə spen′shən), *n.* **1** a suspending: *the suspension of a driver's license for speeding.* **2** support on which something is suspended.

sus·pi·cious (sə spish′əs), *adj.* **1** causing one to suspect; questionable; doubtful. **2** feeling suspicion; suspecting; mistrustful. —**sus·pi′cious·ly,** *adv.* —**sus·pi′cious·ness,** *n.*

sus·tain (sə stān′), *v.t.* **1** keep up; keep going: *Hope sustains him in his misery.* **2** supply with food, provisions, etc.: *sustain a family.* **3** hold up; support: *Arches sustain the weight of the roof.* **4** bear; endure: *The sea wall sustains the shock of the waves.* **5** suffer; experience: *sustain a great loss.* **6** allow; admit; favor: *The court sustained his suit.* **7** agree with; confirm: *The facts sustain her theory.* [< Old French < Latin *sustinere* < *sub-* up + *tenere* to hold] —**sus·tain′a·ble,** *adj.* —**sus·tain′er,** *n.*

sus·te·nance (sus′tə nəns), *n.* **1** food or provisions; nourishment. **2** means of living; support: *give money for the sustenance of the poor.*

SWAT (swät), *n.* Special Weapons and Tactics (a specially trained section of police).

sweet (swēt), *adj.* **1** having a taste like that of sugar or honey: *Pears are sweeter than lemons.* **2** having a pleasant taste or smell: *a sweet flower.* **3** pleasing; agreeable: *a sweet child, a sweet smile, sweet music.* [Old English *swēte*] —**sweet′ly,** *adv.* —**sweet′ness,** *n.*

swore (swôr), *v.* a pt. of **swear.**

sym·bol (sim′bəl), *n., v.,* **-boled, -bol·ing** or **-bolled, -bol·ling.** —*n.* something that stands for or represents an idea, quality, condition, or other abstraction: *The lion is the symbol of courage; the lamb, of meekness.* —*v.t.* symbolize. [< Greek *symbolon* token, mark < *syn-* together + *ballein* to throw]

sym·me·try (sim′ə trē), *n., pl.* **-tries.** a regular, balanced arrangement on opposite sides of a line or plane, or around a center or axis. [< Greek *symmetria* < *syn-* together + *metron* measure]

sym·pa·thet·ic (sim′pə thet′ik), *adj.* having or showing kind feelings toward others; sympathizing. —**sym′pa·thet′i·cal·ly,** *adv.*

syn·chro·nize (sing′krə nīz), *v.*,
-nized, -niz·ing. —*v.i.* **1** occur at
the same time; agree in time.
2 move or take place at the same
rate and exactly together. —*v.t.*
1 make agree in time: *synchronize
all the clocks in a building.*
2 assign to the same time or
period. —**syn′chro·ni·za′tion**, *n.*
—**syn′chro·niz′er**, *n.*

T

tam·bou·rine (tam′bə rēn′), *n.* a
small, shallow drum with one
head, and jingling metal disks
around the side, played by striking
with the hand or by shaking it.

tan·ge·rine (tan′jə rēn′), *n.* a small,
reddish-orange citrus fruit with a
very loose peel and segments that
separate easily. It is widely grown
in the United States. [< French
Tanger Tangier]

tar·iff (tar′if), *n.*, *pl.* **tar·iffs.** list of
duties or taxes that a government
charges on imports or exports.
[< Italian *tariffa* < Arabic *ta'rīf*
information] —**tar′iff·less**, *adj.*

ta·ta·mi (tə tä′mē), *n.*, *pl.* **-mi.** a
woven straw floor mat traditionally
used in Japanese homes.
[< Japanese]

ted·dy bear or **Ted·dy bear** (ted′ē
bâr′), a child's furry toy bear.

tel·e·scop·ic (tel′ə skop′ik), *adj.* **1** of
or having to do with a telescope.
2 obtained or seen by means of a
telescope. **3** visible only through a
telescope. **4** farseeing.

tel·e·thon (tel′ə thon), *n.* a television
program lasting many hours,
especially one soliciting
contributions for a charity, etc.

tem·per (tem′pər), *n.* **1** state of mind;
disposition; mood. **2** angry state of
mind. —*v.t.* **1** moderate; soften:
Temper justice with mercy.
2 check; restrain; curb. [Old English
temprian to temper < Latin
temperare, originally, observe due
measure < *tempus* time, interval]

tem·per·a·men·tal (tem′pər ə
men′tl), *adj.* subject to moods and
whims; easily irritated; sensitive.
—**tem′per·a·men′tal·ly**, *adv.*

tem·per·a·ture (tem′pər ə chər), *n.*
the number that is a measure of
the average kinetic energy of all
the particles in an object or
material, expressed in degrees.

tem·pest (tem′pist) *n.* a violent
windstorm, usually accompanied
by rain, hail, or snow.

tem·po (tem′pō), *n.*, *pl.* **-pos. 1** (in
music) the time or rate of movement.
2 characteristic pace or rhythm.

tem·po·rar·y (tem′pə rer′ē), *adj.*, *n.*,
pl. **-rar·ies.** —*adj.* lasting for a short
time only; used for the time being;
not permanent. —*n.* person hired
for a limited period of time.
—**tem′po·rar′i·ly**, *adv.*

ter·mi·nat·ing dec·i·mal (tèr′mə nā′
ting des′ə məl), a decimal with an
exact number of nonzero digits.

tes·ti·mo·ny (tes′tə mō′nē), *n.*, *pl.*
-nies. 1 statement used for
evidence or proof. **2** evidence:
*They presented their teacher
with a watch in testimony of their
respect and affection.* See **evidence**
for synonym study. **3** an open
declaration or profession of one's
faith. [< Latin *testimonium* < *testis*
witness]

ther·a·py (ther′ə pē), *n.*, *pl.* **-pies.**
treatment of diseases or disorders.
[< Greek *therapeia* < *therapeuein*
to cure, treat < *theraps* attendant]

ther·mal (thèr′məl), *adj.* **1** of or
having to do with heat; thermic.
2 warm; hot. —*n.* a rising current
of warm air. —**ther′mal·ly**, *adv.*

ther·mo·dy·nam·ic (thèr′mō dī
nam′ik), *adj.* using force due to
heat or to the conversion of heat
into other forms of energy.

ther·mom·e·ter (thər mom′ə tər), *n.*
instrument for measuring the
temperature of a body or of space,
usually by means of the expansion
and contraction of mercury or
alcohol in a capillary tube and
bulb with a graduated scale.

thermometer
The **thermometer**
measures temperature
in degrees.

a	hat	**ī**	ice	**ù**	put	**ə** stands for	
ā	age	**o**	not	**ü**	rule	**a**	in about
ä	far, calm	**ō**	open	**ch**	child	**e**	in taken
âr	care	**ȯ**	saw	**ng**	long	**i**	in pencil
e	let	**ô**	order	**sh**	she	**o**	in lemon
ē	equal	**oi**	oil	**th**	thin	**u**	in circus
ėr	term	**ou**	out	**ŦH**	then		
i	it	**u**	cup	**zh**	measure		

ther·mo·nu·cle·ar (thėr′mō nü′klē ər, thėr′mō nyü′klē ər), *adj.* of or having to do with the fusion of atoms through very high temperature, as in the hydrogen bomb: *a thermonuclear reaction.*

ther·mos (thėr′məs), *n.* container made with a vacuum between its inner and outer walls so that its contents remain hot or cold for a long time. [< *Thermos,* a trademark]

ther·mo·stat (thėr′mə stat), *n.* an automatic device for regulating temperature, especially one in which the expansion and contraction of a metal, liquid, or gas opens and closes an electric circuit connected to a furnace, air conditioner, etc.

the·ro·pod (thėr′ə pod′), *n.* a member of a group of meat-eating dinosaurs that had short forelimbs and walked or ran on their hind legs.

thor·ough (thėr′ō), *adj.* **1** being all that is needed; complete: *a thorough search.* **2** doing all that should be done and slighting nothing; painstaking: *The doctor was very thorough in examining the patient.* —**thor′ough·ly,** *adv.* —**thor′ough·ness,** *n.*

three-di·men·sion·al (thrē′də men′shə nəl), *adj.* **1** having three dimensions. **2** seeming to have depth as well as height and breadth; appearing to exist in three dimensions.

thrive (thrīv), *v.i.,* **throve** (thrōv) or **thrived, thrived** or **thriv·en** (thriv′ən), **thriv·ing.** **1** grow or develop well; grow vigorously: *Flowers will not thrive without sunshine.* **2** be successful; grow rich; prosper. —**thriv′er,** *n.* —**thriv′ing·ly,** *adv.*

through (thrü), *prep.* **1** from end to end of; from side to side of; between the parts of; from beginning to end of: *march through a town.* **2** having reached the end of; finished with: *We are through school at noon.* **3** during and until the finish of: *help a person through hard times.* —*adv.* from end to end; from side to side; between the parts: *The ball hit the window and went through.* —*adj.* **1** going all the way without change: *a through flight from New York to Paris.* **2** having reached the end; finished: *I am almost through.*

tradition (def. 2)
The Pipers of Scotland have been a **tradition** for more than 500 years.

through·out (thrü out′), *prep.* **1** in every part of: *The Fourth of July is celebrated throughout the United States.* **2** during the whole of (a period of time or course of action). —*adv.* in or to every part: *This house is well built throughout.*

thun·der·storm (thun′dər stôrm′), *n.* storm with thunder and lightning.

thyme (tīm), *n.* any of a genus of herbs of the mint family, with fragrant, aromatic leaves. The leaves of the common garden thyme are used for seasoning.

tim·id (tim′id), *adj.* **1** easily frightened; shy. **2** characterized by or indicating fear: *a timid reply.* [< Latin *timidus* < *timere* to fear] —**tim′id·ly,** *adv.* —**tim′id·ness,** *n.*

tim·pa·ni (tim′pə nē), *n.pl.* of **tim·pa·no** (tim′pə nō). kettledrums. [< Italian, plural of *timpano* < Latin *tympanum*] —**tim′pa·nist,** *n.*

to·bog·gan (tə bog′ən), *n.* a long, narrow, flat sled with its front end curved upward without runners. —*v.i.* slide downhill on a toboggan. [< Canadian French *tabagane;* of Algonquian origin] —**to·bog′gan·er,** *n.*

tow·el (tou′əl), *n., v.,* **-eled, -el·ing** or **-elled, -el·ling.** —*n.* **1** piece of cloth or paper for wiping and drying something wet. **2 throw in the towel,** INFORMAL. admit defeat; surrender. —*v.t.* wipe or dry with a towel.

tra·di·tion (trə dish′ən), *n., pl.* **tra·di·tions. 1** the handing down of beliefs, opinions, customs, stories, etc., from parents to children. **2** what is handed down in this way. [< Latin *traditionem* < *tradere* hand over < *trans-* over + *dare* to give.]

tra·di·tion·al (trə dish′ə nəl), *adj.* **1** of tradition. **2** handed down by tradition. **3** according to tradition: *traditional furniture.* **4** customary. —**tra·di′tion·al·ly,** *adv.*

trail drive (trāl′ drīv′), during the cowboy era, a long trip in which cowboys drove their herds hundreds of miles to railroad stations for shipment to market.

Trail of Tears (trāl′ əv tirz′), name given to the journey of the Cherokee nation from the Southeast to an area west of the Mississippi when they were forced to leave their ancestral homelands in 1830. Thousands perished from disease, starvation, and other hardships.

tram·po·line (tram′pə lēn′), *n.* piece of canvas or other sturdy fabric stretched on a metal frame, used for tumbling, acrobatics, etc.

tran·quil (trang′kwəl), *adj.* free from agitation or disturbance; calm; peaceful; quiet. [< Latin *tranquillus*] —**tran′quil·ly,** *adv.*

tran·quil·li·ty (trang kwil′ə tē), *n.* tranquil condition; calmness.

trans·ac·tion (tran zak′shən), *n.* 1 act or process of transacting: *She attends to the transaction of important matters herself.* 2 piece of business. —**trans·ac′tion·al,** *adj.*

tran·script (tran′skript), *n.* 1 a written or typewritten copy. 2 copy or reproduction of anything: *The college wanted a transcript.*

trans·fer (*v.* tran sfér′, tran′sfér′; *n.* tran′sfér′), *v.,* **trans·ferred, trans·fer·ring,** *n.* —*v.t.* 1 convey or remove from one person or place to another; hand over. 2 convey (a drawing, design, pattern) from one surface to another. —*v.i.* change from one place, position, condition, etc., to another. —*n.* 1 a transferring. 2 a being transferred. —**trans·fer′rer,** *n.*

trans·fer·al (tran sfér′əl), *n.* transference; transfer.

trans·fu·sion (tran sfyü′zhən), *n.* 1 act or fact of transfusing. 2 transfer of blood from one person or animal to another.

tran·sis·tor (tran zis′tər), *n.* a small electronic device containing semiconductors such as germanium or silicon, used to amplify or control the flow of electrons in an electric circuit. [< tran(sfer) + (re)sistor]

trans·late (tran slāt′, tran′slāt), *v.,* **-lat·ed, -lat·ing.** —*v.t.* 1 change from one language into another. 2 change into other words. 3 explain the meaning of; interpret. —*v.i.* change something from one language or form of words into another. [< Latin *translatum* carried over < *trans-* + *latum* carried] —**trans·lat′a·ble,** *adj.*

trans·lu·cent (tran slü′snt), *adj.* letting light through without being transparent: *Frosted glass is translucent.* [< Latin *translucentem* < *trans-* through + *lucere* to shine] —**trans·lu′cent·ly,** *adv.*

trans·mit (tran smit′), *v.t.,* **-mit·ted, -mit·ting.** 1 send over; pass on; pass along; let through. 2 send out (signals) by means of electromagnetic waves or by wire. [< Latin *transmittere* < *trans-* across + *mittere* send] —**trans·mit′ta·ble,** *adj.*

trans·o·ce·an·ic (tran′sō shē an′ik, tranz′ō shē an′ik), *adj.* 1 crossing the ocean. 2 on the other side of the ocean.

trans·par·ent (tran spâr′ənt), *adj.* 1 transmitting light so that bodies beyond or behind can be distinctly seen: *Window glass is transparent.* 2 easily seen through or detected: *a transparent excuse.* [< Medieval Latin *transparentem* showing light through < Latin *trans-* through + *parere* appear] —**trans·par′ent·ly,** *adv.*

trans·por·ta·tion (tran′spər tā′shən), *n.* 1 a transporting: *The railroad gives free transportation to a certain amount of baggage.* 2 a being transported. 3 business of transporting people or goods.

trea·ty (trē′tē), *n., pl.* **-ties.** a formal agreement, especially one between nations, signed and approved by each nation.

tre·men·dous (tri men′dəs), *adj.* 1 very severe; dreadful; awful: *a tremendous defeat.* 2 INFORMAL. very great; enormous: *a tremendous house.* 3 INFORMAL. excellent; wonderful; extraordinary. [< Latin *tremendus,* literally, be trembled at < *tremere* to tremble] —**tre·men′dous·ly,** *adv.* —**tre·men′dous·ness,** *n.*

tres·pass (tres′pəs), *v.i.* 1 go on somebody's property without any right. 2 do wrong; sin. —*n.* a wrong; a sin. [< Old French *trespasser* < *tres-* across + *passer* to pass] —**tres′pass·er,** *n.*

transportation
a type of
transportation

a	hat	ī	ice	u̇	put	ə stands for	
ā	age	o	not	ü	rule	a	in about
ä	far, calm	ō	open	ch	child	e	in taken
âr	care	ȯ	saw	ng	long	i	in pencil
e	let	ô	order	sh	she	o	in lemon
ē	equal	oi	oil	th	thin	u	in circus
ėr	term	ou	out	ŦH	then		
i	it	u	cup	zh	measure		

tri·an·gu·lar prism (trī ang′gyə lər priz′əm), a polyhedron whose congruent and parallel bases are triangles.

tset·se fly (tset′sē flī′), any of a group of two-winged, bloodsucking African flies that transmit disease, including the one transmitting the trypanosome that causes sleeping sickness, and one that carries a disease of horses and other domestic animals. Also, **tzetze fly.** [*tsetse*, of Bantu origin]

tsu·na·mi (sü nä′mē, tsü nä′mē), *n.* an oceanic tidal wave caused by a submarine earthquake. [< Japanese]

tun·dra (tun′drə), *n.* a vast, level, treeless plain in the arctic regions. The ground beneath the surface of the tundras is frozen even in summer. Much of Alaska and northern Canada is tundra. [< Russian]

tu·pe·lo (tü′pə lō, tyü′pə lō), *n., pl.* **-los.** a large North American tree of the same family as the sour gum, whose flowers are often used by bees in making honey. [of Algonquian origin]

tur·quoise (tėr′koiz, tėr′kwoiz), *n.* **1** a sky-blue or greenish-blue precious mineral which is valued as a gem. **2** a sky blue or greenish blue. [< Old French (*pierre*) *turqueise* Turkish (stone)]

tux·e·do (tuk sē′dō), *n., pl.* **-dos.** **1** a man's coat for semiformal evening wear, made without tails, usually black with satin lapels. **2** the suit to which such a coat belongs. [< *Tuxedo* Park, New York]

ty·coon (tī kün′), *n.* businessman having great wealth and power. [< Japanese *taikun* < Chinese *tai* great + *kiun* lord]

ty·rant (tī′rənt), *n.* **1** person who uses power cruelly or unjustly. **2** a cruel or unjust ruler.

UNICEF

UNICEF is an international organization that helps needy children.

U

u·ku·le·le (yü′kə lā′lē), *n.* a small guitar having four strings. [< Hawaiian, originally, leaping flea]

um·brel·la (um brel′ə), *n.* a light, portable, circular cover for protection against rain or sun, consisting of a fabric held on a folding frame of thin ribs, which slide on a rod or stick. —**um·brel′la·like′,** *adj.*

un·con·nect·ed (un′kə nek′tid), *adj.* **1** not joined together; not fastened. **2** not joined in orderly sequence.

un·daunt·ed (un dòn′tid), *adj.* not afraid; not dismayed or discouraged; fearless. —**un·daunt′ed·ly,** *adv.*

un·der·ground (*adv.* un′dər ground′; *adj., n.* un′dər ground′), *adv.* beneath the surface of the ground. —*adj.* being, working, or used beneath the surface of the ground. —*n.* place or space beneath the surface of the ground.

Un·der·ground Rail·road (un′dər ground′ rāl′rōd′), system by which the opponents of slavery secretly helped fugitive slaves to escape to the free states or Canada.

un·der·rate (un′dər rāt′), *v.t.,* **-rat·ed, -rat·ing.** rate or estimate too low; put too low a value on.

un·der·stand·ing (un′dər stan′ding), *n.* **1** comprehension; knowledge. **2** a mutual arrangement or agreement: —*adj.* that understands or is able to understand: *an understanding reply.* —**un′der·stand′ing·ly,** *adv.*

un·doubt·ed·ly (un dou′tid lē), *adv.* beyond doubt; certainly.

UNICEF (yü′nə sef), *n.* United Nations Children's Fund. [<*U(nited) N(ations) I(nternational) C(hildren's) E(mergency) F(und),* the original name of the fund]

u·nit pric·es (yü′nit prīs′iz), prices that give both the total cost and the cost per unit of measure.

un·nat·ur·al (un nach′ər əl), *adj.* **1** not natural; not normal. **2** shocking; horrible. **3** synthetic; artificial. —**un·nat′ur·al·ly,** *adv.* —**un·nat′ur·al·ness,** *n.*

un·nec·es·sar·y (un nes′ə ser′ē), *adj.* not necessary; needless. —**un·nec′es·sar′i·ly,** *adv.*

un·pro·nounce·a·ble (un prə noun′sə bəl), *adj.* too complicated or too difficult to be pronounced.

un·re·al (un rē′əl), *adj.* not real or substantial; imaginary; fanciful.

un·u·su·al (un yü′zhü əl), *adj.* not usual; not in common use; uncommon; rare. —**un·u′su·al·ly,** *adv.* —**un·u′su·al·ness,** *n.*

u·su·al (yü′zhü əl), *adj.* **1** commonly seen, found, or happening; ordinary; customary. **2** as usual, in the usual manner; as is customary. —**u′su·al·ness,** *n.*

u·su·al·ly (yü′zhü ə lē), *adv.* according to what is usual; commonly; ordinarily; customarily.

u·til·i·ty (yü til′ə tē), *n.*, *pl.* **-ties**, *adj.*
—*n.* **1** power to satisfy people's
needs; usefulness. **2** a useful thing.
3 company that performs a public
service; public utility. Railroads,
bus lines, and gas and electric
companies are utilities. —*adj.* used
for various purposes: *a utility shed.*

V

van·dal·ism (van′dl iz′əm), *n.*
willful or ignorant destruction or
damaging of valuable things.

var·i·a·ble (vâr′ē ə bəl), *n.* a letter
or symbol used to represent a
number.

vaude·ville (vȯd′vil, vȯ′də vil), *n.*
theatrical entertainment featuring
a variety of acts, such as songs,
dances, acrobatic feats, skits,
trained animals, etc. [< French,
alteration of *vaudevire* < *(chanson
de) Vau de Vire* (song of the)
valley of Vire, region in Normandy]

ve·loc·i·ty (və los′ə tē), *n.*, *pl.* **-ties.**
quantity giving both the speed
and the direction that an object is
moving.

ven·det·ta (ven det′ə), *n.* **1** feud in
which a murdered person's
relatives try to kill the slayer or the
slayer's relatives. **2** any bitter feud.
[< Italian < Latin *vindicta* revenge,
perhaps ultimately < *vis* force,
strength + *dicere* say]

venge·ance (ven′jəns), *n.* punishment
in return for a wrong; revenge.
[< Old French < *vengier* avenge
< Latin *vindicare* < *vindex*
avenger]

ven·ti·late (ven′tl āt), *v.t.*, **-lat·ed,**
-lat·ing. 1 change the air in.
2 purify by fresh air. **3** furnish with
a vent or opening for the escape of
air, gas, etc. [< Latin *ventilatum*
fanned < *ventus* wind]

ver·sa·tile (vėr′sə təl), *adj.* able to do
many things well. [< Latin *versatilis*
turning < *versare*, frequentative of
vertere to turn]
—**ver′sa·tile·ness,** *n.*
—**ver′sa·til′i·ty** (vėr′sə til′ə tē), *n.*

vet·er·i·nar·i·an (vet′ər ə ner′ē ən),
n. doctor or surgeon who treats
animals.

ve·to (vē′tō), *n.*, *pl.* **ve·toes**, *adj.*, *v.*
—*n.* the right or power of a
president, governor, etc., to reject
bills passed by a lawmaking body.
—*adj.* having to do with a veto:
veto power. —*v.t.* **1** reject by a
veto. **2** refuse to consent to.
[< Latin, I forbid] —**ve′to·er,** *n.*

vice-pres·i·dent (vīs′prez′ə dənt), *n.*
officer next in rank to the president,
who takes the president's place.

vi·ce ver·sa (vī′sə vėr′sə), the other
way round; conversely: *John
blamed Mary, and vice versa
(Mary blamed John).* [< Latin]

vic·to·ri·ous (vik tôr′ē əs), *adj.*
1 having won a victory;
conquering: *a victorious team.*
2 ending in victory: *a victorious
war.* —**vic·to′ri·ous·ly,** *adv.*

vic·tor·y (vik′tər ē), *n.*, *pl.* **-tor·ies.**
defeat of an enemy or opponent;
success in a contest.

vin·dic·tive (vin dik′tiv), *adj.*
1 feeling a strong tendency toward
revenge; bearing a grudge.
2 showing a strong tendency
toward revenge: *a vindictive act.*
[< Latin *vindicta* revenge < *vindex*
avenger] —**vin·dic′tive·ly,** *adv.*
—**vin·dic′tive·ness,** *n.*

vis·i·ble spec·trum (viz′ə bəl
spek′trəm), part of the
electromagnetic spectrum that
people can see.

VISTA (vis′tə), *n.* Volunteers in Service
to America (agency of
the United States government
established in 1964 to send
volunteers to work and help in
depressed areas of the country).

vo·cal·ize (vō′kə līz), *v.*, **-ized, -iz·ing.**
—*v.i.* use the voice; speak, sing,
shout, etc. —*v.t.* form into voice;
utter or sing. —**vo′cal·i·za′tion,** *n.*

vo·ca·tion (vō kā′shən), *n.*
occupation, business, profession,
or trade. [< Latin *vocationem*,
literally, a calling < *vocare* to call,
related to *vocem* voice]

veterinarian
a **veterinarian**
treating a bird

a	hat	**ī**	ice	**u̇**	put	**ə** stands for	
ā	age	**o**	not	**ü**	rule	**a**	in about
ä	far, calm	**ō**	open	**ch**	child	**e**	in taken
âr	care	**ȯ**	saw	**ng**	long	**i**	in pencil
e	let	**ô**	order	**sh**	she	**o**	in lemon
ē	equal	**oi**	oil	**th**	thin	**u**	in circus
ėr	term	**ou**	out	**ᵺH**	then		
i	it	**u**	cup	**zh**	measure		

311

woodwind instrument

A clarinet is a **woodwind instrument.**

vo·ca·tion·al (vō kā/shə nəl), *adj.*
1 of or having to do with some occupation, business, profession, or trade. **2** of or having to do with studies or training for some occupation, etc.: *vocational guidance.* —**vo·ca/tion·al·ly,** *adv.*

vol·ca·no (vol kā/nō), *n., pl.* **-noes.** an opening in the earth's crust through which steam, ashes, and lava are expelled in periods of activity. [< Italian < Latin *Vulcanus* Vulcan]

volt·age (vōl/tij), *n.* the push needed to move an electron from one place to another, in volts.

vol·ume (vol/yəm), *n.* a number given in cubic units that indicates the size of the inside of a space figure. [< Old French < Latin *volumen* book, roll, scroll < *volvere* to roll]

W

warn (wôrn), *v.t.* give notice to in advance; put on guard (against danger, evil, harm, etc.).

wart (wôrt), *n.* a small, hard lump on the skin, caused by a virus infection. [Old English *wearte*]

weird (wird), *adj.* **1** unearthly or mysterious: *They were awakened by a weird shriek.* **2** odd; fantastic; queer: *The shadows made weird figures on the wall.* [Old English *wyrd* fate] —**weird/ly,** *adv.* —**weird/ness,** *n.*

well-known (wel/nōn/), *adj.* **1** clearly or fully known. **2** familiar. **3** generally or widely known.

wharf (hwôrf), *n., pl.* **wharves** (hwôrvz), **wharfs.** platform built on the shore or out from the shore, beside which ships can load and unload.

wheel·chair (hwēl/châr/), *n.* chair mounted on wheels, used especially by invalids. It can be propelled by the person sitting in it.

white dwarf (hwīt/ dwôrf/), *n., pl.* **white dwarfs.** rather faint, dead star about the size of the earth but containing about as much mass as the sun; the end state of stars containing as much mass as the sun or less.

white light (hwīt/ līt/), light, such as sunlight, that is a blend of visible colors.

wife (wīf), *n., pl.* **wives** (wīvz). woman who has a husband; married woman. [Old English *wīf*] —**wife/less,** *adj.*

wind·ward (wind/wərd), *adv.* toward the wind. —*adj.* **1** on the side toward the wind. **2** in the direction from which the wind is blowing. —*n.* the side toward the wind.

wood·chuck (wŭd/chuk/), *n.* a small North American marmot; groundhog. Woodchucks grow fat in summer and sleep in their holes in the ground all winter. [< Cree *otchek* or Ojibwa *otchig* fisher, marten; influenced by *wood, chuck*]

wood·wind in·stru·ment (wŭd/wind/ in/strə mənt), any of a group of wind instruments which were originally made of wood, but are now often made of metal or plastic. Clarinets are woodwinds.

wran·gler (rang/glər), *n.* (in the western United States and Canada) a herder in charge of horses, etc.

wreck·age (rek/ij), *n.* what is left by a wreck or wrecks.

Y

yacht (yät), *n.* boat equipped with sails or engines, or both, used for pleasure trips or racing. —*v.i.* sail or race on a yacht.

yam (yam), *n.* **1** vine of warm regions with a starchy, tuberous root much like the sweet potato. **2** its root, eaten as a vegetable. [< Portuguese *inhame* and Spanish *ñame*, ultimately < a west African word *nyami* eat]

yel·low jour·nal·ism (yel/ō jėr/nl iz/əm), characterized by sensational or lurid writing or presentation of the news.

Z

Zep·pe·lin or **zep·pe·lin** (zep/ə lən), *n.* a large, rigid, cigar-shaped airship with separate compartments filled with gas. Zeppelins were mostly used between 1914 and 1937. [< Count Ferdinand von *Zeppelin,* 1838–1917, German general who invented it]

Zip Code (zip/ kōd/), **1** system of numbers, each of which identifies one of the postal delivery areas into which the United States and its larger cities have been divided. **2** a number in this system. [<Z(one) I(mprovement) P(lan) Code]

zeppelin

The development of the airplane contributed to the decreased use of the **zeppelin.**

Writer's Thesaurus

Many of your spelling words have synonyms, words with similar meanings. This thesaurus lists those spelling words alphabetically, defines them, and provides synonyms. For many words, you can also look up antonyms, words with opposite meanings. It can even introduce you to new words.

Understand a Thesaurus Entry

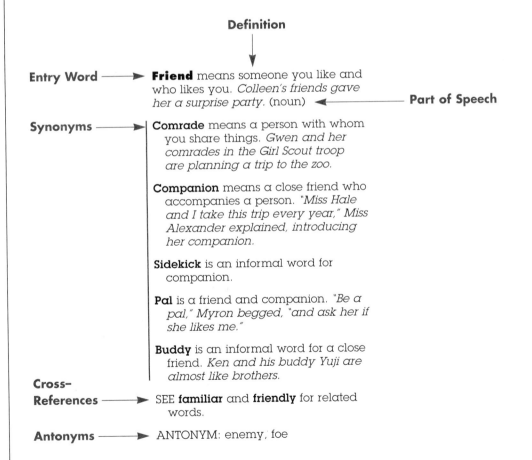

Definition

Entry Word → **Friend** means someone you like and who likes you. *Colleen's friends gave her a surprise party.* (noun) ← **Part of Speech**

Synonyms → **Comrade** means a person with whom you share things. *Gwen and her comrades in the Girl Scout troop are planning a trip to the zoo.*

Companion means a close friend who accompanies a person. *"Miss Hale and I take this trip every year," Miss Alexander explained, introducing her companion.*

Sidekick is an informal word for companion.

Pal is a friend and companion. *"Be a pal," Myron begged, "and ask her if she likes me."*

Buddy is an informal word for a close friend. *Ken and his buddy Yuji are almost like brothers.*

Cross–References → SEE **familiar** and **friendly** for related words.

Antonyms → ANTONYM: enemy, foe

A a

Accompany means to go along with someone or something. *Lightning and thunder often accompany heavy rain.* (verb)

Attend can mean to go along with someone in order to assist. *Attended by two secretaries, the head of the company arrived at the meeting.*

Escort means to go along with someone on official business, or as someone's date. *The President is escorted by Secret Service agents.*

Chaperon means to go along with and supervise young people. *Four parents and two teachers will chaperon the seventh-grade dance.*

Advantage means anything that helps you get what you want, or anything that is in your favor. *Tall people have an advantage in playing basketball.* (noun)

Benefit means anything that does you good or that is good to have. *One of the benefits of taking shop classes is that you can save money by making simple repairs yourself.*

Profit can mean benefit. *"What profit is there in keeping magazines you don't read?" asked Marty's father.*

Gain means anything you get that is valuable or good to have. *Sylvia's biggest gain from summer school is knowing how to study better.*

Ace in the hole is an idiom meaning a secret, strong advantage. *The detective's ace in the hole was a videotape of the crime.*

ANTONYMS: disadvantage, drawback

Ancient means very old. It is generally used to describe things, but can be used to describe people. *Workers digging for the highway have come upon an ancient Native American city.* (adjective)

Antique means of former times. It always describes things. *In the back of the resale store, Joleen found an antique telephone.*

Old-fashioned means out of date in style, working, thinking, or behaving. *I told my mom not to buy those old-fashioned shoes, but she went ahead and did it anyway.*

Archaic means not used since a very long time ago. *Elisabeth enjoyed the old poem, but Mr. Allen had to explain some of the archaic words in it.*

Obsolete means no longer in use. It is often used about machines. *Kenny's computer is obsolete—they don't even make it anymore.*

SEE **old** for related words.

Argue means to disagree strongly and give reasons for your opinion. *Sandy argued with the umpire who called her out at second base.* (verb)

Dispute can mean to argue loudly or at length. *The neighbors are disputing about how late it's OK to play music.*

Squabble means to dispute over something seemingly unimportant. *The children squabbled about who should be first in line.*

Awkward means lacking grace, skill, or ease in action or manner. *Since Nancy broke up with Derek, he acts in a really awkward way whenever they meet. Willie sprained her wrist playing volleyball, so it's awkward for her to write.* (adjective)

Clumsy means stiff and likely to bump into things or drop them. *Tad is so clumsy, I believe he can trip over his own feet while he's sitting down.*

Inept can mean unskilled or clumsy. *"I remembered your party, but I forgot your address," is a completely inept excuse.*

All thumbs is an idiom that means very clumsy, especially in working with one's hands. *If I weren't all thumbs, I would sew on the button myself.*

ANTONYM: graceful

WORDS AT PLAY

There is a young man named Dubose,
So clumsy, as everyone knows,
   He is really all thumbs.
   "But," as he tells his chums,
"it's better than being all toes!"

B b

Because means for the reason mentioned. *Lyle is late tonight, because he missed the bus.* (conjunction)

Since can mean because. It is used when the cause is explained before the effect. *Since Lyle missed the bus, he is late tonight.*

For means because. This meaning is used mostly in writing. *The people rejoice tonight, for the long war has ended.*

So means with the effect mentioned, or for the purpose mentioned. *Tawana washed the dishes, so you don't have to.*

Beg means to ask with deep feeling for something. *John begged to go on the hunt with his brother.* (verb)

Entreat means to beg in order to persuade someone. *Conservationists have been entreating the state government not to dam this river for several years.*

Plead can mean to beg repeatedly or to make an urgent appeal. *Mrs. Turner pleaded with the social worker to help her family.*

Petition means to ask earnestly, especially in a formal request. *The student council petitioned the principal for a relaxed dress code during the heat wave.*

Implore means to beg with very deep feeling. *Joan of Arc implored the prince of France to let her lead his soldiers in battle.*

SEE **request** and **urge** for related words.

Beginning means the time when something first happens or first exists. *The Declaration of Independence marked the beginning of the United States.* (noun)

Start can mean a beginning. *Jason led the sack race from start to finish.*

Creation means the act of making something that did not exist before. *Since the creation of the Cafeteria Committee, we've had better desserts.*

Dawn can mean a beginning, especially the earliest part of a beginning. *World War II marked the dawn of the atomic age.*

Opening can mean a beginning, especially of a story, music, or other works of art. *The opening of the musical, with its great song and fabulous dancers, really grabbed Mike's attention.*

Introduction can mean a beginning in common use. *Since the introduction of the microwave, cooking habits have changed greatly.*

SEE **start** for related words.

ANTONYMS: conclusion, end, finish

Belief means an idea that someone holds to be true. *It is Joanna's belief that Willard sent her that valentine.* (noun)

Trust means belief that someone or something will do what is expected. It suggests expecting good things. *"And this be our motto," wrote Francis Scott Key, "'In God is our trust.'"*

Confidence means trust. It suggests sureness based on experience. *Mr. Anagnos has such confidence in Peter that he lets him help the mechanics work on cars.*

Conviction can mean a belief of which someone is firmly convinced. *The family shares the conviction that education is the ticket to a better life.*

Faith means a very strong, unquestioning belief. *Rev. Martin Luther King, Jr., spoke of his faith in freedom and justice.*

ANTONYMS: disbelief, doubt, mistrust

C c

Clothes means covering for a person's body. *Miguel has grown so much he needs new clothes.* (noun)

Clothing means clothes. It is a slightly more formal word. *New-to-You Fashion Shop sells both women's and men's clothing.*

Dress can mean clothing of a particular type. *It's a softball game and a picnic dinner, so casual dress will be fine.*

Wardrobe means all the clothes a person has. *Most of Ray's wardrobe came from his older brothers.*

Outfit can mean clothes that go together. *Mom has a plaid skirt and a red blouse that she wears as an outfit with her velvet blazer.*

poncho

parka

Complicated means very difficult to understand because of many parts. *Dimitri likes complicated jigsaw puzzles with hundred of pieces.* (adjective)

Complex means having many parts and therefore not easy to understand. *A complex set of instructions came with the new VCR.*

Intricate means having many closely interconnected parts and therefore not easy to understand. *In medical school Uncle Miguel is learning the intricate systems of the human body.*

Elaborate means made with great care, filled with detail, and quite complex. *Engineers may spend many months designing an elaborate computer circuit.*

SEE **hard** for related words.

ANTONYM: simple

Criticize means to point out what is wrong with someone or something. *I hate to go to the movies with Pete because he criticizes everything.* (verb)

Condemn means to criticize strongly and openly. *Everyone condemns cruelty to animals.*

Knock can mean to criticize. This meaning is informal. *Travis says he quit the swimming team because Coach Bronson always knocks him instead of helping.*

Find fault means to look for what is wrong and point it out. *I asked Don to read my report because he's so good at finding fault.*

ANTONYMS: compliment, praise

D d

Describe means to tell about someone or something. *In her report, Ramona described the natural beauty of the Grand Canyon.* (verb)

Portray can mean to describe. *In* Uncle Tom's Cabin, *Harriet Beecher Stowe portrayed life under slavery.*

Characterize means to describe the special qualities of someone or something. *Dachshunds are characterized by short legs.*

Represent can mean to describe, often in an untruthful way. *The man at the door represented himself as a fire inspector, but he left quickly when Mrs. Luna asked him for identification.*

Detail means to describe something fully, telling even the smallest facts. *Mr. Moravcik will detail for us what math assignments are due.*

Different means not alike. *Edgar and Edwin try hard to be different, because they don't want to be known as "the twins."* (adjective)

Various means different. It is used when there are many different things. *Every morning, Babur opens his family's shop and sets out the thirty baskets of various spices.*

Miscellaneous means of many sorts, not all the same. It may suggest no effort to choose. *My sister collects only clear marbles, but she keeps some miscellaneous ones to trade.*

Diverse means varied. *Sue reads books on many diverse subjects.*

ANTONYMS: alike, identical, same, similar

Disaster means something very bad that happens suddenly. *Disasters such as the 1989 San Francisco earthquake remind us of nature's power.* (noun)

Calamity means a disaster that causes great damage or suffering. *The oil spill was a calamity that should never have happened.*

Catastrophe means a huge disaster with terribly destructive effects. *It will be years before the city recovers from the catastrophe of the hurricane.*

Tragedy can mean an event that causes great sadness. *The long war in Vietnam was a tragedy for millions of people.*

Disasters such as the 1989 San Francisco earthquake remind us of nature's power.

Dismiss can mean to get rid of a worker. *After ten years with the company, the bus driver was dismissed.* (verb)

Discharge can mean to dismiss a worker, usually for a good reason. *Maureen was afraid to tell her parents she'd been discharged from her job for being late too often.*

Fire can mean to dismiss a worker suddenly. This meaning is informal. *Late Friday afternoon, six people in the print shop were fired.*

Lay off means to dismiss a worker, often for a specific period of time. *Mrs. Turner was laid off from her job last month, but she hopes to be rehired soon.*

ANTONYMS: employ, hire

Distribute means to give out. *Mr. Raincloud distributed the hay to his six horses.* (verb)

Dispense means to distribute. It suggests a measured amount. *The relief workers will dispense food and blankets as soon as they reach the refugee camp.*

Issue means to make available many similar items. *Darryl thinks the Post Office should issue Michael Jackson stamps.*

Hand out means to distribute, especially by hand. *"Danny, will you please hand out shop safety rules?" asked Mr. Montroy.*

Deal out can mean to distribute. It suggests taking turns. *Standing at the grill, Ms. Escobar dealt out hamburgers to everyone in line.*

ANTONYM: gather

E e

Effect means something that happens because of something else. *One effect of the very cold weather was a great increase in the amount of heating fuel consumed.* (noun)

Result means an effect, especially a particular event. *As a result of the newspaper's support for her, Mrs. Estevez won the mayoral election.*

Outcome means an effect, especially one that happens at the end of many events. *The outcome of the trial is still in doubt.*

Consequence means an effect, especially one that has several causes or happens a while after the cause. *As a consequence of walking in the woods wearing shorts, Mario got poison ivy on his legs.*

ANTONYM: cause

Effort means a use of strength and energy in hope of doing something. *Kerri practices every day in an effort to perfect her volleyball serve.* (noun)

Attempt means an effort, but not always a strong one. *Mr. Paxton asked the chorus to make one more attempt at the song before rehearsal ended.*

Try means an attempt. *Sonia's first try at knitting a scarf didn't get very far.*

Endeavor means a serious effort over time. *Carmen's endeavor to improve her typing speed was successful.*

Stab can mean an attempt, often a brief or casual one. *Sheila took a stab at the video game but gave up quickly.*

Crack, shot, and **whack** can mean an attempt. These meanings are informal. *After Orville took his first shot at making potato salad, Earl had a crack at cooking hot dogs. Later, Billy Joe took a whack at cleaning up the kitchen.*

Eloquent means able to speak or write gracefully and persuasively. *Mrs. Ling's eloquent speeches convinced many of her neighbors to vote for her as assemblywoman.* (adjective)

Vocal can mean able and eager to speak freely. *At the meeting with the landlord, several tenants were extremely vocal about problems.*

Silver-tongued means very eloquent in speaking. *"You always know how to get around me, you silver-tongued rascal," Mom said to Dad as she kissed him.*

Articulate can mean able to speak or write clearly and easily. *Jaime doesn't speak up often, but he's very articulate when he does.*

Glib means speaking cleverly and persuasively, but not necessarily truthfully or knowledgeably. *Maurice gave a glib answer to the question, and we got past the gate.*

ANTONYM: tongue-tied

AROUND THE WORLD: LIVING WITH CONSEQUENCES

You've made your bed, now lie in it.
— **English proverb**

You have cooked the broth, now eat it.
— **German proverb**

He who eats the honey must expect the sting of the bees.
— **Egyptian proverb**

Beans grow where beans are planted.
— **Korean proverb**

You reap what you sow.
— **English proverb**

There is no catching fish in dry clothes.
— **Portuguese proverb**

Emergency means a sudden and dangerous situation that calls for quick action. *The Kims had an emergency last night—Myung had an asthma attack and had to go to the hospital.* (noun)

Crisis can mean a dangerous situation, especially the most dangerous part of a story or set of events. *The crisis in the movie came when all six of the explorers fell into the river.*

Predicament means a difficult or dangerous situation that is hard to get out of. *Trapped in a burning building, the hero is in a terrible predicament.*

Enclose means to shut something in on all sides. *Vinu's father enclosed their field with a thorn fence.* (verb)

Surround means to enclose. *The soldiers moved quietly to surround the enemy camp.*

Envelop can mean to enclose. It suggests being wrapped or covered. *As her grandfather read, Oona sank back on the pillow, enveloped by her big quilt and the smell of cookies baking.*

As her grandfather read, Oona sank back on the pillow, **enveloped** by her big quilt and the smell of cookies baking.

Encircle means to form a circle around something. *Members of the tribe encircled the old storyteller, moving in closer to hear her words.*

Blockade means to keep everything from going in or out of a place. *During the Civil War, Union ships blockaded southern ports.*

Besiege means to surround a city or fort in order to capture it. *For nine days, Shawnee braves besieged Boonesborough, hoping to defeat Daniel Boone.*

Encourage means to help someone gain courage or confidence. *The basketball coach's praise encouraged Rafael to try out for the team.* (verb)

Inspire means to fill someone with courage or confidence. *Mrs. Chernoff's success in night school inspired her husband to learn English there too.*

Hearten means to encourage and make happier. *After weeks of nasty weather, it was heartening to see the sun yesterday.*

Cheer on means to encourage someone by yelling. *The scout troop cheered on their team in the tug-of-war.*

Root for means to cheer on. *"If I have to root for anybody," Lucy said, "I'm rooting for the home team."*

SEE **urge** for related words.

ANTONYMS: discourage, dishearten

Especially means more than others or in a special way. *Luis likes to eat fruit, especially papaya.* (adverb)

Particularly means especially. *"I hate getting out of bed," Minh yawned, "particularly on dark, rainy days."*

Specifically means with attention to a single item or detail. *Isabel wants to be a nurse, specifically to help older people.*

Primarily means more than others or mainly. *Hilary's mother is primarily a children's doctor, but she sees grownups on occasion.*

In particular means especially. *Carly loves to shop, in particular for new clothes.*

Above all means more than anything else. *Luther likes acting class a lot, above all because he's learning sign language.*

Evidence means something that shows what is true and what is not true. *The footprints are evidence that someone crossed the lawn.* (noun)

Clue means something that suggests what may be true. *Since none of us could guess what Emily was holding behind her back, she gave us a clue.*

Testimony means a statement that is used as evidence, especially in court. *Mrs. Daniels gave testimony that Steve and Sammy were at home when the store windows were broken.*

Excitement means strong and active feelings, usually with much sound and motion. *The crowd roared with excitement when the teams ran onto the field.* (noun)

Commotion means a noisy and excited disturbance. *The gerbil caused a commotion in the classroom when it escaped from its cage.*

Hurly-burly means a noisy and excited disturbance. *When BillyBob first came to Atlanta, the hurly-burly of city life amazed him.*

Fuss means a lot of bother and excitement, usually about something unimportant. *"All right," said the police officer, "what's all this fuss about a missing flowerpot?"*

Stir can mean confused excitement. *The school board's suggestion that classes be held year-round has created a stir in the community.*

SEE **noise** for related words.

Exercise means repeated activity that increases strength, endurance, and skill. *Jan and Lou get exercise by skating two miles every day.* (noun)

Training can mean the development of strength, endurance, and skill by exercise. *Jenny's former gym teacher went into training for the Pan American Games.*

Workout means a period of exercise. *Tina ran a mile during her workout this morning.*

Calisthenics and **aerobics** are kinds of exercise. Calisthenics especially increases strength and gracefulness; aerobics especially increases endurance. *Ricki does slow calisthenics to get warmed up and then fast aerobics to raise her pulse.*

Expand means to become larger. *The United States expanded greatly with the Louisiana Purchase.* (verb)

Swell means to become larger by puffing up. *Nelson sprained his wrist, and it's swelling rapidly.*

Bulge means to swell out. *See the hamster's cheeks bulge with food.*

Balloon means to become larger quickly. *The number of applications to the music program ballooned when Ms. Selkirk said she would teach this year.*

Mushroom means to become larger quickly. *The number of robberies in the neighborhood has mushroomed since the police foot patrol stopped.*

Widen means to become larger across. *The street widens just before it meets the highway.*

Snowball can mean to expand faster and faster. It suggests something out of control. *Shortages of food and snowballing popular discontent contributed to the breakup of the Soviet Union in 1991.*

ANTONYM: shrink

F f

Failure means someone or something that does not do well. *The sidewalk sale was a failure because it rained all day.* (noun)

Flop can mean a failure, especially of something that is meant for people to like. *The movie cost thirty million dollars to make, but it was a terrible flop!*

Dud can mean someone or something that fails to function. *Saul's new computer game was a dud, but the store promised to replace it.*

Bust can mean something that fails completely, like a bankrupt business. *With hardly any rain this year, the corn crop was a bust.*

Fiasco means a complete failure. *Chip's breadmaking was a fiasco because he forgot to put yeast in the dough.*

ANTONYM: success

Forbid means to refuse to allow something. *Joetta's dad forbids her to hang around with any gang.* (verb)

Prohibit means to forbid by law or official rule. *Many companies prohibit smoking in the workplace.*

Ban means to prohibit. *Dictators usually ban any criticism of their governments.*

Bar can mean to prohibit. It is used especially about refusal to allow entry. *Hunting is barred in this wildlife refuge.*

Rule out means forbid, especially in a general way for a good reason. *The doctor rules out all sports for Augustin until his sprained ankle is completely better.*

SEE **prevent** for related words.

ANTONYMS: allow, permit

Force means to use power to get someone to do something, usually unwillingly. *The dictator forced the newspaper to stop publishing.* (verb)

Make can mean to force. *"You can't make me believe that!" George said. "I know Alonzo's not a liar!"*

Drive can mean to force. *"Turn that noise down," Linda's father shouted, "or you'll drive us all crazy!"*

Compel means to force, especially unwillingly. *When Ben lost his job, he was compelled to sell his house.*

Coerce means to compel, often by means of threats. *"I don't want you to feel coerced, but—if you don't eat your vegetables, there'll be no TV for you tonight," said Grandma.*

SEE **persuade** for related words.

G g

Gentle means smooth and light and quiet, not forceful or sudden or upsetting. *Fujio closed his eyes as a gentle breeze ruffled his hair.* (adjective)

Soft can mean gentle. *Sissy sang to the crying baby in a soft voice.*

Tender can mean gentle and kind. *The tender touch of Owen's hands soothed his frightened puppy.*

Mild means gentle and calm. *Matt has a mild manner but a strong will.*

Meek means gentle and patient, not quick to anger. *"Be careful," Cynthia warned her new friend. "My cat looks meek, but she's a real tiger."*

ANTONYMS: harsh, rough, violent

Grip means to hold firmly with the hand or hands. *Gripping the bat nervously, Rory stepped into the batter's box.* (verb)

Grasp means to grip tightly. *Consuela grasped the railing as she walked up the dark stairs.*

Clutch means to grasp. *The tiny girl clutched her doll and wouldn't let go.*

Clench can mean to grasp. *Clenching his hat in both hands, Juwon went down the windy alley.*

SEE **catch** for related words.

Grow means to increase in size or amount. *The singer's fame grew with every album.* (verb)

Develop means to grow and change gradually. *Flowers develop from buds into full bloom.*

Flowers **develop** from buds into full bloom.

Evolve means to develop over a long time, with many stages. *Our knowledge of the solar system has evolved over hundreds of years.*

Mature means to become completely grown. It suggests fulfillment. *Lara has matured a great deal during her years in the Navy.*

Ripen means to mature. *When the grain has ripened, the people of Soyan's village begin the harvest.*

ANTONYMS: decrease, shrink

H h

Hard means needing a lot of work or effort. *Making a cherry pie was harder than Sandi expected.* (adjective)

Difficult means not easy to do or figure out. *Chuck keeps practicing the difficult dance that his teacher taught him.*

Tough can mean very hard. *Hauling the fallen tree branches out of the yard was a tough job.*

Laborious means requiring a great amount of effort. *After laborious weight training, Robert has gained 20 pounds.*

Strenuous can mean requiring great effort. *The trip to Echo Cliffs will be a strenuous hike.*

SEE **complicated** for related words.

ANTONYMS: easy, effortless, simple

Help means to do part of the work that someone else has to do. *"Jack, help your father bring up the groceries," said Uncle Tim.* (verb)

Aid means to help, especially by providing something needed by someone. *The research has been aided by a gift of a computer.*

Assist means to help someone do something by working with her or him. *Terralynn assists Mrs. Feldman with cooking in exchange for sewing lessons.*

Lend a hand is an idiom that means to help someone do something. *Mr. Aponte lent Dad and me a hand with moving the sofa to the other side of the room.*

ANTONYMS: hinder, obstruct

Hesitate means to stop and wait before doing something because you have not made up your mind to do it. *Mr. Bryce hesitated before driving onto the busy highway.* (verb)

Waver can mean to hesitate. *Loranne's hearing impairment has never made her waver in her determination to be an actress.*

Falter means to hesitate or stop because of doubts. *Amanda wanted to ask the singer for his autograph, but she faltered when she saw the crowd around him.*

Think twice is an idiom that means to hesitate. It suggests questioning a decision already made. *Dad suggested to Sally that she think twice before spending all her allowance.*

Hide means to put out of sight. *We quickly hid the birthday present we were making for Mom when we heard her at the front door.* (verb)

Conceal means to hide something on purpose so that it won't be found. *Ugo conceals his comic books, but I always find them.*

Camouflage means to hide something by giving it a false appearance. *This caterpillar's dull colors let it camouflage itself as a twig.*

Cache means to store in a safe hiding place. *The explorers cached their supplies at base camp before venturing out onto the ice.*

Bury can mean to hide something by covering it. *When Tana saw the teacher coming, she quickly buried Michelle's note under her books.*

Cover up means to keep something bad from being known. *Company officials covered up the factory's pollution of the nearby river.*

ANTONYMS: expose, reveal, show

I i

Improve means to make something better, increase its value, or correct its faults. *"Your writing will be improved, Priscilla, if you use some synonyms for really," said her teacher.* (verb)

Better is a formal word that means to improve. *The United Nations was created in hopes of bettering the lives of people everywhere.*

Help can mean to make a physical ailment better. *The nurse told Kimi that glasses might help her headaches.*

Reform means to improve, especially by removing faults. *Mr. Chung suggests that we reform the village government by limiting the number of years people can hold office.*

Amend is a formal word that can mean to make a change for the better. *Proposals to amend the Constitution require approval by three-fourths of the states.*

ANTONYM: worsen

Influence means to make someone do or believe something without giving orders. It often suggests not showing that you want to affect someone. *The director said she hoped her new movie would influence young people to stay away from drugs.* (verb)

Sway can mean to influence someone, especially to change a decision or opinion. *The crowd's boos failed to sway the umpire's decision.*

Induce means to influence someone. It suggests an open attempt to lead or persuade. *The social workers try to induce runaway children to return to their families.*

Move can mean to cause someone to do something. *Tanya's concern for the homeless moved her to collect blankets for the shelter.*

SEE **persuade** and **urge** for related words.

WRITING TIP: USING VIVID WORDS

A plan *hidden* in secrecy, or a plan *veiled* in secrecy—which description seems more vivid to you? The word *veil* calls up images of a piece of material worn to protect or hide the face. You can almost see the veiled plan. Other words meaning "to hide something from sight" include *cloak*, *mask*, and *screen*. All of these are also the names of things that are used to conceal or cover, and, like *veil*, they can be used to create vivid descriptions.

Interfere means to get involved in somebody else's business without being asked and in an unwelcome, unhelpful way. *"Stop interfering with Lerice's homework or you're going to bed," Mom told Allen.* (verb)

Meddle means to interfere. *When the editor changed the end of the story, the author asked her to stop meddling with it.*

Tamper means to meddle with something and spoil the way it works. *The janitor says somebody has tampered with the fuse box.*

Kibitz means to interfere by giving unwanted advice. *"Young man, I was repairing cars before you were born, so I'll thank you not to kibitz!" the mechanic told his assistant.*

Intermission means a scheduled pause during a performance. *During intermission, the musician was able to rest his weary arm.* (noun)

Time-out means a short pause during a game. *The basketball team called a time-out to plan their play.*

Recess means a pause during some official activity. *The judge called a recess during the trial.*

Interval means the time between two things. *The interval between World War I and World War II was only twenty-one years.*

Interlude means interval. *Two bitterly cold weeks were separated by an interlude of one warm day.*

L l

Luck means what seems to make things happen, without anyone planning, controlling, or predicting events. *"Just my luck," Paula said, as the bus pulled away without her.* (noun)

Fortune can mean luck. *Ms. Voigt's good fortune at finding the lost ring in the wastebasket was amazing.*

Chance can mean luck. It suggests that things really happen for no reason. *It's not just chance that Manasa and Hank both showed up at the library.*

Accident can mean chance. *By accident, he caught a glimpse of his friend on the street.*

The breaks, the way the ball bounces, and **the way the cookie crumbles** are informal expressions that all mean chance. They are all used when something unpleasant happens. *"I lost my lunch," said Matt. "That's the breaks. And I forgot my wallet, but that's the way the ball bounces. Anyhow, the cafeteria's closed. I suppose that's the way the cookie crumbles."*

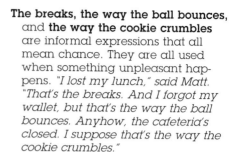

M m

Many means including a large number, not a few. *People have immigrated to the United States from many countries.* (adjective)

Numerous means many. It emphasizes the large number. *On numerous occasions, it was impossible to get good seats at the outdoor concerts.*

Countless means too many to count. *Countless pigeons all took flight.*

Innumerable means too many to count. *Buffalo were once innumerable in the United States, but by 1889 only 551 remained.*

Umpteen means countless. It is an informal word. *"Bianca, you've played that cassette umpteen times," complained her sister.*

A lot of, lots of, and **quite a few** mean many. *Dad took a lot of my friends to the game for my birthday. We had lots of soda pop and quite a few hot dogs.*

ANTONYM: few

N n

Necessary means needed. *Iron, coal, and limestone are necessary to make steel.* (adjective)

Essential means completely necessary. *The keyboard is an essential part of a computer.*

Vital can mean essential. *Lt. Privac returned from her mission with the vital supplies.*

Indispensable means too necessary to do without. *A dictionary and a thesaurus are indispensable tools for a writer.*

Irreplaceable means too necessary to get another instead. *The information stored in my computer is irreplaceable.*

ANTONYM: unnecessary

Noise means an unpleasant sound. *The noise of the jet engine made Gina cover her ears.* (noun)

Racket means a banging noise. *The plumber banging on the pipes downstairs made a terrible racket.*

Clatter means a loud noise of things knocking or banging together. *From the kitchen came a loud clatter of plates being put away quickly and carelessly.*

Din means a mixture of loud, confused noises that may last a long time. *"What did you say?" shouted Toni over the din of the lunchroom.*

Commotion means a noisy, excited disturbance. It suggests disorderly sounds and movement. *"What's all the commotion about?" asked Officer Jimson, as he walked up to the people clustered on the sidewalk.*

Tumult means commotion. *The tumult from the protesters drowned out the speakers on the platform.*

ANTONYMS: quiet, silence

O o

Obstacle means something that stands in the way and prevents or delays action. *"Not knowing how to read," confessed Mr. Fitzroy, "has been the greatest obstacle of my life."* (noun)

Obstruction means an obstacle. *An obstruction in the pipe caused the sink to overflow.*

Barrier means an obstacle. It suggests something like a long, high wall. *The new treaty removes most barriers to free trade between the two countries.*

Hindrance means something that prevents or delays action. It suggests holding back or standing in the way. *Experts fear that environmental problems may be a hindrance to the country's economic progress.*

Hitch can mean a hindrance. *A slight hitch in traffic can clog an expressway for miles.*

SEE **prevent** and **stop** for related words.

Often means many times. *Casimir often earns a few dollars helping people carry groceries.* (adverb)

Frequently means often and at short intervals. *Rain falls frequently in the tropical forest.*

Repeatedly means many times and the same each time. *JoAnne must go repeatedly to the stream for her family's water.*

Regularly means often and at the same interval. *"Buses arrive at this corner regularly," said Mr. Crankshaw, "but I haven't seen one yet."*

ANTONYMS: infrequently, rarely, seldom

Old means having lived for a long time. *The old tortoise at the zoo was born during World War I.* (adjective)

Elderly means old. *Maria's elderly great uncle remembers when there were no radios.*

Aged means having lived to a great age. *The aged couple still live in a small cottage near the lake.*

Getting on in years means having lived on into old age. *Chet Dole may be getting on in years, but he still plays a great saxophone.*

SEE **ancient** for related words.

ANTONYMS: young, youthful

P p

Peculiar means unusual. It suggests that something is not normal or not as it should be. *Fred likes peculiar foods, like salted marshmallows and pickles with chocolate sauce.* (adjective)

Weird can mean extremely peculiar. *What kind of weird person keeps Halloween decorations up all year?*

Odd can mean peculiar. *Chelsea's odd behavior made us wonder if something was wrong.*

Strange means peculiar. It suggests that something is hard to understand. *Marika tried to figure out where the strange crackling sound was coming from.*

Curious can mean strange. *Manny found a curious old tool in the basement.*

Eccentric means out of the ordinary. It is mostly used to describe people and what they have or do. *The artist's eccentric paintings attracted much attention, not all of it polite.*

ANTONYMS: normal, ordinary, usual

AROUND THE WORLD: OLDER IS BETTER

Old crows are not easy to catch.
— **German proverb**

When you see an old lady run, don't ask what's the matter— you run too!
— **Jamaican proverb**

An old horse does not forget his path.
— **Japanese proverb**

An old camel is worth two young ones.
— **Sindhi proverb** (Pakistan)

Most ants have enough **strength** to lift ten times their weight.

Persuade means to make someone agree with you by giving reasons. *"What will it take to persuade you to give up one of those cookies?" asked Tasha with a smile.* (verb)

Convince means to make someone believe that something is true. *Irina convinced Jacob that it wasn't she who told his secret.*

Talk into means to persuade someone by speaking. *Latisha tried to talk her mother into letting her bleach her hair.*

Sell on means to convince someone of an idea as if you were selling it. *Vicky hopes to sell her parents on the idea of an after-school job at Burger Barn.*

Win over means to persuade someone in spite of objections. *At first Clint's parents said no to a skateboard, but he won them over.*

SEE **influence** and **urge** for related words.

Poor means having little or no money. *Many poor people cannot afford doctors if they get sick.* (adjective)

Penniless means without any money, even if only temporarily. *Whoever stole Mrs. Feld's purse left her penniless and miles from home.*

Broke can mean without money. This meaning is informal. *"Oh, no," moaned Sam, "all jeans are on sale, and I'm flat broke."*

Needy means very poor and not having enough to live on. *"Remember the needy," the newspaper urges its readers at holiday time.*

Hard up is an informal phrase that means needing money badly. *We were hard up when Mom was laid off from the battery factory.*

ANTONYMS: rich, wealthy, well-to-do

Power means the ability to do something or to make something happen. *Paul has the power to motivate people with his eloquent speeches.* (noun)

Force means active power. It suggests effort and work. *The force of the blast leveled the building and took out the side of the mountain.*

Strength means the amount of power that someone or something has. *Most ants have enough strength to lift ten times their own weight.*

Might means great power or strength. *Janek took a deep breath and flung himself at the locked door with all his might.*

Vigor means strength and force. *Imagine Miss Henderson's vigor, to run a marathon at 73!*

SEE **force** for related words.

ANTONYM: weakness

Prejudice means an unfair and usually bad opinion formed because of personal feeling. *George grew up with a prejudice against anyone from other countries.* (noun)

Intolerance means unwillingness to let other people think or act differently from you. *Abby is getting over her intolerance of people who disagree with her.*

Narrow-mindedness means intolerance. *Arnie's narrow-mindedness is all that keeps him from admitting that people in wheelchairs can be top athletes.*

Bigotry means an unreasonable belief in your own prejudices. *The refusal to let women vote was the result of bigotry.*

Prevent means to stop something from happening. *Brushing and flossing help to prevent cavities.* (verb)

Block means to stop the progress of someone or something. *Tina leaned out the car window, trying to see what was blocking traffic.*

Avert means to prevent something bad from happening. *By making a backup copy, Jo averted a disaster when her computer crashed.*

Throw a monkey wrench into is an idiom that means to prevent something by interfering with it or sabotaging it. *Our lead singer joined another band, which threw a monkey wrench into our plans.*

SEE **forbid, obstacle,** and **stop** for related words.

ANTONYMS: allow, permit

Promote means to help something toward success. *UNICEF promotes the welfare of the world's children.* (verb)

Further means to promote. *Kevin is studying Spanish to further his career plans.*

Advance can mean to promote. *The breakup of the Soviet Union has advanced the cause of democracy.*

Foster means to help the growth or development of something. *The circus's Clown College continually fosters a search for new silliness.*

Boost can mean to promote something by speaking well of it. *Business leaders met with the mayor to boost a light rail transportation system.*

SEE **encourage** and **help** for related words.

ANTONYMS: obstruct, prevent

R r

Ridicule means to make fun of someone or something. *"Just because I'm taller than anybody in my school,"* Alice sighed, *"do people have to ridicule me all the time?"* (verb)

Mock means to ridicule, especially by imitating. *The clown mocked the lion tamer by pretending a trained poodle was ferocious.*

Kid means to tease someone playfully. *"Bill kids you about your clothes because it's the only way he knows how to be friendly,"* said Mom.

Josh is an informal word that means to make fun of someone in a good-natured way. *Aunt Prue joshes Uncle Al about what a mistake she made in marrying him.*

SEE **scoff** for related words.

S s

Serious means showing deep thought and purpose. *"I am the man of the family now,"* said Tom in a serious voice. (adjective)

Sober can mean serious and not playful. *The story of the UFO sounds strange, but witnesses insist that it's the sober truth.*

Solemn means serious, formal, and impressive. *The President takes a solemn oath to uphold the Constitution.*

Grave can mean very serious and dignified. *What makes Ernesto's jokes so funny is the grave face he uses to tell them.*

Staid means serious and settled in your way of doing things. *Ms. Welles seems staid, but she's the oldest person who ever bungee-jumped from Larkin Bridge.*

ANTONYMS: frivolous, lighthearted

Start means to do the first part of something. It suggests that you will continue to do it. *Jan finally opened her book and started to do her homework.* (verb)

Begin means to start. *"Who would like to begin the lesson?" asked Mr. Suarez.*

Commence is a formal word that means to begin, especially officially or publicly. *The court proceedings commence at ten o'clock.*

Initiate is a formal word that means to start an activity. It suggests that the activity is expected to continue into the future. *Clara was responsible for initiating the after-school tutoring program at the Neighborhood Club.*

Launch can mean to start something. *The store launched a new advertising program for the fall clothes.*

SEE **beginning** for related words.

ANTONYMS: end, finish, stop

Stop means to keep from doing or happening. *Uncle Henry patched the roof to stop the rain from leaking in.* (verb)

Halt means to force to stop for a time. *The police halted traffic until the fallen tree was removed from the road.*

Cease means to stop something that has been going on for a while. *The two countries have ceased fighting, and peace is near.*

Check means to stop forcefully, if only for a short time. *The sandbags have checked the flood—for now.*

Arrest can mean to stop. This meaning is formal. *This city's economic development has been arrested by its pollution problems.*

SEE **prevent** for related words.

ANTONYMS: begin, continue, start

IDIOMS

There are many idioms that mean to get started. Here are some of them:

dive right in
get down to business
get your feet wet
get the show on the road
plunge in
roll up your sleeves
set the ball rolling
take the first step
Can you think of other ways to say this?

Stubborn means insisting on an idea or plan and not willing to change it. *Because Shelby was stubborn about which movie to see, his friends went without him.* (adjective)

Hard-headed can mean stubborn. *Dad says his boss is too hard-headed to listen to Dad's good ideas.*

Obstinate means stubborn. *Both the company and the union are obstinate, and a strike is likely.*

Headstrong means foolishly determined to have one's own way. *Lindsey's headstrong insistence on skating too fast has cost her a broken knee.*

SEE **firm** and **rigid** for related words.

Stupid means very slow to learn or understand. *"Because I don't speak Spanish," Neal told the class, "I felt stupid during my trip to Mexico."* (adjective)

Dull can mean not quick to think, learn, or act. *The dull dog was no match for the squirrel that went scurrying by.*

Dumb can mean stupid or silly. *That dumb cat hisses at her own reflection in the mirror.*

Dense can mean stupid. *I felt dense when Tim had to explain his pun.*

Shortsighted can mean not thinking ahead. *Lakwonda's report ended by saying that it would be shortsighted not to conserve our natural resources.*

ANTONYMS: bright, intelligent, smart

U u

Urge means to try to get someone to do something by saying to do it. *Highway police are urging people not to drive during this blizzard.* (verb)

Press can mean to urge by asking strongly several times. *Since it was so late, the Douglasses pressed us to stay for supper.*

Coax means to urge in gentle, pleasant ways. *"Just a little chicken soup," Mr. Greer coaxed his sick daughter.*

Exhort is a formal word that means to urge strongly. *The speaker exhorted students to take pride in their cultural backgrounds.*

Egg on means to urge or encourage. *If Donna is too nervous to try out for the play, we'll have to egg her on.*

V v

Victory means complete success and defeat of an opponent in a contest, game, or war. *Washington's victory at Yorktown convinced the British that they could not prevent American independence.* (noun)

Conquest means total victory by force. It suggests taking control of the loser's property. *The Spanish conquest of the Aztecs was made possible when thousands of other Indians rebelled against Aztec rule.*

Triumph means supreme victory and joy. *Ms. Walton gained a triumph in the city seniors' golf tournament.*

Mrs. Walton gained a **triumph** in the city seniors' golf tournament.

Win means a victory, especially in sports. With this meaning it is an informal word. *A win today means that Lofaro will wrestle Jackson for the championship.*

Landslide can mean an election victory won by a very large majority of the votes. *Elected in a landslide, the new mayor promised that she would deserve the voters' confidence.*

W w

Weird means very strange and mysterious. *From deep in the forest, She Walks Away heard a weird croaking rumble.* (adjective)

Uncanny means weird. *In "The Hound of the Baskervilles," Sherlock Holmes pursues an uncanny giant dog.*

Spooky is an informal word that means strange enough to make you nervous. *It's spooky how quiet the street gets at night when traffic stops.*

Creepy can mean weird and frightening. *The heroine of the movie saves her friend from some creepy villains.*

SEE **peculiar** for related words.

ANTONYMS: natural, normal

The Word List in English and Spanish

A

abbreviate (33)   abreviar

abduct (33)   secuestrar

abnormal (33)   anormal

abolish (33)   suprimir

abolitionist (CC)   abolicionista

absorb (33)   absorber

acceleration (CC)   aceleración

accessory (2)   accesorio

accompany (2)   acompañar

accumulate (2)   acumular

accuracy (28)   precisión

acknowledgment (25)   reconocimiento

acquaintance (31)   conocido, conocida

addition (33)   adición

adhesive (33)   pegamento

adjacent (33)   adyacente

adjourn (31)   suspender

admiral (35)   almirante

advantage (33)   ventaja

advent (32)   advenimiento

adventurous (3)   aventurero, aventurera

advertisement (32)   anuncio comercial

advocate (15)   defensor, defensora

aerial (19)   aéreo, aérea

affirmative action (CC)   acción afirmativa

aggravate (28)   agravar

aggression (CC)   agresión

aggressive (2)   agresivo, agresiva

aisle (23)   pasillo

alcohol (31)   alcohol

allergic (29)   alérgico, alérgica

Allies (CC)   los Aliados

allot (22)   asignar

allowed (23)   permitido, permitida

all ready (22)   totalmente preparados, totalmente preparadas

all together (22)   todos juntos, todos juntas

allude (16)   aludir

a lot (22)   mucho, mucha

aloud (23)   en voz alta

already (22)   ya

altogether (22)   en general

amateur (17)   aficionado, aficionada

ambulance (28)   ambulancia

analyses (5)   análisis

anchor (35)   ancla

ancient (3)   antiguo, antigua

annex (CC)   anexar

annual rate (CC)   interés anual

antibiotic (27)   antibiótico

antibody (27)   anticuerpo

antidote (27)   antídoto

antifreeze (27)   anticongelante

antiseptic (27)   antiséptico

antisocial (27)   antisocial

any more (22)   uno más, una más

any way (22)   ninguna forma

anymore (22)   ya no

anyway (22)   de todo modos

apart (22)   aparte

a part (22)   un repuesto

appropriate (2)   apropiado, apropiada

archaeology (19)   arqueología

arctic (31)   ártico

argument (25)   disputa

arrangement (25)   arreglo

Art Deco (CC)   art deco

article (28)   artículo

artifact (32)   artefacto

artificial respiration (CC)   respiración artificial

ascent (23)   ascensión

assembly (29)   asamblea

assent (23)   asentimiento

assistance (23)   ayuda

assistants (23)   ayudantes

atom (CC)   átomo

atomic number (CC)   número atómico

attendance (21)   asistencia

automatically (7)   automáticamente

available (21)   disponible

awkward (29)   torpe

Axis (CC)   el Eje

B

baggage (10)   equipaje

balance (CC)   equilibrio

banjo (17)   banjo

barbed wire | conclude

barbed wire (CC)	alambre de púas
barometer (4)	barómetro
barriers (CC)	obstáculos
base (CC)	base
basically (31)	básicamente
batik (17)	batik
batteries (CC)	baterías
bazaar (23)	bazar
because (1)	porque
beginning (31)	principio
believe (1)	creer
benefactor (32)	benefactor, benefactora
beneficial (3)	beneficioso, beneficiosa
biography (15)	biografía
bizarre (23)	extravagante
black hole (CC)	agujero negro
bookkeeper (11)	tenedor de libros
bootleggers (CC)	contrabandistas
Boston Massacre (CC)	masacre de Boston
bounces (CC)	salta
boycott (CC)	boicoteo
breathing (CC)	respiración
budget (CC)	presupuesto
bungalow (35)	casa pequeña de playa o de campo
bureau (35)	cómoda

C

cafeteria (35)	cafetería
calculus (CC)	sarro
calligraphy (17)	caligrafía
camouflage (19)	camuflaje
Canadian (CC)	canadiense
cancellation (2)	cancelación
candid (CC)	sincero, sincera
cantaloupe (19)	melón
canvas (23)	lienzo
canvass (23)	solicitar
capitalism (10)	capitalismo
capture (3)	capturar
cardiologist (CC)	cardiólogo, cardióloga
caries (CC)	caries
catamaran (35)	catamarán
catastrophe (7)	catástrofe
cede (CC)	ceder
centimeter (4)	centímetro
centipede (26)	ciempiés
challenge (2)	desafiar; reto
charitable (21)	caritativo, caritativa

Charleston (CC)	charleston
chemical formula (CC)	fórmula química
Cherokee (CC)	Cherokee
chips (CC)	microchips
chronic (4)	crónico, crónica
chronicle (4)	crónica
chronological (4)	cronológico, cronológica
chuck wagons (CC)	carretas de provisiones
circuit breaker (CC)	interruptor automático
circumvent (32)	enredar
Civil War (CC)	Guerra Civil
civil disobedience (CC)	desobediencia civil
civil rights (CC)	derechos civiles
claim (CC)	reclamar
cleanliness (25)	aseo
clothes (31)	ropa
co-leaders (CC)	dirigentes
coexist (33)	coexistir
cohesive (33)	coherente
collage (16)	montaje
collapse (1)	derrumbe; derrumbarse
collectible (21)	coleccionable
college (16)	universidad
colloquial (15)	coloquial
colonel (23)	coronel
Columbia River (CC)	Río Columbia
commemorate (2)	conmemorar
commission (14, CC)	comisión
commit (14)	cometer
community (33)	comunidad
comparable (31)	comparable
comparison (CC)	comparación
compassionate (2)	compasivo, compasiva
compatible (21)	compatible
compete (33)	competir
competence (21)	competencia
complicate (33)	complicar
composure (10)	compostura
compound (33, CC)	compuesto, compuesta
compound interest (CC)	interés compuesto
comprehend (14)	comprender
comprehension (14)	comprensión
concentrated (CC)	concentrado, concentrada
concentration camps (CC)	campos de concentración
concert (33)	concierto
conclude (34)	concluir

conclusion (34)	conclusión
conductor (CC)	conductor, conductora
cone (CC)	cono
conference (9)	conferencia, entrevista
confession (33)	confesión
congestion (3)	congestión
congratulate (8)	felicitar
congratulations (8)	felicitaciones
connoisseur (19)	conocedor, conocedora
conscience (31)	conciencia
consensus (9)	consenso
consent (9)	consentimiento
consequences (7)	consecuencias
conservation (33)	conservación
conspire (26)	conspirar
construction (9)	construcción
consume (34)	devorar
consumption (34)	consumo
contract (CC)	contraer
controversy (32)	controversia
convenience (21)	comodidad
conventional (32)	corriente
convert (32)	convetir
cooperate (33)	cooperar
coordination (33)	coordinación
corporal (26)	cabo
corporation (26)	corporación
corps (26)	cuerpo
corpse (26)	cadáver
cosmopolitan (20)	cosmopolita
cotton gin (CC)	desmotadora
counterfeit (19)	falso, falsa
courageous (25)	valiente
CPU (CC)	CPU (Unidad Procesadora Central)
credit (CC)	crédito
crises (5)	crisis
criteria (5)	criterios
critical (20)	crítico, crítica
criticism (7)	crítica
critique (20)	crítica
cultural (3)	cultural
cylinder (CC)	cilindro
cymbal (23)	címbalo

D

daydream (11)	fantasear
deceitful (1)	engañoso, engañosa

Declaration of Independence (CC)	Declaración de Independencia
decompose (32)	descomponerse
deductible (21)	deducible
deductions (CC)	deducciones
define (8)	definir
definition (8)	definición
dehydrated (4)	deshidratado, deshidratada
delicate (7)	delicado, delicada
democracy (20)	democracia
demographic (20)	demográfico, demográfica
demonstrations (CC)	demostraciones
dermatologist (CC)	dermatólogo, dermatóloga
describe (15)	describir
desegregation (CC)	eliminación de la segregación
despair (CC)	desesperación
destructive (9)	destructivo, destructiva
detain (14)	detener
detention (14)	detención
diagnoses (5)	diagnóstico
diameter (4)	diámetro
dictators (CC)	dictadores
different (9)	diferente
dilemma (2)	dilema
diluted (CC)	diluido, diluida
disastrous (29)	desastroso, desastrosa
discipline (28, CC)	disciplina
discrimination (CC)	discriminación
disintegrate (31)	desintegrar
dismissed (2)	dejar ir (pasado)
disposable (32)	desechable
distance (CC)	distancia
distribute (7)	distribuir
diversion (32)	distracción
divisible (21)	divisible
doesn't (1)	no (+verbo)
double stars (CC)	estrellas dobles
drowned (29)	ahogarse (pasado)
dwarf (CC)	enano, enana

E

edible (21)	comestible
efficient (3)	eficiente
elastic (CC)	elástico, elástica
electric current (CC)	corriente eléctrica
electron (CC)	electrón

elegance | grievances

elegance (21)	elegancia
eloquent (15)	elocuente
elude (16)	eludir
emancipate (26)	emancipar
emancipation (CC)	emancipación
embargoes (5)	embargos
embarrassment (2)	turbación
emergency (CC)	emergencia
emigrants (16)	emigrantes
emigrates (CC)	emigrar
emotional (3)	conmovedor, conmovedora
empire (CC)	imperio
emulsifier (CC)	emulsionador
encore (17)	repetición
endurance (21)	duración
energetic (CC)	vigoroso, vigorosa
enforcing (CC)	imponer
engagement (25)	compromiso
enslavement (CC)	esclavitud
envelop (16)	cubrir
envelope (16)	sobre
environment (7)	ambiente
epidemic (20)	epidémico, epidémica; epidemia
equation (CC)	ecuación
especially (29)	especialmente
estate (35)	propiedad
evaluate (CC)	evaluar
evenness (25)	equilibrio
eventually (32)	finalmente
every day (22)	todos los días
everyday (22)	cotidiano, cotidiana
everything (7)	todo
evidence (28)	prueba
exaggerate (2)	exagerar
excitement (25)	emoción
exclaim (14)	exclamar
exclamation (14)	exclamación
exercise (29)	ejercicio
existence (29)	existencia
expand (CC)	expandir
expectations (CC)	esperanzas
expire (26)	expirar
expression (3)	expresión
extending (CC)	extendiendo
extraordinary (31)	extraordinario, extraordinaria
extravagant (28)	costoso, costosa

extrovert (32)	extrovertido, extrovertida

F

facilitate (32)	facilitar
faction (32)	facción
failure (10)	falla
farsighted (CC)	hipermétrope
favorite (7)	preferido, preferida
feat (CC)	proeza
ferocious (14)	feroz
ferocity (14)	ferocidad
fertilize (9)	fertilizar
finally (28)	finalmente
finance charge (CC)	gasto financiero
fire extinguisher (CC)	extinguidor de incendios
flammable (21)	combustible
flappers (CC)	jovencitas de los años 20 que vestían trajes no convencionales
floppy disk (CC)	disco flexible
forbidden (2)	prohibido, prohibida
force (CC)	fuerza
foreign policy (CC)	política exterior
forfeit (19)	perder como castigo
formula (CC)	fórmula
franchise (CC)	derecho de voto
fugitive (CC)	fugitivo, fugitiva

G

Geiger counter (CC)	contador de Geiger
generator (CC)	generador
gentleness (25)	gentileza
genuine (CC)	genuino, genuina
geography (15)	geografía
geometry (4)	geometría
ghettos (5)	ghettos
gingham (35)	guingán
giraffes (5)	jirafas
glimpse (1)	vista fugaz
going to (22)	ir a
gondola (35)	góndola
government (7)	gobierno
graduate (8)	graduar
graduation (8)	graduación
granddaughter (11)	nieta
graphic (15)	gráfico, gráfica
great-aunts (5)	tías abuela
great-grandmother (11)	bisabuela
grievances (CC)	agravios

grievous (29)	grave
gross income (CC)	ingreso bruto
grouping symbols (CC)	símbolos de agrupamiento
guarantee (19)	garantía
gullible (28)	bobo, boba

H

halfway (11)	a medio camino
hammock (17)	hamaca
hardware (CC)	soporte físico
hardy (16)	temerario, temeraria
Harlem (CC)	Harlem
harsh (CC)	áspero, áspera
have to (22)	tener que
hazardous (25)	peligroso, peligrosa
hearty (16)	sincero, sincera
heat sources (CC)	fuentes de calor
helmet (CC)	casco
heroism (10)	heroismo
hesitate (28)	dudar, vacilar
hideous (7)	horrible
hindrance (29)	obstrucción
historical fiction (CC)	ficción histórica
homelands (CC)	patrias
hydrant (4)	hidrante
hydraulic (4)	hidráulico, hidráulica
hydroelectric (4)	hidroeléctrico, hidroeléctrica
hydrogen (4)	hidrógeno
hydrophobia (4)	hidrofobia
hypocrite (20)	hipócrita

I

identify (7)	identificar
immediately (2)	inmediatamente
immigrants (16)	inmigrantes
impede (26)	impedir
imperialism (CC)	imperialismo
imply (16)	implicar
import (CC)	importación
imposing (32)	imponiendo
impression (3)	impresión
improvement (25)	progreso
incorporate (26)	incorporar
indigo (35)	índigo
inequality (CC)	desigualdad
inevitable (28)	inevitable
infer (16)	inferir
inference (9)	inferencia

influence (34)	influencia
influential (34)	influyente
initiation (3)	iniciación
injure (CC)	lesionar
inputting (CC)	ingreso (de información)
inscription (15)	inscripción
inspect (8)	inspeccionar
inspection (8)	inspección
installments (CC)	pagos parciales
instructor (9)	instructor, instructora
insulation (CC)	aislamiento
insulator (CC)	aislante
intelligence (21)	inteligencia
intensity (CC)	intensidad
intercept (27)	interceptar
interfere (27)	interferir
intermediate (27)	intermedio, intermedia
intermission (3)	intermedio
international (27)	internacional
intersection (27)	intersección
intervene (27)	intervenir
intramural (27)	intramuros
intrastate (27)	dentro de los límites de un estado
intravenous (27)	intravenoso, intravenosa
introvert (32)	introvertido, introvertida
intrude (14)	inmiscuirse
intrusion (14)	intrusión
invade (14)	invadir
invaders (CC)	invasores
invades (CC)	invade
invasion (14)	invasión
investigate (28)	investigar
investment (CC)	inversión
invoke (15)	invocar
iris (CC)	iris
irrational number (CC)	números irracionales
irrelevant (1)	no pertinente
irritate (28)	molestar
isle (23)	isla
isolationists (CC)	aislacionistas

J

Jazz Age (CC)	Edad del Jazz
journalism (10)	periodismo
journals (CC)	diarios
judgment (25)	juicio
judicial (20)	judicial
judicious (20)	juicioso, juiciosa

jukebox | noticeable

jukebox (17)	rocanola		marathon (28)	maratón
jurisdiction (20)	jurisdicción		mathematical expression (CC)	expresión matemática
jury (20)	jurado		matinee (19)	función de la tarde
justify (20)	justificar		mattress (35)	colchón

K

karate (17)	karate
kayak (35)	cayak
keelboat (CC)	barcaza de río
kernel (23)	grano
keyboard (CC)	teclado
khaki (35)	caqui
kimono (35)	kimono
kind of (22)	en cierta forma
knowledgeable (21)	bien informado, bien informada

L

lariat (CC)	lazo
legislature (10)	legislatura
liable (16)	propensoa
liaison (19)	enlace
libel (16)	difamación
liberal (31)	liberal
liberate (CC)	liberar
liberation (CC)	liberación
life jacket (11)	chaleco salvavidas
limousine (19)	limosina
longhorn (CC)	ganado de cuernos largos
looms (CC)	telares
loquacious (15)	locuaz
Louisiana Purchase (CC)	compra de Luisiana
luckily (7)	afortunadamente
luggage (17)	equipaje
luminous (CC)	luminoso, luminosa

M

machete (17)	machete
macramé (17)	macramé
magnate (16)	magnate
magnet (16)	imán
magnificent (28)	espléndido, espléndida
management (26)	administración
manicure (26)	manicura
manifest destiny (CC)	destino manifiesto
manipulate (26)	manipular
mannerism (10)	manerismo
manufacture (26)	fabricar
manuscript (15)	manuscrito

marathon (28)	maratón
mathematical expression (CC)	expresión matemática
matinee (19)	función de la tarde
mattress (35)	colchón
may be (22)	podría ser, podría estar
maybe (22)	quizá
mediocre (1)	mediocre
melancholy (CC)	melancolía
melanin (CC)	melanina
mementos (5)	recordatorios
memorable (28)	memorable
metropolis (20)	metrópolis
mileage (10)	millaje
minority groups (CC)	grupos de minoritarios
minutemen (CC)	combatientes voluntarios durante la revolución americana
miracle (28)	milagro
miscellaneous (25)	misceláneo, miscelánea
mischievous (29)	travieso, traviesa
mixture (CC)	mezcla
moccasin (2)	mocasín
moisture (10)	humedad
mole (CC)	lunar
momentum (CC)	impulso
monstrous (29)	monstruoso, monstruosa
mortgage (7)	hipoteca
mosquitoes (5)	zancudos
motocross (29)	motocross
muscular strength (CC)	la fuerza muscular
mustangs (CC)	mustangos

N

naive (1)	ingenuo, ingenua
narrate (8)	narrar
narrative (8)	relato
naval (CC)	naval
nebula (CC)	nebulosa
negotiate (3)	negociar
net income (CC)	ingreso neto
neurologist (CC)	neurólogo, neuróloga
neutral (1)	neutral
neutrality (CC)	neutralidad
neutron (CC)	neutrón
neutron star (CC)	estrella neutrón
no one (11)	ninguno
nonviolence (CC)	no violencia
noticeable (21)	perceptible

ENGLISH/SPANISH WORD LIST ■

nuclear fission | prescription

nuclear fission (CC)	fisión nuclear
nuclear fusion (CC)	fusión nuclear
nucleus (CC)	núcleo
nuisance (19)	fastidio

O

objectives (CC)	objetivos
observations (CC)	observaciones
obstacle (CC)	obstáculo
obstetrician (CC)	obstetra
obstruction (9)	obstrucción
occasionally (2)	ocasionalmente
occurrence (21)	ocurrencia
omission (34)	omisión
omit (34)	prescindir
opaque (CC)	opaco, opaca
open range (CC)	pradera abierta
openness (25)	franqueza
ophthalmologist (CC)	oftalmólogo, oftalmóloga
optimism (10)	optimismo
order of operations (CC)	orden de las operaciones
origami (17)	origami
orthopedist (CC)	ortopedista
outgoing (CC)	sociable
outputting (CC)	recuperación
outrageous (25)	excesivo, excesiva
outside (11)	exterior
outstanding balance (CC)	saldo pendiente
overdo (23)	recocer; hacer algo demasiado
overdue (23)	vencido/a y no devuelto
overrated (31)	sobreestimar
overseas (CC)	ultramar
overseer (CC)	capataz
overwhelming (CC)	abrumador, abrumadora
oxygen (CC)	oxígeno

P

pageant (19)	espectáculo
pajamas (35)	pijamas
paragraph (15)	párrafo
parallel circuits (CC)	circuitos en paralelo
parentheses (CC)	paréntesis
parliament (19)	parlamento
passage (10)	pasaje
pastime (29)	pasatiempo
peculiar (31)	peculiar

pedestal (26)	pedestal
pedestrians (CC)	peatones
pediatrician (CC)	pediatra
pedigree (26)	pedigree
pedometer (26)	podómetro
perceive (1)	percibir
percent of decrease (CC)	porcentaje de disminución
percent of increase (CC)	porcentaje de incremento
perception (1)	percepción
perfect square (CC)	cuadrado perfecto
perilous (CC)	peligroso, peligrosa
periodic table (CC)	tabla periódica
perish (CC)	perecer
perjury (20)	perjurio
persecute (16)	perseguir
persevered (CC)	perseverar (pasado)
personal computer (CC)	computadora personal
perspective (1)	perspectiva
perspiration (26)	transpiración
persuade (34)	persuadir
persuasive (34)	persuasivo, persuasiva
pertain (14)	pertenecer
pertinent (14)	pertinente
petition (CC)	petición
phenomena (5)	fenómenos
photography (15)	fotografía
pistachios (5)	pistachos
pitfalls (CC)	trampas
plantations (CC)	plantaciones
plaque (CC)	placa
pleasure (10)	placer
podiatrist (CC)	podiatra
policy (20)	política
political (8)	político, política
politics (8)	políticos, políticas
poncho (35)	poncho
porcelain (19)	porcelana
positive (CC)	positivo, positiva
possessive (2)	posesivo, posesiva
postage (10)	franqueo
postscript (15)	posdata
posture (3)	postura
preferable (1)	preferible
preferred (9)	preferir (pasado)
preliminary (1)	preliminar
prescribe (34)	recetar
prescription (34)	receta

333

presidency | secessionist

presidency (29)	presidencia
pressure (10)	presión
prevent (CC)	impedir
prevention (32)	prevención
principal (CC)	principal
prism (CC)	prisma
probably (7)	probablemente
proclaim (27)	proclamar
proclaims (CC)	proclama
profit (CC)	ganancia
profound (27)	profundo, profunda
programs (CC)	programas
progress (27)	progreso
Prohibition (CC)	Prohibición (de fabricar alcohol)
prologue (27)	prólogo
promote (27)	ascender
proposal (32)	propuesta
prosecute (16)	encausar, procesar
protect (8)	proteger
protection (8)	protección
protest (CC)	protestar
proton (CC)	protón
provocative (34)	provocador, provocadora
provoke (34)	provocar
publication (34)	publicación
publish (34)	publicar
pueblo (35)	pueblo
punctual (3)	puntual
purchase (CC)	comprar
pyramid (CC)	pirámide

Q

quest (CC)	búsqueda
questionable (3)	cuestionable

R

racketeers (CC)	estafadoros
radiation (CC)	radiación
radiologist (CC)	radiólogo, radióloga
rational (16)	racional
rational number (CC)	número racional
rationale (16)	razón fundamental
real numbers (CC)	números reales
realism (10)	realismo
really (7)	realmente
reassure (3)	tranquilizar
recede (14)	retroceder
recession (14)	recesión

reconstruct (9)	reconstruir
rectangular prism (CC)	prisma rectangular
red giant (CC)	gigante rojo
redcoats (CC)	casacas rojas
reference (21)	consulta
referral (9)	referencia
reflective (CC)	reflexivo, reflexiva
reflects (CC)	refleja
refreshment (25)	refresco
refrigerator (29)	refrigeradora
regal (20)	regio
regardless (29)	a pesar
regime (20)	régimen
regiment (20)	regimiento
regional (20)	regional
regular (20)	normal
relative motion (CC)	movimiento relativo
remembrance (29)	recuerdo
remote control (11)	control remoto
removal (CC)	expulsión
rendezvous (31)	reunirse
repeating decimal (CC)	decimal periódico
represents (CC)	representa
resemblance (21)	parecido
resentment (9)	enojo
resistance (CC)	resistencia
resolved (CC)	resolvido
respiration (26)	respiración
respiratory (31)	respiratorio, respiratoria
retrieve (1)	recuperar
reunion (CC)	reunión
revoke (15)	revocar
ricochet (19)	rebote
ridiculous (25)	absurdo, absurda
rodeo (17)	rodeo
role model (11)	ejemplo
rolling friction (CC)	fricción de rodamiento
roundup (CC)	rodeo

S

safari (17)	safari
satisfaction (32)	satisfacción
scientific notation (CC)	notación científica
scientist (29)	científico, científica
scribble (15)	garabatear
sculpture (10)	escultura
sebaceous glands (CC)	glándulas sebáceas
sebum (CC)	secreción sebácea
secessionist (CC)	separatista

segregation (CC)	segregación
self-esteem (11)	autoestima
self-image (CC)	opinión de uno mismo
semester (7)	semestre
sensational (9)	sensacional
sensibility (9)	sensibilidad
sensitivity (9)	sensibilidad
sensitize (9)	sensibilizar
sequin (35)	lentejuela
sergeant (19)	sargento
series circuits (CC)	circuitos en serie
seriously (CC)	seriamente
setting (CC)	ambiente
settle (CC)	colonizar
settlement (CC)	colonización
seventy-two (11)	setenta y dos
shadow (CC)	sombra
shock (CC)	choque
shopping center (11)	centro comercial
silhouette (19)	silueta
simple interest (CC)	interés simple
Sioux (5)	Sioux
sisters-in-law (5)	cuñadas
skyscrapers (CC)	rascacielos
slalom (17)	slalom
sleepiness (25)	somnolencia
sleuth (19)	sabueso
sliding friction (CC)	fricción de deslizamiento
smoke detectors (CC)	detectores de humo
snorkel (17)	esnórquel
software (CC)	soporte lógico
solar collectors (CC)	colectores solares
soliloquy (15)	soliloquio
solute (CC)	soluto
solution (CC)	solución
solve (CC)	resolver
solvent (CC)	solvente
something (31)	algo
sophomore (31)	segundo año (de secundaria o de universidad)
spacious (3)	espacioso, espaciosa
speakeasies (CC)	tabernas clandestinas
species (5)	especie
speed (CC)	velocidad
speedometer (4)	velocímetro
sphere (CC)	esfera
spiritual (26)	religioso, religiosa

square root (CC)	raíz cuadrada
stability (8)	estabilidad
stable (8)	estable
stampede (CC)	estampida
standard form (CC)	forma normal
states' rights (CC)	soberanía de los estados
static friction (CC)	fricción estática
stimuli (5)	estímulos
storage (10)	almacenamiento
strain (CC)	tensión
strategic (8)	estratégico, estratégica
strategy (8)	estrategia
strenuous (CC)	arduo, ardua
structural (9)	estructural
stubbornness (25)	terquedad
subcommittee (13)	subcomité
subdivision (13)	subdivisión
subheading (13)	subtítulo
submarine (13)	submarino
submerge (13)	sumergir
subscribe (15)	suscribir
subsection (13)	subsección
substance (34)	substancia
substantial (34)	importante
subtraction (13)	resta
suede (35)	gamuza
sufficient (3)	suficiente
suite (23)	suite
suitors (CC)	pretendientes
superficial (13)	superficial
supergiants (CC)	supergigantes
supermarket (13)	supermercado
supernatural (13)	sobrenatural
supernova (CC)	supernova
supersede (13)	sustituir
supersonic (13)	supersónico, supersónica
superstition (13)	superstición
supposed to (22)	se supone que
surface area (CC)	área superficial
surgeon (CC)	cirujano, cirujana
surrenders (CC)	capitula
surviving (CC)	sobrevivir
susceptible (31)	susceptible
suspend (34)	colgar
suspense (CC)	suspenso
suspension (34, CC)	suspensión
suspicious (25)	sospechoso, sospechosa
sustain (14)	mantener

sustenance | yellow journalism

sustenance (14)	sustento
sweet (23)	dulce
symbol (23)	símbolo
symmetry (4)	simetría
sympathetic (CC)	compasivo, compasiva
synchronize (4)	sincronizar

T

tambourine (17)	pandero
tariffs (5)	tarifas
telethon (28)	teletón
temperamental (7)	temperamental
temperature (CC)	temperatura
terminating decimal (CC)	decimal finito
therapy (7)	terapia
thermal (4)	térmico, térmica
thermometer (4, CC)	termómetro
thermos (4)	termo
thermostat (4, CC)	termostato
Thomas Jefferson (CC)	Thomas Jefferson
thoroughly (1)	totalmente
three-dimensional (CC)	tridimensional
thrive (CC)	tener éxito
through (1)	a través de; terminado, terminada
throughout (11)	por todo
thunderstorm (11)	tormenta
timid (CC)	tímido, tímida
toboggan (17)	tobogán
traditional (CC)	tradicional
traditions (CC)	tradiciones
Trail of Tears (CC)	Sendero de Lágrimas
trail drive (CC)	arreo
trampoline (7)	trampolín
transaction (13)	transacción
transcript (13)	transcribir
transfer (9, CC)	transferir
transferred (CC)	transferido, transferida
transfusion (13)	transfusión
translate (13)	traducir
translucent (CC)	translúcido, translúcido
transmit (13)	transmitir
transparent (13, CC)	transparente
transportation (13)	transporte
treaty (CC)	tratado
tremendous (1)	tremendo, tremenda
trespass (2)	traspasar
triangular prism (CC)	prisma triangular
turquoise (19)	turquesa

tuxedo (29)	esmoquin
tyrant (CC)	tirano, tirana

U

ukulele (17)	ukelele
umbrella (17)	paraguas
undaunted (CC)	intrépido, intrépida
Underground Railroad (CC)	ferrocarril clandestino
underground (11)	subterráneo, subterránea
underrated (11)	menospreciar
understanding (CC)	comprensión
unit prices (CC)	precios unitarios
unnatural (3)	anormal
unnecessary (2)	innecesario, innecesaria
usually (28)	generalmente
utility (CC)	utilidad

V

vandalism (10)	vandalismo
variable (CC)	variable
velocity (CC)	velocidad
vengeance (21)	venganza
ventilate (CC)	ventilar
versatile (28)	versátil
veterinarian (31)	veterinario, veterinaria
vetoes (5)	vetos
vice-president (11)	vicepresidente
victorious (8)	victorioso, victoriosa
victory (8, CC)	victoria
visible spectrum (CC)	espectro visible
vocalize (15)	vocalizar
vocation (15)	vocación
voltage (CC)	voltaje
volume (CC)	volumen

W

wart (CC)	verruga
weird (1)	extraño, extraña
well-known (11)	famoso, famosa
wharves (5)	muelles
wheelchair (11)	silla de ruedas
white dwarfs (CC)	enanos blancos
white light (CC)	luz blanca
wives (5)	esposas
wrangler (CC)	vaquero, vaquera
wreckage (10)	ruinas

Y

yacht (35)	yate
yellow journalism (CC)	periodismo amarillista